Violence
Renounced

"Attesting to the maturation of reflection on the work of René Girard over the past decade, this compelling and well-crafted volume is a substantive contribution to Girard scholarship. Clearly demonstrating the ongoing importance of Girard's thought, the contributors offer strong, probing, and provocative assessments of its significance.

"Developed from a set of conference presentations and responses, this anthology demonstrates all of the strengths of that genre and none of its weaknesses. Capturing the spirit of a memorable gathering, the contributors engage each other within and across chapters, preserving their conversations in ways that bring alive for the reader contested and varied readings of Girard. Moving reflection on Girard to the next level, the contributors secure this book's import

"Readers newly acquainted with Girard as well as those long steeped in his thought will find much to ponder here. A notable achievement!" —*Martha J. Reineke*

"Adams shows how mimetic desire is not necessarily linked to rivalry and violence, but can form the essence of the kind of love which leads to the well-being of the Other. And Willard Swartley's thorough exegesis of mimesis texts in the New Testament establishes ethical teachings which are theologically and personally inspiring. Sandor Goodhart's sensitive treatment of the Suffering Servant motif from the perspective of scapegoating revealed is a must-read for anyone interested in Jewish-Christian dialogue and understanding. Atonement theology takes on new life as Robin Collins invites us to "an incarnational theory of mimetic participation." James Williams on "King as Servant" blends his profound knowledge of Girard with his creative Hebrew exegesis and passion for Christian discipleship.

"All this and more. This book is a cornucopia of insight—the fruit of theological reflection and the grist for creative imaginings. The hard and thorough scholarly work mingles with the loving spirits of the contributors adding to our understanding of what it takes to resonate with the Spirit of the loving Creator, always acting even when victimization and violence threaten to drain every ounce of energy. Beyond a significant contribution to Girardian studies of mimetic phenomena, it holds its own theologically and there is much to make the discerning reader a better person." —*Vern Neufeld Redekop*

Violence
Renounced

Studies in Peace and Scripture, Volume 4
Institute of Mennonite Studies

Edited by
Willard M. Swartley

Studies in Peace and Scripture Series

Volumes in the Studies in Peace and Scripture Series are sponsored by the Institute of Mennonite Studies, Elkhart, Indiana, and released by a variety of publishers.

Violence
Renounced

RENÉ GIRARD,
BIBLICAL STUDIES,
AND PEACEMAKING

Studies in Peace and Scripture, Volume 4

Edited by
Willard M. Swartley

Foreword by Diana M. Culbertson

Pandora Press U.S.
Telford, Pennsylvania

Copublished with **Herald Press**
Scottdale, Pennsylvania

Pandora Press U.S. orders, information, reprint permissions:
pandoraus@netreach.net
1-215-723-9125
126 Klingerman Road, Telford PA 18969
www.PandoraPressUS.com

All Bible quotations are used by permission, all rights reserved, and unless otherwise indicated are from the *New Revised Standard Version Bible*, copyright 1989, by
the Division of Christian Education of the National Council of the Churches of
Christ in the USA. Scripture marked JPS is from *The Holy Scriptures:
A New Translation* (Philadelphia: Jewish Publication Society, 1917).

Grateful acknowledgment is made for permission to quote, in ch. 9, fom
James G. Williams, "Sacrifice and the Beginning of Kingship," *Semeia 67;
Transformations, Passages and Processes: Ritual Approaches to Biblical Texts*, ed.
Mark McVann (copyright © Society of Biblical Literature, 1995), 73-92.

Library of Congress Cataloging-in-Publication Data
Violence Renounced : René Girard, Biblical Studies, and Peacemaking / edited by Willard M. Swartley ; foreword by Diana M. Culbertson.
    p. cm. -- (Studies in peace and scripture)
    ISBN 0-9665021-5-9 (alk. paper)
    1. Violence--religious aspects--Christianity; 2. Peace--Religious
aspects--Christianity. 3. Violence--Biblical teaching. 4. Peace--Biblical
teaching. 5. Girard, René, 1923- I. Swartley, Willard M., 1936- II. Series

BT736.15 .V495 2000
241'.697--dc21

                                                        00-026147

12 11 10 09 08 07 06 05 04 03 02   12 11 10 9 8 7 6 5

*Blessed
are the peacemakers,
for they shall be called
the children of God.*
—Matthew 5:9

Contents

Foreword

"I SEE VIOLENCE AND STRIFE IN THE CITY . . . but I will trust in you," writes the Psalmist (Ps. 54). The biblical testimony witnesses both to the violence of humankind and the graciousness of God. How can the tension between these realities be reconciled? From the murder of Abel to the killing fields of Kosovo, humankind has struggled in prayer and politics with the single most critical issue in history. Violence is a principal concern of biblical writers and the obsession of modern media. Shall we assert that violence will be punished by God (by even greater divine violence?) Shall we argue that our own violence must be excused so we can save ourselves from the violence of others? Do the scriptural accounts of human violence offer a response to the most searing dilemma of human existence?

One of the most penetrating analyses of human culture and its relationship to religious history and religious texts has been given to us by René Girard. His brilliant exploration of the dynamics of desire and the victimage mechanism has opened Scripture anew to those who seek to understand the God of peace and the mysterious origins of human violence. The essays in this book not only contribute to our understanding of Girard's insights into human culture but also offer valuable interpretive readings of Scripture in light of those insights.

What is at stake in this study of Scripture is not only our understanding of God and the Word of God but the quality of our efforts to work for justice and peace in human history. Implicit in these efforts is the imperative to examine particular religious traditions and how the texts of these traditions have been historically interpreted, not only by believers but by those who dismiss all religious texts as mythological. To suggest that religious believers must constantly reexamine what they understand to be God's revelation is to reaffirm how culture can deform both theology and praxis.

The history of anti-semitism and racial persecution testifies to the often tragic blindness of believers to the message of their own religious heritage. The politics of identity, the zeal that overwhelms humility and crusades in the name of a punishing God, can generate a religion that betrays God. To misread Scripture as a justification for violence is to read it as mythology and not as the subversion of mythology, which is its singular contribution to human history.

The inspired text will eventually resist perverse reading; its inner dynamic will open the minds and hearts of those who seek God not for the sake of political and cultural survival but for the sake of human salvation. The power and depth of the revelatory text can call us to repentance and urge us to help with that transformation of culture that is expressed in the biblical ideal of the Reign of God.

Studying Scripture in the light of René Girard's cultural anthropology helps us to recognize, moreover, the inspiration behind those non-Western religious traditions that are specifically directed to heal the violence of human hearts. In exploring them, we can do no better than to seek what Scripture asks us to seek: the unity that comes from our compassion for the victim, rather than the unity that comes from the shoring up of cultural and national identity.

To those who seek peace and for whom Scripture is the normative textual source of God's revelation, no undertaking can be more important than the kind of study this collection provides. Willard Swartley is to be commended for his efforts to provide us with the record of an important conference and an instructive sequence of readings.

Gratitude must be extended especially to René Girard not only for his extraordinary intellectual achievement but for his openness to critique and debate. These essays constitute a vigorous engagement with a great thinker on a critically important issue. It is hoped that readers will take from this collection of readings a new understanding of the significance of René Girard's work, and a deeper appreciation of the power of Scripture to heal and transform the world.

—*Diana Culbertson, O.P., President of the*
Colloquium on Violence and Religion and
Emeritus Professor of English, Kent State University

Series Editors' Preface

VISIONS OF PEACE ABOUND IN THE BIBLE, whose pages are also filled with the language and the reality of war. In this respect, the Bible is thoroughly at home in the modern world, whether as a literary classic or as a unique sacred text. This is, perhaps, a part of the Bible's realism: bridging the distance between its world and our own is a history filled with visions of peace accompanying the reality of war.

That alone would justify study of peace and war in the Bible. However, for those communities in which the Bible is sacred Scripture, the matter is more urgent. For them, it is crucial to understand what the Bible says about peace—and about war. These issues have often divided Christians from each other, and the way Christians have understood them has had terrible consequences for Jews and, indeed, for the world. A series of scholarly investigations cannot hope to resolve these issues, but it can hope, as this one does, to aid our understanding of them.

Over the past century a substantial body of literature has grown up around the topic of the Bible and war. Studies in great abundance have been devoted to historical questions about ancient Israel's conception and conduct of war and about the position of the early church on participation in the Roman Empire and its military. It is not surprising that many such studies have been motivated by theological and ethical concerns, which may themselves be attributed to the Bible's own seemingly disjunctive preoccupation with peace and, at the same time, with war.

If not within the Bible itself, then at least from Aqiba and Tertullian, the question has been raised whether—and if so, then on what basis—God's people may legitimately participate in war. With the Reformation, the churches divided on this question. The division was unequal, with the majority of Christendom agreeing that, however regrettable war may be, Christians have biblical warrant for participating in it. A minority countered that, however necessary war may appear, Christians have a biblical mandate to avoid it. Modern historical studies have bolstered one side of this division or the other.

Meanwhile, it has become clear that a narrow focus on participation in war is not the only—nor likely the best—way to approach the Bible on the topic of peace. War and peace are not simply two sides of a coin; each is broader than its contrast with the other. Despite broad agreement on this point, the number of studies devoted to the Bible and peace is still small, especially in English. Consequently, answers to the most basic questions remain to be settled. Among questions is what the Bible means in speaking of *shalom* or *eirene*, the Hebrew and Greek terms usually translated as "peace." In addition, what the Bible has to say about peace is not limited to its use of these two terms. Questions remain about the relation of peace to justice, integrity, and—in the broadest sense—salvation. And of course there still remains the question of the relation between peace and war. In fact, what the Bible says about peace is often framed in language of war. The Bible often uses martial imagery to portray God's action, whether in creation, in judgment against or defense of Israel, or in the cross and resurrection of Jesus Christ—actions aimed at achieving peace.

The Bible's close association of peace and war presents serious problems for the contemporary appropriation of the Bible. Are human freedom, justice, and liberation—and the liberation of creation—furthered or hindered by the martial, frequently royal, and pervasively masculine terms in which the Bible speaks of peace? These questions cannot be answered by the rigorous and critical exegesis of the biblical texts alone; they demand serious moral and theological reflection. But that reflection will be substantially aided by exegetical studies of the kind included in this series—even as these studies will be illumined by including just that kind of reflection within them.

The essays in this interdisciplinary volume engage the work of René Girard. They assess, critically and constructively, Girard's theories on the sacrificial origins of violence and its eventual renunciation in the Bible. In so doing, they further the goals of the series.

Studies in Peace and Scripture is sponsored by the Institute of Mennonite Studies, the research agency of the Associated Mennonite Biblical Seminaries. The seminaries and the tradition they represent have a particular interest in peace but even more a shared interest in the Bible. We hope this ecumenical series will contribute to a deeper understanding of both.

Ben C. Ollenburger, Old Testament Editor
Willard M. Swartley, New Testament Editor

Editor's Preface

Since the mid-1980s several among the Associated Mennonite Biblical Seminary faculty had from time to time discussed René Girard's theses on violence, rooted in mimetic desire. They sought to ascertain the significance of Girard's insights for biblical studies and theological perceptions, especially understandings of atonement.

This growing interest led to a special conference on René Girard and Biblical Peace Theology, held at Associated Mennonite Biblical Seminary in June 1994. The conference was folded into a summer seminar class on Biblical Theology of Violence and Peace, taught by Willard Swartley. The forty-five participants consisted of half seminary students and half university and seminary scholars interested in Girard's thought and biblical studies. All participants shared a vision for empowering the peacemaking mission of God's people.

The conference participants and contributors to this volume represent Jewish, Roman Catholic, Protestant, and Anabaptist-Mennonite theological traditions. The main presentations at the conference form the chapters of this book. Several chapters were invited later or developed from the respondents' presentations at the conference. These included those of Charles Mabee, Robin Collins, Jim Fodor, and Rebecca Adams.

Marlin Miller, at the time president of AMBS, wished to participate in the conference but was in Japan, using René Girard's and Raymund Schwager's works as the basis for lectures critically rethinking basic Christian doctrines. The first chapter of this volume was reconstructed by Willard M. Swartley and Professor Miller's daughter, Rachel Miller Jacobs, from Professor Miller's taped lectures.

Special thanks go to the respondents to the main presentations, since those responses have influenced and strengthened the final form of these essays. These respondents included Mary Schertz, Professor of New Testament (AMBS); Daniel Schipani, Professor of Religious Education and Personality (AMBS); Perry Yoder, Professor of

Old Testament (AMBS); Robin Collins, Professor of Philosophy (Messiah College); Loren Johns, Professor of Religion and Bible (Bluffton College); Vern Redekop, Director of Canadian Institute of Conflict Resolution (St. Paul University); James Brenneman, Old Testament scholar and pastor (Pasadena Mennonite Church); Harold Dyck, Professor of Old Testament, Tabor College (Kan.); Millard Lind, Professor Emeritus of Old Testament (AMBS); Ben Ollenburger, Professor of Old Testament (AMBS); Diana Culbertson, Professor of English and Comparative Literature and Director of Religious Studies (Kent State University); Jim Fodor, Associate Professor of Christian/Ethical Moral Philosophy (St. BonaventureUniversity). Three of the participants found it necessary to submit papers in absentia, read by other participants: Gordon Matties (paper presented by James Brenneman); response by Verne Redekop (presented by Willard Swartley); and response by Diana Culbertson (presented by Rebecca Adams).

René Girard himself had planned to participate in the conference but was unable to do so because of other obligations. However, he has now been able to contribute to this book. We are most grateful to have Girard's response to this collection of essays inspired by his work, and certainly his comments greatly strengthen this volume.

The Institute of Mennonite Studies sponsored the original conference. Thus, special thanks go also to Professor Ross T. Bender, then Director of IMS, and the efficient IMS administrative secretaries, Ruth Liechty, and most recently, Barb Nelson Gingerich. Thanks for preparing the index go to Sally Weaver Glick.

Finally, special thanks go to Michael A. King, Pandora Press U.S. publisher, both for his strong interest in publishing this book and for his editorial expertise. We are grateful also for the commitment of copublisher and codistributor Herald Press to help market the book.

My hope and prayer, as editor of this volume, is that these explorations will lead to a more profound appreciation of Isaiah's suffering servant and the cross and resurrection of Jesus Christ, as well as to empower us as peacemakers in this world.

—Willard M. Swartley
Winter 2000

Introduction

Willard M. Swartley

"Amazing Love, How Can It Be,
That Thou, My God, Didst Die for Me?"

Dread violence, how can it be,
Alas, we murdered the Son of God?

"In him we have redemption through his blood. . . ."
"The blood of Jesus [God's] Son cleanses us
from all sin."[1]

MYSTERIES OF FAITH, BEGUN WITH ABRAHAM, revealed fully in Jesus the Messiah. The cross, weapon of ultimate violence and love, confronts us with history's most profound mystery: how can one person's death be salvation for all people?

In the last decade, after the collapse of the Cold War threat of mass nuclear genocide, wars and brutal massacres between closely related peoples have broken out in numerous locations, shocking our moral senses even as we enter the twenty-first century. Why and how do such atrocities occur? Girard identifies and explicates the chief underlying cause of violence. In Girard's writings we encounter new and profound meanings derived from key phenomena that constitute the recurring cycle of violence: mimetic desire, rivalry, scapegoat, sacrificial violence, religion, culture, and "peace." From Girard we learn that "peace" as the aftermath of violence is a universal phenomenon, in ancient to modern cultures. We also learn that the biblical gospel exposes this mechanism and liberates us from its domination of human life and culture.

René Girard has emerged in recent years as a foremost voice in cultural analysis. His theory holds that culture itself and religion are founded on an original and ever-recurring cycle of mimetic desire that breeds rivalry. This in turn leads to sacrificial violence as the unconscious means of restoring peace to the social order. Girard, a literary critic and anthropologist, developed his views from "the literary court," arguing that societal myths the world over, ancient and modern, bear witness to this reality of human experience. In the myths and stories of cultures universally the violent mechanism of scapegoating is concealed, but in Scripture violence is exposed; the biblical narrative has us hear the voice of the victim.

This occurs clearly—but not everywhere—in the Old Testament, especially in the Prophets, the Psalms (see especially 50:12-15, 22-23; 51:16-17), and Job. It is obvious and virtually normative in the New Testament. On discovering this feature as the essence and heart of biblical revelation, Girard became a Christian and a member of the Roman Catholic Church.[2]

In Girard's numerous provocative writings, sacrifice is a key word, weighted with mostly negative valence. But,

"Without the shedding of blood there is no forgiveness of sins." —Hebrews 10:22b

"You were ransomed . . . with the precious blood of Christ . . .
destined before the foundation of the world." —1 Peter 1:18-19

"When Christ came into the world, he said,
Sacrifices and offerings you have not wanted,
but a body you have prepared for me;
in burnt offerings and sin offerings you have taken no pleasure."
—Hebrews 10:5-6, quoting Psalm 40:6

"Through him, then, let us continually offer a sacrifice of praise to God, that
is, the fruit of lips that confess his name." —Hebrews 13:15

Of the texts in Hebrews cited above, one seems to repudiate sacrifice, but the others do not. The same author can reject sacrifice (Heb. 10:5-6), yet use the term to express precisely the joyful and free response of praise to God (13:15). Girard once held (but later questioned his judgment) that Hebrews is the one New Testament book that seems not to have advanced to the level of gospel in repudiating sacrifice, the mechanism that conceals violence and imprisons humans unknowingly in its grip.

How do Girard's theories square with biblical theology and ethics? That question provides the stimulus of this book. Girard's all-encompassing theory—of the causative relation of mimetic desire that leads to rivalry, sacrificial violence, and generates religion and culture—challenges and dismays biblical scholars. Some laud his work as providing a genial descriptive analysis of the human condition that grasps accurately the revelational core of canonical literature. Others groan under this attempt of biblical scholars to hitch their wagon to yet another fleeting Hale-Bopp brilliance. There was Bultmann's existentialism, Cullmann's *Heilsgeschichte*, and currently the liberationist/feminist ideological hermeneutic (often of suspicion), to name a few dominant interpretive trends. Why yet another ideological lens for biblical exegesis and theology? Girard, of course, would counter and contend that his contribution is not an ideology but a banal phenomenological description of human reality!

• • •

The essays of this volume seek to illumine the heuristic dimensions and exegetical payoff of using Girardian thought for biblical-theological understandings. Is Girard a productive ally or an unwitting opponent of what really matters in biblical faith? As Keim puts it in his essay, do Girard's

> ideas represent the "Archimedian point" which will transform the study of culture and religion, or are they just another crazy literary theory meant to befuddle the exegetical types among us? Specifically, has Girard succeeded in revolutionizing our understanding of the relationship between religion and violence? Or is he, as some claim, a God-is-dead theologian in sheep's clothing, selling culture-criticism at the cost of transcendence and other orthodox fundamentals? Or is he, as others have suggested, a reactionary, neo-fundamentalist defender of the old time religious and social order?

These essays disclose fruitful insights in biblical interpretation arising from Girardian theory about mimetic rivalry and the surrogate victim mechanism—sacrificial violence—that generates religion and culture. The first seven lay a foundation for the reader to understand Girard's theories and how they interact with biblical study and basic theological doctrines, especially the atonement. They also represent "soundings" on the crucial key concepts of violence and sacrifice, with significance for understanding atonement. The second set of six show exegetical payoff, go beneath and beyond Girard, and elucidate, probe, and challenge various aspects of Girard's assumptions and theses. As a whole, the essays honor Girard, but even more, I hope and pray, the God of Holy Scripture and Jesus Christ our Savior and Lord.

The purpose of these essays is not to reduce Scripture and biblical revelation to Girardian theory. Indeed, Girard's theories do not adequately explain all aspects of divine revelation. But they do stimulate new insights and sensitize us to the voice of the victim in biblical literature. Does Girard help us to understand better the role of violence in biblical literature; God's wrath; Jesus' death, sacrifice, and atonement? By engaging Girard's thought in critical dialogue with biblical texts, each of these Christian beliefs is explicated in fresh and provocative perspective.

The essays are arranged in an order intended to be user-friendly. The first essays, those of Miller and Grimsrud, introduce the reader to Girard's thought and how it can interact fruitfully with foundational Christian beliefs, especially the Christian doctrine of atonement. Then follow several essays that intend to pose the hard test cases: can Girard's theory about violence help us read Hebrew Scripture texts that are filled with stories of violence? Mabee and Matties help us read the narratives of Deuteronomy and Joshua with new lenses. How does Girard's view of sacrifice square with what the New Testament says about Jesus' death as a sacrifice?

The essays of Hardin and Johns focus on the book of Hebrews—which speaks more about sacrifice than any other NT book—and set forth both a thesis and counter-thesis. Collins' essay focuses on both atonement theory and imitation, forming with Miller's essay on inclusion an atonement emphasis for Part I and signaling a major focus of Part II: how Jesus, in life and death, is a model for human living that breaks the cycle of violence and makes possible a new mimesis.

The second set of essays engages Girard at the presuppositional and philosophical level and at the same time also works at appropriating Girard at the level of biblical textual study. After challenging Girard's views on numerous points, Keim focuses on the ancient Near Eastern Gilgamesh epic myth to test whether Girard's theses are evident there. He offers partial confirmation, then asks how Girard might help us manage scapegoating tendencies in our own Christian or religious communities.

Williams contributes first a scholarly analysis of the "sacrificial crisis" as it manifests itself in cultural myth and practice. He then focuses especially on the Saul narratives to show the extent of "sacrificial crisis" connected with Israel's transition to kingship. He deftly discerns the transformation of kingship-sacrifice categories in the passion narrative of Jesus in the Gospels.

Goodhart proposes that Girard's understanding of sacrificial violence is most important in assessing the relationship between the Testaments and how we understand Jewish and Christian, Christian and Jewish relationships. How Christians interpret the Hebrew Scripture and the New Testament's interpretation of the same is a crucial issue, lest such interpretation do violence to (and sacrifice) the Jewish believer. He examines the Isaiah 52-53 song on the Suffering Servant of the Lord vis-à-vis Girard's theory that biblical revelation enables us to hear the voice of the victim. This provides the backdrop for asking about the actual relation between Jewish faith and what is uniquely Christian in the Gospels. Finally, through a rabbinic story he apprises Christians of proper attitudes toward learning Torah.

Both Williams and Goodhart advocate strongly that Girard, rightly understood, uncovers for us a—perhaps the—most authentic core of divine gospel disclosure in both Old and New Testaments. However, Goodhart also suggests that anti-idolatry is an even more fundamentally distinguishing feature of Hebrew Scripture.

My own essay contends that Girard's theory works well through Good Friday but does not connect adequately—and perhaps by definition cannot—with post-Easter potential for human reality. Presaging James Alison's recent *Raising Abel*[3], my contribution goes beyond Girard to explicate New Testament imitation language in the category of Christ-anthropology, freeing humans from the mimesis that leads to death—which Girard sees as universal in human culture.

The next two essays, by Fodor and Adams, test the foundations of Girardian thought. Fodor carries forward Swartley's proposals on the new Christ-mimesis and persuasively explicates the implications in ethical expression—how this is known in life habits, character, and practice. Further, he asks basic questions about Girard's philosophical presuppositions, testing them against a Trinitarian understanding of salvation and discipleship.

Adams clarifies several crucial aspects of Girard's views, which shows some shift and maturation in Girard's thought itself. Asking us to rethink the Girardian framework, her critique—better, tribute—expands the Girardian model to a Genesis 1–2 dimension of shalom-love *desire* among humans that puts the rivalry-violence model into a second order of reality. She also questions the split between subject and object (as presupposed by Girard's theory) and seeks to reconceptualize a primal, ultimate reality based on intersubjectivity in human relations, so that rivalry is not an inevitable outcome of social relations. In this way she seeks a nondualistic conceptualization of the nature of the human, a model she holds to be primal, and congruent with feminist critique generally. This model—extended from Girard and not uniquely grounded in Jewish-Christian faith-impulses—calls us to a peaceable conceptualization of life and human relations.

The latter chapters suggest that if Girard enables us to see how violence is concealed universally in myth/religion/culture but exposed in the biblical revelation, a new model of mimesis is possible. The essays call us to follow Suffering Servant Jesus as a model who depowers violence and leads us on a journey toward a new city. This city is not that of the Cain legacy in Genesis 4. Rather, its light is the slain-exalted Lamb and its Builder and Maker the God of Peace.

We are most fortunate to have Girard's own response, in which he calls us to assess more fully the mimetic theory, especially in light of the contributions of this volume. He engages directly the essays by Miller, Swartley, and Goodhart and expresses appreciation for all of them. On certain points he challenges, but generally affirms the contributions. He desires that we younger researchers seek further clarity of the meaning of and relation between the Suffering Servant and the Cross, and thus of Incarnation and Redemption, to "reach some day the goal that keeps eluding me." What a task!

• • •

Several findings, together with my own convictions about this project, are here set forth.

1. Girard's work, when used in biblical studies, puts the violence depicted in biblical narrative in a new light. Biblical revelation reveals and exposes sacrificial violence and enables us to hear, see, and side with the victim. But this enterprise works only by positing a duality between myth and gospel. Those stories that condone violence and erase the victim reflect and perpetuate the founding myth of violence. They are thus part of Israel's contextual background myths that depict human cultural experience universally. More important, to be sure, in biblical literature we encounter also the gospel that reveals the lie of the myth. There we hear the voice of the victim. The Gospels' accounts of Jesus' death culminate this biblical strand, thus unveiling the new world of God's truth about and for humans.

At the same time, Girard's axe that cuts between myth and gospel tends too easily to explain the biblical depictions of God executing wrath and judgment on evil as human mythical projections. This "operation" strikes me as too cavalier, leaving one certainly groping for a satisfactory understanding of biblical and canonical authority. Schwager's emphases, presented in Miller's and Hardin's essays, seek to allay this discontent by contending that biblical accounts about God executing wrath are in fact God giving humans over to the fury of their own violence boomeranging back on them. Salvation thus is God's intervention into this ominous spiraling cycle, delivering humans from the evil of the violence in which they are caught ontologically. All this is helpful and mostly to the point—but still begs the issue: is that really how the biblical words of judgment are to be read and understood (whether Joshua or 2 Thess. 1:7-10)?

2. Girard enables us to see more clearly both the scapegoating mechanism at work in biblical narrative and biblical revelation's judgment of this mechanism. But as Adams points out, with Girard's acknowledgement, Girard has tended to scapegoat sacrifice. Girard failed to consider adequately the multivalent view of sacrifice. Sacrifice continues in Christian vocabulary even though Jesus' death is the sacrifice to end sacrifice. In later writings Girard acknowledges positive uses of the term sacrifice.[4]

In Scripture the term has been transformed so that both the Psalmist and writer of Hebrews retain sacrifice after declaring an end to sacrifice (Ps. 50–51 and Heb. 10:5-6; 13:15). Further, even the Christian believer's discipleship is joined to Christ's work of atonement seen as sacrifice, as a voluntary giving of one's energies and life in service to God's will and purpose. Thus in a real daily sense, blood has salvific power: the power of Christ's own blood; derivatively, the power of faithful saints expending themselves in service to Christ; and the power of martyrs who follow Jesus in obedience unto death.

3. Because Girard's thesis rests on the phenomenon of mimetic desire that leads to sacrificial violence and its generative fruit in religion and culture to regulate violence, the Girardian project has enormous power to expose what Walter Wink calls "the myth of redemptive violence" that prevails in politics, culture, economics, and the religion of our everyday world. Further, Girard's reading of biblical narratives together with scholars who use his theories to read and exposit biblical texts[5] have indeed unveiled some central truths of biblical revelation. This highlights the peacemaking core of the gospel and enables sharp criticism of contemporary spirals of violence.

However, Girard, as prophetic critic of culture but not constructive theologian, stops short of explicating the biblical model of mimesis emanating from the new Adam. My own essay and Jim Fodor's move in that direction (see also Alison's brilliant contribution noted above).

Reading Scripture through Girardian lenses strikes many new chords in the theological anthem. Hear a rich one from Alison, on sacrifice. After quoting 1 John 4:8-10 which declares that God's love sent the divine Son to be the atoning sacrifice (or propitiation) for our sins, Alison explicates:

> Here we have the element of the discovery of the absolutely viva-
> cious and effervescent nature of God leading to the realization that
> behind the death of Jesus there was no violent God, but a loving
> God who was planning a way to get us out of our violent and sin-
> ful life. Not a human sacrifice to God, but God's sacrifice to hu-
> mans.[6]

What does this final line mean? Is it a sellout to all that Girard has hoped we would never say again? I think not, since Girard regu-larly celebrates the sacrifice—once for all—in the Catholic mass. For Christians who value the death of Christ as atoning, the Girardian project seems to me to stand or fall in relation to how we view Jesus' own death as sacrifice. If we say it should not have happened as sac-rifice for us, we are left to our own destructive mimesis that perpetu-ates the cycle of sacrificial violence—the very cycle that killed Jesus.

If we say it was a sacrifice for us, we must answer further: in what manner? Then our goal will certainly not be to legitimate the scapegoat mechanism. Rather, our aim will be to expose it as the truth about the human condition, to call us to repent of it, accept Jesus' death as our salvation from it, and then seek to pattern our lives after the Suffering Servant of Isaiah 52-53, whom Christians see supremely but not only in Jesus Christ.

Girard's interpretation contrasts to Joanne Carlson Brown's charge that Christian atonement theology has fostered a view of God that is tantamount to "Divine Child Abuse."[7] Girard at least saves us from this ditch and helps us see just who in the divine-human drama is the abuser and the abused—indeed, that the voice of the victim is the whisper, sometimes resounding as thunder (John 12:29), of God's reign. Whereas Carlson Brown seems to imply that Scripture itself planted the seed that leads to a view of God who violently sacrifices the divine Son to satisfy justice, Girard beckons us to see that Scrip-ture is the only literature in the world that exposes the violence perpe-trated by humans, sides with the victim, and thus calls humans to re-nounce violence in the name of the One who forged for us another way to live and die.

Further, in clarification of Alison's last quoted line above, the sacrifice of the Son is both his own and his Father's sacrifice. The biblical view of atonement does not separate Son from Father, but holds them together in the most costly and intimate embrace of love this world will ever know. It is the cornerstone of our salvation. Praise be to the triune God—Father, Son, and Spirit—who delivers us from this world's persisting cycle of rivalry and violence, reminding us amid our noble strivings that salvation is not by our own making, but the gift of God's amazing grace!

NOTES

1. The first doublette is from an old-time favorite song; the second, my composition; the third, from Eph. 1:7 and 1 John 1:7.

2. See Girard's account of his two-stage conversion from atheistic intellectualism to Christian faith in "Epilogue: The Anthropology of the Cross: A Conversation with René Girard,"in *The Girard Reader*, ed. James G. Williams (New York: Crossroad Herder, 1996), 283-288.

3. James Alison, *Raising Abel: The Recovery of the Eschatological Imagination* (New York: Crossroad Herder, 1996).

4. See Adams's chapter in this book as well as Williams, *Girard Reader*, 69-79, 292-293.

5. E.g., Gil Bailie in his brilliant book *Violence Unveiled: Humanity at the Crossroads* (New York: Crossroad, 1995).

6. Alison, *Raising Abel*, 46.

7. Joanne Carlson Brown, "Divine Child Abuse," *Daughters of Sarah* 18, no. 3 (Summer 1992), 24-28.

Carlson Brown provides a fuller theological analysis, and rationale for her objection to most all views of atonement, in her article published three years earlier, "For God So Loved the World?" in *Christianity, Patriarchy, and Abuse: A Feminist Critique*, ed. Joanne Carlson Brown and Carole R. Bohn (New York: Pilgrim Press, 1989), 1-30. Her trenchant critique, in one sentence: "To argue that salvation can come only through the cross is to make God a sadist and divine child abuser" (p. 3). What is lacking in Brown is any persuasive analysis of the human condition that generates violence, specifically the violence that killed Jesus. To say that patriarchy, not original sin, is the problem from which we need liberation may have elements of truth in it. But what is the cause of oppressive patriarchy (or, conceivably, oppressive matriarchy)? In short, what are the ontological causes behind the symptomatic "sins" she describes?

The longer and deeper analysis, such as Girard's, leads to a bivalent meaning of the cross, represented by two of Brown's quotations, one with which she disagrees and one which she affirms:

On the positive side the cross presents a basic affirmation about God. It says that on the cross God himself is crucified. The Father suffers the death of his Son and takes on himself all the sorrow and pain of history. This ultimate solidarity with humanity reveals God as a God of love in a real and credible way rather than in an idealistic way. From the ultimate depths of history's negative side, this God of love thereby opens up the possibility of hope and a future (p. 23) (From Jon Sobrino, *Christology at the Crossroads*, 371).

The image of a Jesus who, in the prophetic tradition of Israel, despised the blasphemous notion of a deity who likes sacrifice, especially human sacrifice, can assure us that we are not here to give ourselves up willingly to be crucified for anyone's sake, but rather to struggle together against the injustice of all human sacrifice, including our own (p. 26) (From Carter Heyward, *The Redemption of God*, 168-69).

But even then Carlson Brown contends that the Christian tradition is so abusive it must be rejected, the exact opposite move from Girard's upon his perceiving that the Judeo-Christian gospel is unique among, and stands against, the myths of cultures generically, where the victim is hidden and silenced.

Part One

FIRST READING: GIRARD FOR BIBLICAL STUDY AND THEOLOGY

CHAPTER ONE

Girardian Perspectives and Christian Atonement

Marlin E. Miller

THIS ARTICLE IS EDITED FROM A TRANSCRIPT of lectures on the atonement given by Marlin Miller in Japan in the summer of 1994, a few months before his untimely death on November 3, 1994, from a heart attack. We are grateful for this, though it falls short of the finished article he had hoped to write in December 1994. The following paragraphs are a summary of the scope of material Marlin treated at length in preparation for focusing the distinctive perspectives that Girard raises for atonement theology.

The church through the ages has understood atonement in different ways. John Driver has identified and explicated more than twenty biblical images[1]; in the history of the church, these have been used to support several main theories. The early church understood atonement in terms of the ransom/conflict victory model; the medieval church in terms of the satisfaction/ penal substitution model developed most carefully by Anselm; beginning with Abelard and continuing into the modern period, the moral influence model shaped theological emphases; and with Grotius, the Arminians, and John Wesley, the governmental model, stressing God's benevolent ordering of all things including human life and salvation, was influential. To these should now be added the recent contributions of Raymund Schwager, Girardian scholar, who proposes a model he calls the "Drama of Salvation."

There are at least three dimensions of Christ's work of salvation, and all three are essential. The first dimension, reconciliation with God, tends to be emphasized by more conservative theologians. More liberal theologians generally focus on reconciliation and peace in relation to all people. A third element of salvation has to do with reconciliation and peace in the community of believers, even if it doesn't exist in the broader society. Girard's thinking is useful in helping us take into account all three of these dimensions of Christ's saving work. [Ed. Willard Swartley and Rachel Miller Jacobs]

GIRARD'S HYPOTHESES: VIOLENCE AND CULTURE

René Girard has defined his scholarly work primarily as a literary critic, an anthropologist, an ethnologist, and a psychologist. Over the years, he has tried to work toward a comprehensive understanding of human culture focusing on violence, religion, and what he calls mimesis. He himself says he is neither theologian nor biblical scholar. His claim, however, is that the Judeo-Christian Scriptures provide the answers to questions the intellectuals of the last several hundred years, in turning to Marx, Nietzsche, Freud, or the deconstructionists, have been unable to find. These answers involve human nature and the roles of religion and violence in society.

Girard's thinking provides us with four important perspectives in which to re-examine atonement theologies: a hypothesis about the role of violence and religion in tribal societies, the mimetic structure of human desire, the scapegoat mechanism, and the way the Gospels challenge these worldviews.

To develop a general theory of human culture, Girard begins by looking at violence and the role of religion in tribal societies. He questions the post-Enlightenment tendency to characterize humans as primarily rational and well-intentioned, seeing them instead as passionate beings who behave on the basis of hidden impulses. Girard takes special note of anger, pointing out that when people become angry, they are unable to see their own evil deeds and instead project all that is evil onto their adversaries. This anger left to itself becomes violent and even murderous. Girard concludes that violence is a universal human characteristic. The task then becomes one of regulating this violence in human societies.

Girard observes that in primitive societies, unlike modern Western ones, religion played a central role. Furthermore, what primitive societies have in common—despite differences in culture or beliefs about and rules governing sacrifice—is a carefully regulated practice of ritual sacrifice central to religion. From the attention devoted to sacrificial rules both in the Old Testament and in the records of other ancient cultures, Girard posits that sacrifice must have had a necessary function in these ancient societies.

On the surface, of course, sacrifice was important because people felt they were offering something to God. But Girard asks not only about the religious function of sacrifice, but also its *social* function. In analyzing many societies and religions, he hypothesizes that ritual sacrifices in primitive societies secretly provided a substitute object for the violence in society. Ritual sacrifices and related religious practices thus played the roles that government and legal institutions play in regulating human behavior in modern societies, namely, preventing violence from destroying a society and restoring order in times of crisis.[2] Focusing the violence on the victim in the sacrifice provided a catharsis of the violence, restored harmony to the community, and preserved the society.

For Girard, the reason why violence spreads so easily in society, and why it is so threatening, is his understanding of human desire and how it works. Building on his conviction that humans are not so much rational as driven by impulses, Girard notes that these impulses work according to a certain predictable pattern. Just as two children in a room full of toys will both want the same toy, Girard says that it is not only human nature to desire an object, but to desire what another wants *because* the other wants it. This understandably makes life in society difficult.

Girard observes that taboos help regulate the mimetic structure of human desire, but when these taboos break down, the suppressed violence spreads like a disease. Hidden rivalries between people come out into the open and create a crisis, for the spread of violence threatens to destroy the entire society.[3] Girard posits that the way to resolve the mounting crisis is to select a victim onto whom the violence of the entire community can be projected. This projection then enables the society to protect itself from complete destruction. Girard calls the chance or random victim of the society's violence the scapegoat. And he calls this process of transference, and the resulting unity it brings about, the surrogate victim mechanism.

After the victim, seen as a threat by the entire community, has been killed, peace comes to the group. The group then begins to see the chance victim as the one who brought salvation from the crisis and saved the society from possible destruction. The group experiences this projection of violence and its catharsis as sacred or holy. Because anger and violence are blind, the community cannot see that it was the transfer of its collective violence that made the victim holy. The problem is that, sooner or later, more violence and conflict will break out. Girard hypothesizes that primitive societies develop sacrificial rites as a kind of institutionalized crisis and killing that repeats the original experience of expelling and killing the chance victim. This means, finally, that violence is made both sacred and legitimate, and that a kind of regulated violence becomes the basis for human culture. Because it is a sacred means of preserving a society, violence is also therefore legitimately turned against external threats. And according to Girard, because violence is made sacred, it is projected onto God: God becomes the one who requires the violence.[4]

As Girard understands it, the Old Testament begins to reveal the way this scapegoat mechanism works in society. This trajectory reaches its high point in the Gospels, which expose the scapegoat mechanism and therefore rob it of its power.

Unlike myths of ancient religions that assume the guilt of the victim (whether real or imagined), the Gospels emphasize Jesus' innocence as the victim of the forces of evil. In addition, they do not use the language of sacrifice with regard to Jesus. In place of the scapegoat mechanism, the Gospels reveal a loving and nonviolent God who did not require the sacrifice of the Son, but only the full obedience of love for all, including the enemy. Girard believes the Gospels picture a reconciling community which is an alternative to societies structured either directly or indirectly on violence and scapegoating victims.

Girard's views are useful in part because he has a more holistic view of human nature. He emphasizes the community (in contrast to modern Western individualism), and his theories provide a way of understanding sin as rivalry both with God and in the human community. The remainder of this article will explore the application of Girardian thought to the life, death, and resurrection of Jesus Christ and to the formation of an alternative community.

Jesus' Proclamation of the Kingdom

Jesus' proclamation was that the kingdom of God was at hand. In the beginning of Mark's Gospel (1:14ff.) for example, he comes "to Galilee, proclaiming the good news of God, and saying, 'The time is fulfilled, and the kingdom of God has come near; repent, and believe the good news.'" This proclamation of the kingdom is the framework in which Jesus' entire message, his ministry of healing, his relation to Old Testament law, his calling of the disciples, and the conflicts which led to his death must be understood. Girard sees Jesus' message about the kingdom as the key to interpreting all Scripture.

According to Girard, Jesus' message, particularly in the Sermon on the Mount, combines a new worldview and a new ethic. A new kind of conduct is required from humans because of the way God acts toward them (see Matt. 5:43-45 for example). Because God as Father sends rain on the righteous and the unrighteous, Jesus' followers are called to love their enemies and to pray for those who persecute them. This parallel between a new ethic and a new revelation about the nature and behavior of God echoes throughout the Sermon on the Mount. If "you greet only your brothers and sisters, what more are you doing than others? Do not the gentiles do the same? Be perfect [*teleios*—complete], therefore, as your heavenly Father is perfect," (Matt. 5:47-48).

Jesus is teaching not only a new ethic but also a new experience and message about God. Jesus addresses God as "Abba," the heavenly Father who shows compassion to all. Jesus' experience of God as Abba has significant ramifications for the way he relates to those around him, and for the kind of relationship to which he calls his followers. This new experience of God is the basis for Jesus' relationships with tax-gatherers, sinners, and outcasts. His experience and proclamation of God as a God of love and unconditional forgiveness are the basis for his authority to forgive sins.

The Sermon on the Mount also uncovers human sinfulness as a latent will to violence. In the saying about adultery (Matt. 5:27-28) for example, Jesus shows that evil begins in the sphere of desire. Furthermore, in passages such as Matt. 5:38, he calls people beyond what Girard calls the mimetic principle. "You have heard that it was said, 'an eye for an eye, and a tooth for a tooth. . . . But *I* say . . . do not resist the evildoer.'" In other words, don't imitate, but instead act in a way that breaks the cycle of imitation.[5] Desire, mimesis, and violence, as well as their countermeasure presented here by Jesus, correspond to Girard's view of the nature of evil and how it acts in human relations.

It is also important, especially in a Western context, to emphasize that the message of the kingdom is not only to individuals. Jesus seeks to gather a new people of God as an essential part of the kingdom coming near.[6] In Matthew 9:35-36, Jesus, seeing the crowd, has compassion for them. He tries to gather this harassed and scattered people who are like sheep without a shepherd. His calling of the twelve symbolizes a prophetic calling of a new Israel, and he sends them out to minister to villages rather than to individuals (Luke 9).

Furthermore, the prayer that Jesus taught his disciples also assumes that the Father is not only "my Father," but *"our* Father," the Father of the whole people. This emphasis on community becomes even clearer when we see the prayer that invokes the Father's name to be hallowed and that the Father's kingdom come against the backdrop of Ezekiel 36:22-32, where these petitions involve gathering a people who will represent God's name among the nations. The Sermon on the Mount is thus intended to describe the distinctive conduct of a new people of God and demonstrate how the evils that have plagued the history of Israel, and in fact all human history, might be overcome.

At the same time, the gathering of a people includes the repentance and faith of individuals. Repentance is part of the proclamation of the kingdom. And many healing stories note the faith of individuals which helped make their healing possible (Mark 5:34, 10:52; Luke 7:50, 17:19). The opposite was also true: where there was no faith, Jesus was unable to do miracles (Mark 6:5). The gathering of a community does not undermine but supports the call to repentance and faith of the individual.

What happened, however, was that his message of the kingdom and Jesus' gathering of a people provoked a countermovement. The opposition, led by some of the Jewish leaders, tried to unite the people against Jesus, his message of the heavenly Father who loves his enemies, and his movement to gather a new people to God. Jesus himself acknowledged this countermovement as he wept over Jerusalem (Matt. 23:37).

A contemporary Jewish rabbi gives some insight into the kind of opposition Jesus might have aroused. Explaining why, had he lived in the time of Jesus, he would not have become a disciple, he writes that

> [T]he Torah knows nothing of not resisting evil and does not value either the craven person, who submits, or the arrogant person, who holds that it is beneath one's dignity to oppose evil. Passivity in the face of evil serves the purpose of evil. The Torah calls eternal Israel always to struggle for God's purpose; the Torah sanctions warfare and recognizes legitimate power. So I find amazing Jesus' statement that it is a religious duty to fold before evil.[7]

Jacob Neusner says he would have disagreed courteously; one can understand that many rabbis, in the social and political context of the time of Jesus, may have felt less courteous.

However, didn't Jesus also proclaim a God of judgment and punishment? He strongly criticized the Pharisees and other Jewish leaders and talked about the end in apocalyptic terms. It would seem that such teachings imply a God who directly judges and punishes his enemies, those who are sinners (see Matt. 23–24; Mark 13; Luke 10:13-15, 13:31ff.; 21; John 8:39ff.). Girard sees this language as reflecting a realistic appraisal of the consequences of human refusal to accept the message of the kingdom of God.[8] The Gospels' accounts of judgment are thus to be regarded not so much as a direct intervention of God's judgment and punishment, but as the effects of human actions which sinners bring on themselves. Whereas John the Baptist's preaching of the kingdom included a theme of judgment, Jesus' did not. And the so-called apocalyptic chapters in the Gospels (Matt. 24; Mark 13; Luke 21) describe events that take place on earth, without God's direct intervention.

This perspective challenges those explanations of the cross that claim that an expiatory death was necessary to satisfy God's wrath or justice or honor. According to the gospels, the necessity of the cross must be based on something else.[9] Girard suggests that "Jesus had to die because continuing to live would mean a compromise with violence. . . . Here we have the difference between the religions that remain subordinated to the powers and the act of destroying those powers through a form of transcendence that never acts by means of violence, is never responsible for any violence, and remains radically opposed to violence."[10]

JESUS' TRIAL AS A SCAPEGOAT: THE SURROGATE VICTIM MECHANISM AT WORK

Because Jesus so threatened human belief and behavior, he was brought to trial. Raymund Schwager sees this trial as a proclamation of judgment. Those who do not open themselves to Jesus' message exclude themselves from the community of life and condemn themselves to ultimate isolation and hell in their rejection of Jesus.[11] The trial is thus a sham: a satanic spirit, murderous violence, lying, and deceit are at work. As in the parable of the vine-growers (Mark 12:27), the way Jesus is treated exposes humanity's original sin of mimetic desire (Genesis 3-4) and enmity against God which leads to violence. Jesus can't be sacralized because he subverts the scapegoat mechanism. He is therefore satanized by his opponents.

Hermeneutically, Girard's scapegoat mechanism helps us understand what took place according to the New Testament text. Theologically, it clarifies that it was human and not divine violence that killed Jesus. Though God was able to use this violence for our salvation, the violence did not originate with God.

One of the problems arising from Girard's perspective, however, has to do with the role of Jesus. Is Jesus playing only a representative role in the salvation event, either in relation to sinners or to the Father? Is it God (according to Paul) who identifies Jesus with sinners, or is it the people's identification of Jesus with sin and Satan that is operative? To put it differently, sinners alone cannot distance themselves from their sins. As 1 Peter 2:22-23 indicates, Jesus carried or bore the sins of the people and left the judgment to God.

But Jesus is not merely passive or submissive. He actively appeals to God for the people (John 17:9-19; Heb. 4:14-5:10). He prays for their forgiveness (Luke 23:34) and identifies himself with sinners (John 12:32). As a victim himself, Jesus radically intercedes for his enemies, identifying himself with them insofar as they also are harmed by evil: he identifies himself as a victim with all other victims.[12]

In Jesus' identification with victims (Matt. 25:30-45)[13] there is a kind of exchange: he carries their suffering, and they experience the power of his salvation. Paul later persecutes Christ by persecuting his followers (Acts 9), and this persecution influences his theology of the body of Christ (see Acts 9:1-5 and 2 Cor. 5:14). This theology only makes sense if Christ identified himself with victims to the extent that his destiny became theirs (see also Acts 4:27).

Furthermore, Jesus' words at the Last Supper show that he understood his destiny in relation to the salvation of all humans (Luke 22:19-20). Thus he prays for his murderers. The ignorance of the killers shows that they too are victims (see Heb. 5:1-10). This prayer for forgiveness is answered when the Father raises the Son from the dead. Thus he pours out his blood for many (Matt. 26:28).

But it is not only Jesus' self-identification that makes him a victim. Schwager sees Jesus not as a random victim[14] but as the inevitable scapegoat, because Jesus exposed the underlying will of the people to kill.[15] Furthermore, he fueled this desire to kill by making exalted claims about himself (Mark 2:10, 28, and 3:6).

However, what we see in the trial and crucifixion of Jesus is not just a conspiracy against a random person.[16] The gospels reveal a universal human grudge against and resentment toward God. This truth emerges only in the confrontation with the message of pure love and the nonviolent living of Jesus, God's son.[17] Here Schwager criticizes Girard for underplaying or failing fully to take into account the New Testament's implicating of God as ultimate scapegoat.

As Schwager sees it, judgment thus comes not from God, but from people declaring what they think is God's will: in scapegoating Jesus, human beings unknowingly judge themselves.[18] Though they think they are judging another, they are in fact projecting their own sins onto one who is innocent. By identifying with sinners and accepting their judgment, Jesus transforms that judgment into something else: he opens a new way of salvation, a way dependent not on compromise with violence and deceit but on the resurrection and the sending of the Holy Spirit. In this sense, the Father gave the Son, not to judge and punish him in the place of sinners, but to give sinners another opportunity to repent and return to God.[19]

One might argue that if God is omniscient, God planned or wanted Jesus' death. But this cannot be true in a direct way. The actions of Jesus and of his enemies in relation to the cross are very different. Both cannot in the same way reflect God's will. Therefore, phrases like "God sent his son" (Rom. 8:3; Gal. 4:4) and "God has made Christ sin" or "he has condemned sin in his flesh" (2 Cor. 5:21; Rom. 8:3) must be understood differently. In the case of the first phrase, human and divine will agree. In the other instances, human will works against divine will. Hence it is necessary to differentiate between the direct expression of God's will and God's allowing people to respond by opposing and killing Jesus. God allowed the Son to choose obedience unto death as an alternative to killing enemies with supernatural power (Matt. 26:52). God wills to suffer violence rather than to use it to avenge evil.

THE UNIQUE CHARACTER OF CHRIST'S SACRIFICE

The book of Hebrews and a few other places in the New Testament refer to Jesus' death as a sacrifice. As we have seen above, Girard is critical of a sacrificial view of Christ's death and sees Hebrews in particular as leaving open the possibility for Christianity to understand the crucifixion sacrificially and to see God as violent. His sense is that "sacrifice" has been so misused in Christianity that it should be discarded. He also prefers to take Hebrews less seriously, pointing out that he's in good company since Luther didn't like Hebrews either. Both Michael Hardin[20] and Schwager[21] criticize Girard on this point, contending that the word "sacrifice" is being used in a unique way in Hebrews and can therefore be retained.

In contrast to the victim mechanism, Hebrews portrays Jesus as offering himself, as becoming both the subject and object of the verb "to offer." But where does this "offering himself" language come from? Schwager proposes that the Aramaic-speaking congregations portrayed Jesus as a passive victim of the mob (Acts 2:23, 3:15). The language of "offering himself" comes from the Greek-speaking early Christians who also speak of Jesus' death "for us." This is virtually synonymous with "he gave his life for us" and thus seems to denote intentionality. This accords with the New Testament practice of usually avoiding the cultic language of *thuō* (sacrifice) and its cognates in favor of the language of *pherō* (bear or carry) and its cognates.

The nature of the self-giving in Hebrews is distinct from *do ut des*, that is, giving something to God to get something from God. Hebrews 7:1-10:18 is written against the backdrop of Psalm 110. But, as Hardin points out, whereas the figure of Melchizedek in the Qumran scroll (11QMelch) is vengeful, this element of vengeance is absent in Hebrews.[22] Jesus' high priestly work is of a different nature: he lays down his life voluntarily, and in so doing, speaks a word of mercy and forgiveness rather than one of an eye for an eye and a tooth for a tooth (see Heb. 8:3; 9:14, 26-27; 10:10-12; 12:24).

Hebrews 10:1-18 also contains a direct quotation from Psalm 40, an anti-sacrificial text. Thus Christ's death is not portrayed as the spilling of even innocent blood demanded by vengeance, but as an act of self-offering that reveals the scapegoat mechanism. God neither wanted the sacrifice nor was pleased with it. Rather, the new covenant makes clear that sins and lawless acts are forgiven on the basis of repentance rather than sacrifice.

Jesus' self-giving becomes the pattern for the Christian life, which also involves self-offering (10:19-25; 12:14-28; 13:1-16). Thus the ongoing use of the offering language transforms sacrifice. As Schwager notes, this new view of sacrifice constitutes a transformation of evil. Both Jesus and the people were victims of the power that kills, namely, sin, rather than victims of God. But by identifying with humanity in suffering a sin-inflicted death, Jesus typified the death of all and revealed his love for the enemy. So Paul says, "We are convinced that one has died for all; therefore all have died" (2 Cor. 5:14).

The Gospels also emphasize Jesus' death as being active rather than passive. Crying out, he gave up the Spirit (Mark 15:37; Matt. 27:50). In Luke, he gives his Spirit back to the Father (23:46), thus completing his mission as one anointed by the Spirit (Luke 4:16-22). What Hebrews describes as sacrifice includes this act of dying, the completion of his mission and calling as herald and inaugurator of the kingdom.

Furthermore, in his dying, Jesus entrusts himself entirely to the Father. He makes himself completely open and dependent on the Father and thereby transforms death, which is above all something to which human beings are subjected and which they suffer, into an act of self-giving to God. Thus Jesus' radically being delivered over to his enemies is transformed into his radically being delivered over to his Father. In this way Jesus breaks open and transforms all dimensions of human existence.

THE WRATH OF GOD

In the Old Testament, wrath is frequently associated with Yahweh, the covenant God, but it is rarely unmotivated or arbitrary. Rather, as Schwager points out, God's wrath has to do with God's jealousy to preserve the covenant relationship and is therefore directed primarily against an unfaithful Israel. God's wrath is also sometimes seen in unpredictable and catastrophic events that affect all people, but even these are increasingly seen as the result of Israel's covenant violation. Hence the "response of God's wrath" is called forth by unfaithfulness to the covenant.[23]

Several New Testament texts also speak of God's wrath (John 3:36; Rom.1:18, 5:9; Eph. 2:3ff., 1 Thess. 1:10), following the pattern established in the Old Testament: God's wrath appears in the context of God's covenant-making love. God's own people are the primary objects of God's wrath.[24] This wrath is not so much directed against individual sinners as it is the result of the people's rejection of covenant love made known in Jesus Christ. Though God's wrath sometimes appears personal, it usually operates through inexorable consequences (see Rom 1:18ff.; 1 Pet. 2:8).[25] God does not so much directly express wrath as he delivers humans to themselves, their desires, passions, and perverse thinking. In the "little apocalypse" in the Gospels (Matt. 24:1-46; Mark 13:1-37; Luke 21:5-36), nothing is said about a direct violent act of God, only that human beings will attack each other violently. Schwager interprets the book of Revelation in a similar way but on a cosmic level, understanding the angels to be representatives of human communities or nations.[26]

John Driver, in his work on atonement,[27] contends that in the Old and especially in the New Testament there is a strong movement away from the language of propitiation (emphasizing the need to placate the deity) and toward expiation (emphasizing the deity's move to heal the breach between the human and the divine). This stands in contrast to the beliefs of the surrounding cultures. He implicitly criticizes nineteenth- and twentieth-century revivalist or pietist theology that tends to focus God's wrath on individuals and to direct its expression towards those who have never heard of God or responded to him. Though Driver uses varieties of biblical images for atonement and thus does not have to deal with how they are connected with each other, he manages to take the sharpest edges off the worst misuses of conceptions of God's wrath.

There is one specific point of convergence between Schwager and Driver, but Schwager makes a much more systematic use of it than

Driver does. Both interpret Romans 1:18-32 to indicate that God's wrath is not directly exercised on human beings, but is a handing over of human beings to the consequences of their own action. This becomes Schwager's primary point of departure for his systematic interpretation.

Jesus also seems to understand God's wrath in this way. For example, in Matthew's Gospel, as opposition to Jesus begins to grow, he sends out his disciples to proclaim the message of the kingdom. The disciples must have been wondering about what to do with the unrighteous. According to apocalyptic views common at the time, the people who considered themselves righteous, like the Maccabees and the Zealots, for example, tried to drive out the wicked, or, like the Essenes, withdrew completely. In this context, Jesus tells the parable of the wheat and the tares (Matt. 13:24-30, 36-43). In this parable, and Jesus' explanation of it, his main point is that his servants should not tear out the weeds that are growing in the field. That is, the ones who consider themselves children of the kingdom should not destroy those who have rejected the message of the kingdom. The disciples are to let the weeds live, and they will be taken care of at the end of the age. There will still be judgment, but they are not the ones to carry it out.

Regarding hell or eternal punishment and how this relates to God's wrath or forgiveness of sins, Schwager's key point is that because God is nonviolent, God respects human freedom.[28] God is also always willing to forgive, as Jesus' kingdom message makes clear. God's willingness to forgive reached a preliminary limit, however, in the human rejection of Jesus' offer of forgiveness, a rejection that prefigures the killing of the Son. The cross is a sign that God allows himself to be deeply touched by the rejection of his Son. But even then, God so respected human freedom that he was willing to permit his own Son to be killed rather than force humans to preserve his Son. God's response to this rejection is to raise Jesus from the dead and in doing so again to extend peace to humans. After the resurrection, Jesus always said, "Peace be with you." So God's response is to continue to seek a free human response to his offer of pardon rather than forcibly and violently to change people. This does not fully answer the hell question but points to the last-resort nature of eternal punishment. The emphasis of the gospel falls on the offer of salvation, even to those who ignorantly crucify Jesus.

THE RESURRECTION, THE COMING OF
THE HOLY SPIRIT, AND A NEW GATHERING

God's action on Easter should then be understood as a judgment between the claims of Jesus and those of his adversaries (see 1 Peter 2:23). But it is also, and above all, a decision for the Son who gave himself over to death for his adversaries. Thus is it also a judgment for the good of sinners, for whom God once again opens the way of salvation. God acted differently than the vineyard owner in the parable of the tenants (Mark 12:1-12) by sending the resurrected Son back with the message of peace (see Luke 24:36; John 20:19, 21, 26). The resurrection both confirms the message of the Son and makes a new offer of salvation, but it does so in a manner that is not directly victorious in earthly terms. For those who believe, it is a powerful sign that confirms the Son's message and action, but it does not overrun those who were "defeated."

Pentecost then begins a new dimension of the salvation event. The Spirit's coming brought new certainty that equipped the early disciples to witness in and confront the world (see Acts 2:29; 4:13, 29, 31; 28:31). Before the Spirit arrived, the believers had received the message of a kingdom still in some ways external to them. Even the postresurrection appearances of Jesus aroused fear and doubt in the beginning. But the events at Pentecost brought about a bold inner transformation that enabled Jesus' followers to witness to and praise God in new and more immediate ways.

The events at Pentecost are also a proclamation of a healing of the divisions that occurred at the Tower of Babel (Genesis 11). Pentecost does not mark the return to one language; rather, it enables understanding in the midst of diversity, so that multiplicity of language is no longer a barrier between believers. It also demonstrates that new understanding and unity cannot be forced and are finally not in human power to assure, for they depend on the working of the Spirit in the lives of humans. Pentecost marks the inauguration of a new kind of community that, while it is not without division, overcomes social, language, gender, and religious differences. This new community comes about as a result of Jesus' offering himself on the cross and therefore cannot be ignored; it is an important part of the atoning work of Christ (see John 12:24). Though it cannot be explained simply as a sociological phenomenon, it has sociological implications.[29]

The new community is also a sign of the kingdom of God and the activity of the Spirit in history. First, it is a sign of the mission of Jesus Christ in the world, in the preaching of good news, in baptism, in the

Lord's supper, and in service. Second, it is a sign of the unity the Spirit provides in a common praise of God, in communication across ethnic divisions, in fellowship, and in sharing of material resources. Finally, it is a sign of the moral character of the kingdom of God. The ethical and religious conduct of the new community is to be an alternative to the kinds of communities in the world around it (see especially Matt. 5 and 6, texts that are broadly analogous to the New Testament as a whole).

SUMMARY

We began with the question of whether Girard's views are potentially helpful for understanding and interpreting the doctrine of the atonement. Several considerations provide the background for this question:

1. In Scripture, salvation through Jesus Christ essentially includes both reconciliation with God and reconciliation with human beings. Sin as disobedience to God results simultaneously in enmity to and separation from God and in enmity to and separation from others. Most Western doctrines of atonement, however, limit their concern to reconciliation with God, or at most they consider reconciliation with others a secondary consequence of reconciliation with God.

2. Jesus' life, teachings, ministry, call to discipleship, and death on the cross are all intrinsically related to his rejection of violence. Therefore, a theological understanding of the work of atonement should also provide the basis for a Christian ethic of nonviolence. But most Western doctrines of atonement, especially after Christus Victor, do not specifically relate Jesus' nonviolence to his work of atonement. Traditional doctrines of atonement implicitly either justify violence or consider the question a matter of secondary importance.

3. On the surface there seems to be a sharp contrast between the violent Old Testament God and the nonviolent God revealed through Jesus Christ. This observation about the different ways God is portrayed led to one of the early Christian heresies, the Marcionite heresy, and remains a problem for some contemporary peace churches. The question we face is how to take seriously the God revealed as nonviolent in Jesus Christ without dismissing the Old Testament. Or to put it the other way around, most traditional doctrines of atonement assume that there is violence in God that is somehow worked out in the doctrine of atonement, at least in the sense that God is the one who demands the death of Christ.[30]

EVALUATION

Girard's views seem to be helpful in uncovering the legitimation of violence that is incorporated either implicitly or explicitly into most traditional views of the atonement. Though Girard's views cannot and should not discredit all the traditional models of atonement, they do help uncover the legitimation of violence in many of the traditional views, and by extension criticize these doctrines' implicit justification for human violence against the enemy.

By assuming that the revelation of God in and through Jesus Christ is the central focus of theology and faith, Girard provides an alternative to both historical-critical and traditional noncritical methods of interpreting Scripture. Specifically, Girard emphasizes that Jesus' death on the cross has a certain coherence with his life and ministry, his resurrection, and the formation of a new community of people. Most traditional doctrines of atonement do not build on this coherence of Jesus' birth, life, death, resurrection, and formation of the new community. They tend either to focus on his incarnation, his death, or perhaps his resurrection.

Girard also highlights Jesus' rejection of violence in all the aspects of what Schwager calls the "Drama of Salvation." This alternative to violence is evident even in the biblical stories about the birth of Christ, which, in contrast to mythological stories of unions between gods and humans, involves not the rape of a woman, but her willing consent to become God's servant in a pregnancy by the Holy Spirit.

Girard's views are also helpful in demonstrating the pervasiveness of violence and deceit in the mythologies and realities of various cultures, religions, and societies. Girardian perspectives help us interpret what he calls "texts of persecution": the myths of culture and religion which are the stories victors tell to justify their persecution of the weak and the enemy.

A Girardian perspective highlights the God revealed in and through Jesus as the God whose love is perfect, to use the word from Matthew 5. God's love is without violence and without limits. God calls human beings to a nonviolent mimesis: to accept God's forgiveness, to love one another, and to follow Jesus in life and death.[31] Jesus calls his disciples to follow him not only by his words but by his whole existence. Since his own desires and ambitions were focused on the will of the Father, he assigns the same goal to his disciples.

Finally, at least in Western cultural context, Girard provides a useful critique of individualistic and rationalistic anthropologies, and he may also be helpful in *constructing* a theological anthropology in the context of Western culture.

Although Girard's own work and the contributions of Girardian scholars are useful in a number of ways, some problems still remain. To begin, Girard's anthropological model for explaining the pervasiveness of violence in human culture, religion, and society has not been tested and proven in Eastern religions and cultures. Whether it is accurate in those contexts remains to be shown.

In addition, Girard himself does not contend that his views provide an adequate alternative theological model of the atonement, and they in fact do not. This critique can be expressed in several ways: that a social sciences approach cannot fully perceive and articulate the particular truth of revelation, or that Girard's view of sin and salvation may be too limited (see above), whereas the Bible makes universal claims. Schwager's "Drama of Salvation," so far the only attempt to work out a systematic or constructive account of atonement based on Girard's views, also needs further examination and critical assessment. Biblical scholars have given significant attention to the topic of sacrifice and pertinent texts in the Synoptics on Jesus' death, but more complete work remains to be done.

In addition to unanswered theoretical and theological questions, the pastoral implications of Girardian scholarship are not clear. How does the Girardian emphasis bring release from guilt and shame? How does it empower believers to live a new life in Christ?

Some questions remain about the final outcome of judgment in a Girardian framework. Although some biblical scholars have interpreted the separation of humans into an eternal heaven and an eternal hell in metaphorical terms, there are some problems with reducing this expression of judgment entirely to metaphor. But there is also a contradiction between the sovereign goodness and power of God, on the one hand, and the eternal punishment of evil (hell), on the other.

Some biblical passages emphasize the continuity between the present and future life by portraying the eternal state as flowing from current experiences of good and evil. Other texts seem to speak of the destruction of all evil, including the destruction of unrighteous people, and the eternal existence of the righteous. These texts resolve the tension between God's sovereignty and evil in the world by destroying rather than redeeming evil. And some texts hold to the view of universal restoration, though this perspective seems not to satisfy the demands of justice. However, if this view maintains that restoration cannot happen without the cross and without repentance, then the consequences of sin are not arbitrarily canceled to overcome death and hell. There is, rather, a genuine triumph of God over all sin and evil. But we cannot hold to this view if we do so in a way that cancels out the justice of God or makes Christ's costly death vain. We cannot cover and condone violence rather than exposing and judging it.

It may be, then, that what is called for, in addition to further research and study, is the ability to live with paradox. For while Girard contributes to our understanding of the nature of God as good and the nature of human evil, the paradox of God's sovereignty and human freedom remains.

NOTES

1. John Driver, *Understanding the Atonement for the Mission of the Church* (Scottdale, Pa.: Herald Press, 1986).

2. Raymund Schwager, *Must There be Scapegoats? Violence and Redemption in the Bible* (San Francisco: Harper and Row, 1987). See p. 6 for the quotation from Girard.

3. Schwager discusses the signs of a mounting crisis in *Scapegoats*, p. 15ff.

4. For other consequences, see Schwager, *Scapegoats*, 22-25.

5. See Schwager, *Scapegoats*, 171-176.

6. See ibid., 180-83; also Schwager, "Christ's Death and the Prophetic Critique of Sacrifice," *Semeia* 33 (1985), 111-113.

7. Jacob Neusner, *A Rabbi Talks with Jesus: An Intermillennial, Interfaith Exchange* (New York: Doubleday, 1993), 27.

8. René Girard, *Things Hidden Since the Foundation of the World* (Stanford, Calif.: Stanford University Press, 1987), 203ff.

9. See Schwager, "Christ's Death and the Prophetic Critique," 113-119.

10. Girard, *Things Hidden*, 213.

11. Schwager, "Christ's Death and the Prophetic Critique," 113-119.

12. Cf. Girard's reasons for Jesus' identification with victims (*Scapegoats*, 118ff.) Note also Jesus' relation to the Father in obedience and intercession for sinners.

13. Raymund Schwager, "La mort de Jesus: René Girard et la Theologie," *Recherches de science Religieuse* 73/4 (1985), 495ff.

14. Schwager, *Must There be Scapegoats*, 195-197.

15. Ibid., 191.

16. Ibid., 195ff.

17. Ibid., 197.

18. Raymund Schwager, *Jesus in the Drama of Salvation: Toward a Biblical Doctrine of Redemption*, trans. James G. Williams and Paul Haddon (New York: Crossroad, 1999), 118; *Jesus im Heilsdrama: Entwurf einer biblischen Erlösungslehre* (Innsbruck-Wein: Tyrolia, 1990), 154.

19. Cf. Schwager, "La mort de Jesus."

20. Michael Hardin, "Sacrificial Language in Hebrews: Reappraising

René Girard," in this volume, pp. 114-16. See also Loren Johns, pp. 120-28.

21. Schwager, *Scapegoats*. Note also the critique of sacrifice beginning with Amos 5:21-25.

22. Hardin, *Hebrews*, 111 in this volume.

23. Schwager, *Scapegoats*, 57.

24. Ibid., 150-54.

25. Ibid., 60-66; *Drama of Salvation*, 164-66 // *Heilsdrama*, 209-211.

26. Schwager, *Scapegoats*, 218-219.

27. John Driver, *Understanding the Atonement*, 147-155.

28. Schwager, *Drama of Salvation*, 67-68 // *Heilsdrama*, 92-93.

29. Schwager, *Drama of Salvation*, 143-45 // *Heilsdrama*, 184-86.

30. For more on the unity of Christ's life in revealing the nonviolence of God, see Michael Hardin, "Violence: René Girard and the Recovery of Early Christian Perspectives," *Brethren Life and Thought* 37 (Spring 1992), 107-120.

31. See Schwager, *Scapegoats*, 176ff.; Robert G. Hamilton-Kelly, *Sacred Violence: Paul's Hermeneutic of the Cross* (Minneapolis: Augsburg Fortress, 1992), 173ff.; and Willard M. Swartley, "Discipleship and Imitation of Jesus/ Suffering Servant: The Mimesis of New Creation," in this volume, pp. 218-245.

CHAPTER TWO

Scapegoating No More: Christian Pacifism and New Testament Views of Jesus' Death

Ted Grimsrud

THERE IS A PARADOX IN HUMAN RELIGIOUS experience. On the one hand, religion is a main (perhaps *the* main) dynamic in death-dealing violence in the world. On the other hand, religious faith also often provides the main basis for the fruitful *rejection* of violence.

Religion has been a key dynamic in the death-dealing violence of generation after generation of "holy" wars—the Crusades, the seventeenth-century Thirty Years War between Protestants and Catholics, 1940s conflicts between Hindus and Muslims in newly liberated India, strife between Catholics and Protestants in Northern Ireland, ongoing Middle East hostilities among Muslims and Jews.

Most premeditated death-dealing violence requires a fueling ideology that justifies human taking of human life. Often this ideology has a clear religious element, claimed to be a *divinely* sanctioned rationale for coercion, even for taking human life.

At the same time, religious faith inspires people seeking means to break this spiral of violence. For many, faith affirms that what is beautiful and worthwhile about the human project comes from God—the merciful and loving creator, who desires human flourishing and well-being, who grieves at the costly spiral of violence. The heart of many people's religious faith moves them to care passionately about escaping this spiral of violence.

Many see Christianity as offering in Jesus a model of living that enables such escape. Jesus models—in life and in teaching—a way toward genuine peace. Therefore, despite the bloody hands apparent throughout the history of Christianity, many people believe the story of Jesus remains a main source of hope.

Christian pacifism has always held that the story of Jesus points toward rejection of all violence.[1] However, the question of how to overcome violence confronts everyone with renewed urgency. René Girard asserts that, in the light of contemporary weapons of mass destruction, human beings are essentially faced with a choice: total destruction or total renunciation of violence.[2]

The Christian response to violence, even among Christian pacifists, has not taken seriously enough the centrality of violence in the Bible. The biblical materials take violence seriously as something central to human reality. At least some of those materials ultimately show that at the heart of God, the very heart of reality, violence has no place. As Walter Wink puts it,

> The violence of Scripture, embarrassing to us, [actually] became the means by which sacred violence was revealed for what it is: a lie perpetuated against victims in the name of a God who, through violence, was working to expose violence for what it is and to reveal the divine nature as nonviolent.[3]

A major ingredient of the Bible as a resource for peacemaking is actually that part of the biblical materials often seen as most problematic—the Bible's portrayal of violence. One especially important instance is the portrayal of Jesus' death. Here the two sides of the paradox of religion come into focus. On the one hand, Jesus' death reveals a great deal about religious ideology as a major dynamic *in* death-dealing violence. On the other hand, Jesus' death reveals a great deal about religious faith as a source of freedom from giving in to the cycle of violence.

The work of René Girard and biblical theologians directly influenced by him provides a needed challenge to consider these issues. Girard has asserted that the issue of violence is central to human existence. Only by facing this, understanding it, and coming to terms with it can we hope to break free from the dominion of violence.

Girard helps us see that conceptions of the sacred are based on violence turned on scapegoats, then attributed to God. This is sacred violence. For him, the revelation of the true God involves exposing the falsehood of sacred violence. The justification of such violence does not come from the true God. With such a revelation, it becomes increasingly clear that "the actual initiative to kill does not originate in God after all, but in human beings." Sacred violence is not from God, but simply "human beings attacking one another."[4]

Girard also points out that mythology is generally told from the point of view of those on top, who often are killers. *Demythification,* on the other hand, retells "the story from the point of view of the victim." The Bible is uniquely characterized by such demythification, by emphasis on the victim's point of view.[5] So the Bible is a unique resource for exposing mythology that blinds us to the reality that social structures that victimize the many on behalf of people on top are themselves violent.

Seeing Jesus' death primarily as a sacrifice offered to a holy God to effect salvation actually reflects such mythification. Thus such a view buttresses structural violence. For Girardians, demythifying Jesus' death helps us to see that Jesus did not die as such a sacrifice. Rather, Jesus' death reveals God's love as that which *refuses* "to participate in the cycle of mimetic desire and vengeance."[6] Jesus' death is *not* an act of violence *God* needs.

Girardians associate sacrifice with sacred violence. Sacrificial theology does not help us overcome the problem of violence. Rather, such theology pictures ultimate reality (the heart of God itself) as requiring violence—the death of innocent victims. Thus ultimately sacrifice does not provide the means to genuine salvation and *shalom* but only feeds the spiral of violence.

The central violent event in the Bible is the death of Jesus. In the manner it portrays this death, the Bible itself reflects the paradox characteristic of religious faith—where religious faith both adds to the spiral of violence and also provides the best means to break free from it. In the New Testament, Jesus' death is in places interpreted in sacrificial terms, as a cosmic transaction through which an act of violence enables God to effect human salvation.

However, such an interpretation reflects a perspective on God different from that revealed by Jesus himself. Jesus portrayed God not in terms of vengeance and wrath, but in terms of unconditional love and forgiveness. This loving God needs no blood sacrifice. The church, though, came to portray God differently. Jesus' infinitely merciful God came to be seen as one whose wrath required blood atonement. This leads to God requiring Jesus to die on behalf of us all. In Wink's words:

> The nonviolent God of Jesus comes to be depicted as a God of unequaled violence, since God not only allegedly demands the blood of the victim who is closest and most precious to him, but also holds the whole of humanity accountable for a death that God both anticipated and required.[7]

Sacrificial theology stands in tension with thoroughgoing pacifism because it posits a violence deep in the heart of God. Such violence ultimately undergirds inter-human violence. And though it is attributed to God, such violence is in actuality only a projection of human violence.[8]

However, the Bible contains other understandings of the death of Jesus which take us beyond sacrificial thinking. My focus in this paper is not primarily that of arguing against sacrifice. Rather, my aim is to present an alternative way of thinking of Jesus' death which I believe is more relevant to Christian pacifism and more congruent with how Jesus himself portrayed God. The New Testament does contain sacrifice-theology which requires analysis in its own right.[9] Nevertheless, my focus is on selected New Testament materials that provide a basis for an interpretation of Jesus' death *not* determined by sacred violence.

Stimulated by Girardian thinking, I want to consider Jesus' death in relation to several issues—namely, Jesus' relationship with *religious institutionalism* (use of institutional power in oppressive and self-serving ways) as portrayed in Mark's Gospel, especially in relation to the Jerusalem temple; Jesus relationship with *cultural exclusivism* (self-protective policies and actions that exclude people from kingdom blessing) as portrayed in some of Paul's letters, especially in relation to the law; and Jesus' relationship with beastly *political authoritarianism* (political policies and actions that oppress and kill people) as portrayed in the Book of Revelation, especially in relation to the Roman empire.

Jesus' cross, I contend, is significant more for its historical content than as a basis for an ideology of sacrifice. The historical significance is the shameful death of a good person through an act of violence on the part of the established order. Jesus' death does not destroy these social structures. Instead, though leaving them intact, it reveals their true nature, thus providing a basis for withdrawal of credibility and allegiance. In this way, their effective power is overcome.[10]

When we focus on the historical content of Jesus' death, and the applications New Testament writers make based on that content, we find two main themes. First is exposure of the violence of major social structures. This exposure undercuts the authority given to these institutions and in this way enables freedom to break the spiral of violence. Second, the life of Jesus, especially the way he faced the violence of these institutions, which he brought to surface, points to freedom from violence.

JESUS EXPOSES INSTITUTIONAL POWER (THE GOSPEL OF MARK)

The stories in the latter part of Mark's Gospel leading up to Jesus' crucifixion highlight Jesus' conflict with the religious institution of the temple.

The temple was vital to established life in Jerusalem and Judea. It was the *economic* center of Jerusalem. An estimated eighty percent of Jerusalem's employment was dependent on the temple.[11] The temple was the *political* center. Since Israel was a religious state, its religious code was also its state and civil code. The temple leadership, the Sanhedrin, also carried legislative and executive power. This power was heightened due to the Sanhedrin's cooperation with Roman rule. However, most of all, the temple was the *religious* center. The temple was where God was present on earth. It was "a religious center and theological symbol of tremendous emotive power."[12]

As Mark's drama approaches its climax, Jesus is seen entering Jerusalem (11:1). This begins the last week and final stage of Jesus' life. Immediately (11:11), Jesus visits the temple. The sense of conflict is established: Jesus versus the religious leaders, the temple authorities. The conflict escalates when Jesus returns to the temple a second time and proceeds to "drive out those who were selling and those who were buying in the temple, and he overturned the tables of the money changers and the seats of those who sold doves; and he would not allow anyone to carry anything through the temple" (11:15). With these actions, Jesus judges these transactions as defiling the temple's true purpose.

Mark brackets this confrontation in the temple with a two-part account of Jesus cursing a fig tree, causing it to wither (11:12-14; 11:20-21). The tree symbolizes Israel, and its fate parallels that of the temple. Jesus' challenge to the temple is an acting out of God's judgment on the temple. The problem with the temple is that it has failed to be "a house of prayer for all the nations," becoming instead a center for religious exclusivism and economic exploitation.[13]

Jesus quotes two Old Testament prophets here: Isaiah 56:7 ("My house shall be called a house of prayer for all the nations") and Jeremiah 7:11 ("You have made it a den of robbers"). The context of the Isaiah text is a portrayal of an eschatological hope of foreigners flocking to Jerusalem. The Jeremiah quote is part of Jeremiah's condemning the people of Judea for presuming that God would continue to sustain the temple even in the face of their sinful living.[14] Jesus uses Israel's prophets to challenge Israel's present temple practices, which he asserts are corrupt and counter to God's intentions.

We are told that in response to this so-called cleansing of the temple, "the chief priests and scribes . . . kept looking for a way to kill [Jesus]" (11:18). These religious leaders were for a time restrained by Jesus' popularity. But they fully intended to do away with Jesus. He was a major threat to their purity-based system of religious control. He had not only trifled with the purity regulations but was also widely known and supported. These factors alone were cause for alarm. Added to these was his direct confrontation with the temple.

The parable of the vineyard which immediately follows (12:1-12) is one of Jesus' most allegory-like parables. He likens the vineyard to the people of Israel, the watchtower to the temple, and the tenants to the religious leaders. The temple was intended by God from of old to be a center for justice among Israel but instead became a center for *in*justice. God sent messengers, "slaves," to restore the vineyard to its intended purposes. But the tenants murdered those messengers— analogous to the fate of prophets throughout the history of Israel. Finally, the master sends his "beloved son," who is also murdered. This is the last straw for the owner, and he promises to come to "destroy the tenants and give the vineyard to others."

These tenants (the religious leaders) have shown that they are *rivals* to the owner (God). The practices of the temple are hence seen to be not faithful responses to God's wishes but, rather, efforts to usurp God's place as Israel's object of worship.[15] This is harsh criticism. The parable is patterned after Isaiah's Song of the Vineyard (Isa. 5:1-7), itself a strong critique of unfaithful eighth-century Israel. The parable ends with a quote from Psalm 118:22-23, a temple psalm. Temple imagery thus pervades the parable. That the parable was meant to criticize current temple practices and the religious leaders is seen in their response. "When they [the chief priests and scribes of 11:18 and 11:27] realized that [Jesus] had told this parable against them, they wanted to arrest him" (12:12).[16]

Jesus speaks in Mark 13 of the destruction of the temple. One of the disciples exclaims regarding the greatness of the temple: "Look, Teacher, what large stones and what large buildings!" The temple, constructed by Herod, was famous for its splendor. This exclamation likely reflects precisely that sense of security about the great temple as guarantor of God's ongoing protection for the chosen people Jeremiah scored in the text Jesus earlier quoted. These wonderful buildings were seen to symbolize God's presence with Israel.[17]

Jesus, however, was not impressed. "Do you see those great buildings?" he replied. "Not one stone will be left here on another.

All will be thrown down" (13:2). This in part is an allusion to the impending physical destruction of this great edifice. Perhaps it also reflects that the spiritual authority of this institution was collapsing. Immediately after the discourse of chapter 13, we are told again that "the chief priests and the scribes were looking for a way to arrest Jesus by stealth and kill him" (14:1).

Finally, they do arrest and bring him to trial. One of the main allegations is that Jesus said he would destroy the temple (14:58). This charge is false on the surface. Jesus did not say *he* would destroy the temple. Yet, ironically, it is true in the sense that Jesus' actions and words render the temple's functions meaningless.[18]

Mark's Gospel does not picture Jesus as actually threatening to destroy the temple. However, the prominence of the accusation— 15:29 continues the accusation against Jesus—reflects the reality that Jesus' enemies did understand him to be a threat to the temple.[19]

Mark's treatment of the temple concludes in 15:38. When Jesus died, "the curtain of the temple was torn in two, from top to bottom." The significance of this final event, in part at least, is connected with what immediately follows, the Roman centurion's confession that "Truly this man was God's Son" (15:39). The torn "curtain of the temple" juxtaposes Jesus and the temple as alternative places of divine presence. It provides perspective on what follows, the centurion's confession. The death of the Servant opens the way to God for all the world by exposing sacred violence and depriving the temple of its mystique.[20]

For Mark's Gospel, there is a clear connection between Jesus being put to death and Jesus' conflict with the temple, Jerusalem's center of religious institutional power.[21] In several cases—the cleansing of the temple, the parable of the vineyard, the apocalyptic vision, and the accusation before the tribunal—we see a connection between Jesus being perceived as a threat to the institution and the promise that he will be killed for this.

In the end, though, for Mark Jesus' death does not signal that the religious authorities are victorious over him. Jesus' death actually signifies the opposite. The temple curtain is torn. Jesus, even on the cross, fulfills what the temple was meant to do and did not—engendering worship of God by Gentiles as well as Jews.

Jesus, as interpreted by Mark, challenges the misuse of institutions head on. He does so by denying the ultimate legitimacy of his culture's central religious institutions. He does not answer the religious leaders when they have him on trial (14:61). This refusal to answer, in effect, is a statement that he rejects their legitimacy as representatives of God.

Mark contains several references to Jesus' mission to the nations, in the context of the conflicts in the temple. The temple in Jerusalem, in its institutional power, had lost touch with God's will that the word of mercy be expressed to all peoples. Jesus came to express that word and met only with hostility from the religious leaders. So, in effect, the old temple must be torn down. A new, open, and inclusive temple, erected by Jesus himself, must take its place (as Rev. 21:22 states a few decades later: "I saw no temple in the city, for its temple is the Lord God the Almighty and the Lamb").

Mark's Jesus criticized the temple system. That system originally had a mission, to provide creative, communally faithful ways of living for all in Hebrew society. But by behaving as institutions so often do and ultimately placing priority on survival and support of a static unjust status quo, the temple had left its original mission far behind.

Institutionalism stifles creativity. When the priority is on institutional survival, then order, security, and peace at all costs take precedence. Few risks can be taken. Few new thoughts can be pursued. The people who thrive are not visionaries or prophets but bureaucrats and yes-men. A prophet such as Jesus is not welcomed as a messenger from God. He is not seen as one sent to provide much-needed light into new ways of responding faithfully to the many and great crises faced by first-century Judaism. Rather, he is seen as a threat, an upsetter of the applecart, a voice to be stilled.

Jesus' conflict with the temple was costly. Many forces in his world benefited from people being subservient to institutions. Seeking to break free from that subservience provoked resistance. Yet Jesus' example highlights the need to seek such freedom and witnesses that such freedom is at least partly attainable.

As Mark tells the story, Jesus' witness led to his death. However, in facing death as he did—fully committed to the *life* of the Spirit and free from the dominance of spirit-*denying* hierarchies and religious ideologies—Jesus' life of freedom *amid* the struggle points to an alternative to life lived in obeisance to the sacred violence of religious institutions turned in on themselves.

JESUS' DEATH AND THE LAW OF THE SPIRIT (PAUL'S LETTERS)

Paul treats some elements of Jewish law as implemented by his opponents as aspects of sacred violence. This is especially evident in his letters to the Galatians and the Romans. Paul essentially argues that the central issue is trust. He contrasts trust in "works of the law" as an approach to salvation with trust simply in God's mercy apart from rituals, boundary markers, and other forms of cultural exclusivity.

My understanding of Paul and the law is greatly influenced by the work of James D. G. Dunn. In Dunn's view, "'Works of the law' are not understood, either by his Jewish interlocutors or by Paul himself, as works which earn God's favor, as merit-amassing observances." Rather, these works play the role of indicators that show that the Jews are God's people. They demonstrate covenant status. "They are the proper response to God's covenant grace, the minimal commitment for members of God's people." Paul, though, sees adherence to works of the law as too exclusive. He denies that God's justification extends only to those who wear the badge of the covenant.[22]

Throughout its history, Israel had placed high priority on the law as a key element distinguishing Israel from the nations. Two centuries before Paul's time, the Maccabean crisis had pushed a few key elements of law observance to the forefront as boundary markers crucial for Jewish self-identity. Two of the most important were circumcision and food laws, and they remained central in Paul's time for the same reason. Hence when Paul speaks of works of the law, he in particular has circumcision and food laws in mind. "Not because they are the only 'works' which the law requires, but because they had become the crucial test cases for covenant loyalty." They were crucial for maintaining Jewish identity as God's special chosen people. They marked the boundary between who was in and who was out.[23]

For Paul, such an emphasis on these works as required for Christian faith was unacceptable. Because they put so much emphasis on cultural exclusivity, works of the law are no different than "works of the flesh" (Gal 5:19). "These works of the law in effect imprison God's righteousness in a [cultural, a] racial and national, that is, [a] fleshly, framework."[24]

For Paul, placing one's trust in works of the law leads to a misunderstanding of God's mercy. It distorts the meaning of salvation by tying it to cultural exclusivity. And this can lead to violence. Trust in works of the law focused on particular boundary markers—circumcision, food purity regulations, and Sabbath observance. Such a focus inevitably led to emphasis on demarcating who is in and who is out. Resistance to such demarcation, a hallmark of Jesus and to some degree at least of the early church, met with the hostility of those zealous for works of the law.

Paul identifies himself as having been one such zealot. In his zeal, he was "violently persecuting the church of God and trying to destroy it" (Gal 1:13). In fact, he was one of the most zealous of the zealous. He was, as he wrote, "advanced in Judaism beyond many among my people of the same age" (Gal 1:14).

Paul's zeal was to defend Israel's covenant distinctiveness by the sword. His intent was to enforce his conviction that salvation is only for Israel—no one else. Together with other Pharisees, he wanted to draw a tighter, stricter line round the "righteous," to mark them off even more clearly from the Gentile "sinner." This was why he was so violent to the early Hellenist Christians. They were opening the door to Gentiles. Paul persecuted Christians out of his "zeal for the law as a boundary marking off righteousness with God as a special privilege to be promoted and defended."[25] The Hellenist Christians likely threatened Paul's own identity as a covenant member with their inclusiveness. For Paul, this was a threat to the covenant itself.

Paul constructed his whole system of life around works of the law and exclusivity. He did so out of a heartfelt desire to do good, to serve God, to remain faithful to "the traditions of [his] ancestors" (Gal 1:14). However, while on his way to Damascus, he had his system turned upside down. Paul was so shattered by this confrontation with the risen Jesus that he could not see nor speak for days (Acts 9:1-9).

A major aspect of Paul's experience was to realize that in the name of service to God's law, he was actually a murderer. The way to faithfulness to God was not via trust in works of the law but simply through unadorned trust in God's unconditional mercy—especially as expressed in the life, death, and resurrection of Jesus of Nazareth.

Paul came to see that trusting in works of the law, even when in the name of purity and out of zeal for living faithfully to God, actually leads into slavery to sin. Even while delighting with one's heart in the law of God, when one is focusing on works of the law more than all-inclusive mercy, one's practices actually reflect one's captivity to the law of sin (Rom. 7:21-25). Such imprisonment is actually captivity to sacred violence. Here, in the name of purity and holiness, one excludes, boasts, and even literally persecutes and kills.

Paul believes that the law is indeed of God but has always been meant to be secondary to the promise. The point of the law was and is to order life in the community of those who have received God's promise and trusted in God's mercy. Appropriation of the law becomes problematic when it becomes a basis for restricting God's mercy only to people who follow certain rituals and observances. Such appropriation is contrary to the God-given purpose of the law. It reflects trusting in works of the law for one's standing before God rather than trusting in God's unconditional mercy. This empowers cultural exclusivity based on boundary markers that have become rigid, absolute, and pride-inducing weapons to be used against outsiders.

Paul affirms that Jesus Christ points to a different way—trust in God's mercy. Life in the Spirit replaces life focused on the flesh. In fact, such a life leads to fulfillment of the genuine purpose of the law—living in love (Rom. 8:4).

The law itself could not effect freedom from the power of sin and violence. When people live as if it can, then the law becomes another of the "elemental spirits" that binds people and actually separates them from God's mercy (Gal 4:3).

The law itself is of God. The law is good and useful to human well-being when properly understood. However, it all too often is misappropriated, as works of law, and then trusted as the foundation of peoples' identity as God's chosen. When thus appropriated, the law becomes "weakened by the flesh" (Rom. 8:3). As such, the law not only cannot set people free from bondage to sin and violence, it actually only tightens those chains, itself causing more sin and violence. Paul knew this from bitter personal experience, both as a chief persecutor himself and later as the recipient of such sacred violence by those defending the Truth (violently).

For Paul, when the law is appropriated in ways that become forms of nationalism, bases for cultural exclusivity, driving forces in setting up and enforcing rigid boundary markers, then its appropriation is idolatry. This is a drastic claim. But Paul himself knew only too well that drastic measures were required to uncover the powerful hold this idolatry had on religious people.

When Jesus asserted that the Sabbath was made for humans, not humans for the Sabbath (Mark 2:27), he exposed this idolatry. An institution that justifies violence against human beings in the name of law is worshiping rules and regulations more than the merciful God, who desires works of mercy more than rituals and sacrifices.

The alternative to trusting in works of the law is simple trust in God's mercy, in God's promise. Paul develops this contrast in Romans 4 by discussing Abraham, who he asserts was "reckoned righteous" *before* the beginning of the rite of circumcision. It was not Abraham's obedience to this regulation that justified him, but his simple trust in God's unconditional mercy. Circumcision was secondary, temporal, relative.

Now in Paul's day, through the work of Jesus and the outpouring of the Spirit, Gentiles were making apparent the truthfulness of God's order of salvation with Abraham. *Trust* first. Trust as the basis for salvation. Then the law follows, to guide and direct life in the Spirit.

The Gospel accounts make it clear that Jesus' life reflected these same dynamics. Jesus healed on the Sabbath, emphasizing the relativity of Sabbath regulations in relation to human well-being—the former is meant to serve the latter, not vice versa, as he accused the scribes and Pharisees of advocating. Jesus welcomed unclean people, people on the margins (lepers, tax collectors, women, children, various other "sinners"[26]), unconditionally. He announced that the kingdom of God was at hand, available, requiring only trust in God's mercy as a basis for entrance.

Jesus argued that genuine fulfillment of the law had to do with loving God and other people. He asserted that he did not mean to abolish the law at all. However, he did mean to call people to a different approach to the law—seeing it as a means to encourage love and forgiveness, even toward enemies and outsiders. He rejected the law as a basis for setting boundaries, for facilitating exclusiveness and pride. As a result, he was seen by Pharisees as breaking, even abandoning, Israel's covenant with God—a covenant witnessed to by faithful adherence to works of the law.[27]

Paul knew from his own life that such an approach to the law would bring about a violent response. The perspective Jesus opposed, which turns works of the law into cultural exclusivity, as Paul himself had done, is based on deep-seated and often hidden violence.

Paul refers to Deuteronomy 21:23: "Cursed is everyone who hangs on a tree" (Gal 3:13). By applying this verse to Jesus' crucifixion, Paul implies that Jesus was regarded as a covenant breaker. Jesus was seen to violate the boundaries set by the law and suffered justifiably violent consequences. What Paul came to believe after his Damascus road experience, however, was that in fact God affirms the one the so-called law cursed.[28] What Jesus brought to the surface was sacred violence, thereby revealing that the law as Paul had understood it was not *God's* actual law. Paul's focus on works of the law had led him to commit violence.

Paul himself had joined the forces that had put Jesus to death. By challenging exclusiveness and boasting, Jesus had laid bare the reality that such a system was based on violence. And when the system is challenged, its underlying violence becomes explicit and overt. In Jesus' case, this violence contributed to his death.

The sacred violence inherent in the law understood primarily in terms of cultural exclusivity is revealed in the murder of Jesus, the one Paul came to see as a genuine upholder of God's true law of love. After Paul came to know Jesus and his way as the revelation of the true God, he came to see that the death of Jesus uncovers the violence of trusting in works of the law. For Paul, Jesus' death also points toward life. Jesus' death followed by resurrection effects salvation by making God's mercy more apparent and the Spirit more accessible.

In light of the life Jesus witnesses to, Paul asserts that the genuine law is the life of love, living freely in light of God's mercy and showing that mercy toward others (Rom. 13:8-10). This love is modeled after the very heart of God. For Paul, then, Jesus' death both reveals the sacred violence of trust in works of the law that leads to cultural exclusivity *and* violence-free living, through which may be experienced God-given blessings of appropriate law observance.[29]

Jesus' Death and the Powers That Be (Revelation)

Jesus' way as criticism of the empire is a central theme in the Book of Revelation. Especially in chapter thirteen, Revelation presents an image of the Roman empire as a demonic Beast.[30] The most direct reason John, author of Revelation, would have expressed such antipathy was the Roman demand that people render to Caesar and to the state what belongs to God alone. Such demands compelled the early church to resist the empire, even to the point of death.

Another image John uses of Rome is "Babylon." John's Babylon also represents totalitarian political authority. For first-century Jews and Christians, Babylon is a code name for Rome. Both Babylon and Rome had destroyed Jerusalem and the temple.[31]

John's central emphasis is to encourage Christians to faithfulness in the face of political authoritarianism. At the core of John's argument is that the Lamb that was slain is the one who is genuinely powerful and reveals God's ways with the world. Jesus' death is crucial for John's case, crucial for John's judgment of the empire, crucial for John's words of encouragement, in several ways.

1. Jesus' death brings to the surface the actual nature of the Beast. John's revelation strips off the mask of benevolence and reveals the true spirit of Rome. He sees a monstrous deformity bent on supplanting God (Rev. 13). He sees a harlot seated on Rome's seven hills who seduces kings of the earth (17:1-18).[32]

The empire, ultimately, is violent. The empire is the force that nailed Jesus to the cross (16:4-7; 18:24). John presents evil not as the threat of anarchy but as the system of order. This system of order institutionalizes violence as the foundation of its way of being. Jesus was a threat to order, so he was eliminated. The new insight here is that order is not the opposite of chaos. Instead, the empire's order is actually the means by which a system of chaos among the nations is maintained. Empire is not, then, the bulwark against disorder. Empire actually is disorder epitomized.[33]

2. Jesus' death also serves John's purposes by pointing to a way to break *free* from the spiral of violence. In response to the violence of the Beast in chapter 13, John calls on the "relentless persistence and fidelity of the saints" (13:10).[34] The only way to opt out of the dynamic of an eye taking an eye taking an eye is simply to refuse to retaliate, simply to refuse to add fuel to the fire. What this relentless persistence means in John's day—and supremely with Jesus—is nonretaliation, even in the face of death. Retaliation inevitably adds to the spiral of violence and enhances the power of the demonic.

The point is to be convinced that one's essential identity as a child of God has to do with living with relentless persistence in the ways of love. For Jesus, and his followers, living consistently with this identity provides power to accept even the utmost suffering. Such living *breaks* the spiral of violence.

3. Jesus' death also engenders encouragement. That is because this death is not capable of destroying God's loving involvement with human beings. In Revelation, John uses various images to symbolize that the Lamb who was slain lives. God in Christ conquered death through resurrection. Death lost its sting and the relentless persistence of Jesus in the ways of peaceableness was vindicated.

To support this understanding of John's argument, I want to look at two texts: 5:1-12 and 19:11-20.[35]

Chapter five is the key to the entire book. We are shown a scroll, perhaps a legal document relating to the destiny of humankind. The content of the scroll reveals God's redemptive intentions for the creation.[36] However, the scroll at first cannot be opened. "Who is worthy to open the scroll and break its seals?" (5:2). No one. So John "wept much" (5:4). Presumably if the scroll remains unbroken the promised healing will remain ineffectual and the spiral of violence will continue.[37]

One of the elders, however, tells John not to weep. Someone *has* been found. "The Lion of the tribe of Judah, the Root of David, has conquered" (5:5). What John *hears*—the traditional Old Testament expectation of military deliverance—is reinterpreted in 5:6 by what he *sees*—the historical fact of Jesus' death. He sees a "Lamb" who bears the marks of slaughter, which are later explained by the heavenly choir: with his lifeblood he has set free "for God people from every tribe." The Lamb is the symbol of suffering and redemptive love.[38] And the Lamb is "standing," an image of resurrection.

The lamb's death is not weakness and defeat, but power and victory. God's power and victory lie in suffering love. This is contrasted to the power of Satan, whose Beast looks like a lamb but speaks like a dragon (13:11).

The Lamb, through his death, is called "conqueror." The Lamb conquers (3:21; 5:5; 17:14), as do faithful Christians (2:7, 11, 17, 26; 3:5, 12, 21; 12:11; 15:2; 21:7). He does this through relentless persistence, even to the point of death. Conquering happens through suffering love, not destructive judgments on enemies. John sees Jesus' death as powerful even over against the empire.

Many visions in Revelation picture the fall of the great Powers, of the Beast, of Babylon the great, in large part due to the effects of the death of Jesus. One such vision is found in 19:11-20. The vision begins with Jesus riding a white horse (19:11) which symbolizes victory. He comes to this apparent battle scene as the one who has *already* conquered sin, death, and evil through his death and resurrection. As the following verses make clear, he comes to this apparent battle with the forces of the Beast already victorious.

The rider is called "Faithful and True"; that is, "the faithful and true witness" of earlier in the book (1:5; 3:14). He remained faithful and true even when it meant death. That is how he gained the white horse.[39] Verse 13 contains a key image. The rider approaches this battle "clad in a robe dipped in blood." The blood has been shed before the battle begins. This alludes to Jesus' blood in death and is the reason no actual battle takes place here. Jesus can already ride the white horse. The actual battle is over. Jesus won it when he faced the violence of political authoritarianism and refused to retaliate, remaining faithful to the God who loves enemies.[40]

The Beast and the kings and armies are ready for battle (19:19). They genuinely are deceived to think one will occur. However, the battle is past. Jesus simply captures the Beast and false prophet and throws them into the fiery lake (19:20). There is no battle.

The judgment of the Beast, of Babylon, has a great deal to do with the mere revelation of their true nature as violent. They are *not* servants of God, worthy of reverence and blind obedience. In his portrayal of this judgment, John is particularly intending to help his Christian readers see political authoritarianism for what it is.

John provides a picture which reveals that the "order" of our seemingly all-powerful political structures may well include the demonic. That is, the order of Babylon is actually chaos. It is the power of chaos, not authentic peace, that puts to death one such as Jesus. This revelation can help those with eyes to discern that Caesar does not have the sovereignty he claims. John points out the Beast's role in Jesus' death. He pictures this type of violent response to God's messengers of peace as endemic in the ways of the Beast. This stands as a reminder to remain wary of all claims that the Beast might be changing its spots.

John's visions also encourage his readers not to accept the *Beast's* definition of reality. Revelation 13 talks about a second Beast, the first Beast's false prophet, an ancient allusion to what we today call propaganda.[41] The basic idea is that the legitimacy of the Beast depends on the masses believing in it. If we see what happened to Jesus as typical of Beast ways, we will grow a great deal in our skepticism toward the propaganda we are fed. As Walter Wink writes,

> When anyone steps out of the system and tells the truth, lives the truth, that person enables everyone else to peer behind the curtain too. That person has shown everyone that it is possible to live in the truth, despite the repercussions. Living in the lie can constitute the system only if it is universal. Anyone who steps out of line therefore denies it in principle and threatens it in its entirety.[42]

John's visions challenge his readers to be aware of where they are getting the material that shapes their view of reality. John invites us to open our imaginations to the way of the Lamb—and to let the Lamb's way help us find freedom from accepting too easily and uncritically the ways of the powers-that-be.[43]

The death of Jesus, as understood by John, engenders resistance to the Beast by bringing to the surface the Beast's violence. Hence, this violence becomes visible for those with eyes to see. Such sight undercuts the Beast's claim to be the people's "benefactor." Jesus' way of facing death also provides encouragement by pointing to the power of relentless persistence. Trust in that kind of power is the key to breaking the spiral of violence.

CONCLUSION

All three areas of concern discussed—temple, law, empire—point to two different aspects of understanding Jesus' death which have relevance to our questions regarding the spiral of violence.

The first is that Jesus' death exposes the tendencies of three powers (religious institutions, cultural ordering systems, and political structures) toward fueling the spiral of violence. The temple (or church or mosque or synagogue) asks at times for loyalty that values the survival of the institution above the well-being of human beings. The law (or churchly mores or the middle-class North American way) asks at times for loyalty that excludes outsiders. The law may even blame or scapegoat outsiders as the cause of the culture's problems and as legitimate recipients of "sacred violence." The empire (or all other states, including democratic ones) asks at times for loyalty that buttresses power politics and treats with violence any who threaten the peace and tranquility of the status quo.

Jesus bumped up against all three areas of social life. He brought to the surface their wrath, their intolerance of people who resist their demand for highest loyalty. In other words, Jesus—by acting deeply in harmony with God's will for peace and compassion for all people—brought out deep-seated violence in the major structures of his society.

Jesus' fate helps those with eyes to see to perceive how these structures work. His fate reveals that the emperor has on no clothes. So much of the power of these structures is primarily the power of *belief* or *trust*. If people believe in, trust in, the supremacy of religious institutions, of cultural systems, or of empires, they provide the basis of much of the power these structures have. But Jesus' fate—for those who see him as embodying God's will for human beings—reveals these structures to be unworthy of such trust. These structures did violence to Jesus, the Son of God. When people no longer give supreme trust to these structures, one of the main elements of the spiral of violence will be broken.

The thinking might go like this: the Roman state nailed Jesus to the cross. I realize most states do that kind of thing, so maybe I'll no longer let my state tell me to kill for its sake. Or: the strictest defenders of the religious institutions sought ways to kill Jesus because he was, to them, a heretic—I realize now that most religious institutions are capable of focusing on ideology and survival at all costs, and willing to scapegoat and sacrifice so-called heretics. So maybe I'll no longer let a religious institution define my enemies or assert heresy.

As well as exposing violence, Jesus' death also points toward life. Jesus modeled a life lived in the power of the Spirit right up to the bitter end. The powers of death did not conquer him because he chose not to respond with an eye for an eye; he chose to live (and die) free from the spiral of violence.

In Matthew's account, when Peter fought back and cut off a soldier's ear in Gethsemane, Jesus ordered him to sheathe his sword. "Put your sword back into its place; for all who take the sword will perish by the sword. Do you think that I cannot appeal to my Father, and he will at once send me more than twelve legions of angels?" (Matt. 26:52-53).

In effect, this was the temptation Satan gave Jesus in the wilderness back at the beginning. Exert your force and make things work out right. But that would only add more violence to the spiral. Jesus' life in the Spirit witnesses to the possibilities of not adding to the spiral. That life was vindicated when God raised Jesus from the dead. Jesus shows that the power of the Spirit of life remains vital despite the all-out assault of the powers of death.

NOTES

1. For a recent statement, see Douglas Gwyn, George Hunsinger, Eugene F. Roop, and John Howard Yoder, *A Declaration on Peace: In God's People the World's Renewal Has Begun* (Scottdale, Pa.: Herald Press, 1991).

2. René Girard, *Violence and the Sacred* (Baltimore: Johns Hopkins University Press, 1977), 240.

3. Walter Wink, *Engaging the Powers: Discernment and Resistance in a World of Domination* (Minneapolis: Fortress Press, 1992), 147.

4. Raymund Schwager, *Must There Be Scapegoats? Violence and Redemption in the Bible* (San Francisco: Harper & Row, 1987), 66-67.

5. Robert Hamerton-Kelly, *Sacred Violence: Paul's Hermeneutic of the Cross* (Minneapolis: Fortress Press, 1992), 38.

6. James G. Williams, "The Innocent Victim: René Girard on Violence, Sacrifice, and the Sacred," *Religious Studies Review* 14, no. 4 (October 1988): 325.

7. Wink, *Engaging the Powers*, 149.

8. Schwager, *Must There Be Scapegoats?* 66-67.

9. Williams, "The Innocent Victim," 325; Wink, *Engaging the Powers*, 153; James G. Williams, *The Bible, Violence, and the Sacred: Liberation from the Myth of Sanctioned Violence* (San Francisco: HarperCollins, 1991), 188.

10. Hamerton-Kelly, *Sacred Violence*, 60.

11. Robert Hamerton-Kelly, *The Gospel and the Sacred: Poetics of Violence in Mark* (Minneapolis: Fortress Press, 1994), 15; James D. G. Dunn, *The Partings of the Ways: Between Christianity and Judaism and Their Significance for the Char-*

acter of Christianity (Philadelphia: Trinity Press International, 1991), 32.

12. Dunn, *The Partings of the Ways*, 33.

13. Willard M. Swartley, *Israel's Scripture Traditions and the Synoptic Gospels: Story Shaping Story* (Peabody, Mass.: Hendrickson, 1994), 159-160; Hamerton-Kelly, *The Gospel and the Sacred*, 17-18.

14. Swartley, *Israel's Scripture Traditions and the Synoptic Gospels*, 161; Hamerton-Kelly, *The Gospel and the Sacred*, 19.

15. Raymund Schwager, "Christ's Death and the Prophetic Critique of Sacrifice," *Semeia* 33 (1985), 114.

16. Swartley, *Israel's Scripture Traditions and the Synoptic Gospels*, 162.

17. Morna D. Hooker, *The Gospel According to St. Mark* (Peabody, Mass.: Hendrickson, 1991), 304.

18. Swartley, *Israel's Scripture Traditions and the Synoptic Gospels*, 165.

19. Hamerton-Kelly, *The Gospel and the Sacred*, 52.

20. Ibid., 57; Swartley, *Israel's Scripture Tradition and the Synoptic Gospels*, 168.

21. I am not arguing that Jesus himself was necessarily hostile toward the temple. Some scholars in fact see him as essentially positive, such as Bruce Chilton, *The Temple of Jesus: His Sacrificial Program in a Cultural History of Sacrifice* (University Park, Pa.: Pennsylvania State Press, 1992). The Gospel of Luke pictures Jesus as much more positive toward the temple than does Mark (Swartley, *Israel's Scripture Tradition and the Synoptic Gospels*, 185-192). My point is that *Mark* pictures a major conflict. Certainly all the synoptics picture Jesus as concerned with abuses in the temple. I find Mark's picture of Jesus being put to death because he was perceived as a direct *threat* by religious institutionalism eminently believable—a similar dynamic to the response of Dostoyevsky's Grand Inquisitor to Jesus.

22. James D. G. Dunn, "The New Perspective on Paul," in *Jesus, Paul and the Law: Studies in Mark and Galatians* (Louisville: Westminster/John Knox Press, 1990), 194.

23. Dunn, "The New Perspective on Paul," 210.

24. Ibid., 199-200.

25. Dunn, *The Partings of the Ways*, 121-122.

26. It is probable that the term *sinners* often is used in a kind of technical sense in the Gospels. It likely reflects the Pharisees' characterization of those with whom they disagreed and who they considered unclean. Jesus welcoming "sinners," then, was not simply a blanket acceptance of everyone no matter what kind of bad things they had done. It was a matter of him purposely denying the cultural exclusiveness of the Pharisaic emphasis on "works of the law." Jesus was emphasizing that God's mercy welcomes *all* who genuinely trust in it, regardless of their ritual purity; see Dunn, *Jesus, Paul, and the Law*, 79-80; Michael J. Wilkins, "Sinner," in *Dictionary of Jesus and the Gospels*, ed. J. B. Green and S. McKnight (Downers Grove, Ill: InterVarsity Press, 1992), 759-760.

27. Dunn, *The Partings of the Ways*, 110-111.

28. Ibid., 123.

29. Paul's harsh criticism of trust in "works of the law" and the violence that he sees likely to follow from such trust must not be interpreted as a blanket rejection of the law or of Judaism. One of the greatest tragedies of human history is how Paul's words were interpreted in ways that supported the exact evils that he was trying to counter—sacred violence in the name of cultural exclusivity (in this case, Christians doing violence to Jews—the mirror of what he had done as a "zealot"). A legitimate Christian appropriation of Paul's critique of trust in "works of the law" would lead to a critique of *Christian* versions of such idolatrous trust, not to a Christian critique of Judaism and certainly not to sacred violence against Jews.

Krister Stendahl, *Paul Among Jews and Gentiles* (Philadelphia: Fortress Press, 1977); and E. P. Sanders, *Paul and Palestinian Judaism* (Fortress, 1977) as well as *Paul, the Law and the Jewish People* (Fortress, 1984), followed now by many others, have persuasively made the case that Paul was *not* a "Lutheran" posing a mutually exclusive contrast between law and grace. I have tried in the above discussion to be precise in focusing on works of the law as Paul's concern and not Judaism as a religion. Paul always saw himself as a Jew, and he affirmed his Jewish tradition. So I agree with Jewish scholars such as Daniel Boyarin, in "Was Paul an 'Anti-Semite'? A Reading of Galatians 3-4," *Union Seminary Quarterly Review* 47 (1993), 47-80, and Alan Segal in *Paul, The Convert: The Apostolate and Apostasy of Saul the Pharisee* (New Haven, Conn.: Yale University Press, 1990), who argue that Paul was not anti Judaism, even if at times in his frustration he makes intemperate remarks which could be so construed.

30. Elisabeth Schüssler Fiorenza, *Revelation: Vision of a Just World* (Minneapolis: Fortress Press, 1991), 83-87; M. Eugene Boring, *Revelation* (Louisville: John Knox Press, 1989), 155-157; G. B. Caird, *The Revelation of St. John the Divine* (New York: Harper & Row, 1966), 160-177.

31. Schüssler Fiorenza, *Revelation*, 89.

32. Wink, *Engaging the Powers*, 89-90.

33. Ibid., 90-91.

34. Ibid., 92.

35. For a fuller discussion see, on 5:1-12, Ted Grimsrud, *Triumph of the Lamb: A Self-Study Guide to the Book of Revelation* (Scottdale, Pa.: Herald Press, 1987), 49-59; on 19:11-20, *Triumph*, 149-150; and Grimsrud, "Peace Theology and the Justice of God in the Book of Revelation," in *Essays on Peace Theology and Witness*, ed. Willard M. Swartley (Elkhart, Ind.: Institute of Mennonite Studies, 1988), 144-146.

36. Caird, *The Revelation of St. John the Divine*, 72.

37. Gerhard A. Krodel, *Revelation* (Minneapolis: Augsburg Press, 1989), 162-163.

38. Caird, *The Revelation of St. John the Divine*, 74.

39. Ibid., 240.

40. Boring, *Revelation*, 196.

41. Wink, *Engaging the Powers*, 93.

42. Ibid., 98.

43. Tina Pippin, *Death and Desire: The Rhetoric of Gender in the Apocalypse* (Louisville: Westminster/John Knox Press, 1992), using Girardian categories, recognizes Revelation's critique of Roman power politics. However, she argues, Revelation retains a scapegoat mechanism, transferring it "from the Lamb to the symbols of oppression (beasts and the dragon) and to the women who have seductive power (Jezebel, the Woman Clothed with the Sun, and the Whore—and the unnamed women who are excluded from the New Jerusalem)" (84).

Whereas I am sympathetic with Pippin's political commitments, I do not agree with her interpretation of Revelation. I believe that John's enemies in the text are not literal people so much as the spiritual forces of evil. John is opposed to the ways these powers enslave even the kings of the earth. The war he envisions does not result in the obliteration of the kings of the earth, but results in their conversion (Rev 21:24).

Whereas Pippin dismisses Revelation as hopelessly misogynist (91-92), Elisabeth Schüssler Fiorenza recognizes that it is possible to interpret Revelation in a way which, while recognizing its embeddedness in a first-century patriarchal worldview, also allows the contemporary interpreter to benefit from Revelation's underlying liberationist perspective (*Revelation*, 12-15). I am grateful to Loren Johns for alerting me to Pippin's work and for his analysis of it.

CHAPTER THREE

Text as Peacemaker: Deuteronomic Innovations in Violence Detoxification

Charles Mabee

INTRODUCTION: THE CENTRALITY OF DEUTERONOMY AND ITS ROOT CONCEPT

I begin this article with a disclaimer. I have purposely left out references to the thought of René Girard in this study of the book of Deuteronomy and peacemaking. I have not done that to hide my personal attachment to the Girardian understanding of culture and religion, which is considerable. Rather, I have followed an alternate strategy of Girardian interpretation. As profound and powerful as the Girardian insights are, they have not yet had great impact on the rather technical discipline of biblical studies. I hope this chapter and the book in which it appears will help change this situation for the better.

I believe that in the long run what will make a difference is not only Girardian biblical studies emanating from committed scholars showing how Girard's insights are part and parcel of the biblical message. Also needed are studies that show how Girard-inspired interpretation can proceed in ways much closer to traditional models of biblical scholarship. That is the approach I have taken here. I believe the points I discuss should be evaluated on their own merit without reference to Girardian theory. The truth or falsity of his approach is irrelevant in that sense. However, I want to acknowledge at the outset that this article would never have been written without the entirely new light in which Girard has allowed me to see everything in the book of Deuteronomy.

The central place of Deuteronomy in the Old Testament has become clear in modern biblical scholarship.[1] Half a century ago, Martin Noth established the close connection between Deuteronomy and the block of four books that follow in the canon, the so-called "Former Prophets," or historical books of Joshua–2 Kings.[2] More recent scholarship has shown that as insightful as Noth was in establishing this primary link, in effect a kind of Pentateuch of History, he was shortsighted in not seeing a broad literary and theological integration between Deuteronomy and the initial four books of the canon that precede it, the traditional Pentateuch. In fact, Deuteronomy lies at the heart of the block of material that runs from Genesis–2 Kings. Recently, David Noel Freedman has provided us with significant help in understanding the literary dynamics at work here:

> The book of Deuteronomy, the fifth book, is at the center of the nine books in the narrative sequence and thus serves as the pivot or apex of the entire work. . . . Moses, the central figure of the Primary History, dominates the whole book, which is devoted to a series of addresses by this greatest of Israel's leaders toward the end of his life. . . . [Here] Moses not only reviews the precedent history of his people (thereby providing legitimate reason to bring in the Ten Commandments, a climactic experience at the beginning of a new era), but also, as a true prophet, he forecasts what is going to happen to the people in the future, depending on their behavior. Thus the Book of Deuteronomy encompasses practically the entire Primary History and deservedly occupies the central and dominant position in the narrative.[3]

Viewing Deuteronomy as the apex of the newly termed "Primary History" is an especially favorable way to begin our discussion of peacemaking from the general perspective of the book. For here, as Brevard Childs has reminded us, the writer "strives to inculcate the Law into the will of the people."[4] If the Old Testament is itself in some sense an elaboration of Torah and specifically the Decalogue— and at some level it is—then it is so through ancient Israel's Deuteronomization of all life.[5] It follows that if the Bible is the aid we take it to be for peacemaking, the Deuteronomic piece is arguably the cornerstone on which the edifice of peace is to be built.[6]

Central to an evaluation of the book's contribution to peacemaking is the determination of its basic structure and its genre. In my view, Dennis T. Olson's work on the importance of the death of Moses in the book represents an especially penetrating analysis of Deuteronomy. Olson argues that the form of the book is *torah*, which he translates as "a program of 'catechesis.'"[7] By catechesis, he means "the process of education in faith from one generation to another based on a distillation of essential tradition."[8] Structurally, he points to the "five important editorial superscriptions that mark the major sections" which we shall presuppose in our discussions:

1. "These are the words" (1:1) [community-forming foundation of God's grace from the past];

2. "This is the *torah*" (4:44) [Decalogue];

3. "This is the commandment—the statues and the ordinances" (6:1) [community-sustaining law to guide the present];

4. "These are the words of the covenant" (29:1) [community-sustaining provisions for a new covenant with future generations];

5. "This is the blessing" (33:1) [God's ultimate blessing of the community as it moves through death to life].[9]

Olson considers item 2 above to be "a miniature version of the structure of the whole book."[10] From this perspective the remainder of Deuteronomy is interpreted as a "secondary commentary or exposition of the primal Decalogue."[11] The meaning of the overall structure is that "the community of faith is rooted in the past, active in the present, but always open to and yearning for God's new future."[12] In this way, "in both form and structure, the book of Deuteronomy intends to bring readers of every age to claim its *torah* as their own."[13]

While maintaining the centrality of the Decalogue for the structure of the book, Patrick Miller also rightly insists on the central role of the Shema in Deuteronomy 6:4ff., which is itself a reiteration of the Great Commandment found at the beginning of the Decalogue.[14] For him, "Moses' speech, in chapters 5–11 especially but also to some extent in later chapters, is in effect a kind of sermon on the primary commandment in its positive (6:4-5) and negative (5:6-10) formulations."[15] Such scholarly discussions undergird the recognition that if Deuteronomy itself represents a cornerstone of Old Testament thought, then surely the stipulation that Yahweh alone must be embraced as Israel's God stands as a cornerstone of Deuteronomy itself. All discussion of Deuteronomic theology, including its contribution to peacemaking, begins with this recognition.

Although a detailed discussion of the Decalogue (and Shema) is beyond the scope of this chapter, one feature deserves mention that has particular relevance for the topic of peacemaking. In terms of its own internal dynamic, the Decalogue moves from the initial commandment concerning the exclusive sovereignty of Yahweh in Israel's religious life to stipulations concerning coveting and desiring in human community at its conclusion. I take these stipulations to be the summary and culminating point of this dynamic in the Decalogue: it says, in effect, that the exclusive worship of Yahweh leads to a cessation of coveting and desiring for the wrong ends, such as the property of an other, in human community.[16] Even more to the point, it provides us with the *purpose* or *intention* of this demand for Yahwistic exclusivity, namely, as a means of eliminating this very cessation of coveting and desiring. In other words, the Deuteronomic prescription for social solidarity and peaceful coexistence begins at this crucial point of redirecting desire toward Yahweh rather than the (things of the) other (personified as the neighbor's wife) and the property of the other (house, field, slave, ox, donkey, and the like).

Presupposed here is the anthropological perspective that human beings have the capacity to "choose" Yahweh, and that this choice breaks the back of misdirected human desire. In Deuteronomic theology, this capacity to choose Yahweh is based on Yahweh's prior choice of Israel. It is only made possible based on the work of Yahweh in Israel's historical experience: "You have seen all that the Lord did before your eyes in the land of Egypt, to Pharaoh and to all his servants and to all his land, the great trials that your eyes saw, the signs, and those great wonders" (Deut. 29:2b-3).

That Israel has the capacity for such choice really constitutes the "goodness" of its existence. To become fully human, to fulfill their lives as a people and as individuals, Israel must only reciprocate in kind to the love of Yahweh. In this way, the *chosen people* concept is not allowed to indicate the superiority of Israel over the nations. Yahweh's choice of Israel functions theologically to eradicate all self-referential claims that Israel of all nations *deserved* Yahweh's special consideration.

This point functions as a safeguard against Israel's assumption of the same strong-against-weak morality Yahweh's presence is meant to eliminate. In other words, Yahweh's choice of Israel has theological priority over the "natural" human desire of its people, and thereby becomes the key to transform their human desire from an evil into a good, or into a choice *for* Yahweh. By implication, without this choice the story of Israel would mimic that of the other nations. That is, its historical script would play out yet again the recurring story of the moral tyranny of the powerful—thereby eliminating the societal basis for peacemaking. In this way, Deuteronomy can best be understood as a catechetical handbook designed to instruct the community of faith in the fundamentals of life liberated from the drive of destructive coveting and desiring which always lies embedded in the soul of human society.

Doing the Word: The Death of Moses and the Birth of the Text (Deut. 12-28, 33-34)

The unfolding and application of the general commandments and prohibitions of the Decalogue in Israel's historical experience begins in ch. 12. It is rooted in Moses' word to all of the Israelites: "These are the statutes and judgments which you are to *keep, to do* in the land which Yahweh the God of your fathers has given you. . . " (Deut. 12:1a, emphasis added). The written text as peacemaker begins with this statement of double emphasis on *keeping* and *doing* the Law. The text can only generate the social solidarity on which authentic peace is built insofar as it presents not a word simply to be learned as an end in itself, but a word to be acted on by all Israel—the rich and powerful as well as the poor and powerless.

This perspective is theologically grounded in the emphasis in the book that *all* Israel exists in dependence on Yahweh's act of liberation. All Israel has its roots in slavery, the rich and powerful as well as the poor and exploited. The Exodus is the great democratizing reality that stands in the middle of Israel's identity. In the Exodus liberation, class and economic distinctions did not exist. The imaginative return to this experience in the text is *de facto* a call to reconceptualize societal equality as a basis for social order.

The purpose of intellectually reconstituting its origins in release from slavery is to shape Israel's behavior—behavior which in and of itself constitutes its choice of being for or against Yahweh (or, for or against *itself*). This understanding of the term *torah* is the precise reason why it cannot be translated into modern European thought categories, which tend to separate understanding from doing. Here thinking functions as a kind of prologue to action. The text is not so much to be *learned* as *done*.

The text leads to a certain kind of relationship to others. If that relationship is not instituted, the text has not been understood. This is why, in Israel's mind, behavior has priority over thinking. Thinking always takes place in the context of desire, whether wrongful desire or desire for Yahweh. This understanding of the intrinsic power of the text distinguishes it from the traditional law-codes of Israel's neighbors. The law-code is based on the morality of the powerful, on those who by definition have the means in society to force their will on others. Such a morality is imposed top-down and is essentially blind to the will of those whom it binds. In this context, the text functions in a way that eliminates action by sanctifying the status quo. The catechetical *torah* of Deuteronomy, on the other hand, demands the participating will of those whom it binds and motivates them to *change* the ever present corruptions of society that always fall short of the vision of the text.

The plea of Deuteronomy is that the people freely choose the societal constraints that limit human desire and make authentic community possible. Only a community so constituted can long endure and have a reasonable hope for internal and external peaceful existence. If the community can embrace such a group affirmation of the meaning of its existence, it can drive out the social toxins of coveting and wrongful desiring of the (things of) the other from its midst. The text becomes, essentially, an agent of detoxification.

As mentioned above, Olson has shown how the death of Moses thematically pervades the book of Deuteronomy. In my construal of the text as peacemaker, it is indeed crucial to appreciate that it only comes into existence in, around, and through the death of Moses. The text is, in other words, the continuing spirit of Moses—only now deepened and made available to all Israel. The text can do what the actual figure of Moses cannot: it can democratize the will of Yahweh throughout the body of the people of Israel throughout the generations. I believe the entire concept of canonicity in the Judeo-Christian tradition is rooted in this "resurrection" of Moses through the text and the democratization of his teaching to all throughout the generations of Israel. If my interpretation is correct, this dynamic is central to understanding the text itself as peacemaker.

However, I also believe the centrality of Moses' death for the life of the text underscores a deeper reality than Olson's informative interpretation indicates. The Deuteronomic text concludes its account of Moses' death with this extraordinary remark: "no one knows his burial place to this day" (Deut. 34:6b). What a strange notation set in the context of traditional religious thought: *the community has lost contact with the body of its heroic founder!* Here in Girardian terms we see the transformation of the Primitive Sacred into authentic religion. But on reflection, the elimination of Moses' tomb from community control is precisely the obviation that unleashes the power of the text. We can only imagine that as long as Israel had the tomb as its spiritual center, the Mosaic text would have served it rather than the people.

In this sense, the book of Deuteronomy is an authentic heir of

Moses' life rather than the mythological traditions associated with his tomb. We are left to imagine a counterfeit history in which the tomb would have been constructed by societal "authorities"—authorities that would use it to construct and maintain a hierarchical society precisely in opposition to the present text.

In the real history, however, the path is cleared for the Mosaic *torah* to replace the Mosaic body and give rise to a different set of authorities, namely, the scribe whose religious life is lived in dependence on the text. Now the possibility exists and the way established by which the land as well as its inhabitants might become holy. The holy land is holy because all means will be removed to divinize Moses as god/hero/king. It is holy because it is the first land where the tomb is not worshipped. It is the first "land of the text" in human history. This unprecedented possibility in the human struggle for peace through the demythification of the death of Moses is the fundamental achievement of the Deuteronomic text.

To grasp the further significance of the demythification of Moses that takes place in the context of Deuteronomy, we need to set it against the presumed power of the mythological beings against which the text must combat. Something of the power of the false mythological beings is captured in Deuteronomy 1:28: "Where are we headed? Our kindred have made our hearts melt by reporting, 'The people are stronger and taller than we; the cities are large and fortified up to heaven! We actually saw there the offspring of the *Anakim!*'" (emphasis added).[17] We cannot pinpoint precisely who these mythological giants were thought to be, but they clearly are related to other such peoples as the Emim, Rephaim, and Zamzummim.

Whatever the historical details may be, they are clearly heroic elements of the religion which the Deuteronomic text is to replace. And these mythological heroes strike fear in the hearts of the Israelites, for whom, we are to suppose, the strangeness of the new textually based religion is initially as incomprehensible as it is for all.

Miller summarizes the point this way:

> All the references describe the Anakim as many and tall and mention their great fortified cities. In the context of these chapters, therefore, the Anakim are a *paradigmatic symbol*. They embody the problem that is too great, that strikes fear into the hearts of the people. They point to the power of the Lord as the one who is able to overcome such mighty heroes as the Anakim.[18]

The question is, how can the written text overcome the might of religious belief sanctified by heroic tales of the Anakim that tell of superhuman power and valor? The fortified cities associated with them in the tradition stand in mute witness to the contrast with the Yahwistic cities of refuge set apart by Moses at the culmination of the opening section of the book (Deut. 4:41-43). The Mosaic text itself is a kind of refuge from the violent world of the mythological hero; it promotes the establishment of societal forms that embody its spirit of compassion and social solidarity.

By eliminating the tomb of its "heroic" founder and opposing the mythological Anakim, the Deuteronomic writers in effect propose the written text as a weapon of peace (replacing the weapons of war), as the new means to effect social change. The hero forces social change based on imposition; Deuteronomy relies solely on the catechetical tools of teaching and persuasion and places the fundamental motivation of war—vengeance—out of human hands and under divine control. By placing vengeance in the hands of God alone, no societal role exists for the mythological human hero to effect vengeance. This is the achievement of the text which sets in motion the primary strategy of Deuteronomic detoxification of human community.

From the traditional mythological way of thinking, this may well have roots in the warlike nature of primitive Yahwism. Now, however, with the ascendancy of textual Yahwism taking place through the rising importance of Deuteronomy, we are moving toward a new point of view. To maintain holy war conducted by Yahweh removes the entire activity from the hands of the human despot and places it into the hands of Yahweh, subject to his initiation. The practice of *herem*, outlined in chapter 20, must be seen in this light. Here, as elsewhere, Deuteronomy is wresting traditional power away from the king and effectively placing it in the hands of the prophet who will interpret Yahweh's will to the people.

THE PEOPLE'S COVENANT AT MOAB: A NEW SONG FOR THE NEW ORDER (DEUT. 29-32)

Rising out of and standing as the apex of the textual prescription for eliminating human violence appear the new stipulations of the so-called Moabite covenant in Deuteronomy 29-32.[19] According to 28:69 (29:1 in English), this covenant is enacted in addition to the covenant previously enacted by Moses at Horeb (Sinai). All the previous stipulations given in the book of Deuteronomy from the Decalogue and Shema onward (chs. 5, 6) build up to this crescendo. The nature of this Moabite covenant, especially in relationship to the new covenant emphasis in Jeremiah (31:31-34) has been widely discussed among Old Testament scholars. Clear similarities exist between these reformulated "post-Sinai" covenants; much of what one says of one can also be said of the other.[20]

Although the resolution of the issue of the specific relationship between these two concepts of covenant lies beyond the scope of this chapter, one important point is clear: in both cases *all* members of the community are brought into covenantal relationship with Yahweh. We read in 29:14ff.: "I (Moses) am making this covenant, sworn by an oath, not only with you who stand here with us today before the Lord our God, but also with those who are not here with us today." This statement recalls Jeremiah 31:34a: "No longer shall they teach one another, or say to each other, 'Know the Lord,' for they shall all know me, from the least of them to the greatest, says the Lord."

Whatever the exact connection between them, no doubt exists as to the common extension of covenantal blessing to each and every member of the community. By extending the benefits to all members of the community, the text intends to open space for a new basis for eliminating community violence.

The task of extending covenantal blessing to each individual replaces the control of the community by the traditional means of statecraft. In its traditional legal manifestation, covenant is enacted *on behalf of* the people by the elite leaders of society. But this structure of covenant-making had historically failed the people by the time of the writing of Deuteronomy (and Jeremiah).

Yet what dimension of this traditional covenant conceptuality could be used by the Deuteronomic writer to draw all people into the process? The answer lay in a hermeneutical move which uncovered the metaphorical nature of covenant language itself. Through the preceding centuries the legal fabric of the covenant language had not convicted either the leadership of the state or its citizens. It was at its root, after all, "only" a borrowed metaphor from the social realm of law, no matter how stringently interpreted and used by the state.

This metaphor, however, had been often misused for aggressive nationalism. The false prophets of the state had falsely used this covenantal idea as a means of propagating a divine cover for state-sponsored violence. In contradistinction to this traditional covenantal metaphysic, the new Moabite covenant is written on the heart.[21]

It is important not to be overly sentimental about this new covenantal prescription. The point is the directness by which Yahweh will now relate to the people, *without benefit of institutional intermediaries*. The state prophets are now revealed for what they truly are: appendages of state-supported violence. Deuteronomy, in conjunction with authentic Yahweh prophets, speaks a message of creative possibility that bypasses such institutions. The text holds the creative potential by which this new reality may be established without the corrupting influence of the ruling elite.

As the final segment of the Moabite covenant, and at the point of his imminent death, Moses recites the words of a song which concludes the new covenant effected at Moab (ch. 32). The legal portions of this covenant, as well as the entire book itself, reach a crescendo here. The Song of Moses is the summary of the entire message of Moses—and it is a message by which the people are to be inculcated into community life through song. In effect, this song replaces sacrifice as the means of building nonviolent community solidarity.

In a recent study of Deut. 32: 6-12, Stephen A. Geller, partly following G. E. Wright,[22] analyzes the introductory verses of the first part of the song (covering at least the initial 25 verses), commonly interpreted as a prophetic *ribh* (lawsuit). He notes that in this historical introduction of the ribh, the meaning is clear: "Israel's disobedience to its God is all the worse for its insensate ingratitude to a loving benefactor."[23] In this historical prologue, the central couplet is v 9:

> But Yahweh's own portion was to be his own people,
> It was Jacob that was his own allotment.

This couplet links up with those in vv. 6b and 12 to establish the theological ground of the poem:

> Isn't he the father who created you,
> He made you and brought you into being? (6b)
> Yahweh alone led him;
> No foreign god was with him. (12)

In this way, the central proposition of the Deuteronomic prescription for peacemaking comes full circle. Whereas the Decalogue and Shema at the outset of the book propositionally set forth the conceptual basis for textual peacemaking, now the text itself is strengthened by means of poetry. This song brings about the communion of Moses with his people—who become, in effect, the sons and daughters of Mosaic *torah*. What is particularly striking about this song is its affinity with prophetic teaching.[24]

The song inculcates the theme that the Old Testament prophets are the correct interpreters of the will of Yahweh. In its historical existence, Israel is to live in obedience to these prophets. They are the lifeline to Yahweh. Without these prophets, there is no communication between Yahweh and Israel. This is not true of the other key officials in Israel's societal existence: judges, priests, or kings. None of these officials have direct contact with Yahweh. Rather, they represent the very institutions that have led Israel toward exile. None of the functionaries of the state communicate the initiative of Yahweh to the people. Only the authentic Yahweh prophets do this. That is why they are the most important officials in Israel's existence. That is why they are singled out in 13:1-11 as a concern immediately after the crucial chapter 12, which initiates the elaboration on the Decalogue.

The Song of Moses confronts the Israelite reader directly with the issue of vengeance. Should they interpret the historical reality of the loss of their land in terms of blaming their enemies? Should future societal activities be directed toward exacting vengeance from these enemies? The answer of the song is "No." Thus the song can be seen as one of nonviolence and peacemaking. Israel's enemies act under the guiding hand of God, not their own (Deut. 29:27-28). In this framework of understanding, retribution makes no sense for the people of Yahweh. Israel cannot play the part of the innocent victim in their failure to maintain the gift of the land—a fact which itself would enable them to continue the retributive cycle of violence against their enemies.

CONCLUSION:
BOUNDARY EXISTENCE AS A BASIS OF PEACEMAKING

The achievement of Deuteronomy for the cause of peacemaking is extraordinary. In this brief chapter I have tried merely to suggest some of the innovative ways that the text establishes new terrain in this age-old human struggle. Certainly more remains to be discussed. More could be said, for instance, about the concept of chosenness that appears in the book and the potential that the concept itself holds for acts of violence against the other. As a safeguard against such a potential, Deuteronomy makes clear that Israel, as the chosen people, is not chosen because of any particular achievement on its own part. Israelite chosenness lies exclusively in the initiative of Yahweh, and Yahweh alone. The book makes clear that this concept of chosenness must never be used against others in a hierarchically superior way.

More could also be said about the specific laws of Deuteronomy, and how they promote social stability and well-being. Among the least noticed but more interesting ones, especially from a Girardian perspective, are the laws concerning forbidden mixtures (Deut. 22:9-11).[25] If Girard is correct in locating violence in sameness and in interpreting societal structures that establish differentiation as the necessary means of social order, then surely such laws have deeper meanings that provide important clues for the Deuteronomic approach to peacemaking. The text seems to be telling us that differentiation is structured into the very order of creation and that the potential for violence in human community increases when such boundaries are inappropriately transgressed.

More could be said as well about the restrictions that the text of Deuteronomy place on warfare itself (Deut. 20). Especially interesting here is a stipulation concerning charitable acts toward those among Israel's enemies who are not located in the Promised Land (Deut. 20:15) and whose rituals are less likely to tempt the Israelites than the ever-present violent religious practices of the Canaanites. The phenomenon of Holy War itself, with particular emphasis on the way it removes the declaration of war from the Israelite ruling elite and places it in the realm of Yahweh's initiative, would form a significant part of any complete discussion of this topic.

We conclude with this thought: It has rightly been said that Deuteronomy is written from the standpoint of boundary existence. We began our discussion by noting its preeminent role in the Old Testament. It is ironic to conclude with a reference to the book's boundary ambiance. This "boundary" feel of the book is not simply a reference to the location from which Moses delivers his words. It is also felt in the thoroughly dialectical way the book proceeds. Deuteronomy is rightly called the "second law." As such it accomplishes much that the Sinaitic law could not, especially for the cause of peacemaking in the community. Everything here is in relation to what has preceded it in the biblical narrative, especially the Sinaitic law. Everything is also, however, simultaneously in relation to what will come afterwards.

The book is the bridge between the people's experience of liberation and their settlement in the new land. It demands that words become deeds, that ideas become actions. It informs us that the present is always dependent on the past for understanding, but that the past does not absolutely determine the understanding of the present. Everything Moses tells us presupposes the existence of an immutably loving God, but also a God who links up with the historical experience of the Israelites and shapes and adapts that love accordingly.

Finally, the genius of the book is most profoundly evident in the way that it continues to inspire us to become involved in the same struggle for peacemaking that it advocates. It is in bringing about this life-changing movement from text to reader that the true significance of the book for peacemaking lies and the way open to understanding it as a strong ally to Girard's insights into the nature of violence and the prospects for peace.

NOTES

1. Generations ago Julius Wellhausen made the claim that the "connecting link between old and new, between Israel and Judaism, is everywhere Deuteronomy," in *Prolegomena to the History of Ancient Israel* (New York: Meridian Books, 1957), 362. Dennis T. Olson has noted that "contemporary scholars have lauded Deuteronomy as 'the theological center of the Old Testament' (Brueggemann), 'the middle point of the Old Testament' (von Rad), the 'center of biblical theology' (Herrmann) and the most 'theological' book in the Old Testament' (Reventlow)," in Olson, *Deuteronomy and the Death of Moses: A Theological Reading* (Minneapolis: Fortress, 1994), 1. Elizabeth Achtemeier has argued that "there is no book of more importance in the Old Testament and no Old Testament book more basic for understanding the New Testament than Deuteronomy," in *Deuteronomy, Jeremiah.* (Philadelphia: Fortress, 1978), 9.

2. Cf. Martin Noth, *The Deuteronomistic History* (JSOT Supplement 15; Sheffield, England: University of Sheffield, 1981).

3. David Noel Freedman, *The Unity of the Hebrew Bible* (Ann Arbor: University of Michigan, 1993), 15f.

4. Brevard S. Childs, *Old Testament Theology in a Canonical Context* (Philadelphia: Fortress, 1986), 56.

5. In a remarkable introduction to his recent book *Capital and the Kingdom: Theological Ethics and Ethical Order* (New York: Maryknoll, 1994), Timothy J. Gorringe writes: "What is attempted, then, is a sketch of a new Deuteronomy. Like the first Deuteronomy this can only be a collaborative enterprise. Throughout the world there are thinkers and activists concerned with bringing a new society into being and these are, in effect, the new Deuteronomists. . . . The recovery of virtue we so sorely need can only be effected by establishing new forms of social and economic structures but, as the Deuteronomists understood, discussion of what is wrong with the present and sketches of the shape of the future are essential to the emergence of this society. To participate in this Deuteronomic task is the purpose of this book" (xf.).

6. Gorringe also makes the following insightful point: "The two most profound students of Deuteronomy we know of are Jesus and Paul. Paul's

inspired summing up of the vision of human community opened up by the life, death, and resurrection of Jesus of Nazareth—"No Jew no Greek, no slave or free, no male or female" (Gal 3:28)—can be understood as a radicalization of the Deuteronomic imperatives. . . . [Here] the program of Deuteronomy was deepened and extended to cover all people; it was no longer a programme for Israel, but for all nations" (ix).

7. Dennis T. Olson, *Deuteronomy and the Death of Moses: A Theological Reading* (Minneapolis: Augsburg Fortress, 1994), 2.

8. Ibid., 11.

9. Ibid., 15.

10. He terms Chapter 5 "the *torah en nuce,*" or "Torah in a nutshell" (15f.). He also notes that Stephen Kaufman "has argued very specifically for an arrangement of the laws of 12-26 along the order of the Decalogue," in "The Structure of the Deuteronomic Law," in *Maarav* 1:105-158 (1979).

11. Olson, 16. Georg Braulik has recently reviewed the literature which structurally ties the Decalogue to the remainder of the Book of Deuteronomy in "The Sequence of the Laws in Deuteronomy 12-26 and in the Decalogue," in *A Song of Power and the Power of Song: Essays on the Book of Deuteronomy,* ed. Duane L. Christensen (Winona Lake, Ind.: Eisenbrauns, 1993), 313-335. Braulik notes that the first scholar to draw attention to this relationship was F. W. Schultz, who wrote: "In Deuteronomy . . . the Law . . . is itself, in a certain sense, a commentary," because in it Moses "by means of the order in which he treats them, has placed each section of the Torah in close relationship to one of the commandments of the Decalogue. In this way he has made the Decalogue the key to the rest of the Law, but equally and at the same time has made the rest of the Law an interpretive expansion on the Decalogue" (Schultz, *Das Deuteronomium* [Berlin, 1895], iii).

12. Olson, 16.

13. Ibid., 17.

14. Patrick D. Miller, *Deuteronomy* (Louisville: John Knox, 1990), 15.

15. Ibid., 98.

16. Cf. K. D. Schunck, "Wanting and Desiring," in *The Anchor Bible Dictionary 6,* ed. David Noel Freedman (New York: Doubleday, 1992), 866f.

17. Cf. Deut. 2:10, 20-23; 9:2 for other references to the Anakim.

18. Miller, 35.

19. The structure given at the beginning of our discussion indicates that the textual delineation of the new covenant is chs. 29-32, not simply chs. 29-30. Cf. Norbert Lohfink, "Der Bundesschluss im Land Moab: Redaktionsgeschichtliches zu Dtn. 28, 69-32, 47," in *Biblische Zeitschrift* 6 (1962), 32-56.

20. The major difference lies in the two contexts in which the covenantal language appears, i.e., the context provided by the books of Deuteronomy and Jeremiah themselves. The important question for our topic concerns the relationship between the previous legal language in Deuteronomy and the Moabite covenant.

21. The book of Ezekiel also uses the language of the heart in establish-

ing a new foundation of relationship between Yahweh and Israel (cf. Ezek, 11:19-20, 36:26-28).

22. Wright, "The Lawsuit of God: A Form-Critical Study of Deuteronomy 32," in *Israel's Prophetic Heritage*, ed. B. W. Anderson and W. Harrelson (New York: Harper, 1962), 26-67.

23. Geller, "The Dynamics of Parallel Verse: A Poetic Analysis of Deut. 32:6-12," *Harvard Theological Review* 75, no. 1 (1982), 40.

24. Cf. Cornil *(Einleitung,* 13:5): This poem is characterized as a "compendium of prophetical theology." Driver (347) wants to date the song at the time of Jeremiah and Ezekiel, i.e., 630 B.C.E. This is because he sees a greater affinity with the prophets of the Chaldaean age than with earlier prophets: "the terms in which idolatry is reprobated, the thought of Israel's lapse, punishment, and subsequent restoration, various traits in vv. 16, 21, 25, 36, 41-42, the contrasts established between Jehovah and the gods of the nations, though there are isolated parallels in earlier prophets, recall strongly, as a whole, the tone and manner of Jeremiah, Ezekiel, and the Deuteronomic writers in the historical books. Where Israel's recent disasters are referred to (vv. 20-30), or Jehovah's coming triumph is portrayed (vv. 41-43), the terms used are figurative and general, . . . [they seem to point more to] a prophetic meditation on the lessons to be deduced from Israel's national history."

25. For recent treatments of these passages, cf. Calum M. Carmichael, "Forbidden Mixtures," *Vetus Testamentum* 32 (1982), 394-415, and C. Houtman, "Another Look at Forbidden Mixtures," *Vetus Testamentum* 34 (1984), 226-228.

CHAPTER FOUR

Can Girard Help Us to Read Joshua?

Gordon H. Matties

I always cherished the hope that meaning and life were one. Present-day thought is leading us in the direction of the valley of death, and it is cataloguing the dry bones one by one. All of us are in this valley but it is up to us to resuscitate meaning by relating all the texts to one another without exception, rather than stopping at just a few of them. —Girard[1]

WITH THAT PLEA RENÉ GIRARD ends his book *Things Hidden Since the Foundation of the World*. Perhaps for good reason the book of Joshua has been one of those texts that has been avoided and may need to be brought into relation with all other texts. But can we thereby resuscitate meaning? Although Girard's focus is primarily on Gospel texts, he suggests that the Hebrew Bible participates in the same dynamic as do Gospel texts. The Hebrew Bible is a "text in travail." It is not simply a record of a developing theme or process, but "a struggle that advances and retreats."[2] Reflecting on Jeremiah's use of the Jacob tradition, for example, Girard writes,

> The books of the Old Testament are rooted in sacrificial crises, each distinct from the other and separated by long intervals of time, but analogous in at least some respects. The earlier crises are reinterpreted in the light of the later ones. And the experience of previous crises is of great value in coping with subsequent ones."[3]

The attempt to read Joshua through Girard's hermeneutical perspective will not evade problems. Like recent efforts at historical reconstruction of the settlement period, Girard's theory proposes that understanding *origins* reveals the meaning hidden in the text.[4] In Girard's case, however, what is sought is not the hiddenness of what actually happened, but a meaning that exposes the original violent act. Such discovery offers human beings a way of seeing the truth about themselves and of taking responsibility for their own violent reality. In other words, understanding what is hidden in the text exposes the violent origin of culture by means of revealing the sacrificial (and mimetic) crisis at the heart of the conflict.

Because conflict is central to Joshua, Girard's perspective can raise questions about traditional ways of reading that book. The questions are important, even if not every detail of our analysis of Joshua fits Girard's hermeneutic rubrics. Bringing Girard and Joshua together is significant in at least two ways: first, as the conversation seeks to find its way through the tensions between literary and historical approaches to the text; and second, as interaction focuses on how to deal with the matter of warfare and violence in the book.

Joshua is a "text in travail" even as we are readers in travail; we struggle to resolve the tension between biblical historiography and ethics, or between narrative representation and our own theological affirmation, or between particular texts and the larger canon of Scripture. Our attempt to "make sense" of the text may rebound as we discover that the text makes sense of us and the ethnic violence that continues to emerge in our time.

I hope my reflections will begin to clarify how Girard's theory can enlarge the scope for discussion of those matters. This chapter does not, therefore, present a critique of Girard's hypothesis. Rather, it asks whether Girard's theory offers conceptual tools for reading the narrative of Joshua.

Let me state at the outset where my interests lie. I am writing a commentary on Joshua intended for general readers. My reflection on Joshua and Girard is therefore nontheoretical in that I do not want simply to resolve critical questions related to the book of Joshua. Moreover, the commentary aims to bring to bear hermeneutical perspectives and insights from the Anabaptist tradition, along with its commitment to peace and nonviolence as a way of life.

This chapter falls into two parts. In the first part I reflect on observations that spring from literary analysis of Joshua as it intersects with Girard's theory. In the second I pose a number of questions that arise from a reading of Joshua in the light of Girard's theory.

LITERARY ANALYSIS OF JOSHUA IN DIALOGUE WITH GIRARD

The starting point for most recent analyses of Joshua is that the narrative presentation is opaque: it is not transparent to historical events nor to literary coherence. The narrative requires either rewriting or rereading. Historical criticism tends to write a new story; narrative analysis tends to present a new reading. I do not wish to take sides here. I would like to ask, however, whether a reading in dialogue with Girard might not share some of both interests and strategies.

A Girardian reading seeks to uncover an original—and historical—act of violence that accounts for what is disguised in the narrative presentation (Girard speaks mostly of myth and tragedy, a topic to which I shall return). The narrative, therefore, points to something behind it. Such a reading is interested in narrative dynamics insofar as the narrative also reveals what is hidden in front of it, namely, the threat of violence breaking out in the community that discovers its identity in the narrative. The narrative stands between what Girard calls the generative act of violence and the danger of violence in the community.

SACRIFICE REDIRECTS VIOLENCE

The book of Joshua, therefore, disguises the reality of the past to prevent a similar outbreak of retributive violence in the community in the present. But it is not the narrative itself that serves the preventive function, but the ritual of sacrifice as presented in the narrative. As Girard writes in *Violence and the Sacred*:

> There is a common denominator that determines the efficacy of all sacrifices. . . . This common denominator is internal violence—all dissensions, rivalries, jealousies, and quarrels in the community that the sacrifices are designed to suppress. The purpose of sacrifice is to restore harmony to the community, to reinforce the social fabric. Everything else derives from that. If once we take this fundamental approach to sacrifice . . . we can see that there is no aspect of human existence foreign to the subject.[5]

The role of sacrifice, therefore, is to "redirect violence into 'proper' channels."[6] Sacrifice is "primarily an act of violence without risk of vengeance."[7] This "risk of vengeance" is important for reading Joshua, due to its deuteronomistic flavor. If, according to Girard, "The function of sacrifice is to quell violence in the community and to prevent conflicts from erupting,"[8] then the violence represented in the narrative of Joshua, and hence the narrative itself, functions to prevent vengeance, which Deuteronomy 32 ascribes to Yahweh alone. Taking vengeance on enemies is Yahweh's doing (Deut. 32:35, 41, 43). Since, according to Girard, "Vengeance . . . is an interminable, infinitely repetitive process,"[9] sacrifice functions as "an instrument of prevention in the struggle against violence."[10] The spread of violence is kept in check, therefore, by the sacrificial process.[11] And since "no aspect of human existence is foreign to the subject,"[12] the violence presented in the book of Joshua must be sacrificial.

Before further exploration of violence and sacrifice in Joshua, I would like to point out why current literary studies of Joshua serve as a resource to our reading of Joshua in dialogue with Girard. One such resource comes from recent analyses of Joshua, which seek to account for ambiguity in the narrative sequence or plot of the book, or to explain the tension between competing themes. Although the book as a whole (on the surface) gives the impression of a rather ideal situation (which in popular discussion is often contrasted with the chaos of Judges), attention to detail exposes numerous tensions, inconsistencies, and even outright contradictions in Joshua itself. Hawk suggests, for example, that

> the book's tensions and contradictions arise either because contrary events are juxtaposed or because the events narrated and the narrator's evaluation of these events are inconsistent. In other words, the reader's sense of textual incongruity is a result of the way the story's events are organized and interpreted; it is a circumstance of the story's *plot*.[13]

Hawk introduces the notion of "textual desire" as a way of understanding why the plot of Joshua is fraught with ambiguity.[14] The text promises, as it were, an outcome that is not, and perhaps cannot be, fulfilled. In this respect, suggests Hawk, "the making of plots is a mimetic activity."[15] The function of plot in Joshua, with its dissonances and incoherences,

> mirrors the difficulty of applying dogma to the experience of life. Our structuring operations are essential. We cannot effectively engage the world without them. Yet experience often seems to exceed our constructs. Reality resists and provokes our concords and dissonances and uncertainties. Israel laid claim to fulfillment, but continued to tell its story under the impulse of a promise yet to be realized.[16]

Unlike historical reconstructions of events "behind the text," the competing facets of the book of Joshua support the moral and theological identity of Israel "in front of" the text. The mimetic function of the plot, in this literary model, reflects tensions in the worldview of the community of readers.

JOSHUA'S FRAME: NARRATION OF LITURGICAL ACTS

A second example of the resource of literary analysis involves recognition that the entire book of Joshua has been framed by narration of liturgical acts. Episodes at the beginning interpret the conquest itself as a liturgical act modeled in many ways on the Exodus narrative. Episodes at the end highlight, again in liturgical terms, both fragmentation and unity of the newly settled community.

This literary feature intersects with Girard's linkage of ritual and violence. Does the liturgical structuring device in Joshua conceal or reveal a desire to maintain harmony through liturgical action and through sacrifice in particular? Attention to the sacrificial motifs in the book (the story of Achan in ch. 7; the sacrificial destruction of the enemy; the sacrifice in ch. 8; and the episode concerning an altar in ch. 22) suggests that the text invites us to do more than construct historical and literary models as ways of explaining the book of Joshua.

JOSHUA AS CRITICAL TRADITIONALISM

A third example of literary analysis illustrates why Girard's theory may add significantly to our understanding of Joshua. Robert Polzin's work explores the tension between Deuteronomic speech and commands, and reported speech and action in the book of Joshua. The tension between Deuteronomy and Joshua represents, as he sees it, the conflict between different voices in Israel: "authoritarian dogmatism" and "critical traditionalism." The book of Joshua reflects the voice of critical traditionalism that "recognizes the constant need for revision and varying interpretations of the traditions that formed the core of its message."[17]

The fact that Rahab and the Gibeonites are spared, for example, are significant revisions of Deuteronomy's commands not to spare anyone, and not to make treaties with any of the inhabitants. Those who act as "exceptional outsiders" in the story function, according to Polzin, as "types of Israel":[18]

> The underlying ideological position of the Rahab story as a preview of the entire Book of Joshua is that some nations (represented by Rahab) will be spared a punishment they deserve, just as Israel (also represented by Rahab) obtains a land they do not deserve.[19]

Polzin concludes his analysis of Joshua by suggesting that

> The complicated relationship between God's mercy and justice is bound up with Israel's self-understanding as both citizen and alien in the community of the Lord. As the narrative describes Is-

rael-the-community settling in Israel-the-land, it never ceases to emphasize how much of the "outside," both communally and territorially is "inside" Israel. Doubtless the Deuteronomic narrator's audience, which appears from the text to be situated outside Israel-the-land, was to take comfort in the realization that they had always been outsiders, even when inside the land.[20]

So also the transjordanian tribes could be a model of those who are clearly "inside" even though they live "outside" Israel-the-land.[21]

This insider-outsider dynamic in the book of Joshua is important from the perspective of Girard because the victim is always ambiguously both insider and outsider. In the substitution of ritual victim for surrogate victim, the ritual victim must come from outside; this prevents the community from choosing someone from within. That helps prevent a new outbreak of reciprocal violence.[22]

Usually, however, the ritual victim is not outside or inside but marginal: "This marginal quality is crucial to the proper functioning of the sacrifice."[23] Girard suggests that since the ritual victim must be situated "between the inside and the outside, they can perhaps be said to belong to both the interior and the exterior of the community. . . . but never in both at the same time."

Yet no victim "perfectly meets this requirement."[24] Thus there are two approaches to sacrificial preparation: "The first seeks to make appear more foreign a victim who is too much a part of the community. The second approach seeks to reintegrate into the community a victim who is too foreign to it."[25]

In light of the above observations we can suggest that elements of literary observation (Hawk, Polzin) and theoretical reflection Girard) merge in the narrative function of Joshua. Consider, for example, the story of Rahab in Joshua 2. Here Rahab is not sacrificed; rather, she is incorporated into the community. By profession she is marginal. Spatially she is on the fringe; she lives on the wall. She moves between inside and outside in both Canaanite and Israelite communities. It is only her confession that identifies her now as an insider. The narrative, by refusing to do what must be done to enemies, subverts or uncovers the violence of the sacrificial *herem* by drawing her into the community of Israel.

As the first, and possibly paradigmatic narrative in Joshua, Rahab's story offers a way of seeing through the hidden mechanism of the sacrifice of war. Could it be that here we find a reason why the commands of Deuteronomy regarding warfare are not explicitly carried through in Joshua? The emphasis on keeping Torah (Josh. 1:8) is given a particular shape by the story in Joshua 2. At the beginning of the narrative Rahab participates in the creation of a new community of those who "put away the foreign gods" (Josh. 24:14, 23). The trajectory her story sets in motion comes to completion only in chapter 24 where the divine "I" states, "it was not by your sword or by your bow" (24:12). Although the narrative does not deny the violent acts of warfare that were sanctioned by God's command, the story as a whole calls into question the validity of the assumption that sacrificial warfare against the outsider is the preferred way of shaping the boundaries of the new covenant community.

I suggest this because Girard explicitly identifies the sacrificial act with the act of warfare. He suggests the following as

> the principle behind all "foreign" wars: aggressive tendencies that are potentially fatal to the cohesion of the group are redirected from within the community to outside it. Inversely, there is reason to believe that the wars described as "foreign wars" in the mythic narratives were in fact formerly civil strifes.[26]

According to Girard, these foreigners are presented "in terms of a 'fictive' foreign threat."[27] In this case, therefore, the insider-outsider dynamic in the plot of Joshua is not at all about shaping the identity of a community in front of the text; rather, it obscures a conflict behind the text in a generative act of violence. Reading Joshua with Girard's interests in mind would not simply describe how the narrative functions to shape corporate identity in the present, but would uncover how the hidden violence inherent in the community is linked, through the narrative, to original violence against the outsider.

By contrast, Theodore Mullen Jr. suggests that from the perspective of an exilic community,

> the deuteronomistic writer was not only recreating the boundaries that should define and refine the ethnic identity of Israel and its members, but was also producing the authoritative traditions that supported and legitimized the claims made by the narrative and its prophetic author. This fictive way of presenting reality provides a basis for the creation of a new community out of the remnants of the people scattered and dislocated by the exile.[28]

Such a reading, building on observations by Polzin about reinterpretation of Mosaic commands in Deuteronomy, offers a way of explaining tension that differs from Girard's approach. According to Mullen, modifications of Deuteronomy's instructions regarding conquest, particularly in matters concerning the inclusion and exclusion of foreigners, changing the rules of warfare, and so on, have to do with the "formative prophetic voice" and the "prophetic authority of the writer."[29] This literary prophetic act of reimagining the past is, in fact, a constitutive act: "the 'ideal' Israel is recreated in a new context."[30] Thus, "By virtue of the ritual participation of those who would identify themselves with this group and who would accept the responsibilities of the covenant demands, a people were both defined and created."[31]

That kind of generative act seems not to be what Girard is describing. For Girard the narrative reflects an original act of violence and communal breakdown that functions to preserve and protect the community from the threat of reciprocal vengeance. Nor does the narrative offer a paradigmatic world that could be or ought to be imitated. The narrative itself does not suggest that the communal identity ought to be formed by imitating the actions depicted in the narrative. Rather, the narrative criticizes by exposing the terror of the original act of violence. The categories of insider and outsider, then, cannot function to direct the identity formation process. Girard's notion of insider/outsider belongs in the realm of sacrificial ritual, which is concerned with preventing chaos from running rampant in the community. It assumes a threatened community seeking to maintain order, not a disordered exilic community seeking to rebuild.

That point has been developed in George Pattison's application of Girard's theory to the warfare texts in Joshua in an article entitled "Violence, Kingship and Cultus." There Pattison begins by addressing Girard's thesis that collective violence is generative in that it reestablishes order in society. Through the sacrificial act,

> maleficent violence is replaced by beneficent violence, violence drives out violence, and the victim who was initially blamed for the violence is now hailed as the one who delivers the community from its own self-destructive tendencies.[32]

The sacrificial act in Joshua, according to Pattison, is the act of warfare against the Canaanites. This is not a historical conflict.

For Girard, the ritual act imitates the historical act: "The function of ritual is to 'purify' violence; that is, to 'trick' violence into spending itself on victims whose death will provoke no reprisals."[33] Ritual is then "the regular exercise of 'good' violence" that resembles the nonsacrificial.[34] Thus the *herem* ritual in particular, and warfare in general, must resemble the nonsacrificial act so as "to prevent the resurgence of violence and its spread throughout the community."[35]

Pattison suggests, therefore,

that many of the accounts of violent engagements against an external enemy can be interpreted as retellings of what may originally have been intra-tribal conflicts. One can even take this one step further and say that the division between internal and external is itself a part of the process of resolving the sacrificial crisis, part of the process of expunging the memory of reciprocal violence from the life of the community. In the resolution of this crisis . . . projection and substitution are everything.[36]

BENJAMIN: SURROGATE VICTIM AMONG THE TRIBES?

Through Girard's lenses, both the intra-tribal tension and the insider-outsider conflict are seen to be significant for shedding light on the narratives in Joshua and Judges that highlight the tribe of Benjamin. In Joshua most of the conquest accounts take place in Benjaminite territory or have to do with the tribe of Benjamin, the youngest brother of the sons of Jacob. Yet Achan (of the tribe of Judah) is singled out as the sacrificial victim after the failure of the assault (Josh. 7). And in Judges the first judge is Othniel the son of Kenaz (3:9). The tradition identifies him as an outsider become insider.

The next judge is Ehud, a Benjaminite. Why is an outsider juxtaposed with a Benjaminite at the beginning of the sequence of narratives in Judges? And why, then, is Benjamin highlighted at the end of Judges as the tribe that committed the atrocity against the Levite's concubine (Judg. 19)? That text, by the way, gives this narrative a communal identity-forming function when the community itself reflects negatively on the behavior of the Benjaminites in Judges 19:30 and 20:6-7. In those verses we read of "advice" and "counsel" sought from the community.

The story continues to tell of battle against Benjamin, with Judah leading the way (Judg. 20:18). It tells of Benjamin's victories on the first two days of battle, with victory for Israel coming only on the third day (Judg. 20:29-48). Judges 21 recounts the violence against all the inhabitants of Jabesh-Gilead (on the east of the Jordan), except for four hundred young women who are given to the Benjaminites as wives. All of this finds echoes in Girard's work: violence between brothers, sacrificial victims, associations with marriage (exogamous marriage customs), and so on. Nothing seems hidden here. Yet there is more than meets the eye. Even the fact that Judah is chosen to go first against Benjamin may reflect the fact that it is from Benjamin that Saul, Israel's first king is chosen, and that from Judah comes the usurper, David. So also we find echoes of Benjamin's distress in the Joseph narrative when he is singled out by Joseph (who represents, of course, the other elder brother Ephraim, the Northern Kingdom).

But these may simply be fanciful projections on my part. According to Pattison, however, that is not the case. In fact, "Benjamin is *chosen* as the focus of internal violence, the surrogate victim for the community as a whole."[37] He points out the similarity between the story of the ruse in Judges 20 and the action against Ai in Joshua 8. In both stories the same sequence occurs. This could simply be a similar military tactic. Yet there seems to be more to it. In both cases the narrative records a failure of the first attempts (see Josh. 7). Although Pattison does not adduce all the details that I have noted here, he does draw a conclusion that fits Girard's theoretical proposal:

> In both these parallels the line between Benjamin and non-Israelite peoples is broken down. Can we not then go on to infer that these duplications actually reflect a process of substitution whereby, firstly, Benjamin is substituted for the violence pervading the tribal situation in general; and, secondly, the internal, intra-tribal violence is projected out on to an external enemy. The various "wars" of Joshua-Judges need not have been wars waged by Israel against the nations but intra-Israelite wars of all against all. The defining of the enemy as external itself reflects the resolution of the sacrificial crisis and the deliverance of Israel from its own blood-bath.[38]

Pattison argues that the resolution of the crisis hinted at in those narratives is not effected until Solomon founds the temple and offers "the sacrifice which restores harmony to the community."[39] But how is it that Benjamin, youngest and most favored son of Jacob, becomes associated with the most violence in Israel? According to Pattison, "In the light of Girard's theory the identity between the surrogate victim and the deliverer should come as no surprise."[40] Although Saul attempts a sacrifice (1 Sam. 11), he is not able to break the sequence of retributive violence. Nor is David (from Judah), whose life is immersed in the violence of his own family and community, able to create harmony.

It is only in the cult that the violence is tamed. According to Pattison,

> these enemies, clearly regarded in most (but interestingly not all) cases as "outsiders" are in fact the distorted memory of the now-mastered plague of intra-communal violence, exteriorized in the

words and actions of the cult and in the national enemies of Is-rael.[41]

I might add that Pattison's application of Girard's theory does not pay attention to the narrative structuring of the book of Joshua with all its ambiguities and tensions. Nor does it consider the cultic fram-ing of the entire narrative. It does not consider the "exceptional out-siders," the problems associated with geographical boundary defini-tion, and the matter of inclusion in and exclusion from the new com-munity. These concerns seem to raise questions for a straightforward application of Girard's hermeneutic to the narrative of Joshua.

Girard's approach seems unable to do two things: first, it does not pay enough attention to all details of a text; second, in its focus on the world hidden behind the text, it does not clearly address recep-tion of the text by later readers in front of the text. With respect to both concerns, Girard's hermeneutic seems to offer a limited understand-ing of the formative and transformative function of the narrative. What it does well, however, is to offer critical tools by which to offer a critique of the violent mechanisms so often justified by texts like Joshua. These I highlight briefly in the second part of this paper.

QUESTIONS RAISED BY JOSHUA IN LIGHT OF GIRARD

The following observations and questions are intended to signal either points that need to be developed or items that may fill out sug-gestions in the preceding section.

1. The most important question concerns the genre of Joshua. What is the relationship between myth, tragedy, tradition, and his-tory in Girard's thought? How does Joshua participate in that ma-trix? How does Joshua echo exodus motifs (which I think for Girard might constitute a mythic element)? Gil Bailie, for example, suggests that Joshua militarizes the burning bush story of Exodus 3: "The armed angel of Joshua's vision is purely and simply a specter of sa-cred violence expressed militarily."[42] Are the narratives in Joshua like Girard's "tragedy"? Or does the book function more like Girard's understanding of prophecy? According to Girard,

> Tragic and prophetic inspiration do not draw strength from his-torical or philological sources but from a direct intuitive grasp of the role played by violence in the cultural order and in disorder as well, in mythology and in the sacrificial crisis.[43]

In particular, then, can Girard's hermeneutic be integrated with a more functional view of narrative such as reflected in the work of

Theodore Mullen (noted above)? Related to that, of course, is the question of whether conquest accounts of other ancient Near Eastern peoples betray the same substitutions as does Joshua?

2. Is the herem a significant element in this process of substitution? Does the radical elimination of the enemy support a sacrificial reading of the narrative? Or does the presentation of the narrative of Joshua undermine or subvert the ancient practice by means of the tensions and ambiguities in the narrative? Are we dealing here with sacrificial substitution, in other words, or with narrative subversion of a common ancient Near Eastern practice? According to Philip Stern, "Israel integrated the herem into its religion because the herem helped meet its need to bring order and security to a hostile and chaotic environment."[44]

What is the relationship between that kind of "ordering" and the "taming" that Girard speaks of in relation to sacrificial violence? And how does the herem and warfare fit Girard's categories of "good violence" and "bad violence"? Does the narrative of Joshua reflect a unanimous perspective or a mixed or ambiguous view? Is the entire narrative, in Girard's terms, representative of beneficent sacrificial violence? Or does the narrative complexity suggest a more nuanced reading?

3. How would the perceived similarities and differences between Canaanites and Israelites function in Girard's understanding of the sacrificial crisis? A sacrificial crisis emerges, according to Girard, on the loss of distinctives. But the "destruction of the adversary"[45] actually fails in Joshua (cf. Polzin). There is indeed a "crisis of distinctions" in terms of the cultural order.[46] On the surface Joshua seems to reflect the danger of assimilation and blurring of distinctions between Canaanites and Israelites. This seems a carryover from Deuteronomy's prohibition against imitation (Deut. 12:30-31; 18:9; 20:18). Joshua, however, does not continue the motif of imitation from Deuteronomy. The nations are not viewed as a religious threat.[47] There is a marked absence of imitation terminology (especially lamad, which appears throughout Deuteronomy).

The narrative of Joshua as a whole, therefore, actually demonstrates that reestablishing distinctives according to patterns of geography and ethnicity do not work to maintain holiness (a term that Deuteronomy employs to identify Israel's distinctiveness, an identity rooted in divine love; e.g., Deut. 7:6-8). It is those distinctives that actually lead to violence, even though loss of distinctives appears to be the real threat. Therefore the narrative of Joshua subordinates all distinctives to Torah (faithfulness to the divine word) and covenant loyalty (so also Schwager[48]). The *narrative* functions, in fact, to discredit warfare as a means of dealing with difference because war fails to clarify the separation by ridding the land of the outsider. Even as a sacrificial act, it fails to end warfare. Instead, Joshua 24:12 offers a critical principle that functions to advocate the elimination of human violence: "not by your sword or by your bow."

In Joshua the notion of a community of *torah*-keepers redefines the meaning of distinction. And that notion is underlined by the framework of liturgical and *torah* motifs at the beginning and end of the book. Even the altar built on the eastern side of the Jordan (Josh. 22) may be "meant to prevent violence, expulsion, and difference— precisely *because* no sacrifice will be offered on it."[49] After the east Jordan tribes appealed, "may the Lord himself take vengeance" (22:23), and asserted that no sacrifice be offered on the altar, the west Jordan tribes "blessed God and spoke no more of making war against them" (22:33).

4. That brings us to the question of divine involvement. Why is the divine command and the divine sanction of violence in warfare significant in Joshua? I offer first of all an extended quotation from Girard about the function of religion:

> Religion, then, is far from "useless." It humanizes violence; it protects man from his own violence by taking it out of his hands, transforming it into a transcendent and ever present danger to be kept in check by the appropriate rites appropriately observed and by a modest and prudent demeanor. Religious misinterpretation is a truly constructive force, for it purges man of the suspicions that would poison his existence if he were to remain conscious of the crisis as it actually took place.
>
> To think religiously is to envision the city's destiny in terms of that violence whose mastery over man increases as man believes he has gained mastery over it. To think religiously (in the primitive sense) is to see violence as something superhuman, to be kept always at a distance and ultimately renounced.[50]

This is important in relation to the book of Joshua because the narrative clearly reflects, in Girard's categories, "religious" concerns. It operates in a primitive and ritualistic context. Using Girard's terms, then, could the story itself reflect a desire to renounce violence? I suggest that the Joshua narrative reflects a renunciation of violence through its depiction of it. This requires no reconstruction of the historical events behind the narrative, even though original acts of violence may well be unmasked by the narrative. Similarly, this approach does not require us to read the narrative as fiction, but as a text that shapes identity and transforms vision through its own subversion of the exclusively violent sacrificial act of warfare.

Such a reading resonates with the work of Lawson Stone, who argues that the writers already believed that holy war traditions "represented an unusable past." Thus, "Clear moves were made to guide the reader to a nonmilitaristic, nonterritorial actualization of the text in which the conquest first illustrated the necessity of an affirmative response to Yahweh's action, then became a paradigm of obedience to the written Torah." The historian "transformed the historical tradition of the conquest into a gigantic metaphor for the religious life."[51]

That may well be how the narrative functions as a whole, but Stone's analysis does not address the question of how the divine actor is construed in the narrative. Concerning this, Girard writes, "Throughout the Old Testament, a work of exegesis is in progress, operating in precisely the opposite direction to the usual dynamics of mythology and culture. And yet it is impossible to say that this work is completed." It is not completed, says Girard, because of the "ambiguity regarding the role of Yahweh" who continues to be presented as the instigator.[52] He continues:

> This ambiguity in the role of Yahweh corresponds to the general conception of the deity in the Old Testament. In the prophetic books, this conception tends to be increasingly divested of the violence characteristic of primitive deities. Although vengeance is still attributed to Yahweh, a number of expressions show that in reality mimetic and reciprocal violence is festering more and more as the old cultural forms tend to dissolve. Yet all the same, in the Old Testament we never arrive at a conception of the deity that is entirely foreign to violence.[53]

According to Girard, then, the depiction in the narrative of Yahweh as agent of violence suggests the text still shares in the dynamics of mythology and primitive culture. But could it be that, given tensions and ambiguities observed in the narrative of Joshua, Joshua subverts the mimetic character of violence by the overarching theological perspective reflected in Joshua 24:12, "It was not by your sword or by your bow"? As J. M. Oughourlian states in conversation with Girard, the Old Testament "deconstructs" more primitive notions. "The myths are worked through with a form of inspiration that runs counter to them, but they continue in being."[54]

What is criticized continues. "And even though he is presented in a less and less violent form, and becomes more and more benevolent, Yahweh is still the god to whom vengeance belongs. The notion of divine retribution is still alive." Girard responds by stating that only the gospel texts "achieve what the Old Testament leaves incomplete."[55] James Sanders's notion of the process or trajectory of canonical hermeneutics seems, in some respects, to suggest the same thing: "the ancient biblical thinkers depolytheized what they learned from others, monotheized it, Yahwized it, and then Israelitized it."[56]

Perhaps I am asking the narrative of Joshua to do too much. What if Girard is right in saying: "Ascribing the violence to God, that violence has a sacred origin, is an illusion"?[57] If so, then Vernard Eller puts it correctly: Israel only thought they heard God tell them to fight.[58] But Girard's contribution is more profound than that.

> Its [Israel's] concept of the deity therefore still contains vestiges of sacralized violence, as does the sacrificial version of Christianity. Violence is still laid at the door of the divine victim and has not yet become the responsibility of the *generation* that will hear the gospel message.
>
> As the barriers between people start to disappear, mimetic antagonisms multiply. People become for each other the stumbling block that the Old Testament shows Yahweh placing before their feet.[59]

What might it mean, then, for a reading of Joshua to say, with Girard: the motif of divine intervention "produces exclusively maleficent results. Every supernatural visitation is prompted by the spirit of revenge. Benefits accrue only after the divinity has departed"?[60] Must we conclude, as Walter Wink does, that the violence in the Old Testament "is in part the residue of false ideas about God carried over from the general human past"? Wink continues by suggesting that in the narratives we find "the beginning of a process of raising the scapegoating mechanism to consciousness, so that these projections on God can be withdrawn"?[61] Raymund Schwager suggests, similarly, that "when the true God begins to reveal himself, then this unconscious process that produces false ideas of God must gradually be exposed."[62]

I have suggested that the narrative of Joshua itself functions implicitly as a critique of human violence. The motif of divine intervention in Joshua is not simply an illusion that must be rejected, but is an integral element in undermining human violence (which is usually organized along ethnic and geographic lines). Does not Girard's approach to human responsibility make the human community solely responsible for making sure that history comes out right? It seems to me that Joshua implies otherwise. Perhaps we can admit with Girard that "dressing up God" in cultural garb is inappropriate.[63] But Girard also states that "'demythification' works with mythology but not with the Bible, because the Bible already does it itself. The Bible really invented it ['demythification']. The Bible was the first to replace the scapegoat structure of mythology with a scapegoat theme that reveals the lie of mythology."[64] Perhaps the Book of Joshua begins that revelation even as it narrates the creation of a new and alternative community that emerges out of the violence of war.

The commander of the Lord's army gives an ambiguous answer to Joshua's question: "Are you one of us, or one of our adversaries?" (Josh. 5:13). The response indicates that the question is wrongly worded: "Neither; but as commander of the army of the Lord I have now come" (5:14). Perhaps distinctions are irrelevant, as is loss of distinction. The root of the sacrificial crisis that generates violence has already been undercut.

Girard's hope remains that we "resuscitate meaning by relating all the texts to one another without exception, rather than stopping at just a few of them."[65] From another text we hear that Yahweh's aim is to do away with the weapons of war altogether (Ps. 46:9). Joshua might not be as unrelated to that hope as we usually think.[66]

NOTES

1. René Girard, *Things Hidden Since the Foundation of the World* (Stanford, Calif.: Stanford University Press, 1987), 447.

2. Girard, in a chapter with Walter Burkert and Jonathan Z. Smith, "Ritual Killing and Cultural Formation," in *Violent Origins* (Stanford, Calif.: Stanford University Press, 1987), 141.

3. Girard, *Violence and the Sacred* (Baltimore: Johns Hopkins University Press, 1977), 66.

4. Girard, Burkert, and Smith, *Violent Origins* (entire thesis).

5. Girard, *Violence and the Sacred*, 8.

6. Ibid., 10.

7. Ibid., 13.

8. Ibid., 14.

9. Ibid.

10. Ibid., 17.

11. Ibid., 18.

12. Ibid., 8.

13. Daniel L. Hawk, *Every Promise Fulfilled: Contesting Plots in Joshua.* Lit-

erary Currents in Biblical Interpretation (Louisville, Ky.: Westminster/John Knox Press, 1991), 16-17.

14. Ibid., 40.

15. Ibid., 28.

16. Ibid., 145.

17. Robert Polzin, *Moses and the Deuteronomist: A Literary Study of the Deuteronomistic History* (New York: The Seabury Press, 1980), 84.

18. Ibid., 145.

19. Ibid., 90.

20. Ibid., 145.

21. Ibid.

22. Girard, *Violence and the Sacred*, 269.

23. Ibid., 271.

24. Ibid., 272.

25. Ibid.

26. Ibid., 249.

27. Ibid.

28. Theodore E. Mullen Jr., *Narrative History and Ethnic Boundaries*. Society of Biblical Literature *Semeia* Studies (Atlanta, Ga.: Scholars Press, 1993), 97.

29. Ibid., 98-99.

30. Ibid., 92.

31. Ibid., 118.

32. George Pattison, "Violence, Kingship and Cultus," *Expository Times* 102, no. 5 (1991), 136.

33. Girard, *Violence and the Sacred*, 36.

34. Ibid., 37.

35. Ibid., 42.

36. Pattison, 137.

37. Ibid.

38. Ibid.

39. Ibid., 138.

40. Ibid., 137.

41. Ibid., 139.

42. Gil Bailie, *Violence Unveiled: Humanity at the Crossroads* (New York: Crossroad, 1995), 159.

43. Girard, *Violence and the Sacred*, 66.

44. Philip D. Stern, *The Biblical Herem: A Window on Israel's Religious Experience*. Brown Judaic Studies 211 (Atlanta: Scholars Press, 1991), 218.

45. Girard, *Violence and the Sacred*, 48.

46. Ibid., 49.

47. Gordon Mitchell, *Together in the Land: A Reading of the Book of Joshua*, Journal for the Study of the Old Testament Supplement 134 (Sheffield: Sheffield Academic Press, 1993), 127, 189.

48. Raymund Schwager, S.J., *Must there be Scapegoats? Violence and Redemption in the Bible* (San Francisco: Harper & Row, 1987), 112.

49. Ben C. Ollenburger, Response paper during Conference proceedings, 1994.

50. Girard, *Violence and the Sacred*, 134-35.

51. Lawson G. Stone, "Ethical and Apologetic Tendencies in the Redaction of the Book of Joshua," *Catholic Biblical Quarterly* 53 (1991), 36.

52. Girard, *Things Hidden*, 157.

53. Ibid.

54. Ibid., 158.

55. Ibid.

56. James Sanders, *Canon and Community: A Guide to Canonical Hermeneutics* (Philadelphia: Fortress Press, 1984), 56.

57. Girard, *Things Hidden*, 190.

58. Vernard Eller, *War and Peace from Genesis to Revelation* (Scottdale, Pa./ Kitchener, ON: Herald Press, 1981), 78.

59. Girard, *Things Hidden*, 423-24.

60. Girard, *Violence and the Sacred*, 267-68.

61. Walter Wink, *Engaging the Powers: Discernment and Resistance in a World of Domination* (Minneapolis: Fortress Press, 1992), 147.

62. Schwager, *Must there be Scapegoats?* 67.

63. Girard, *Things Hidden*, 256.

64. Ibid., 118.

65. Ibid., 447.

66. I am grateful to James Brennemann, Ben Ollenburger, and James G. Williams, who read an earlier draft of this paper and gave helpful responses.

CHAPTER FIVE

Sacrificial Language in Hebrews: Reappraising René Girard

Michael Hardin

IN RECENT YEARS THE WORK OF RENÉ GIRARD has been used by biblical scholars to elucidate the structure and function of religion in the biblical texts.[1] Girard's hypothesis has not been without its critics. Nevertheless, its heuristic potential to illumine biblical texts is considerable. Biblical studies can ill afford to bypass Girard. Whereas this essay is aware of and uses scholarship on Hebrews, our concern is not historical-critical exegesis of Hebrews. Rather, our interest is whether Girard's hypothesis gains from a Girardian reading of the text itself.[2]

Girard contends that the biblical texts, more so than others, deconstruct the relation between religion and culture and bring to the fore the role of violence in structuring both religion and culture. In this regard, texts that criticize violence and alleged divine referents point to a strategic biblical hermeneutic. This self-critical nature of the Bible is perhaps its most important asset—in that the religious culture that produced writings to justify violence also canonized writings that critique violence.

Girard holds that the biblical writings begin this demystification process in the Hebrew Scriptures and more completely demystify violence in the New Testament. However, according to Girard and many of his interpreters, the Epistle to the Hebrews did not escape the "sacrificial hermeneutic," which justifies mimetic violence and in turn interprets the death of Jesus in a sacrificial manner. In contrast, our contention is that Hebrews subverts the sacrificial process, albeit under cover of sacrificial language. We will present a summary of Girard's hypothesis, then demonstrate the power of Girard's hypothesis by examining the atonement theory of Hebrews.

GIRARD'S THEORY

ary critic. In the works of modern writers, particu-
al, and Dostoyevsky, Girard found that humans
_ through the mechanism of mimetic desire. *Mi-
...metic desire*, is the fundamental way we imitate each
...er's desires.[3] Our self-understanding is therefore locked into the
mechanism of mimesis. From mimesis stems conflict, where two parties become undifferentiated as they imitate one another's desires. This process of becoming the same culminates in violence over the object wanted.

From this mechanism of mimesis, Girard extends his insights into the fields of anthropology and psychology. He contends that inter-mimetic rivalry in a community leads to community breakdown, so a common outlet for mimetic hostility is necessary. He argues that a common scapegoat who receives the mimetic hostility grounds the community. This is because collective violence is the primary unifying act.

Girard in turn argues that human community, or culture itself, is grounded in the scapegoat or victimage mechanism, whereby the continued repetition of such sacrificial scapegoating continues to regenerate the community. Thus religion justifies sacrificial activity and joins culture in supporting the scapegoating mechanism. The assuaging of mimetic conflict in the sacrificial crisis issues prohibitions which seek to end subsequent escalating mimetic conflict. Rituals re-enacting the sacrificial mechanism give the community an outlet for mimetic hostility, and myths develop to justify the victimage of the community.

Central to Girard's thesis is the process of *sacralization*. As such, the victim is the first polyvalent symbol.[4] The victim is first judged guilty by the community and sacrificed to bring an end to the hostility. Then, as a consequence of the community's "reconciliation," the victim is valued as source of saving power, since it appears that communal peace and cohesion come from the sacrificed victim.

Girard has pointed out that most ancient mythologies cover up this process of sacralization. The lie is necessary for the community to remain grounded. However, certain Greek poets, namely Euripedes and Aristophanes, and especially the biblical writers, begin to expose this mechanism of sacred violence.[5] The Hebrew Scriptures began the process of demystification by asserting the innocence of the victim.[6] The New Testament writers carry through this project by exposing the innocence of Jesus and showing that the violence against him is the result of mimetic hostility in the community, not the appeasing of an angry God.[7]

For the church or synagogue to read the biblical texts as though God demanded a sacrifice to appease his wrath is to engage in a "sacrificial hermeneutic." To discern the implicit hermeneutic in the text is to read the text from the perspective of the victim, not the persecutor, and thus to read "nonsacrificially."[8]

Both Girard and some of his interpreters have felt that the epistle to the Hebrews engaged a sacrificial rendering of the text. Girard said in 1978 that

> according to this epistle, there is a difference between Christ's passion and the sacrifices that have gone before. But this difference is still defined in sacrificial terms. Consequently the real essence of the sacrificial is never examined. Like all variants to follow, this first Hebrews attempt at a sacrificial theology is based on analogies between the Passion and the form of all other sacrifices, but it allows the essential feature to escape.[9]

The major objection to this sacrificial theology of Hebrews can be observed in that its author did not include a reference to the persecution by the unjust mob against an innocent victim. Thus Hebrews strips humans of responsibility for the death of Christ. As Girard puts it, "the murderers are merely the instruments of the divine will." That is, when God is deemed responsible for the death of Christ, we are dealing with sacrificial theology. When the account of Jesus' death is placed squarely on humanity, we see the beginnings of nonsacrificial theology.

We are in fundamental agreement with Girard that the demystification of violence and the sacred forms a significant theologoumenon of biblical theology. However, against Girard, it can be shown that the epistle to the Hebrews does indeed demystify violence but through personalist categories.

With the advent of Jesus Christ, violence is demystified; there is no longer any positive function to it. In the story of Jesus, according to Girard, it is not only violence per se that is demystified but the notion of divine punishment. Girard contends that violence continues to be frightening only because

> through the mediation of the scapegoat mechanism can violence become its own remedy, and the victimage mechanism can only be triggered by the frenetic paroxysm of the mimetic crisis ... As the whole of humanity makes the vain effort to reinstate its reconciliatory and sacrificial virtues, this violence will without doubt

tend to multiply its victims, just as happened at the time of the prophets."[10]

Violence is both poison and remedy. As its own remedy, it is involved in ever increasing escalation. Greater numbers of victims are required to pacify the mimetic hostility of the community, or a few victims of great status will suffice.

However, Christian biblical exegesis has long understood the references to the "wrath of God" (ὀργὴ θεοῦ) to refer to the necessity of victims to appease the divine anger. According to this perspective, Jesus became the sacrificial substitute upon whom God could pour out his wrath. Raymund Schwager has argued vociferously against such a connotation for the phrase "wrath of God" in the New Testament. Schwager contends that references to the "wrath of God" typically involve God giving humanity over to the boiling mimetic crisis.[11]

One can see how Girard could read Hebrews and suggest that the author of this epistle had lapsed back into the sacrificial hermeneutic. Jesus is compared to the sacrificial institution *par excellence*, the high priesthood of the Jerusalem temple. Does this mean that the author was not aware of the sacrificial unmasking of the early Christian theologies, found, namely, in the Gospels and Paul?

NONSACRIFICIAL THEOLOGY IN HEBREWS

In Hebrews, it is personalist categories that allow the author to unveil how victimage is unmasked. To do this requires great skill, for using sacrificial language and accepting the victimage mechanism are two different things.

As the revealer, Jesus is similar to those to whom he brings the word of God. Jesus shares in their humanity (2:14); he was made like his siblings in every way (ὁμοιωθῆναι, 2:17); he was tempted just as they would be (4:15); he is the pioneer of their salvation (2:10) and the perfecter of their faith (12:2). This likeness of Jesus to all humans has a double function. On the one hand it allows Jesus to be a mediator with compassion. On the other hand, it turns him into a potential double. His similarity to humans is such that his divine character cannot be known apart from his absolute undifferentiation in regard to humankind.

Girard has pointed out that sacrificial crises occur when there is an abolition of all distinctions, when mimetic conflict and mediated desire renders each person in the community like to the other. The demand for differentiation escalates until one is found who can indeed be deemed different, the victim. What the author of Hebrews recognizes in the discussion that precedes his comparison of Jesus to the sacrificial system is this: revelation of God's self occurs precisely in the midst of a sacrificial crisis. To use the later language of Martin Luther, "God reveals himself under his opposite."[12] That is, for God to reveal the hideous character of violence and victimage there are only two options: join with the victimizers, which brings nothing to revelation, or become the victim.

In the gospel tradition, the similarity of Jesus to other humans with his concomitant claim to reveal God also constitutes a mimetic crisis. His "being known" is a scandal, a stumbling block. For the author of Hebrews, the similarity of Jesus to humans is explored in terms of Jesus as mediator. What is significant is that the mediating function of Jesus is not compared to that of the sacrificial lamb but of the high priest. Jesus is not so much offering as offerer. This distinction is crucial. Had the author of Hebrews compared Jesus to the passive lamb, he would have joined in the mad chorus of victimage, but by comparing Jesus to the high priest, he introduces an entirely new element. It is neither just that the mob takes the life of Jesus, nor is Jesus in collusion with the mob in his death. Something else is occurring.

For Jesus to share in common humanity specifically means that he puts an end to the sacrificial system: he "dies once for all" (9:26, 28). The difference between Jesus and all others consists in his innocence; he is without sin (4:15).[13] Jesus' incarnation and death is not to be repeated. Repetition is indigenous to the sacrificial mechanism, where ritual repetition of sacrifice recalls the originary murder which originally grounded the community. Jesus' life and death is ἅπαξ, once for all. It is precisely the repetitive character of the sacrifices in the Hebrews cultus which is deemed one of its major liabilities (7:27; 9:25).

However, the character of Jesus' death in Hebrews does raise the question as to how the author understood that death as a sacrifice. If the priests in the Jerusalem temple year after year repeatedly offered sacrifices, what is the unique character of Jesus' sacrifice? In Girardian terms, what is the relation of the death of Christ to that of Abel, the founding murder in the Judeo-Christian tradition?

The first time the author uses the term ἅπαξ, it is to recall that "Christ sacrificed for the sins of humanity once for all when he offered himself" (7:27). The critical value of this text is that Christ is both the subject and object of the verb, viz., "he offered himself (ἑαυτὸν ἀνενέγκας)." When the victimage mechanism is discussed, it is always in terms of the taking of the life of another. One observes this, for example, in the founding murder myth of Romulus and Remus. One could object that in mythology when the victim countenances the violence against him or her, this brings about the necessary unanimity required for the mechanism to function. When myth records that victims have also participated in the judgment rendered on them by the community, the victim shares in sacrificial mythology.[14] Is this what Hebrews is suggesting?

In this letter one finds Christ to be the subject and object of verbs related to his self-offering, verbs that have to do specifically with his death. The early Jewish Christian Hellenists may just as well have been the first to deduce this. One can for example find such argumentation in the so-called *carmen christi* of Philippians 2:5-11.[15] Indeed, Martin Hengel has contended that the connection between Jesus' death and his self-giving could have been made in this community.[16] The ὑπὲρ ὑμῶν ("for you") of the eucharistic tradition may have governed this connection, since it is found in all the major writers of the New Testament. As the apostle Paul phrases it, if Christ's death is for us, neither he nor God is against us (Rom. 8:31ff.).

However, in the Hebrew Scriptures, there appears to be a genetic connection between violence and God in which sacrificial violence is necessary to appease God's wrath, or atone for sin. Raymund Schwager, following suggestions made by Girard, has demonstrated that as traditions develop in the Hebrew Scriptures, God becomes less and less identified with violence, death, and killing.[17] The process of demystification begins with the Hebrew Scriptures. Girard sees in the Servant Songs of Deutero-Isaiah, texts that had a profound influence on both Jesus and the early church, and even which have

> the character not of a ritual but of the type of event from which, according to my hypothesis, rituals and all aspects of religion are derived. The most striking aspect here, the trait which is certainly unique, is the innocence of the servant, the fact that he has no connection with violence and no affinity for it. A whole number of passages lay on humans the principal responsibility for his saving death.[18]

The interpretive problem clearly comes to the fore here inasmuch as Yahweh's role in this text is ambiguous and corresponds to the general conception of the deity found throughout the earliest traditions of the Hebrew Scriptures. It is a mixed portrait of Yahweh, one which shares in both the structure of myth and gospel. However, Yahweh's relation to the sacrificial cultus is certainly challenged in many of the prophetic books. According to Schwager, the critique of the sacrificial cultus begins as early as the first written prophets (Amos 5:21-25; Hos. 10:1-5; Mic. 6:16-17). However, it is only in the gospel tradition that God is finally cleared of any culpability in the death of his servant.[19]

A glance at the earliest communities in Jerusalem and their respective preaching allows us to point out that a Girardian interpretation is invited. The death of Christ in the early Aramaic-speaking community is predominantly passive (Acts 2:23; 3:15; 4:10, 28; 5:30; 10:39). The death of Christ is communicated in those terms reminiscent of the founding murder. Jesus is wrongly accused, arbitrarily judged and condemned. The mob who executes Jesus includes the "crowds," Pilate, Herod, and the listeners of the apostolic proclamation. The earliest kerygma is the preaching of the murder to end all murders. It is the exposition of the clear boundaries that had been blurred by the juxtaposition of violence and the sacred. Jesus is the ultimate victim, and his death reveals the victimage mechanism with utmost clarity.

The author of Hebrews reflects only certain aspects of this pattern of thinking when talking of Christ's death. If God is not responsible for the death of Jesus—if God does not demand the sacrifice of his son—then who is responsible? Girard has argued, as seen earlier, that Hebrews failed at this point in that the author did not indicate the culpability of the mob, as did the earliest apostolic proclamation.[20]

If no one is implicated, then who is responsible? The place of responsibility in Hebrews shifts away from the mob in a slight but significant linguistic nuance. Jesus offers (ἀναφέρω) himself. But whence did this language arise? Hengel argues that it is the early Greek-speaking Jewish Christians who point out the significance of Jesus' death "for us" (ὑπὲρ ὑμῶν). It is a short step from "Christ died for us" to "Christ gave his life for us."

It could be argued that in addition to the many unique linguistic contributions of the Greek-speaking Jewish Christian communities, e.g., εὐαγγέλιον, κοινωνία, ἐκκλησία (gospel, fellowship, church), it is possible to suggest that in this community, which clearly saw the implications of the founding murder, that words meaning "to offer," here προσφέρω and ἀναφέρω, were also coined with reference to the death of Jesus. It is the language of self-giving which is here highlighted. To give one's life bespeaks intentionality, a substantially different way of conceiving victimage, in contrast to a passive victim. Although we are not arguing for a straight line from the early Greek-speaking community in Jerusalem to the letter to the Hebrews, a common stock of vocabulary would certainly influence theology as it developed in the early decades of the early church.

Language related to the cultus, namely, θύω and its cognates, is avoided in the New Testament; rather, language related to φέρειν and its cognates occurs. The New Testament uses the more cultic terminology only once at 1 Corinthians 5:7. Oscar Cullmann has argued that even here sacrificial terminology is clearly related to the active self-giving of the "servant of Yahweh."[21] The reason for this is that θύω belongs to the process of propitiation, the God-directed activity of the creature, whereas φέρω and its cognates, especially ἀναφέρω and προσφέρω have more of the sense of bringing a gift.[22] But this gift giving is not a *Do ut des* (giving to get in return). To offer a gift, as the author of Hebrews later argues, is to offer it as an extension of one's very self. Simply put, one cannot bribe or fix things with God. How then does the writer of Hebrews understand the self-giving of Jesus?

It is generally acknowledged that Psalm 110 plays a key role in Hebrews. George Buchanan in his commentary contends that Hebrews is a homiletic midrash on Psalm 110.[23] The heart of the letter is the section on the high priesthood of Christ, 7:1–10:18. The comparison of Jesus to Melchizedek is unique to Hebrews in the New Testament canon. Oscar Cullmann argues that the earthly high priestly work of Christ outlined here in Hebrews is derived from the Jesus tradition, and Jesus' own exegesis of Psalm 110:1.[24]

If the writer had oral tradition about Jesus available, as implied by 5:7-8, one could argue that Jesus' exegesis of Psalm 110:1 might also have been at hand. But Hebrews uniquely connects Psalm 110:1 and 4: "you are a priest forever, after the order of Melchizedek."

The priesthood of Jesus is compared to that of Melchizedek in a midrash on Genesis 14 and Psalm 110:4. Most commentators who have written since the discoveries at Qumran make reference to possible messianic interpretations of a high priestly figure in Judaism. In Qumran writings, Melchizedek is interpreted to mean both "king of uprightness" and "king of peace."[25] While the designation "king of peace" is found in both Philo and Hebrews, commentators have not usually exploited the difference between other Melchizedek speculations and Hebrews.[26]

The publication of the fragments from Qumran known as 11Q Melchizedek provides a crucial text for comparison. In these fragments, Melchizedek is described as the figure who will proclaim the jubilary year, who will restore the captives [Israel] at the end of days. His function is to restore Israel to its kingly state. 11Q Medchizedek reads,

> Melchizedek will avenge the vengeance of the judgments of G o d . . . and he will drag them from the hands of Satan and from the spirits of his lot. And all the gods of justice will come to his aid to attend to the destruction of Satan. And the height is . . . all the sons of God . . . this . . . this is the day of shalom concerning which God spoke through Isaiah the prophet.[27]

The year of jubilee that will be announced by this high priestly figure, called a day of *shalom*, peace or salvation, is followed by an explicit reference to the peace-bringing messenger of Isaiah 52:7. In Qumran, vengeance is to be exacted by this figure. Richard Longenecker notes that warrior characteristics are stressed in 11Q Melchizedek.[28]

In the letter to the Hebrews there is no mention of vengeance exacted by Jesus. Jesus does not repay humanity with violence, which it dealt him. By not participating in violence, Jesus breaks the mechanism of violence and opens the way for a new obedience. Vengeance is not part of the high priestly work of Christ.[29] In 9:28, the only explicit reference to the second coming of Christ in the New Testament, the second appearance (ἐκ δευτέρου) of Christ is to bring salvation to those who wait patiently for him. The message of the Christian community is that God invites repentance and offers unconditional forgiveness apart from sacrifice.

Jesus does not exact vengeance upon his return because his blood, the blood of an innocently murdered victim, "speaks a better word than that of Abel" (12:24). Here the explicit reference to the founding murder in the biblical tradition invites us to reflect on the character of Jesus' death. Abel's response to murder is to call for retaliation, a vengeance he expects God to enact. It is the cry of innocent blood spilled for no reason. It is the cry of the older legislative code which calls for "an eye for an eye, and a tooth for a tooth." The blood of Jesus speaks a better word, a word of mercy and forgiveness.

The exegesis of Jesus as 'king of peace' takes on significance inasmuch as it reflects the character of one who voluntarily lays down his life. There does not appear to be any notion of a high priestly sacrifice in Judaism.[30] Jesus is both the offering as the victim and, more so, the one who came to "give his life a ransom for many." The writer to Hebrews reflects the active character of the LXX Isaiah 53 when he speaks of Christ having offered himself (9:27).[31] It is the active willingness to become the victim who is extruded (ἔξω τῆς πύλης, 13:12) that is emphasized.[32]

It has been argued that the author of Hebrews drew on texts common to early Christian circles and exegeted those texts in line with the thinking of the Jewish Greek-speaking community in Jerusalem, a community whose thought had no little effect on Paul. It has also been contended that the character of the high priestly work of Jesus was explicated in this community with dramatic results for moving away from a sacrificial hermeneutic and propitiatory understanding of the death of Christ. This is most clearly enunciated in Hebrews 10:1-18 and its use of Psalm 40.

Schwager, following Girard, first pointed out the relation of the death of Christ to the founding murder. This has been followed up by James G. Williams.[33] Christ's death at the hands of humanity as the victim of humanity's collective murder is now seen not as an act of innocent blood spilled and vengeance demanded. Rather, it is interpreted as an act of self-offering which yields to and reveals the scapegoat mechanism in all of its fury.

The author begins by arguing that the law, as a designation of the older dispensation, is but a shadow of the good things that are to come. He underscores this by saying that the law was not the reality. The Platonic underpinnings of this text have been widely discussed. However one construes the background of the author, it is clear that a transcending of the old has occurred. As the old is a shadow (σκιά), it is weak and useless (7:18), by implication it is inferior (8:6), something is wrong with it (8:7), and it is obsolete and fleeting (8:13).

The author's critique of the older covenant is grounded in his exegesis of Psalm 40. Psalm 40 is most likely a critique of the Deuteronomic hermeneutic found in the Hebrew Scriptures which justifies sacrifice and often attributes violence to Yahweh. This Psalm is now found on the lips of the pre-incarnate Christ. The writer expressly connects the desire of God in the Psalm with the intention of Jesus in the incarnation. These personalist categories sharpen to cutting edge the critique of the sacrificial system. There is no distinction between the will of the Father and the will of the Son. This is crucial for those who contend for a propitiatory understanding of the atonement and also for those who would contend that Hebrews intends a sacrificial hermeneutic.

The sacrificial system is completely named: sacrifices, burnt offerings, and sin offerings. The citation of Psalm 40 makes clear that God does not desire sacrifices, nor were they something that he ever wanted. In an editorial comment the author also adds that God was not pleased with them. It would appear that the divine is in no way to be connected with the sacrificial system.

The exegesis of Psalm 40 in Hebrews 10:8-10 is one of the most critical exegeses in the New Testament and frequently overlooked.[34] In the sense that the author of Hebrews discerns a crisis in the old sacrificial system, he exposes its weaknesses and limitations and transcends the old with the new. Girard has done this as well, only he uses the language of ritual, myth, and prohibition. That is, the violent underpinnings of religion that have previously been ignored are now shown to be false through the revelation of the victimage hypothesis which occurs in the biblical writings.

Those texts that reveal the victimage mechanism and the relation of violence to the sacred are texts concerning which one can speak of revelatory significance. These texts have the power to deconstruct other texts and themselves. Perhaps in this sense one can speak of an inner biblical hermeneutic.

The author of Hebrews saw the distinction between revelation and religion when he contended that God neither wanted sacrifice nor was he pleased with it. Yet, the law required them. This is the conundrum that faces the exegete, who, if not prejudiced by theological assumptions, will have to admit that Marcion lurks at the door, yet with good cause. I have elsewhere contended that the problem with the relation of the two Testaments lies in the fact that neither separation nor equalization is a proper hermeneutic. That is, Augustine's view of Scripture is just as wrong as Marcion's.[35]

Yet if the law required sacrifice but God neither wants nor is pleased with it, what does this say for the nonsacrificial critique of the Law? Only this: just because a text claims God is speaking does not mean God is speaking. Rather, any notion of the "Word" of God or God's revelation must come under the truly critical control of the distinction between religion, which grounds violence, and revelation, which is nonsacrificial. Sacrifice and violence have never been part of the divine economy; as one early Christian letter put it, "violence is no attribute of God."[36] Perhaps the opening christological hymn in 1:1-4 is meant to initiate this critical hermeneutic when it speaks of "ways and means" in which revelation earlier took place. But now God speaks through his intermediary, the Son, Jesus.

As Girard has shown, particularly in *Violence and the Sacred*, sacrifice arises when mimetic desire reaches a feverish pitch and the necessity for differentiation culminates in the extrusion of an innocent life. The peace that the community experiences is attributed to the victim whose sacrifice must have pleased the "gods." The deception, or the lie, is that the whole community must participate in the verdict—that is, the entire community creates the mythology of guilt. The victim is sacralized. The founding murder becomes the basis for an anthropological mechanism of self-preservation equivalent to salvation.

The author of Hebrews will use the LXX version of Psalm 40 to sharpen his critique of religion and sacrifice. In what Leonhard Goppelt called a "bold interpretation,"[37] the author identifies the taking of a body in the incarnation with doing the will of God. Here, Jesus takes on himself human flesh and, becoming in all respects like every other human, does the will of God. It is precisely by that "will" that Jesus becomes the author of salvation and makes them holy (2:10-11). That is, as the author of Hebrews puts it, God's primordial rejection of religion grounded in violence is seen to effect a choice on the part of the Son who plays the only role available to him in the incarnation process: he becomes the ultimate victim.

Since the citation comes at the end of the long christological section 7:1–10:18, it seems clear that the author's final arguments sum up all he has said. One could object that earlier in 9:22 the author pointed out expressly that "there is no forgiveness without the shedding of blood," thus arguing for a sacrificial interpretation. However, as we have seen, the internal critique of the sacrificial mechanism is also here, in that the text specifically points out that the law requires that there be no forgiveness without the shedding of blood, a law that is powerfully criticized for its apparent justification of religious violence and sacrifice.[38] The author also points out that whereas the law required the shedding of blood, it was not yet effective, inasmuch as the blood of bulls and goats cannot take away sin (9:9, 12-13; 10:4; 11). It is no mistake that there is no new temple theme in the Letter to the Hebrews.[39]

In the new covenant, sins and lawless acts are forgiven apart from sacrifice (10:18). Before sacrifice and apart from sacrifice there is forgiveness. Thus the two major motifs of both Jesus and the prophets appear here albeit under a different form, viz., repentance and forgiveness. Robert Daly has shown that there is an ethicizing of the sacrificial system that takes place as Scripture develops. He demonstrates that the paranetic sections of this letter which follow theological discussion speak of the Christian life as a self-offering (10:19-25; 12:18-28; 13:10-16).[40]

In short, the Christian life is to be modeled on that of Jesus who gave his life for the world. The demands "to be at peace with all" (12:14), to "spur one another to good deeds" (10:24), to love each other and entertain strangers (13:1-2), to remember those unjustly imprisoned (13:3)—all reflect a community whose sacrifices consist not in the taking of the life of another (θύω), but of self-giving (προσφέρειν). This giving is constituted by praise, sharing, and deeds that benefit others (13:15-16). There is a fundamental reorientation that takes place when one comes to the knowledge of sacrifice and the self-giving of the Son of God.[41]

This leaves us with one final problem text to handle, that of the so-called second repentance. In 10:26, the author points out that there is no hope for those who keep on sinning after having been enlightened about the structure of sacrifice, violence, and religion. Why is this? The answer had already been suggested earlier in the letter. Already in 2:1 the author implies that it is possible to drift away and in 3:12 suggests that an unbelieving heart can turn one away from God. Further, 4:1 suggests that one can fall short of the sabbath rest promised for those who listen to God's voice. Thus 6:1-8 is a *crux interpretum*. One recalls that Martin Luther rejected the Epistle to the Hebrews due to this passage.

The phrase that bears scrutiny is ἀπὸ νεκρῶν ἔργων, "acts which lead to death" (6:1).[42] The author could mean that sinful acts bring spiritual death, but the ethical sections suggest that it is the concrete care for those unjustly extruded, that is, for those who have been made victims of society, that is being addressed. To not care for those who have been scapegoated, to expose them to further victimage would be to commit "an act leading to the death [of another]." Furthermore, apostasy is clearly defined as victimage, "since they crucify the Son of God on their own account and hold him up to contempt" (6:6).

The qualifications of those who cannot repent are clear. They have been enlightened. They have tasted the heavenly gift, shared in the life of the Spirit, and heard the word of God. The text speaks of those who have participated in the rule of God and have forsaken "acts which lead to death" as having escaped the rule of violence.

If these then, who know their Lord and Master to reveal the victimage mechanism through his own story, and who calls them to give their lives as he did, should turn and participate by victimizing others, they would be crucifying Jesus all over again. The significant difference is that when humanity crucified Jesus, they did so nonconsciously,[43] whereas now they commit "acts which lead to the death of others" with full awareness of their evil deeds.

The call to persevere is thus an invitation to continue the self-giving in which recipients of this letter have shared (10:23, 32ff., 12:1, 4). The Christian life calls one to intentionally care for victims and if necessary to become the victim. This does not mean the Christian accepts the mythology of the persecutor and the judgment of guilt. Rather, the Christian protests their innocence and seeks for justice.

We have argued that Girard and some of his interpreters have contended that the Scriptures reveal the relation of violence and the sacred. We have observed that Girard and others have rejected Hebrews (as did Luther) since it appears to give in again to a sacrificial hermeneutic. Our observations have sought to show that Girard's insights can be extended to Hebrews and that this letter, while using the language of sacrifice, rejects all connections between violence and the sacred. Instead Hebrews offers a new paradigm of what real self-giving (human and divine) is all about.[44]

NOTES

1. See e.g., Robert North, "Violence and the Bible: The Girard Connection" *CBQ* 47 (1985), 1-27; Norbert Lohfink, ed., *Gewalt und Gewaltlosigkeit im Alten Testament* (Freiberg: Herder, 1983); Raymund Schwager, *Must There Be Scapegoats?* (New York: Harper, 1987); James G. Williams, *The Bible, Violence, and the Sacred* (New York: Harper, 1992); Robert Hamerton-Kelly, *Sacred Violence: Paul's Hermeneutic of the Cross* (Philadelphia: Fortress, 1992); Walter Wink, *Engaging the Powers* (Philadelphia: Fortress, 1992); Garland Knott, "The God of Victims: René Girard and the Future of Religious Education," *Religious Education* 86 (1991): 399-412.

2. James G. Williams ("The Innocent Victim: René Girard on Violence, Sacrifice, and the Sacred," *RSR* 14 [1988], 325) believes it "unlikely that Girard will get a full hearing from biblical scholars until his theory is appropriately adapted to take into account the modern tradition of historical and literary exegesis." This has been done by Raymund Schwager, *Jesus im Heilsdrama* (Innsbruck: Tyrolia, 1990) // *Jesus in the Drama of Salvation*, (New York: Crossroad, 1999), who argues that "this method of questioning [the historical critical] is itself an inner problematic of the New Testament, and at the same time is a continuation of the criticism of the Enlightenment idea of the autonomous moral subject which Girard has discussed under the heading of 'the romantic lie.'"

3. Girard's new approach to mimesis is to observe the fundamental acquisitive character of mimesis, ignored in both the ancient (Plato) and modern philosophies (Hegel). On mimesis in general, though with no mention of Girard, see William Schweiker, "Beyond Imitation: Mimetic Praxis in

Gadamer, Ricoeur, and Derrida," *JR* 68 (1988): 21-38.

4. The victim is the primordial symbol from which language is derived. See e.g., Eric Gans, *The Origin of Language* (Berkeley: University of California Press, 1981); Andrew McKenna, *Violence and Difference: Girard, Derrida, and Deconstruction* (Chicago: University of Illinois Press, 1992).

5. Girard's bibliocentrism has been challenged by Lucien Scubla, "The Christianity of René Girard," in *Violence and Truth*, ed. Paul Dumouchel (Stanford: Stanford University Press, 1985), 160-178.

6. René Girard, *Job: The Victim of His People* (Stanford: Stanford University Press, 1987); originally published as *La route antique des hommes pervers* (Paris: Grasset, 1985).

7. On the early church's shift in atonement theories see Raymund Schwager, *Der Wunderbare Tausch* (Munich: Kosel, 1986); Michael Hardin, "Violence: René Girard and the Recovery of Early Christian Perspectives," *Brethren Life and Thought* 37:2 (1992), 107-120.

8. On which see René Girard, *The Scapegoat* (Baltimore: Johns Hopkins, 1986); originally published as *Le bouc émissare* (Paris: Grasset, 1982).

9. René Girard, *Things Hidden Since the Foundation of the World* (Stanford, Calif.: Stanford University Press, 1978), 228; originally published as *Des choses cachées depuis la fondation du monde* (Paris: Grasset, 1978), 330.

10. Girard, *Things Hidden*, 195-196; *Des choses*, 287.

11. Schwager, *Must There Be Scapegoats?* 202-203.

12. Martin Luther, *Luther's Works* (Philadelphia: Fortress Press, 1975), 31.39ff.

13. Oscar Cullmann, *Christology in the New Testament* (Philadelphia: Westminster, 1963), 93ff. In his exegesis of 4:15, Karl Barth, *Church Dogmatics 1/2* (London: T&T Clark, 1959), 152, comes close to Girard when he points out that the difference between Jesus' incarnation and that of other figures in the history of religion is that Jesus was made sin and became a curse for us. The advance Girard makes over Barth is the hermeneutical exposure of the sacrificial lie in the history of religion and the Bible.

14. As Oedipus does, cf. Girard, *Violence and the Sacred* (Baltimore: Johns Hopkins, 1972), 68ff.; originally published as *La violence et le sacré* (Paris: Grasset, 1972), 105ff.

15. Ralph Martin, *Carmen Christi* (London: Cambridge University Press, 1967).

16. Martin Hengel, *The Atonement* (Philadelphia: Fortress, 1981).

17. Schwager, *Must There Be Scapegoats?* 43-135; Norbert Lohfink, "Altes Testament—Die Entlarvung der Gewalt," *Herder Korrespondenz* 32 (April 1987), 187-193. See also Girard's comments in Robert Hamerton-Kelly, ed., *Violent Origins* (Stanford: Stanford University Press, 1987), 141, "In the Hebrew Bible, there is clearly a dynamic that moves in the rehabilitation of victims, but it is not a cut and dried thing. Rather, it is a process under way, a text in travail; it is not a chronologically progressive process, but a struggle that advances and retreats."

18. Girard, *Things Hidden*, 157; *Des choses*, 235.

19. Schwager, *Scapegoats*, 196-200. See also R. G. Hamerton-Kelly "Sacred Violence and the Messiah: The Markan Passion Narrative as a Redefinition of Messianology" in *The Messiah*, ed. James Charlesworth (Philadelphia: Fortress, 1992), 461-493, who speaks of two levels in a text: one which is generative, the other which is thematic. On the thematic level, texts "play" within the spectrum myth-gospel. Hamerton-Kelly suggests that the detection of myth (generative scapegoating) in texts calls for a "repentant reading" of these texts.

20. Girard, *Things Hidden*, 227-231.

21. Cullmann, *Christology*, 71ff.

22. Harold W. Attridge, *Hebrews* (Philadelphia: Fortress, 1989), 213 n 102, argues that ἀναφέρω and προσφέρω are synonyms.

23. George Buchanan, *To The Hebrews* (Garden City: Doubleday, 1972). C. H. Dodd, in *According to the Scriptures* (London: Collins, 1952), 35, contended a generation ago that Psalm 110:1 underlay all the fundamental texts of the New Testament.

24. Mark 12:35-37. For our purpose it matters little whether or not the pericope is authentic, but simply whether it is possible that it underlay Hebrews' use of Psalm 110. R. Bultmann, *History of the Synoptic Tradition* (New York: Harper & Row, 1963), 136ff., ascribes this saying to the vague "hellenistic church." Jeremias, *New Testament Theology, I* (New York: Scribners, 1969), 259, contends that exegetical tools do not exist to determine its authenticity. Vincent Taylor, *The Gospel According to Mark* (New York: Macmillian, 1957), suggests that "the content of the story and its linguistic features suggest it was derived from Palestinian Judaism" (490). Martin Hengel, *Between Jesus and Paul* (Philadelphia: Fortress, 1983), 180, and Ragnar Leivestad, *Jesus in His Own Perspective* (Minneapolis: Augsburg, 1987) both accept the authenticity of the saying. See also the study by David M. Hay, *Glory at the Right Hand: Psalm 110 in Early Christianity* (Nashville: Abingdon, 1973), 159, who accepts its origins in the historical Jesus.

25. Joseph Fitzmyer, *Essays on the Semitic Background of the New Testament* (Missoula: Scholars Press, 1974), 231f. L. H. Schiffman, "Messianic Figures and Ideas in the Qumran Scrolls" in *The Messiah*, ed. James Charlesworth, 126, comments that 11Q Melchizedek speaks of no messiah but rather of "stages of history."

26. Although Attridge observes that themes which are crucial to a nonsacrificial reading of the text, viz., Jesus' self-sacrifice and rejection of vengeance, are not paralleled in Judaism (*Hebrews*, 99). Garth Lee Cockerill, "Melchizedek or `King of Righteousness,'" *Evangelical Quarterly* 63:4 (1991), 312, concludes that "the interpretation of 11Q Melchizedek further distances it from the Epistle to the Hebrews and makes any connection between their understandings of Melchizedek less likely."

27. Geza Vermes, *The Dead Sea Scrolls in English* (London: Penguin 1975), 265-68.

28. Richard Longenecker, "The Melchizedek Argument of Hebrews," in *Unity and Diversity in the New Testament* (Grand Rapids: Eerdmans, 1978),

166ff.

29. James W. Thompson, "The Conceptual Background and Purpose of the Midrash in Hebrews 7," *NovT* 19/fasc. 3 (July 1977, 209-223), observes that "Hebrews has none of 11Q Melchizedek's interest in Melchizedek as avenger and judge."

30. Cullmann, *Christology*, 91. Although see Käsemann, *The Wandering People of God* (Nashville: Augsburg, 1984), 212ff., whose argument from a gnostic-influenced midrash is not convincing.

31. Contra Attridge, *Hebrews*, 102.

32. Buchanan, *To The Hebrews*, 130, "the fact that Jesus offered himself as a sacrifice was very important to the author's understanding of the atonement (8.3, 9.14, 26, 10.10-12)."

33. Williams, *The Bible, Violence and the Sacred*, 185-211.

34. Attridge, *Hebrews*, 275, is incorrect to argue that Psalm 40 had no acquaintance with the prophetic critique of the sacrificial cultus. Note the Psalms' juxtaposition of idolatry and sacrifice, found particularly in the Prophets. He also argues for a difference between interior and exterior obedience, a thought foreign to Judaism, on which see E. P. Sanders, *Jesus and Judaism* (Philadelphia: Fortress, 1985), 63.

35. Michael Hardin, "The Biblical Testaments as a Marriage of Convenience: René Girard and Biblical Studies" presented to the *Colloquium on Violence and Religion*, AAR/SBL Annual Meeting, November 1990; also "Violence . . . Recovery," 107-20.

36. The Epistle to Diognetus, 7.4 (βία γὰρ οὐ πρόσετι τῷ θεῷ in Kirsopp Lake, ed. *The Apostolic Fathers* (Cambridge: Harvard University Press, 1970), 364.

37. Leonhard Goppelt, *Typos* (Grand Rapids: Eerdmans, 1982), 169.

38. Contra Frances Young, *Sacrifice and the Death of Christ* (London: SCM, 1975), 70ff., who misses the argument of the internal critique of the Law.

39. Robert Daly, *The Origins of the Christian Doctrine of Sacrifice* (Philadelphia: Fortress, 1978), 69.

40. Ibid., 75.

41. On positive imitation see Michael Hardin, "The Dynamics of Violence and the Imitation of Christ in Maximus Confessor," *St Vladimir's Theological Quarterly* 36 (1992): 373-385.

42. The term νεκρῶν ἔργων is also found in 9:14 where it is contrasted with a purified (baptismal?) συνείδησις and could refer to acts that lead to the death of victims, if our nonsacrificial reading of 6:1 is correct. The greater part of the paranetic chapter 13 speaks of care for victims.

43. Girard, *The Scapegoat*, 111 (*Le bouc émissaire*, 165-66), pointed out that the Lukan saying "Father forgive them for they know not what they do" is the first literary allusion to the "unconscious" (Girard uses the French *meconnaisannce*, which arguably should be translated as "non-conscious," thus avoiding all the post-Freudian baggage that the former term implies).

44. An exposition can be found in Arthur C. McGill, *Suffering: A Test Case for Theological Method* (Philadelphia: Westminster, 1982).

CHAPTER SIX

"A Better Sacrifice" or "Better Than Sacrifice"? Response to Michael Hardin's "Sacrificial Language in Hebrews"

Loren L. Johns

WHAT HARDIN DOES: CENTRAL THESES

Central to Michael Hardin's essay, "Sacrificial Language in Hebrews: Reappraising René Girard," are three theses. First, contrary to Girard's early[1] negative assessment of Hebrews' amenability toward his theory, Hebrews "subverts the sacrificial process, albeit under cover of sacrificial language" (p. 103). "The epistle . . . does indeed demystify violence but through personalist categories" (p. 105).

Second, the absence of reference to vengeance in Hebrews—even where its presence might be expected, based on the letter's dependence on Melchizedek traditions[2]—is more than fortuitous; it is intentional. "Jesus does not repay humanity with the violence it dealt him. By not participating in violence, Jesus breaks the mechanism of violence and opens the way for a new obedience" (p. 111).

Third, "Girard's insights can be extended to Hebrews. . . . This letter, while using the language of sacrifice, rejects all connections between violence and the sacred, offering instead a new paradigm of what real self-giving (human and divine) is all about" (p. 116).

THE ISSUES

As Robert North says in his article, Girard has not always been careful to define the word *sacrifice* as used by him.[3] He has tended to use *sacrifice* as a casual equivalent of primary violence or its reenactment. Girard's repudiation of the sacrificial or scapegoating mechanism in religion has led him to reject the sacrificial hermeneutic of Christendom—a hermeneutic based on parts of the New Testament itself. He bases this rejection of a theology of sacrifice on the nonsacrificial theology of the Gospels, which function for him as the hermeneutical key to the competing atonement theologies of the New Testament.

However, it may be possible, theoretically, to speak of Christ's death as a sacrifice *without* engaging in a sacrificial hermeneutic of the cross. That is, the language of sacrifice does not always—or at least *need* not always—express or even reflect subtextually the scapegoating mechanism. According to Raymund Schwager,

> Christ's death can be correctly called a sacrifice, if this is understood to mean an offering which includes the following [three] elements: (1) obedience to the Father as willingness to be persecuted even to the point of death; (2) the identification with all persons who find themselves in similar situations and who are victims of evil; (3) intercession for his brothers and sisters before God, an intercession which is essentially linked to that obedience which led to being rejected and being killed.[4]

These three elements of obedience, identification, and intercession are clearly emphases in the epistle to the Hebrews. Along similar lines, James Williams argues that in Mark, "sacrificial language is used, necessarily, to break out of a sacrificial view of the world."[5]

The question before us is, Does Hebrews use sacrificial language "to break out of a sacrificial view of the world," or does it in fact explicitly—or even worse, *implicitly*[6]—support the scapegoating mechanism?

That sacrifice and the language of sacrifice are near the heart of the rhetoric of Hebrews is undeniable. But how that rhetoric was designed and which elements of the discourse of sacrifice are assumed, tolerated, modified, or embraced is another question.

Few writers have discussed the work of Girard on sacrifice when commenting on sacrifice in Hebrews. This silence is particularly puzzling in works that specifically address the irony of the book's ambivalence about sacrifice. The irony is that Hebrews seems to reject the sacrificial cultic system itself, while appropriating all that is important in it for Christology.[7]

Various ways of relieving this logical problematic have been suggested. Some talk about quantitative *and* qualitative comparison and contrast between the Old Testament sacrificial system and the "sacrifice" of Christ.[8] Others argue that the heart of Hebrews' theology is sacrificial; Jesus' death was a sacrificial death and his priestly ministry and office will last forever.[9] Still others, like Hardin, suggest that the *critique* of sacrifice in Hebrews is thoroughgoing. For instance, Chauvet has argued that Hebrews "subverts" rather than reifies the sacrificial system. Michaud agrees: "To interpret the death of Jesus as a sacrifice is not to support the notion of sacrifice, as Vanhoye claimed, but to subvert it, to give it another sense."[10]

In the Hellenistic context, it was commonplace to question the efficacy of sacrifice on metaphysical grounds.[11] As a result, there was a tendency to "spiritualize" sacrifice, or to reinterpret it. The "spiritualization" of sacrifice at Qumran and in Philo is well-known.[12] Already in 1967, Valentin Nikiprowetzky argued that the critique of the cultus in Hebrews owes more to Hellenistic critique of sacrifice generally than it does to the prophetic critique of the cultus.[13]

SOME SPECIFIC COMMENDATIONS
WITH FURTHER QUESTIONS

I would like to highlight several important contributions by Hardin in his essay and raise several questions about some of his statements. First, Hardin claims that the author of the epistle to the Hebrews develops the solidarity of Jesus with humans in terms of his function as *mediator*, as *high priest*, *not* as the lamb or as the sacrifice, thus vitiating, rather than supporting, the sacrificial hermeneutic (p. 107).

It is true, I think, that the author is not particularly interested in portraying Jesus as sacrifice in Hebrews. He is much more concerned with Jesus as high priest.[14] The language of partnership,[15] fellowship,[16] and community solidarity seems to confirm this.

At points the standard translations obfuscate the issue by making explicit in translation a sacrificial hermeneutic that is not clearly supported in the text. For instance, in 9:26, διὰ τῆς θυσίας αὐτοῦ is translated "by the sacrifice of himself" in the REB, RSV, and NRSV ("by sacrificing himself," NJB), instead of "through his sacrifice." The latter phrase in English is capable of the sort of objective-subjective ambiguity that is present in the Greek.

At a few places, Jesus does appear to be the *sacrifice*. Are these instances simply concessions to the logic of the analogy[17] or subtle pointers to the sacrificial hermeneutic implicitly at work here?[18] Jesus offers himself, which is different from saying that Jesus is offered. Although the passive *is* used in 9:28 to refer to Jesus, the author seems reluctant to refer to Jesus or to his death as a sacrifice.[19] In any case, the fact that Jesus offers *himself* supports the critique of the sacrificial hermeneutic.[20]

Second, blaming the mob or blaming God are not the only alternatives for explaining Christ's death. Although in my opinion Hebrews fails to expose as profoundly as do the Gospels the victimization mechanism, I would agree with Hardin that it does not support that mechanism through a reification of sacrifice theology; rather, it emphasizes Jesus' death as a *self*-offering—a self-offering that attenuates or repudiates the scapegoat mechanism.[21] Girard has lamented that Hebrews fails to attribute Jesus' death to a mob action. However, it also avoids blaming God or some cosmic mechanistic "need" for propitiation by identifying the will of God and the will of Christ as one. When it does speak of sacrifice, Hebrews treats Jesus' death as exemplary rather than substitutionary.[22]

Third, the Christus Victor explanation of the meaning of Christ's death in Hebrews 2:14-15 is another Hardin might have indicated in favor of his thesis. "Since, therefore, the children share flesh and blood, he himself likewise shared the same things, so that through death he might destroy the one who has the power of death, that is, the devil, and free those who all their lives were held in slavery by the fear of death." At the very least, this text would suggest that the author's atonement theology is not singularly substitutionary.

Fourth, it is in Hebrews 10:1-18 and its use of Psalm 40 that the author most clearly repudiates a sacrificial hermeneutic. Here the author makes most "clear that God does not desire sacrifices, nor were they something that he ever wanted. . . . God was not pleased with them" (p. 113). It is here that the author of the letter comes closest to repudiating the scapegoating mechanism as such, and Hardin rightly emphasizes its importance for a Girardian reading of Hebrews. Nevertheless, it is precisely here that a closer look at analogous Hellenistic and Jewish critiques of the temple cult is crucial for understanding the author's underlying hermeneutic of the cross.

Fifth, Hardin claims that in arguing the inferiority of the Law in contrast to the heavenly pattern, the author effectively repudiates the sacrificial system as such, not just the Mosaic form of it. Here, it seems to me, one must be careful. It would be possible to argue that the author effectively repudiates the sacrificial system even if he or she were not aware of it, but is that what Hardin wants to say? Hebrews 10 does seem to provide Hardin with the strongest evidence for an explicit repudiation of the sacrificial system, but I am not sure that it is enough in the face of other apparent appeals to the logic of sacrifice. The questions here are, first, whether the author is simply repudiating the Mosaic *form* of the sacrificial system; second, whether he is repudiating the reductionism of religion to the sacrificial system, much in the same way that the prophets did;[23] or third, whether he is repudiating the sacrificial system as such.

The word νόμος appears only in chapters 7–10 in Hebrews, but this is the key, central section and the word occurs fourteen times in these chapters.[24] It should be pointed out here that νόμοι is not to be equated with תּוֹרָה, understood more broadly as life-giving instruction or the will of God. In fact, the author appeals to the תּוֹרָה in his argument that the νόμος with its commandments (ἐντολαί) is or was inferior.[25] It could be argued that the fundamental theological movement in Hebrews is from the Law understood as *mechanistic religion* (supported by νόμος as the equivalent of ἐντολή)[26] to the Law understood as *relational faith*.[27] If this were the case, it would support a Girardian reading of the letter/sermon.

Sixth, Hardin translates νεκρῶν ἔργων in 6:1 and 9:14 as "acts which lead to death" and thus, by implication, a synonym of "victimization" (p. 115). The verse that most clearly links this phrase with victimization is 6:6: "they then commit apostasy, since they crucify the Son of God on their own account and hold him up to contempt" (RSV). Confirmation is provided by Hebrews 13, which speaks at length of the community's care for victims of violence. Such care is not an *accepting* of the logic of victimization, but resistance to it through solidarity.

The word ἔργον occurs frequently in Hebrews.[28] At several points, the word refers to the work of God in creation.[29] In 4:10 the author appeals to the resting of God from work as a model for human rest from work. Hebrews 6:10 and 10:24 refer to human work in a positive way—as in service of and love toward the community. The remaining two (6:1 and 9:14) are the examples in question. The verb ἐργάζεσθαι occurs in 11:33 in the sense of effecting or "working" justice. Thus, Hardin's rendering of νεκρῶν ἔργων, although attractive in some ways and certainly supportive of Girardian thought, seems to me to be an over-reading of the text and exegetically illegitimate.

Seventh, according to Hardin, "the once-for-all character of Jesus' death amounts to a repudiation of the sacrificial system" (p. 107). However, this is not necessarily so, because repudiation of the sacrificial system is not intrinsic to its once-for-all character. Whether the once-for-all character of Jesus' death really does amount to a repudiation of the sacrificial system will depend on other evidence in the letter/sermon. It is quite possible for a "once-for-all death" to sustain and even support a sacrificial understanding of Jesus' death. As James Williams puts it,

> The traditional Christian doctrine of the sacrificial death of Christ is purportedly different in that it is a sacrifice made once and for all because of human sin to appease a justly angry God, and so is supposed to be the sacrifice to end sacrifice, but it nonetheless preserves the structure of sacrifice at its very core, just like other ancient religions.[30]

Eighth, the language of sacrifice in the concluding paranetic section could support Hardin's thesis. While arguably devoid of the sacrificial hermeneutic, the concluding paraenesis is full of "sacrificial" language: "We have an altar" (13:10). "Jesus suffered outside the gate" (13:12). "The bodies of those animals whose blood is brought into the sanctuary by the high priest as a sacrifice for sin are burned outside the camp" (13:11). "Let us continually offer up a sacrifice of praise" (13:15). "Such sacrifices are pleasing to God" (13:16). "By the blood of the eternal covenant" (13:20).

Finally, the language of imitation in Hebrews seems to refer to a good or "benign" *mimesis* in that the object of imitation is those who refuse the violence of scapegoating.[31] The association of imitation with a nonviolent ethic is not direct in Hebrews. Nevertheless, despite the infrequency of the word forms, mimesis is an important concept in Hebrews. The entire parade of the faithful in Hebrews 11 is predicated on it, as is the paraenesis in the chapter that follows.

OTHER POTENTIAL PROBLEMS

There are several other potential problems with Hardin's reading of Hebrews. In Hebrews 9:22 the generalizing statement, "There is no forgiveness without the shedding of blood," seems to support directly a sacrificial hermeneutic. Yet the context here is one in which the covenant takes effect only on the death of the person who wrote the will or covenant (διαθήκη; cf. 9:15-18). Much has been written on the meaning or meanings of διαθήκη in 9:15-22. I would agree with Hardin that the qualifier "under the law" or "according to the law" (κατὰ τὸν νόμον) is significant in a negative sort of way. The author is expressing the economy of an order that is now superseded precisely because Jesus' death effected a new covenant or will with its own economy.[32] Thus, this potential problem does not appear to me to be a serious one.

Second, does not the Platonic parallelism of earthly and heavenly realities imply that Jesus' sacrifice—however it may be nuanced—is somehow analogous to the sacrificial system of Moses? That is, is there not logically an *economic* parallelism at work here? And doesn't such a parallelism essentially support the *logic* of the sacrificial system despite minor attenuations of that analogy? Put in other terms, is Christ's death portrayed in Hebrews as a "better sacrifice" or "better than sacrifice"? Hebrews 10:26 implies that apart from deliberate sin after acknowledgment of the truth, Jesus' death should be understood as "a sacrifice for sins"—a *better* sacrifice, perhaps, but a sacrifice nonetheless.

To answer this question fully would require a careful examination of Hebrews theology of Christ's "betterment." Is Christ and his death *qualitatively* better, and if so, how?[33] An interesting case study would be 12:24. Why does the sprinkled blood that Jesus offers speak "better" than the blood of Abel? Is it because it speaks in a qualitatively different way?

My tentative conclusion is that although Hebrews understands the system of Melchizedek as revealed in תורה to be a qualitatively "better" system, the superiority of that system is not due to the inferiority of the Mosaic system *as sacrifice*. That is, whereas there are significant departures from the mechanism of violence inherent in Moses' sacrificial system, *and* God's will is linked with the repudiation of violence (10:32-39), the letter does not specifically repudiate the violence of the sacrificial system as such even if it has embarked on a theological trajectory that will logically arrive at such a repudiation.

Third, the connection of Jesus' sacrificial death with the purification of sins effectively supports a sacrificial hermeneutic. I do not mean to imply that the connection of Jesus' death with atonement for sins *necessarily* supports a sacrificial hermeneutic. My question is how the author understands Christ's death to be *effective* with regard to sin. The problem is that dealing with sin in Hebrews is usually discussed in language that derives from the temple cult. Thus we have the "purification of conscience" (καθαρίζω) in 9:14; purification as an analogy for forgiveness of sins in 9:22; and the association of Jesus' death by implication with both purification (καθαρίζω) and sacrifice (θυσία) in 9:23.[34]

Hardin does not address the frequent linking of Christ's death with the purification of sins.[35] The portrayal of Jesus as model—a model of self-offering and obedience—does *attenuate* the sacrificial hermeneutic, but it does not *repudiate* it.

Fourth, at several points in the essay, Hardin traces the language of the letter to Greek-speaking Jewish Christians, even though this judgment is not strictly relevant to any of his arguments. Years ago, Yigael Yadin shook up Hebrews scholarship by postulating that the letter was written to correct certain theological convictions held by the Qumran community. Although his claims have been tempered,[36] Yadin's judgment that Hebrews speaks well in an Essene-like environment continues to be respected. Those who see a more exclusive connection between Hebrews and Hellenistic or Philonic Judaism appear to be in a minority.[37]

This historical-critical issue may actually be relevant to a Girardian reading of Hebrews. If Hebrews were written to Essenes, ex-Essenes, or Essene-like believers who valued highly a sacrificial system, the letter may speak more clearly as a repudiation of the sacrificial system. That is, to readers who assumed a sacrificial hermeneutic of the cross, the letter may actually appear more shockingly deconstructive than it would to those who have no awareness of or interest in sacrifice.

Fifth, the language of vengeance and wrath may weaken Hardin's thesis. Note, for instance, 10:26-31:

> For if we willfully persist in sin after having received the knowledge of the truth, there no longer remains a sacrifice for sins, but a fearful prospect of judgment, and a fury of fire that will consume the adversaries. Anyone who has violated the law of Moses dies without mercy on the testimony of two or three witnesses. How much worse punishment do you think will be deserved by those who have spurned the Son of God, profaned the blood of the covenant by which they were sanctified, and outraged the Spirit of grace? For we know the one who said, "Vengeance is mine, I will repay." And again, "The Lord will judge his people." It is a fearful thing to fall into the hands of the living God.

The crucial issue here is whether the author implies that sacrifice is designed to placate or somehow deal with God's wrath. There does seem to be some implication that it is the sacrifice that is meant to "remain" that effectively holds back the wrath of God.

The author seems to avoid attributing θυμός to God as a word for wrath, using ὀργή instead (3:11; 4:3). θυμός appears only at 11:27, where it is Pharaoh's wrath. θυμός can mean both wrath and intensive (mimetic?) destructive desire.[38] In both 3:11 and 4:3, however, the author is quoting Ps. 95:11 (LXX).

CONCLUSION

In conclusion, I express my sincere respect for what Michael Hardin has done here. He has successfully, in my opinion, articulated a credible Girardian reading of Hebrews. I am not convinced that Hebrews represents as clear a repudiation of the sacrificial hermeneutic as do the Gospels. I am convinced, however, that the letter qualifies in a number of significant ways such a hermeneutic. If at a few points I think Hardin goes too far with his Girardian reading, I am nevertheless taken by the overall result.

NOTES

1. This raises immediately the issue of whether and how Girard has changed in recent years in his use of terms such as *sacrifice* and/or in the articulation of his theory. Burton Mack defines the word *sacrifice* as referring "ultimately to the structuring mechanism of the hidden level" (*Violent Origins: Walter Burkert, René Girard, and Jonathan Z. Smith on Ritual Killing and Cultural Formation.* [Stanford: Stanford University Press, 1987], 10), which seems automatically to place all sacrifice and sacrificial understandings in the service of the generative mimetic scapegoat mechanism (GMSM). Mack's definition accords with Girard's earlier tendency to equate sacrifice as such with the GMSM.

However, there seems to be some further differentiation in Girard's recent use of the word *sacrifice*. He seems more ready now to acknowledge that not all sacrifice or the rhetoric of sacrifice necessarily reflects the GMSM. This question of whether all sacrifice results from the GMSM accounts for some of the ambiguity in Girard's own comments about the Epistle to the Hebrews. Compare *Things Hidden Since the Foundation of the World* (p. 228) and *The Scapegoat*, 200 (originally published as *Le Bouc Émissare*, 279); cf. also the comments of R. Schwager in "Christ's Death and the Prophetic Critique of Sacrifice," *Semeia* 33 (1985), 119–120, and *Des Choses cachées depuis la fondation du monde*, 252, 264.

2. Cf. 11Q Melchizedek at Qumran.

3. Robert North, "Violence and the Bible: the Girard connection," *Catholic Biblical Quarterly* 47 (1985), 8. Awareness of potential distinctions in one's understanding of "sacrifice" is clearly reflected in Girard's "Sacrifice in Levenson's Work," *Dialog* 34 (1995), 61–62.

4. Schwager, "Christ's Death and the Prophetic Critique of Sacrifice," 121.

5. James G. Williams, *The Bible, Violence, and the Sacred: Liberation from the*

Myth of Sanctioned Violence (San Francisco: HarperSanFrancisco, 1992), 224.

6. One of the tricky issues here is that the scapegoat mechanism need not be articulated or understood in order to work in culture. In fact, it works *only* when it is unarticulated. This is why Girard can claim that the Judaeo-Christian tradition actually escapes the scapegoat *mechanism* by developing a scapegoat *theory*. What this means for our understanding of Hebrews is that one must look past the explicit statements about Jesus' sacrifice to understand the implicit logic at work in the theology. It is this implicit logic that is ultimately determinative of whether, as Hardin says, the author "rejects all connections between violence and the sacred, offering instead a new paradigm of what real self-giving (human and divine) is all about" (p. 116).

7. The absence of such discussion in the following works seems particularly conspicuous: Paul Ellingworth, *The Epistle to the Hebrews: A Commentary on the Greek Text*, New Testament Greek Commentary (Grand Rapids: Eerdmans, 1993); Harold W. Attridge, *The Epistle to the Hebrews: A Commentary on the Epistle to the Hebrews*, Hermeneia Commentaries (Philadelphia: Fortress Press, 1989); S. W. Sykes, ed., *Sacrifice and Redemption: Durham Essays in Theology* (Cambridge: Cambridge University Press, 1991); Barnabas Lindars, *The Theology of the Letter to the Hebrews*, New Testament Theology (Cambridge: Cambridge University Press, 1991).

For a helpful discussion of Girard's thought in terms of the logic of sacrifice in Hebrews, see Louis-Marie Chauvet, "Le sacrifice de la messe: un statu chrétien du sacrifice," *Lumière et Vie* 29 (1980), 85–106; and É. Jean-Paul Michaud, "Le Passage de l'Ancien au Nouveau, selon l'Epître aux Hébreux," *Science et Esprit* 35/1 (1983), 33–52, esp. 49–51.

8. Johannes Behm, "θύω, θυσία, θυσιαστήριον" in *Theological Dictionary of the New Testament*, ed. Gerhard Kittel (Grand Rapids: Eerdmans, 1965), 3.180–190.

9. See, e.g., Walter E. Brooks, "The Perpetuity of Christ's Sacrifice in the Epistle to the Hebrews," *Journal of Biblical Literature* 89 (1970), 205–214.

10. Michaud, "Le Passage," 51.

11. See James W. Thompson, "Hebrews 9 and Hellenistic Concepts of Sacrifice," *Journal of Biblical Literature* 98 (1979), 567–578. For examples of the critique of sacrifice in Hellenism generally, see Behm, "θύω, θυσία, θυσιαστήριον."

12. Note, e.g., 1QS 9.3-5; Philo, *De Sacrificiis Abelis et Cain* 107; *De Somniis* 2.183; *De Specialibus Legibus* 1:200–204, 271–272, 277; *Quaestiones et Solutiones in Genesin* 2:52; 3:3.

13. Valentin Nikiprowetzky, "La Spiritualisation des Sacrifices et le Cult Sacrificiel au Temple de Jérusalem chez Philon d'Alexandrie," *Semitica* 17 (1967), 98–114.

14. Cf. Heb. 2:17; 3:1; 4:14, 15; 5:1, 5, 10; 6:20; 7:26, 27, 28; 8:1, 3; 9:11; 13:11; cf. also 9:7, 25.

15. Cf. μέτοχοi and μετέχω in 1:9; 2:14; 3:1, 14; (5:13); 6:4; (7:13); and 12:8.

16. Cf. the κοινωνία and κοιν cognates in 2:14; (9:13); 10:(29), 33; and

13:16.

17. As, for instance, appears to be the case in 8:3: "For every high priest is appointed to offer gifts and sacrifices; hence it is necessary for this priest also to have something to offer."

18. As, for instance, appears to be the case in 9:11-12: "But when Christ came as a high priest of the good things that have come, then . . . he entered once for all into the Holy Place, not with the blood of goats and calves, but with his own blood, thus obtaining eternal redemption."

19. For θυσία, see 5:1; 7:27; 8:3; 9:9, 23, 26; 10:1, 5, 8, 11, 12, 26; 11:4; and 13:15, 16.

20. See Girard, "Sacrifice in Levenson's Work," 61–62.

21. The language of sacrifice (e.g., θύω) is generally avoided, but the language of offering (φέρω and φέρω cognates) abounds. φέρω cognates clearly predominate in Hebrews.

22. Cf. 12:3 *et passim.*

23. Cf., e.g., Isa. 1:11; Jer. 7:21-26; and Amos 4:4-5; 5:21-24.

24. Heb. 7:5, 12, 16, 19, 28 (*bis*); 8:4, 10; 9:19, 22; 10:1, 8, 16, 28.

25. All of 7:1-19 is really a careful appeal to הרות in the author's argument that the sacrificial system of the Mosaic cult was inferior to the system (or priesthood) of Melchizedek.

26. νόμος is linked with, modified by, or explicated by ἐντολή in 7:5, 16, 18-19, and 9:19.

27. Cf. 2:11b-13; 3:6, 12-14; 4:12-16; 5:1-3; etc.

28. See 1:10; 3:9; 4:3, 4, 10; 6:1, 10; 9:14; and 10:24.

29. See 1:10; 3:9; 4:3, 4 [and, indirectly, 4:10].

30. Williams, *Bible, Violence*, 2.

31. Cf. μιμητής in 6:12 and μιμέομαι in 13:7.

32. The problem of "supersessionism" is a difficult one. The author of Hebrews treats the old covenant and the new covenant as two separate systems, the latter of which "supersedes" the former. Thus, in this sense, intellectual honesty requires that one acknowledge that the theology of Hebrews is essentially "supersessionistic."

This word should be placed in quotation marks, however, since admitting this is not at all the same as saying that "Christianity" supersedes "Judaism" in Hebrews, nor is there even a hint of anti-Semitism or anti-Judaism in this supersessionism. Furthermore, there are various "supersessions" of a more minor nature within the Hebrew Bible itself (cf. Isa. 56 [cf. Deut. 23]; Jer. 31:31-34; Ezek. 18). The problem is that subsequent history, tainted as it has been with anti-Semitism, has twisted our thinking on this matter. Even the writer of Hebrews ultimately presupposes the oneness of God and the unity of God's relation to humanity: God spoke formerly and God spoke recently.

33. See 1:4; 6:9; 7:7, 19, 22; 8:6, 6; 9:23; 10:34; 11:16, 35, 40; and 12:24 for 13 of the 18 appearances of κρείττων in the New Testament. James W. Thompson argues that "what is 'better' in Hebrews is, in most instances, metaphysically superior" (Thompson, "Hebrews 9," 570 n 20).

34. For καθαρίζω and καθαρ cognates, see 1:3; 9:13, 14, 22, 23; 10:2, 22. For ἱλάσκεσθαι, see 2:17; and ἱλαστήριον, 9:5. For ἅγια cognates, see 2:4, 11, 11; 3:1, 7; 6:4, 10; 8:2; 9:1, 2, 3, 3, 8, 8, 12, 13, 24, 25; 10:10, 14, 15, 19, 29; 12:10, 14; 13:11, 12, 24.

35. See 1:3; 2:17; 5:1; 9:7, 22, 26, 28; 10:12, 26; and 13:11; but see also 12:4.

36. For instance, P. E. Hughes argues that the recipients of Hebrews were not necessarily Qumran covenanters as such, but "Hebrew Christians who, facing hostility in a Jewish setting, were tempted to ease their position by reverting in a compromising fashion to Judaism of the idealistic Qumran type." See "The Epistle to the Hebrews," chap. 13 in *The New Testament and Its Modern Interpreters* (Atlanta: Scholars Press, 1989), 352.

The question of the intended recipients of Hebrews is a difficult and complicated one. Certainly we must recognize that the *title* ΠΡΟΣ ΕΒΡΑΙΟΥΣ likely was not original to the letter. Even then, as W. Bauer showed long ago, the designation "Hebrews" can mean Jewish or Jewish-Christian people who spoke Greek; cf. *Orthodoxy and Heresy in Earliest Christianity*, Philadelphia Seminar on Christian Origins, trans. Georg Strecker, ed. Robert A. Kraft and Gerhard Krodel (Philadelphia: Fortress Press, 1971), 52. On the other hand, the letter does seem to reflect an awareness of secular Greek writing; cf. Martin Hengel, *The 'Hellenization' of Judaea in the First Century After Christ* (Philadelphia: Trinity Press, 1989), 55.

37. See Hughes, "Hebrews," 353.

38. See Louw and Nida, *Greek-English Lexicon of the New Testament Based on Semantic Domains*, 1.291 (25.19). On the other hand, see ἐπιθυμέω at 6:11; ὀρέγω/ὀρέγομαι, 11:16.

CHAPTER SEVEN

Girard and Atonement: An Incarnational Theory of Mimetic Participation

Robin Collins

INTRODUCTION

Christians committed to peacemaking have long recognized that peace, nonviolence, and reconciliation are at the heart of the gospel. Yet standard Western theories of the atonement appear to paint a picture in which violence is at the core of the divine order of things. To elaborate, conservative and much traditional Roman Catholicism and Protestantism have promoted an understanding of the atonement largely based on the *satisfaction* and *penal* theories of atonement or variations of them. The basic idea behind each theory is that the moral order of reality requires that God punish our sin—and hence render violence against us—by sending us to eternal Hell unless some substitute can be found to pay the penalty for sin. In the satisfaction theory (first systematically developed by St. Anselm in the eleventh century), Christ turns away this purportedly righteous violence against us by paying our debt of obedience to God the Father. Christ does this through being perfectly obedient to the Father, even to death on the cross.

On the other hand, in the penal theory (first systematically advocated by the Protestant reformers), Christ takes the violence on himself—he accepts the punishment *we* deserve. So in both theories violence is in some sense necessary: in the satisfaction theory violence is affirmed as an option that *must* be taken *unless* our debt of sin is paid. In the penal theory, violence—whether directed at us or at Christ—is absolutely necessary to meet the demands of the moral order.

Given that the doctrine of atonement—that is, the claim that through Jesus' life, death, and resurrection we are saved from sin and reconciled to God—is at the core of the Christian gospel, it has become increasingly recognized in peacemaking and other circles that alternative understandings of the atonement are needed.[1] One cannot simply avoid the issue by claiming that the atonement is a mystery, since how we understand Christ's atonement is central to our understanding of the nature of salvation and hence to the gospel message and its implications for our lives and the world.

In light of the ethically problematic image of God in the penal and satisfaction theories and many other purported difficulties with them, numerous Christians have looked for alternative theories and understandings of atonement.[2] For the last thousand years, the main alternative theory in the West has been the *moral influence* theory, a theory that has been the mainstay of liberal Christianity. According to this theory—originally advanced by theologian/philosopher Peter Abelard (1079-1142)—the moral example of Christ's life and death saves us by revealing the depth of God's love for us. This in turn liberates us from false understandings and inspires us to love and good deeds. Or in another version, Christ's life and death save us by giving us a perfect moral example of love, humility, and obedience to follow.

Recently, cultural theorist René Girard has presented a theory of the atonement that is essentially a highly original version of the moral influence theory, as I explain below. Unlike most previous versions of this theory, Girard's atonement theory is a natural outgrowth of a highly fruitful theory of culture, violence, and religion: namely, his own mimetic theory of culture, a perspective he has been developing for thirty years. Because of its link with a larger theory of culture, religion, and violence, and because it rests on an understanding of the gospels in which nonviolence is central, many Christians committed to a nonviolent understanding of Christianity have become enthusiastic about his theory.

As I show below, however, despite its sophistication, Girard's atonement theory suffers from some of the critical defects of the standard moral influence theory, defects that largely form the basis for why conservative and many orthodox Christians have rejected the moral influence theory. Nonetheless, after explicating and critiquing Girard's theory, I will show in part three below how Girard's more general theory of the mimetic basis of culture—which could be plausibly considered to form the heart of this cultural theory—is an exceptionally rich resource for further development of an alternative, thoroughly nonviolent theory of the atonement, with deep roots both in Scripture and in church tradition, particularly that of the Eastern Orthodox and Greek Fathers. Indeed, this alternative theory, which I call the incarnational theory and have worked out elsewhere independent of Girardian thought, follows naturally from Girard's mimetic theory of culture when applied to the New Testament claims about Christ.

GIRARD'S THEORY OF DESIRE, THE SCAPEGOAT, AND ATONEMENT

GIRARD'S THEORY OF DESIRE

According to Girard's mimetic theory of desire, all our desires originate via the process of *mimesis*, commonly translated as imitation. Because it suggests a conscious copying, the word *imitation* here is somewhat misleading. Conscious copying is only one special case of what Girard considers mimesis or imitation. More generally, as Paul Dumouchel notes, for Girard mimesis involves a "disposition of agents to act in similar ways, without the agents intending to imitate each other."[3]

Put differently, Girard's theory should be understood as claiming that individuals obtain their desires by contagiously picking them up from—or patterning them after—other people, something that often occurs unconsciously. Once we think about the mimetic basis of desire as being like contagion, we recognize something else about this theory: it implies that to a large extent our desires are not simply our own but rather a sort of common property that gets passed around among the members of the community. So another way of thinking about Girard's mimetic theory of desire (which will be useful later) is that we typically participate in the desires of the community, instead of merely generating or having them individualistically.

How does this theory account for the ultimate origin of desire, the generation of new desires, and the differences in desire among individuals? First, concerning the origin of desire, Girard does not claim that desire entirely and completely originates in mimesis. If he claimed this, then there would be no way of accounting for how desire among human beings as a whole began. Instead, as Richard Golson comments, "Girard does not challenge the existence of innate, instinctual impulses and drives necessary to the survival of the organism. Rather, he believes that these impulses and drives are channeled by the mimetic process."[4]

Second, new desires can arise because we are creative in our imitation: we modify the imitated desire in accordance with our own needs, goals, situation, and personality traits, often at an unconscious level. So imitation is typically not strict copying.

Finally, each of us has a different conglomeration of desires both because we are creative in our imitation and because, given our environment and our innate characteristics, we do not imitate everyone or every desire, but only a select group of individuals and desires. The drug pusher in the city, for instance, imitates other drug pushers in his immediate environment, not the wealthy businessman across town.

GIRARD'S THEORY OF THE SCAPEGOAT MECHANISM

According to Girard, because of the mimetic nature of desire, acquisitive desire—that is, desire to possess or control an object—quickly results in rivalry and hence violence between individuals. For example, if one person desires an object, then others will imitate the desire and hence become that person's rival in trying to gain possession or control of the object. To control this violence, societies erect rules and taboos that attempt to create social distance between individuals so that they do not become each other's rivals.

For example, because of the social distances between them, princes do not tend to imitate commoners and vice versa. Hence they typically do not become each other's rivals. These social mechanisms, however, do not work perfectly to inhibit mimetic rivalry. This allows the rivalry and the violence associated with it to reach crisis proportions. When this happens, order in society is restored by finding a scapegoat to which all the violence of the community gets redirected, thereby reuniting the community and bringing peace. Crucial to this whole process is that the scapegoat is portrayed as really guilty. Consequently, the order of society depends on concealing both the innocence of the victim and the scapegoat mechanism.

GIRARD'S THEORY OF ATONEMENT

Essentially two theories of atonement are found in Girard and his followers, what I will call the *unmasking theory* and the *imitation theory*, each of which is a version of the moral influence theory. Although Girard does not claim that these theories are complete, his writings and those of his followers suggest that they believe that they have captured a major component of how Christ's life, death, and resurrection save us from sin and reconcile us to God. According to the unmasking theory, Jesus' life and death, in conjunction with the gospel accounts, save us by unmasking the victimage mechanism. Indeed, James Alison, who develops Girard's thought in a theological context, claims that this unmasking is "identical with salvation or redemption," since once the unmasking has occurred it "impels us to the construction of a different social order, one built *from* the self-giving victim, rather than one built *by exclusion of* the victim."[5]

Although Girard recognizes that other texts could be said to have partly unmasked the scapegoat mechanism—such as the anti-sacrificial texts by Empedocles[6] or Plato's account of the death of Socrates in the *Apology*—Girard claims that Jesus is "the only one capable of revealing the true nature of violence to the utmost."[7] The reason for this, Girard and followers claim, is that Jesus, being the Son of God, was the only one entirely outside the cultural system which is founded on the scapegoat mechanism. Hence Jesus was the only one not infected by human culture, which as stated above is based on *concealment* of this mechanism. Such reasoning is what leads to the claim that knowledge of this mechanism cannot be obtained by merely human means.[8]

Against Girard, critics have argued that "the devaluation of sacrifice is neither the distinctive attribute of Christianity nor the major theme of Christ's teaching" and that "the Gospels cannot lay exclusive claim to the revelation of the violent foundations of human society."[9] Although I am to some extent sympathetic with this sort of critique, here I want to focus my critique elsewhere. What I shall argue is that *even if* Christianity uniquely unmasks the scapegoat mechanism as Girard claims, this does not provide an adequate theory of the atonement.

As explained above (note 1), a theory of the atonement must explain how Christ's life, death, and resurrection save us from sin and reconcile us to God. The major problem with Girard's unmasking theory of atonement is that the operative concept of salvation seems too weak. We can see this by asking what the effects of this unmasking might be for us individually and for society as a whole. As Scubla points out,[10] in the worst-case scenario, such unmasking will deprive us of the scapegoat mechanism and thus leave us with no means of resolving the mimetic crises of violence when they occur. In the best-case scenario, by recognizing the mimetic origin of violence and the scapegoat mechanism, we will be able to develop an effective, democratic, nonscapegoating means of keeping acquisitive mimetic desire in check.

At best, therefore, in Girard's unmasking theory Christ's atonement will have been necessary for the development of a nonviolent, democratic society. This, however, seems far too weak a notion of salvation to be compatible with the New Testament. When Paul the apostle, for instance, says that through Christ's atonement we are justified and given new life (e.g., Rom. 5:9 and 8:3), or when John the apostle tells us that the blood of Christ "cleanses us from all sin" (1 John 1:7), it seems they have something much stronger in mind than Christ's death being necessary for the eventual development of a nonviolent society. For one thing, Christ's atonement was supposed to save those to whom the apostles preached, not simply the beneficiaries of a nonviolent society more than two millennia later.

In fact, if this is all Christ's atonement does, then arguably the Buddha's teaching of strict nonviolence does better. After all, as John Kohler notes, Buddhism, unlike Christianity, has a perfect record of nonviolence: "In the twenty-five hundred years since its beginning, Buddhism has spread throughout Asia and has made its way even to the other continents, claiming over four hundred million followers. During that time no wars have been fought and no blood shed in propagation of its teaching."[11] Moreover, historically predominately Buddhist cultures have had a relative lack of war, revolution, or violence of any kind—a record much better than that of the Christianized West.[12] To do better than simply keeping violence at bay, therefore, Christ's atonement must somehow give us an infusion of positive, nonrivalrous, and nonviolent desire, an issue we will pick up later.

The other "imitation theory" of atonement advocated by Girard and his followers is also a version of the moral influence theory, one influence in which Christ saves us by providing a perfect moral example for us to imitate.[13] According to James Alison, for instance, through imitating Christ, the apostles and, by implication, all Christians, "learn to receive their identities as human beings through an entirely nonrivalrous, nonenvious, nongrasping practice of life."[14]

Since, like his unmasking theory, Girard's imitation theory is a version of the moral influence theory, it is open to the same objections. These are worth elaborating on at this point. The most common objection to the moral influence theory is that it is "subjective." Although authors who raise this objection typically do not explain what they mean by calling it subjective, they clearly could not mean it in the normal sense of subjective. Christ acting as a moral exemplar can objectively change his followers for the better, so the effect of the atonement under this theory is "objective" in the normal sense of the word. Rather, as Alister McGrath comments,[15] what they mean by the atonement being subjective under this theory is that the atonement works by effecting a change in us, whereas in the so-called "objective" theories, the atonement works by rendering a change in God—such as satisfying God's demand that we be punished for our sins, as in the penal theory.

Now it seems to me that being "subjective" in this sense is a merit of an atonement theory and fits nicely with the New Testament's stress on the ability of Christ's death on the cross actually to effect a change in us. To cite two of many examples, in Romans 6:1-14 and elsewhere, Paul emphasizes that Christ's atonement has freed us from our slavery to sin. And in 1 John 1:7, John claims that Christ's blood actually cleanses us from sin. That is, it somehow actually works to eliminate sin in our lives; it does not merely satisfy the demand that we be punished as in the penal and satisfaction theories. So I argue that the accusation that the moral influence theory is subjective is really no objection at all, but a merit of the theory.[16]

A more serious objection is that the theory is "Pelagian," meaning that it negates God's grace by suggesting that we can save ourselves through our own effort to imitate Christ. Of course, there is some element of God's grace in the moral influence theory, since God had to provide Christ's moral example. As often presented, however, the element of grace tends to be no more than it would be in a merely prophetic religion, or in religions such as Therevada Buddhism: God must graciously provide the prophet for guidance, but the work of following the prophet is up to us. And in the case of Therevada Buddhism, the Buddha showed us the Noble Eightfold-Path to Nirvana, but it is our job to follow it.

Related to this objection is that the moral influence theory does not take the depth of sin seriously enough. As the apostle Paul (e.g., Rom. 7), St. Augustine, Martin Luther, and anyone who has seriously struggled with sin knows, sin cannot be eradicated merely by our own efforts, even the effort to follow the example set by Christ. Put differently, the structures of what Walter Wink calls the "Domination System,"[17] which are based on violence and oppression, have become too much a part of our psychic structures to be broken through mere conscious imitation. Girard himself is well aware of this in the context of acquisitive mimetic desire, which for him seems to be the basis of sin:

In reality, no purely intellectual process and no experience of a purely philosophical nature can secure the individual the slightest victory over [acquisitive] mimetic desire and its victimage delusions. Intellection can achieve only displacement and substitution, though these may give individuals the sense of having achieved such a victory. For there to be even the slightest degree of progress, the victimage delusion must be vanquished on the most intimate level of experience. . . .[18]

Girard then goes on to claim that such victory over the acquisitive mimetic structures is "only truly accessible through an experience similar to what has traditionally been called religious conversion."[19]

Now in actual practice those who subscribe to or are sympathetic towards the moral influence theory often emphasize the necessity of God's grace through the Holy Spirit in helping us imitate Christ and thereby undergo a "religious conversion" to a new set of desires. According to philosopher Phil Quinn, even Abelard, originator of the moral influence theory, recognized the necessity of God's grace. Indeed, as Quinn shows, this idea of God's grace can be extended in the moral influence theory to completely eliminate its Pelagian element. Specifically, says Quinn, the love of Christ expressed on the cross could have "a surplus of mysterious causal efficacy [to produce a similar love in us] that no merely human love possesses."[20] Once one moves in this direction, however, the type of imitation involved goes from being mere conscious imitation to a form of nonconscious imitation—that is, contagion or participation—specially empowered by the Holy Spirit to be effective. This in turn naturally leads to the theory I will now elaborate.

A NEW AND ORTHODOX THEORY

I call the theory I present below the *incarnational theory*. Although I have developed the incarnational theory elsewhere independent of Girardian thought,[21] here I will develop a version of this theory starting with Girard's hypothesis of the mimetic origin of desire, then show that it has a strong basis in both Scripture and church tradition.

Before developing this theory, two preliminaries should be addressed. The first is to extend Girard's theory of mimesis. To do this, we note that in the broadest sense there is no clear-cut distinction between "desire" and other intentional states: that is, states such as attitudes, orientations, perspectives, commitments, beliefs, and the like. When taken together as forming an inseparable whole with the agent's internalized system of mental, symbolic, and linguistic representation, the totality of these states could be called the agent's subjectivity. Given these definitions, the mimetic theory of the origin of desire can be naturally extended to what could be called a mimetic theory of the origin of intentional states or subjectivity—that is, the hypothesis that in general our subjectivity is not simply generated in ourselves, but to a large extent mimetically picked up from others. It is this extended theory that we will be invoking below. (It should be noted here that use of the term "subjectivity" in this context is not to be confused with use of the term as discussed earlier, in relation to speaking of theories of atonement being "subjective" or "objective." Nor should the handling of "subjective" be confused with how it is used below in discussing Rebecca Adam's definition of love as "desiring the subjectivity of oneself and the other.")

The second preliminary is to understand mimesis as really involving both contagion and participation, as explained in section II above. Specifically, to imitate Christ's intentional states—such as his desires—is to contagiously pick them up, which in turn results in our participating in them. Further, to *participate* in Christ's intentional states implies that they are not something we simply imitate and then possess on our own, but rather something we share in only insofar as we remain connected to Christ and his body. (As Jesus says in John 15, a branch that is disconnected from the vine withers away.) Since the mechanism of this connection is mimesis (understood as contagion), we will often use the phrase "mimetic participation" to refer to this participatory connection with Christ.

The incarnational theory begins by postulating that salvation consists in an ongoing participation in the life of God as it exists in Christ, as indicated by Jesus' metaphor of the vine and branches (John 15:5), and many other New Testament passages, such as John 6:53-56; Colossians 3:4; 2 Peter 1:4; and Hebrews 3:14. Because of the incarnation, this life is both fully divine and fully human. Hence because of its fully human component, we can participate in it.

Our next key step is to postulate that the core of this sharing in the life of Christ consists in mimetically participating in Christ's subjectivity as expressed in his life, death, and resurrection—participation in which our own subjectivity is redemptively transformed as the intentional states in Christ are creatively individualized and integrated into our own. This mimetic participation takes place in several ways: through normal psychological channels, such as consciously imitating Christ or contagiously picking up his intentional states from other exemplary Christians; through reading and hearing the

New Testament and related texts, by which we can absorb and digest their subjectivity—that is, the web of beliefs, attitudes, orientations, perspectives, and system of representation embodied in the texts; and finally, through a more direct "supernatural" operation of the Holy Spirit and God's grace in the Sacraments.

Moreover, in this theory the Holy Spirit is conceived of as supernaturally empowering the transmission of Christ's subjectivity in the normal psychological and linguistic channels mentioned above. Accordingly, because the natural and supernatural means are intermixed together and are continuous with one another, there is no dualistic opposition between the spiritual and the natural, or nature and grace. Rather, they work together: if we merely rely on our own natural ability to partake of Christ's subjectivity, we will be unlikely to participate in it in any deep way, and similarly, if we simply rely on a supernatural miracle, such as a religious conversion. As Philippians 2:12-13 suggests, salvation is a joint operation of natural and supernatural means.

Next we need to elaborate on some particularly redemptive aspects of Christ's subjectivity. We begin by examining some aspects of Christ's subjectivity particularly associated with his death. First, as the kenosis hymn of Philippians 2:6-11 reminds us, during his death on the cross Jesus experientially entered into the depths of the human life-situation of vulnerability, dependence, death, suffering, brokenness, and alienation, even the depths of our alienation from God the Father as evidenced by his cry on the cross, "My God, my God, why have you forsaken me?" (Mark 15:34). Moreover, in some mysterious way, on the cross Jesus experienced the depths of human sin, the "shadow-side" of humanity: "For our sake he made him to be sin who knew no sin, so that in him we might become the righteousness of God" (2 Cor. 5:21). Finally, according to the gospel accounts, during his life Jesus established a subjectivity that was in complete solidarity with the poor, the marginalized and oppressed, a solidarity he took to its experiential depths by dying as a criminal "outside the city gate" (Heb. 13:12).

Now in many ways this new subjectivity created in Jesus is radically at odds with and hence undercuts the "fallen" subjectivity of humanity. To elaborate, most of us try to avoid confronting our own vulnerability, dependence, brokenness, and alienation. Indeed, thinkers as diverse as theologian Reinhold Niebuhr (1941), Pulitzer Prize-winning author Ernest Becker (1973), and psychologist M. Scott Peck (1983)[22] have claimed that this unwillingness to confront our own vulnerability and other "threatening" aspects of our human condition is one of the prime roots of human sin, wickedness, sickness, and neurosis, along with the world-system of status, domination, and oppression. Instead of recognizing that we are vulnerable, dependent, and insecure human beings, for example, we attempt to possess, dominate, and control people and things to give ourselves the illusion of invulnerability, security, and status. Instead of acknowledging our own shadow, we project it onto others and then demonize them.

In fact, it has become a common thesis in this century—for example, René Girard and Michel Foucault, in addition to thinkers mentioned above—that the world-system of psychic and social domination, oppression, bondage, and its associated values rests on expulsion, scapegoating, and marginalization of both aspects of our own psychic lives and the subjectivity of various individuals in society. Given that these thinkers are at least partly correct, it follows that the "fallen" human subjectivity characteristic of the world-system is partly based on the denial of the subjectivity established in Christ on the cross. Consequently, mimetically participating in this new subjectivity established in Christ will tend, as yeast leavens a lump of bread, to undercut the entire world-system of psychic, spiritual, and social bondage in both our personal and social lives.

So far we have suggested one way in which the mimetic participation in the new, fully human and fully divine subjectivity of Christ during his life and death serves to deconstruct the world-system of social and psychic bondage and oppression, in which we all participate to some degree. This deconstructing of the world-system is, I suggest, at least part of how the cross of Christ crucifies us to the world and the world to us, as Paul states in Galatians 6:14. Further, I believe, to partake in the above aspects of Christ's subjectivity is part of what it means to share in Christ's death (Rom. 6), and part of what underlies the New Testament emphasis on acknowledging our weakness, powerlessness, and vulnerability and its emphasis on confession of sin—that is, acknowledgment of our shadow-side.

However, salvation is more than being crucified to the world: it also involves sharing in the resurrection life of Christ. As Girard notes, simply to live in denial of the world-system with its concerns amounts to no more than a "living death."[23] Moreover, such a denial too easily leads to another false attempt to render the self invulnerable to the world, but this time by trying to become dead to worldly concerns, as the Stoics tried to do. Instead, the New Testament teaches engagement with the world, being in the world but not of the world.

To fully redeem us, therefore, the subjectivity created in Christ must include positive intentional states that promote human flourishing in full engagement with the world. Now appropriative desire—by which I mean the entire set of intentional states oriented towards possessing, controlling, and dominating persons and things to sustain the illusion regarding our true human condition—seems to be at the heart of human sin and is at the root of much of the violence in society. Accordingly, these positive intentional states in Christ should, among other things, serve as an antidote to appropriative desire.[24]

Love, as understood in the sense of desiring the subjectivity of oneself and others, an idea that Rebecca Adams has carefully developed in her essay in this collection, is one such intentional state that meets this condition. According to this idea, to desire the subjectivity of another is to desire them to be separate centers of consciousness and will, who not only are presently in relationship with oneself but who are rich with future possibilities of growth and interrelationship. In accordance with Christ's example on the cross, this implies a commitment to treat others in faith and hope of what they are and could be instead of trying to change their beliefs and behavior through brute force or to manipulate and dominate them in any other way.

Further, as Adams shows, when imitated, love in this sense not only unites people together into a noncompetitive, reciprocally sharing community, but gains a creative, generative dynamic of its own which ultimately leads to maximal human flourishing. If through valuing you in love I imitate your desiring of my subjectivity, then I will in turn desire my own subjectivity, your subjectivity, and that of others, and the others will in turn do the same, and so on.[25]

The second positive intentional state we need is that of faith: we must trust that if we give ourselves completely over to God's care, and if we seek first the kingdom of God, our needs will ultimately be met. Further, we must trust that the "will of God" will ultimately be accomplished for us and those around us, insofar as that is compatible with human free will. For a prime reason we want to possess and control things and people is that we fear there are not enough human goods to go around to satisfy our needs. Or we try to control things and people—instead of desiring their subjectivity—because we fear that unless we do, "God's purposes" will not be accomplished in them or the world.

Given these fears, appropriative desire with its attempt to control people and things is virtually inevitable. Moreover, only in the context of faith is it possible to "lay down one's life" for another and still truly desire one's own subjectivity and hence love one's own self, because without faith such "love" will simply mean desiring another's subjectivity at the cost of doing violence to one's own. That is, one must have faith that by losing one's life one will gain it (Matt. 10:39).

Finally, we need to live in hope of God's providence in the historical process and the ultimate fulfillment of God's kingdom of peace, justice, and righteousness. Instead of negating our present history, this hope gives it meaning and allows us to fully nurture and "desire the subjectivity" of our world and its inhabitants as being rich with historically realizable possibilities for the reign of God's kingdom and the fullness of human flourishing it implies.

Given our life-situation, however, we must be able to continue to act in this faith, hope, and love despite severe uncertainty, doubt, fear, unjust persecution, and alienation from God and others. That is, we must be able to act in faith, hope, and love despite every temptation that arises out of our life-situation. Thus if Christ is going to be the perfect mimetic source of the kind of faith, hope, and love we need, he must also experience every type of temptation common to human beings. Moreover, in the face of those temptations, he must continue to act in love, hope, and trust instead of succumbing to the attempt to "secure the self" through violence, injustice, or Stoicism—as is characteristic of fallen humanity.

Indeed, this is just what the book of Hebrews implies about Christ: he experienced every kind of temptation common to humans and was yet without sin (Heb. 4:15). Further, Hebrews indicates that through his sufferings and temptations Christ was made perfect— that is, perfect as our Savior (Heb. 2:10; 5:9; 7:28). If Christ did not experience these temptations, then he would not have been the perfect mimetic source of love, trust, and hope. This is because then he would not have modeled for us continuing to act in accordance with these virtues under the most serious temptations we encounter.[26]

Moreover, I suggest that it is these fully divine and fully human intentional states of love, trust, and hope established in Christ that the Pauline epistles are implicitly referring to when they state that we should put on the "new self" and the "new creation" in Christ. To elaborate, the "old self" seems to be their way of referring to the old "sinful" subjectivity—that is, the set of sinful desires and its associated attitudes, orientations, and the like (e.g., see Col. 3:9, Rom. 6:6).

Hence, by parallelism it makes sense that the "new self" refers to a new, positive subjectivity.

Further, both Ephesians 4:24 and Colossians 3:9-10 speak of this "new self" being created by God. Other passages imply that it exists only in Christ (Eph. 2:10; 2 Cor. 5:17; Gal. 6:15). Taken together, these passages seem to imply that a new fully human and fully divine subjectivity was created by God in Christ and that the Christian life consists of partaking of this new subjectivity—i.e., we are to put on the "new self" (Eph. 4:24; Col. 3:9-10).

In addition, just as the old subjectivity was mimetically obtained from others, and ultimately the first humans (represented by Adam), the new subjectivity is mimetically obtained from Christ, the "second Adam." Thus this theory makes sense of much of Paul's discussion of "original sin" in Romans 5 and elsewhere, especially of the parallelism he draws between the transmission of sin from Adam and the transmission of righteousness from Christ (see Rom. 5; 1 Cor. 15:22, 45-49).[27]

Not only does the incarnational theory make sense on its own terms and shed light on the biblical passages cited above, but it also gives us a deeper understanding of both Old and New Testament rituals intended to express our fundamental relationship to God.

First, the incarnational theory makes it possible to see a new, yet very traditionally Jewish meaning in the Old Testament sacrificial ritual, a ritual that the book of Hebrews tells us is a type or image of Christ's sacrifice. Essentially, this ritual involved the worshiper laying hands on the head of an animal (for example, a lamb or a bull), then slaying the animal. The priest then took the blood and poured it on the altar as a sacrifice to God. Now, as many commentators have noted, the Old Testament never really tells us how such a sacrifice is supposed to provide atonement, except for laying down the principle that the "life is in the blood" (Lev. 17:11-14).

Given this principle, and the claim, advanced by many commentators,[28] that laying on of hands is best interpreted as an act of identification with the one on whom hands are laid, a straightforward Christian interpretation of the Hebrew sacrificial ritual follows. The animal can be seen as analogous to Christ, and the offering of its blood can be seen as analogous to Christ's offering his life over to God and others in love, hope, and trust. Thus the laying on of hands can be seen as analogous to our identification with and sharing in that love, hope, and trust expressed by Christ on the cross—a sharing that results in our redemption.

From this analysis it follows that we are saved by Christ's blood shed on the cross. His blood cleanses us from sin (1 John 1:7), but not in the magical way commonly conceived. Rather, Christ's blood represents his life completely given over to God and others in love, hope, trust, and self-sharing. Or, put in the terminology of the incarnational theory, it represents his subjectivity completely oriented toward giving his life to God and others in faith, hope, love, and self-sharing. Thus we are saved from sin by partaking of this life, or subjectivity, oriented towards God and others in perfect love. This is why, I suggest, Jesus says in John 6 that we must drink his blood to have eternal life.

This account also provides an insightful understanding of the Christian practice of communion. Under the incarnational theory, taking communion by eating the bread and drinking the cup vividly symbolizes (or enacts) partaking of Christ's brokenness, life, and love poured out on the cross—that is, in the language of the incarnational theory, it symbolizes (or enacts) the partaking of the Christ's fully divine and fully human subjectivity which both entered into the depths of our brokenness and was at the same time given over in complete love to God and others. Further, just as we assimilate food and drink into our bodies, we symbolically enact the assimilation of this subjectivity into our own by partaking of Christ's "body and blood."

Finally, the incarnational theory provides an insightful understanding of the Christian practice of baptism. According to Paul's "model" of atonement in Romans 6, it is through being baptized— that is, identified—with Christ in his death that we break the power of sin and share in his resurrection life: "If we have been united with him in a death like his, we will certainly be united with him in a resurrection like his" (Rom. 6:5). According to the incarnational theory, being identified with Christ during his death involves sharing in Christ's subjectivity during his death, and hence, as explained above, becoming "crucified" to the world-system of status and psychic and spiritual bondage (cf. Rom. 6:6). Yet at the same time, to partake of Christ's death is also to share in the perfect love, hope, and trust that Christ exercised during his life and passion—a love, hope, and trust that in turn overcomes our alienation towards ourselves, others, and God. The result is resurrection life.[29]

Next it would be useful to compare this account of "salvation" with that of the great religious/philosophical systems of Asia, particularly Mahayana Buddhism, philosophical Taoism, and Neo-Confucianism. Each of these traditions has recognized that the root of the human problem is appropriative desire. Moreover, they have recognized that we cannot overcome this desire by our own efforts but must somehow participate in a new source of positive desire, such as the Buddha Mind, the Tao, or the Great Ultimate.

Although Therevada Buddhism—which Western scholars tend to agree most closely represents what the Buddha taught—teaches that we are to overcome appropriative desire by our own efforts, in several hundred years after the Buddha's death the need for a source of positive desire, namely Love or Compassion, was recognized. This led to development of the Mahayana tradition, which today represents the vast majority of Buddhists. For Mahayana Buddhists, the source of this Love is ultimately the Buddha-Mind or Buddha-Nature, and it expresses itself through Bodhisattvas, fully enlightened beings full of Compassion who realize their oneness with the Buddha-Nature. Buddhists then try to get in touch with this Buddha-Mind both through emulation of the Bodhisattvas and through existentially realizing their own identity with it through meditation.

In philosophical Taoism—i.e., the Taoism traditionally attributed to Lao Tzu and his successors—appropriative desire is also seen as the source of strife, disharmony, and human dissatisfaction. The heart of the Taoist solution is to effectively gain a new set of "desires" or intentional states based on the mimetic participation in Nature—which is perceived as harmonious and nonappropriative.

Over a thousand years later, the Taoist tradition and the Confucian tradition were conjoined to form what is called the neo-Confucian synthesis, which became the predominant philosophical system of thought in China until the communist revolution in the twentieth century. In both the so-called rationalist and idealist schools of this synthesis, the needed desire is *jen*. Jen is often translated as love or deep empathy toward others in which one attempts to desire the other's subjectivity, such as by trying to see things from the other's perspective. Our job is to "clarify" our nature so we can more fully participate in this jen, which is considered to be at the heart of the "Great Ultimate" and hence of the cosmos and human nature.[30]

According to the incarnational theory, the Christian gospel is in agreement with these other traditions in their affirmation of the need for a source of positive intentional states to supplant appropriative desire. From the perspective of the incarnational theory, however, one key difference is that in Christianity these positive intentional states are part of the subjectivity of a particular historical individual (Jesus), a subjectivity in full acknowledgment and engagement with the world and depths of our life-situation and in solidarity with the marginalized and scapegoats of society. The consequence is that, in partaking of Christ's subjectivity, we are called to fully engage with the world and our life-situation. We are asked fully to acknowledge all those things that we have repressed and scapegoated, both in our own psychic lives and in society. Only by doing this can we also fully partake of the faith, hope, and love that are in Christ.

Finally, it is useful to mention how the incarnational theory can be seen as an elaboration of certain prominent themes regarding atonement and salvation in church history. First, as indicated above, the incarnational theory can be thought of as extending and deepening the traditional moral influence theory in such a way as to eliminate the elements in it that more conservative Christians find problematic.[31] Second, the incarnational theory can be thought of as a new way of developing a basic idea of salvation that not only has ancient roots in the Greek Fathers such as Origin, Athanasius, and Irenaeus, but which has been further developed by Eastern Orthodox theologians through the centuries and has turned up here and there in Western Christianity, for example in the theology of the medieval mystic Julian of Norwich, and in many contemporary theologians. The basic idea is that human nature was restored in Christ, and salvation consists in partaking of this new human nature in Christ.[32]

The unique feature of the incarnational theory is that it spells out what this new nature is and gives us some idea of how we partake of it. Namely, under the incarnational theory, this "unfallen" human nature in Christ is the fully divine yet fully human subjectivity developed in Christ during his life and death, as discussed above. Thus, according to the incarnational theory, we are saved by mimetically partaking of the incarnated subjectivity of God the Son, hence the name, the incarnational theory.

Finally, this view of atonement helps explicate how the atonement defeats the forces of evil in the much-discussed Christus Victor understanding of atonement.[33] Identifying these forces of evil with what theologian Walter Wink has called the "domination system,"[34] Christ's atonement can be seen as defeating the forces of evil by providing a new subjectivity that deconstructs this system. The result can be new, positive, nonappropriative desires of faith, hope, and love of the kind we need for full engagement with the world.[35]

Notes

1. It is useful at this point to distinguish between the *doctrine* of the atonement, an *understanding* of the atonement, and a *theory* of the atonement. Unlike the doctrine, an understanding attempts to provide an idea of what exactly Christ accomplished for us through the atonement and what it means for us to be saved from sin and reconciled with God. Often, understandings are expressed in terms of metaphors or images, such as that Christ's atonement defeated the forces of Satan, as in the much-discussed Christus Victor understanding. Finally, a theory of Atonement goes beyond an understanding in that it explains *how* Christ's life, death, and resurrection save us from sin and reconcile us to God, and *why* it made sense for God to use this method. For example, a theory might explain how Christ's atonement defeated Satan, instead of simply saying that it did.

2. Among these purported additional difficulties with the satisfaction and penal theories are that they are contrary to Scripture and that their key claims do not make sense, such as the claim that divine justice is satisfied by one person accepting the punishment of another.

3. Paul Dumouchel, "Introduction," in *Violence and Truth*, ed. Paul Dumouchel (Stanford, Calif.: Stanford University Press, 1988), 7.

4. Richard Golson, *René Girard and Myth: An Introduction* (New York: Garland Publishing, Inc., 1993), 1, note.

5. James Alison, *The Joy of Being Wrong: Original Sin Through Easter Eyes* (New York: Crossroad Publishing Company, 1998), 84.

6. René Girard, *Things Hidden Since the Foundation of the World* (Stanford, Calif.: Stanford University Press, 1987), 206.

7. Ibid., 209

8. Dumouchel, "Introduction," 18.

9. Lucien Scubla, "The Christianity of René Girard and the Nature of Religion," in *Violence and Truth*, 161.

10. Ibid, 172-73.

11. John Kohler, *Oriental Philosophies*, 1st ed. (New York: Scribner, 1985), 192.

12. Ibid, 192.

13. Girard, *Things Hidden*, 430; Rebecca Adams, "Violence, Difference, Sacrifice: A Conversation with René Girard," in *Violence, Difference, Sacrifice: Conversations on Myth and Culture in Theology and Literature: A Special Issue of Religion and Literature* 25, no. 2 (Summer 1993), 24-25.

14. Alison, *The Joy of Being Wrong*, 168.

15. Alistair McGrath, *What Was God Doing on the Cross?* (Grand Rapids, Mich.: Zondervan Pub. House, 1992), 87.

16. Actually all major theories of the Atonement have both subjective and objective elements in the above sense of the terms, and thus the terms "subjective" and "objective" are doubly misleading. The differences between these types of theories really have to do with which element is logically primary. In the typical "objective" theories, the Atonement first

changes God's attitude toward us, opening the door for the Holy Spirit to change us through the process of sanctification. In the typical "subjective" theories, the Atonement changes God's attitude by changing us, or, more precisely, since this change in us is not immediate, God's "new" attitude towards us is in response to the eschatological event of our full redemption through Christ's Atonement.

17. Walter Wink, *Engaging the Powers: Discernment and Resistance in a World of Domination* (Minneapolis, Fortress Press, 1992).

18. Girard, *Things Hidden*, 399.

19. Ibid, 400.

20. Philip Quinn, "Abelard on Atonement: Nothing Unintelligible, Arbitrary, Illogical, or Immoral about it," in *Reasoned Faith: Essays in Philosophical Theology in Honor of Norman Kretzmann*, ed. Eleonore Stump (Ithaca, N.Y.: Cornell University Press, 1993), 296.

21. "Understanding Atonement: A New and Orthodox Theory" (unpublished manuscript, 1995).

22. Reinhold Niebuhr, *The Nature and Destiny of Man*, Vol. I (New York: Charles Scribner's Son, 1941, 1964). Ernest Becker, *The Denial of Death* (New York: The Free Press, 1973). M. Scott Peck, *The People of the Lie: The Hope for Healing Human Evil* (New York: Simon and Shuster, 1983).

23. Girard, *Things Hidden*, 400.

24. I use the term "appropriative" desire, coined by Rebecca Adams, instead of the term "acquisitive" desire used by Girard and his followers, because it is not always wrong to want to acquire things. It is not wrong, for instance, to marry someone in part to "acquire" the benefits of a loving relationship with that person. It is wrong, however, to treat others as a mere means to something, such as money, that is external to the development of their own subjectivity, or to treat them as an object to be controlled or possessed.

25. Extending this idea of desiring the subjectivity of others to the rest of God's creation suggests that we need to see even material things in a different light: not as items to be possessed and controlled, but as gifts from God: that is, we need to view them sacramentally as embodiments of God's grace to us.

26. The claim that, in general, an effective mimetic source of an intentional state needs to share our life-situation as much as possible is most clear in the case of conscious imitation, though it applies as well to imitation in the more general sense of contagion or participation. A poor person who shares her goods in spite of her poverty, for example, is a much better model of love for other poor people than a rich person who gives out of his abundance. And this is true even if her influence as a model is largely unconscious.

27. Although I do not claim that the incarnational theory is necessarily a complete theory of Atonement, I do claim that it can account for the various New Testament statements used in support of the traditional so-called "objective" theories: namely, statements such as that through Christ's Atone-

ment we are justified, made righteous, reconciled to God, forgiven of sin, and freed from the wrath of God.

To see this, first note that, as New Testament scholar J. D. Dunn argues, for Paul, being justified or made righteous did not primarily have to do with acquittal of guilt, but rather primarily with being in right relationship with God, and secondarily being in right relationship with other human beings (J. D. Dunn and Alan Suggate, *The Justice of God : A Fresh Look at the Old Doctrine of Justification by Faith* [Grand Rapids, Mich.: Eerdmans, 1993]). A right relationship with God and others in which we mutually desire each other's subjectivity, however, can only occur in a context in which we are freed from bondage to our old, "fallen" subjectivity through Christ's Atonement. Further, as Taylor argues, in the New Testament, reconciliation and forgiveness of sins should primarily be understood as a removal of any hindrance to full communion with God, which under the incarnational theory is essentially our alienated and sinful subjectivity (Vincent Taylor, *Forgiveness and Reconciliation* [New York: St. Martin's, 1946]).

The incarnational theory, therefore, would claim that Christ's atonement justifies us, makes us righteous, reconciles us to God, and results in forgiveness of sin by providing us a new, fully redeemed subjectivity in Christ. Although this new subjectivity must still be worked out in each individual's life, its existence in Christ means that the barrier to a right relationship with God and others has already been effectively removed in Christ. Hence the New Testament can speak of us as already being justified, made righteous, reconciled, and forgiven in Christ. Put in traditional terminology, *justification* (that is, the existence of a new subjectivity in Christ) precedes *sanctification* (the full working out of this subjectivity in our lives). This makes the incarnational theory in some sense both an "objective" theory and a "subjective" theory of atonement in the sense of these terms discussed in the second section above: it is "objective" since the change in Christ is logically prior to a change in us, yet "subjective" in that this change in Christ is intimately linked with a change in us through mimetic participation.

Finally, along the same lines as above, the incarnational theory would claim that Christ's atonement saves us from "God's wrath" by saving us from our sinful subjectivity. Because this subjectivity distorts and perverts our relationship to God and others, God, out of love, is absolutely opposed to it. Hence, as George MacDonald states ("The Consuming Fire," in *George MacDonald: Creation in Christ*, ed. Rolland Hein [Wheaton, Ill.: Harold Shaw Publishers, 1976], 162), God could be said to be opposed to us—our desires, aims, and attitudes—insofar as, and while, we are wedded to it. That is, we could be said to be under God's wrath. Or, one could understand the "wrath of God" as the inevitable destructive consequence of this fallen subjectivity, as Paul seems to do in Romans 1:18-32 when he speaks of the wrath of God as involving a "giving over" of humans to their own desires—that is, their fallen subjectivity.

28. Vincent Taylor, *Jesus and His Sacrifice* (London: MacMillan, 1937), 53-54; J. D. G. Dunn, "Paul's Understanding of the Death of Jesus as Sacrifice,"

in *Sacrifice and Redemption: Durham Essays in Theology*, ed. S. W. Sykes (Cambridge: Cambridge University Press, 1991), 44-45.

29. Those familiar with Alcoholics Anonymous (AA), and the many therapy programs its purported success has spawned, will note the similarity between the understanding of the process of transformation of subjectivity involved in sharing in Christ's death and resurrection and the well-known Twelve Step program of AA. Specifically, the core of the Twelve Step program is to first admit one's own powerlessness, vulnerability, and dependence and then to give oneself over to the transforming grace of "a higher power": that is, in the language of the incarnational theory, to the transforming grace of the love and faith in Christ. Thus the purported success of AA and related therapy programs provide good evidence that something similar to the process of transformation described by the incarnational theory actually works in practice. I also suspect that historically many religious transformations have followed the same pattern.

It should also be mentioned here that "sharing in Christ's death" is different for those who are marginalized and oppressed since they already largely recognize their vulnerability and dependence, so, unlike the "rich," it is probably not as difficult for them to partake of the subjectivity of Christ in his death. (As Jesus says, it is particularly difficult for the rich—whether in money, talent, or position—to enter the kingdom of God.) Nonetheless, it is true that, unlike Jesus, the oppressed are often not in solidarity with the true "subjectivity of the oppressed," but rather end up adopting the subjectivity of the oppressors—such as implicitly viewing themselves as inferior or as chattel—and hence still partake of the world system of status, oppression, and domination, but from the other end. In addition, they often still try to solve their problems through their own strength or through violent means and oppress those lower in status, such as oppressed men treating their wives as chattel.

30. Yu-Lan Fung, *A Short History of Chinese Philosophy* (New York: The Free Press [Macmillan] 1947), 281-318. At least with respect to the need for a positive source of desire, the above sort of analysis not only applies to the religions of Asia mentioned above, but also to some Western religions such as Judaism in which the Torah could be thought of as embodying God's desires. One could then understand much of Jewish practice as reflecting the idea that one can participate in God's desires as embodied in the Torah either: i) through the mediation of the community of faith in combination with the various "texts" that the community has developed as commentaries and interpretations of the Torah; or ii) directly, as claimed in certain mystical or pietistic branches of Judaism.

31. For example, unlike the traditional version of the moral influence theory, the incarnational theory explicitly incorporates the supernatural operation of the Holy Spirit in bringing about our participation in Christ's subjectivity, and thus removes the Pelagian element often associated with the moral influence theory. Further, in the incarnational theory imitation is conceived in a deeper way as actually involving a participation in Christ's

subjectivity instead of merely involving following or being inspired by Christ's example. This not only makes the incarnational theory fit very well with scripture, but it also gives it an "objective" component lacking in the standard more influence theory. (See footnote 16.)

32. As I argue elsewhere (unpublished manuscript, 1995), however, the Eastern Orthodox development of this idea is deeply problematic from the perspective of Western modes of thought. (For a discussion of the history of the Eastern Orthodox view, see for instance, Demitru Staniloae, *Theology and the Church*, trans. and ed. by Robert Barringer [Crestwood, N.Y.: St. Vladimir's Seminary Press, 1980], 181-212). Among the many theologians who have suggested a view along the lines of this basic idea of Atonement are Stanley J. Grenz, *Reason for Hope* (Oxford: Oxford University Press, 1990), 121-22, and Michael Ramsey, one of the great Anglican Archbishops of the Twentieth Century. (For an exposition of Ramsey's views in this regard, see Kenneth Leech, "'The Real Archbishop': A Profile of Michael Ramsey," *Christian Century* [March 12, 1986], 266-69). Further, I have been informed that something related to this idea of Atonement is part of Wesleyan thought on the subject. I do not know, however, of anyone in the West who has systematically worked out this idea, at least in the way I have done.

33. Gustaf Aulén, *Christus Victor: An Historical Study of the Three Main Types of the Idea of Atonement* (New York: Macmillan, 1951).

34. Wink, op. cit.

35. Although many people have helped me develop the incarnational theory, I would particularly like to thank my wife and colleague, Rebecca Adams, for encouragement and many helpful insights, along with encouraging me to study the work of René Girard.

Part Two

SECOND READING: GIRARDIAN THEORY, BIBLICAL AND CRITICAL ANALYSES, AND THEOLOGICAL CRITIQUE

CHAPTER EIGHT

Reading Ancient Near Eastern Literature from the Perspective of Girard's Scapegoat Theory

Paul Keim

INTRODUCTION

The works of René Girard have aroused considerable interest and controversy recently. Do his ideas represent the "Archimedian point"[1] which will transform the study of culture and religion? Or are they another crazy literary theory meant to befuddle exegetical types among us? Specifically, has Girard succeeded in revolutionizing our understanding of the relationship between religion and violence?[2] Is he, as some claim, a God-is-dead theologian in sheep's clothing, selling culture-criticism at the cost of transcendence and other orthodox fundamentals? Or is he, as others have suggested, a reactionary, neo-fundamentalist defender of old-time religious and social order?[3]

In its eloquent simplicity, Girard's unified theory of culture and religion has the impact of a screaming headline: The Sacred is Violence. It has become a compelling and exciting lens through which old texts seem to reveal new textures; familiar plots and stereotypical characters spring transformed off the page; a seemingly static moral universe is turned inside out like slain Tiamat. In the steaming carcass of chaos an ominous truth is revealed: Our community was born in fratricide, and we deny the horror of our complicity by sacralizing the cultural mechanisms that allow us to sacrifice innocent victims in our place. In Girard's words, "Violence is the heart and secret soul of the sacred."[4]

Girard's theory asserts that violent aggression is not just one human drive among many. Rather, it is, to paraphrase a certain Near

Eastern sage, "the mother of all human drives," the inevitable by-product of social interaction.[5] Our greed for what others possess leads to conflict ("mimetic desire") which eventually results in a violence so intoxicating it overwhelms even our greed. At the same time this violence breeds violence and threatens to engulf the entire community in ethnocidal chaos. To contain and control this violence, all ancient societies utilize a form of scapegoat mechanism, whereby the guilt and anger and impurity of all can be concentrated on one innocent victim who personifies the collective guilt and impurity.

Sacrifice of the scapegoat cathartically restores the community's equilibrium, simultaneously transforming the victim into an agent of peace and salvation. What is most polluting and abhorrent is also most sacred. This mechanism is routinized as a sacral rite to be performed whenever a community faces sacrificial crisis. In recurring experiences of social disintegration, when the projected differences that make up the conceptual framework of culture appear to be dissolving, the scapegoat mechanism can bring the community atonement and reintegration. The sacred, then, is comprised of that complex of myths, religious rituals, and customs that hide and obscure the underlying violent mechanism of our community's salvation.

My contribution to this discussion does not represent a systematic attempt to test and apply Girard's theory to texts not yet covered in his writings, though preliminary steps of this nature are indeed attempted. The Girardian corpus of the past thirty years is substantial and not easily absorbed, trampling as it does the holy ground of several disparate and traditionally antagonistic disciplines in the humanities, including cultural anthropology, classical and modern literary criticism, philosophy, theology, and biblical studies. The secondary works are already legion.[6]

As one who has read too much Girard too rapidly adequately to digest, yet too little to claim comprehensiveness, I concede that a little knowledge is a dangerous thing. Thus I confine myself to observations, questions, and brief interpretive forays from the perspective of Ancient Near Eastern and cognate studies—all impressionistic and preliminary. I conclude with suggestions of ways the radicality of Girard's vision may contribute to contemporary peacemaking.

A CRITICAL REVIEW

If, as Henry James has said, "To criticize is to appreciate,"[7] then it is perhaps fitting to start with those nagging reservations that have dogged my reading of Girard and some of the secondary literature. This critical appraisal is intended not only to identify what in my view are problematic aspects of the Girardian program, but also to expose my own incomplete understanding of Girard's theory to critical scrutiny and invite correction.

My first concern is a general one and has to do with the highly reductive nature of Girard's theory. This has been identified as one of the principal objections to Girard's reconstruction.[8] As brilliant as his theory is for elucidating a wide variety of cultural and religious *topoi*, it rests on an assumption that many philosophers and ethnologists today would challenge, viz., that the vastly heterogeneous phenomena of culture and religion may be reduced to a unified theory of origin and development. Is the fear of unchecked violence, as Girard claims, really at the heart and origin of all cultural and religious institutions?[9] I remain intrigued but skeptical.

In response, Girard points out that such criticisms are based on an a priori assumption that the diversity of religious phenomena is too great and that the contradictions between particulars are too striking for any unitary theory to be possible.[10] What he has proposed, he asserts, is "a *model* for religious phenomena ... [which] includes the possibility of infinite variation precisely because the event it describes is never concretely observed—it is, in fact, the object of a fundamental and founding misrecognition."[11]

Another concern of mine has to do with the evolutionary paradigm that informs Girard's reconstruction. There is the typical appeal to primitive religion and the recurrent vocabulary of origins and development, all borrowed from ethnologies he otherwise criticizes.[12] As reasonable as his explanation of religious origins might be, it remains a hypothesis that is ultimately neither verifiable nor falsifiable as an *origin* myth.

Apart from its functionalist aspects which stand on their own merits and correlate in varying degrees with observed phenomena, the theory's insistence that it has uncovered the very origins of the sacred in the scapegoat mechanism is reminiscent of those psychological theories of religious origins criticized by Evans-Pritchard. These, he says, rest on suppositions of the "If I were a horse I would do what horses do" variety.[13] It is just as "reasonable" to posit the origins of religion in notions about the spirits of dead ancestors, or in the worship of the community.

The point is that there is little heuristic value in insisting on a reconstruction that ultimately cannot be tested. Not only were we not present at the act of violence which constituted our community, but according to Girard's theory, every cultural and religious product throughout history (except for the Bible) has conspired to deflect, erase, transform, and sacralize that event into obscurity, misunderstanding, and/or self-righteous confidence in the justness of that violence.[14]

At one point Girard explicitly evokes the analogy of biological evolution. In making the undoubtedly valid point that "no single text—mythic, religious, or tragic—" will reveal the surrogate victim theory, but only a comparative method, he likens this to "[t]he theory of evolution [which] depends on the comparison and linkage of evidence—the fossil remains of living creatures—corresponding, in the case of my hypothesis, to religious and cultural texts. No single anatomical fact studied in isolation can lead to the concept of evolution."[15] I like the point he makes here and the manifestation of it in the richness of his field of inquiry. I have no particular problem with the theory of biological evolution. What I object to is the analogy drawn (albeit implicitly) between biological evolution and the "evolution" of the human spirit and culture.

Several characteristics of Girard's analysis seem to fit this profile. The framework of his theory places him and his "kind" at the center of knowledge. As Nemoianu points out in his article "René Girard and the Dialectics of Imperfection,"[16] the underlying thesis of Girard's earliest work is that

> only novelists, not scientists, can grasp and express the truth. Truth is aesthetic, because the structures of wholeness and its internal contradictions can be caught neither by deforming ideologies and philosophies, nor by the simplifications of rationalist science. Art is our only reliable access to reality, because it is the only mode which incorporates and preserves imperfection, rather than trying for coherence and uniformity.[17]

The contemporary Girard has not abandoned this early thesis, which has become the methodological key to his mixture of anthropology, literary theory, and cultural philosophy. Naturally the diviners and prophets of this art are the literary theorists, among whom Girard stands as *primus inter pares*.

The hermeneutics of suspicion has taught us to examine carefully such seemingly self-serving assertions. We must always ask of an intellectual product: *Cui bono*? This is nothing more than an acknowledgment that vested interests may inadvertently steer the course of an inquiry and/or unwittingly determine the outcome. With Amos we wonder, "Do two walk together unless they have made an appointment? Does a lion roar in the forest when it has no prey?" (3:3-4).

Thus one may rightly worry that Girard's theory is the product of and ultimately an apologetic for Western culture and religion. Notwithstanding his assertions that "we are now in a position to get to the truth about all non-Christian religious phenomena by means of purely scientific and hypothetical procedures," one can't help but notice that Girard's theory affirms and indeed does not stray far from the central tenets of orthodox Christianity in significant respects. Raymund Schwager, the Catholic dogmatician who introduced Girard to German theological circles, revels in the thought that the European intellectual tradition, plagued in the modern period by a secularism inimical to religion, has "arrived where the evangelists had already stood some 2,000 years ago."[18]

In Girard's view, it is ultimately the Judaeo-Christian Scripture, above all the Gospels, which confirm this reading already "fully demonstrated on the basis of the anthropological texts."[19] The Christian pretension to absolute singularity, categorically rejected by virtually all ethnological research, is, according to Girard, not just another confirming analogy, but "the source of all analogies, which is situated behind the myths, hidden in their infra-structure and finally revealed, in a perfectly explicit way, in the account of the Passion."[20] Is Saul, in fact, really one of the prophets?

Girard himself anticipates and addresses this concern. "The thesis of the scapegoat," he asserts, "owes nothing to any form of impressionistic or literary borrowing."[21] He maintains that the outline of his earlier work, *Violence and the Sacred*, retraces his own intellectual journey which, as he says, "eventually brought me to the Judaeo-Christian writings, though long after I had become convinced of the importance of the victimage mechanism." Sharing Western intellectualism's long hostility to Christian Scripture, he nevertheless reaches the conclusion, in what he calls "an astonishing reversal," that the gospel accounts of Christ's Passion "—initially revered blindly but today rejected with contempt—[. . .] will reveal themselves to be the only means of furthering all that is good and true in the anti-Christian endeavors of modern times: the as-yet-ineffectual determination to rid the world of the sacred cult of violence."[22] "These texts," he concludes,

> supply such endeavors with exactly what is needed to give a radically sociological reading of the historical forms of transcendence,

and at the same time they place their own transcendence in an area which is impervious to any critique by placing it in the area from which a critique would derive.[23]

Finally, I must raise an issue addressed by Sandor Goodhart in his article on "Prophetic Law" in the Girard Festschrift, *To Honor René Girard*. Is the revelation of the scapegoat mechanism in Girard's theory essentially an insight of the gospels and the New Testament— a "Christian" truth—or is it a *biblical* contribution? Using a wonderful old Hasidic story for illustration,[24] Goodhart asks whether

in opposing the Old Testament to the New, in reading the old god as the sacrificial god of vengeance or anger and the new as the anti-sacrificial God of love (a reading which, of course, is central to a certain Christian understanding of the two books), we have not unwittingly already slipped into the very structure we have wished to displace, believing in a new law or "part two" which it has already been . . . the goal of the Old Testament itself to reveal to us, an Old Testament which is thus that much richer by virtue of its having foreseen our sacrificial misunderstanding of it.[25]

Though he speaks of "Judaeo-Christian Scripture" and discusses isolated Old Testament texts as "biblical myths," it is apparent already in *Things Hidden Since the Foundation of the World* that Girard considers the Passion narratives of the gospels the primary key to deciphering the origins of human culture in collective violence. The Old Testament is "at work on the myths, undoing them to reveal their truth," tending to deconstruct them by placing responsibility for collective violence on the members of the community. In this way, he says, the Old Testament "paves the way for the full and final revelation."[26] In *The Scapegoat*, Girard affirms that it is the Christian Bible, Old and New Testaments, that enables us to decipher the persecutors' accounts of persecution, and to decode the whole of religion. But, he continues, "The Gospels will be seen as that universal force of revelation,"[27] and it is the Gospels' rejection of persecution that will be responsible for the collapse of the scapegoat mechanism.

The dogmatician Schwager understands Girard's hermeneutic as the functional equivalent of patristic allegorizing, whereby the Old Testament is interpreted exclusively in light of Christian theology.[28] Texts that seem to present an immutable and dispassionate God are emphasized and treasured. Meanwhile, the more offensive texts are neglected and obscured, considered little more than pedagogical concessions of a merciful God for an as yet unenlightened people.[29]

This orientation distorts the OT texts in a number of ways and ironically denies the power of anti-substitutionary OT redemption. Goodhart's article eloquently illustrates the singular contribution Old Testament texts have to make in this regard. His dramatic re-reading of the Joseph narrative culminates in Judah's offer of his own life in place of his brother Benjamin, which leads immediately to the demystifying revelation that all, "victim, master, and sacrificers, all [are] doubles, all [are] brothers."[30]

To uncover the revelatory character of this text which leads to the demystification of sacrifice, however, Goodhart must redefine the Girardian terms of revelation, using "anti-idolatry" rather than the Passion of the Gospels as the deciphering key. I wonder whether it might not be possible to push the boundaries even farther. The biblical traditions unfolded and were recorded in a specific cultural and historical context, that of the Ancient Near East. It should be possible to test those cognate traditions for instances or tendencies to demystify the scapegoat mechanism. Of course, the expressed form of demystification will need to be redefined again, since the criterion of anti-idolatry will put Mesopotamian culture at a disadvantage, just as the evocation of the nonsacrificial Christ of the Passion set the OT traditions at disadvantage.

Is there perhaps a vested interest informing the Girardian "canon?" It seems that regardless of our expressed willingness to overcome the sacral mystification of collective violence in reference to particular issues, it is difficult to eradicate it as an orientation, a *Weltanschauung*. We still like to plot out lines of demarcation, to separate revelation from divination, canonical from noncanonical, biblical from extra-biblical.[31] Goodhart affirms a unified revelatory voice in OT and NT expressly exclusive of ANE roots and Platonic corruption. But what might a Girardian reading of Mesopotamian myth and ritual texts reveal?

VICTIMAGE AND SACRED VIOLENCE IN ANE LITERATURE: A PRELIMINARY READING[32]

The Gilgamesh epic is one of the most popular and widespread of Mesopotamian epic legends, judging from the geographical and diachronic dispersal of its remains. It is the principal heroic tale of the Ancient Near East and has been called the *Odyssey* of the Babylonians. As far as we can tell, Gilgamesh apparently was a historical figure, ruler of the city of Uruk (biblical Erech) around 2600

B.C.E.[33] His name is mentioned in the Sumerian king list among those who ruled after the flood. The kings of the Ur III Dynasty counted Gilgamesh as their ancestor. Though there is no historical evidence for the exploits narrated in the epic, the legendary Gilgamesh was famous for his building of the great wall of Uruk. Only fragments remain of the Old Babylonian epic proper, which was composed in Akkadian around 1600 B.C.E. The most complete version available to us, made by a certain Sîn-liqi-unnini, is preserved on copies of twelve tablets found in the famous library of Ashurbanipal in Nineveh, dating to the seventh century B.C.E.

Scholars have long identified the central theme of the Gilgamesh epic as the problem of human mortality. According to Babylonian and Assyrian wisdom, not only humans and the plant and animal kingdoms, but also the gods were susceptible to the destructive power of death. And although the immortal deities did not die of natural causes, they could lose their lives in violent clashes, as did some of the primeval gods in the Mesopotamian creation myth, *enuma elish*.[34]

The story, as recounted in Thorkild Jacobsen's masterful book *The Treasures of Darkness*,[35] and on which the following account is based, begins with young Gilgamesh ruling Uruk with a vigor and zeal that threatens to fully overcome his exhausted subjects. They appeal to the gods for help. It is determined that a companion be created for Gilgamesh. The creator Aruru fashions Enkidu, a wild man of enormous strength, who roams the steppes with the animals, protecting them from the traps of the hunters.

The trappers of the area find their livelihood threatened by Enkidu's exploits, but he is so large and powerful there is nothing they can do. Finally they take a harlot, Shamhat, along to seduce Enkidu away from the animals. At a watering place three days' journey into the desert, the harlot is able to attract Enkidu's attention. For six days and seven nights, Enkidu "knows her in the biblical sense" and is thereby initiated into the ways of the world (this, by the way, is one of the few instances in the mythological literature of antiquity in which human sexuality is affirmed as a humanizing rather than a dehumanizing act).[36]

When at last he is satisfied, he attempts to go back to the animals, but they run off when he approaches. He chases after them, only to find that he has lost his former speed. Bewildered, he returns to the harlot and sits at her feet.[37] Looking up into her face, he listens intently as she says to him,

I look at you Enkidu, you are like a god!
Why do you roam the desert with the animals?
Come, let me lead you into Uruk of the wide streets,
To the holy temple, the dwelling of Anu,
Enkidu, rise, let me take you to Eanna, the dwelling of Anu,
Where Gilgamesh is administering the rites.

Enkidu is pleased with her suggestion, and they set out for the shepherd's camp, where they are received with hospitality. Here Enkidu has his first encounter with civilization. The shepherds set food and drink before him, which he has never seen. He stares at the food and squirms, for he does not know how to eat bread, has never been taught to drink beer. The harlot again addresses Enkidu:

Eat the bread, Enkidu, it is the staff of life.
Drink the beer, it is the custom of the land!
Enkidu ate bread, until he was full up,
Drank beer, seven kegs;
He relaxed, cheered up,
His insides felt good, his face glowed.
He washed with water, and rubbed his hairy body with oil;
He became a man.
He put on a garment, and was like a young noble.
He took his weapon and fought off the lions,
And the shepherds slept at night.

Hearing that Gilgamesh is about to be married, they immediately set out for Uruk. When they arrive, the people gather round and gape at Enkidu, noting his tremendous strength and stature. He is slightly shorter than Gilgamesh but as strong. Just then Gilgamesh approaches on his way to the house of his father-in-law for his wedding. But Enkidu bars the way and does not let him go in to his bride. They seize each other and wrestle like young titans, shattering the threshold and shaking the walls. Eventually Enkidu gains the upper hand and Gilgamesh sinks down on one knee, conceding defeat. But instead of gloating as a victor, Enkidu speaks to Gilgamesh, full of admiration and respect:

Matchless your mother bore you,
The wild cow of the corral Ninsûna,
Raised above men is your head,
Enlil has assigned you
Kingship over the people!

Out of their battle a lasting friendship is formed. They become like brothers. All is happiness and bliss. But a deadly chain of events is set in motion when Gilgamesh proposes an excursion to the cedar forests of the west to kill the terrible monster called Huwawa. Their trip to the Lebanon is described in great detail. Though the section recounting their actual fight with the monster is badly damaged, it is clear that Huwawa is defeated and begs for his life. Gilgamesh is inclined to spare him, but at Enkidu's insistence the monster is killed.

On their return to Uruk, they wash up and put on fresh clothes. Gilgamesh is so attractive that Ishtar, goddess of Uruk, becomes enamored of him and proposes marriage. Instead of politely declining, however, Gilgamesh so insults the goddess that she runs to her father Anu, god of heaven, and demands that he give her the "bull of heaven" to kill Gilgamesh. Anu reminds her that the bull of heaven is such a destructive animal that if let loose there will be seven years of famine on the earth. Ishtar assures him that she has stored enough grain and provisions for humans and animals to last for seven years, and finally he relents.

Ishtar takes the bull of heaven to Uruk. Its first snort blows a hole in the ground that swallows up 100 men. The second traps 200 more. But Gilgamesh and Enkidu team up and show themselves to be old hands at handling cattle. Enkidu gets behind the bull and twists its tail while Gilgamesh plunges his sword into the neck of the bull like a matador. The slaying of the bull of heaven shocks and enrages Ishtar. She hurls curses at Gilgamesh and sets up a wailing lament over the carcass of the bull. The two friends now stand at the pinnacle of their power and fame. There seems to be nothing they cannot do.

But now their deeds catch up with them. In killing Huwawa, Gilgamesh and Enkidu have angered Enlil, who appointed the monster to guard the cedar forests. In a dream, Enkidu sees the gods assembled to pass judgment on the friends. Enlil demands death for them, but sun god Shamash intercedes and is able to save Gilgamesh. Enkidu, however, is condemned to die. He falls ill. Struck with horror at his impending death he curses the harlot and the shepherd who brought him to Uruk. But Shamash reminds him how much he has gained in his new life, of his friendship with Gilgamesh. Reconciled, Enkidu balances the harlot's curse with a long blessing and dies.

Until now, Gilgamesh has flaunted the typical heroic attitude of glorious death in battle and eternal fame.[38] But in the death of Enkidu, his only friend, he suffers a loss that is unbearable and incomprehensible. Refusing to accept it as real he muses,

He who always went through every hazard with me,
Enkidu whom I love dearly,
Who always went through every hazard with me,
The fate of man has overtaken him.
All day and night I have wept over him
And would not have him buried—
As if my friend might yet rise up at my (loud) cries—
For seven days and nights,
Until a maggot dropped from his nose.
Since he is gone I can find no comfort,
I keep roaming like a hunter in the plains.

The fear of death now becomes an obsession with Gilgamesh. The thought of his own mortality haunts him day and night, and he can find no peace. Hearing of an ancestor of his, Utnapishtim, who achieved eternal life and now lives far away at the ends of the earth, Gilgamesh decides to go find him and learn the secret of immortality.

Shamash tries to dissuade him from his quest, but Gilgamesh will not listen. Eventually he comes to an inn run by an alewife named Siduri. At first his appearance frightens her. But after listening to his tale of Enkidu who died and of his search for Utnapishtim and the secret of eternal life, she sees the hopelessness of his quest and, like Shamash, tries to talk him out of it with words of wisdom.[39]

Gilgamesh, where are you roaming?
Life, which you seek, you shall never find.
(For) when the gods created humanity,
They set death as share for him, and life
They snatched away into their own hands.
You, Gilgamesh, fill your belly,
Day and night make merry,
Daily hold a festival,
Dance and make music day and night.
Wear fresh clothes,
And wash your head and bathe.
Look at the child that is holding your hand,
And let your wife delight in your embrace.
These things alone are the concern of man.

But Gilgamesh cannot be touched:

Why, my (good) alewife, do you talk thus?
My heart is sick for my friend.
Why, my (good) alewife, do you talk thus?
My heart is sick for Enkidu.

Eventually he finds Utnapishtim, also known as Atrahasis, the Noah figure of the Babylonian flood story, who lives on an island in the Persian Gulf. The boatman Urshanabi takes Gilgamesh to the house of Utnapishtim. He tells Gilgamesh about the flood, how he built an ark and saved his family and pairs of all the animals. He explains how after the flood he was granted eternal life by the gods as a reward. It was a unique event, he tells Gilgamesh, which will never recur. It is not a secret recipe for immortality which others might follow. It offers no hope for Gilgamesh. His quest has been in vain.

Wishing to reinforce his point with an object lesson, Utnapishtim challenges Gilgamesh to try not to sleep for six days and seven nights. Gilgamesh accepts this challenge with Death's younger brother Sleep, but as he sits down, Sleep overwhelms him, and Utnapishtim comments wryly to his wife,

> Look at the strong man who craved life!
> Sleep is sending a blast down over him like a rainstorm.

Utnapishtim knows that humans are by nature deceitful, so he instructs his wife to prepare food for Gilgamesh every day and to mark the days on the wall behind him. She does so. When Utnapishtim wakes Gilgamesh up on the seventh day, his first words, as Utnapishtim had anticipated, were:

> As soon as sleep poured down over me
> You quickly touched me
> So that you awakened me.

But the marks on the wall and the stale loaves tell a different story. Robbed of all hope for immortality, Gilgamesh is gripped by terror even more desperately than before. He pleads with Utnapishtim,

> What can I do, Utnapishtim, where will I go?
> The one who followed behind me, the rapacious one
> Sits in my bedroom, Death!
> And wherever I may turn my face,
> There he is, Death!

Utnapishtim has no consolation to offer, but his wife intercedes for Gilgamesh, and so he tells him of a thorny plant that grows at the foundation of the sweet waters deep under the earth. It has the powers to rejuvenate. Its name is "As an Old Man Becomes a Child." Overjoyed, Gilgamesh dives for the plant and brings it to the surface. He shows it to Urshanabi the boatman, and tells him how he plans to take it back to Uruk, where he will eat it when he grows old and thus become a child again.

But on his journey back home, Gilgamesh stops at a cool pond to rest and bathe. As he does, a snake comes out of its hole, snatches the plant, and eats it. As it disappears into its hole, it slips out of its old skin and emerges new and shiny and young. Thus ends the quest of Gilgamesh. It has come to naught. He sits down and weeps at his fate. But out of his resignation comes a composure at once humorous and ironical. No longer is he gripped by terror and despair. Gilgamesh's belated acceptance of reality is made complete by his return to the walls of Uruk, which will stand for all time as his lasting achievement, the tangible expression of his immortalization. He proudly shows the walls to Urshanabi the boatman.

> Go up, Urshanabi, on the wall of Uruk, walk around!
> Examine the terrace, look closely at the brickwork!
> Is not the base of its brickwork of baked brick?
> Have not seven masters laid its foundations?
> An acre town and an acre orchards,
> An acre riverbed,
> Also precinct of the Ishtar temple.
> Three acres and the precinct comprises Uruk.

Thus the story ends, dramatizing the journey which Everyman must take, conscious of mortality yet able to find equilibrium while life shall last in building a piece of the stable community which will outlive him.

A "Girardian" reading of the Gilgamesh epic would anticipate that here, as in other myths from antiquity, the underlying collective violence which is affiliated with social origins is obscured.[40] Elements of mimetic conflict and the sacrificial crisis which leads to sacred violence should be discernible to the careful reader. We can test the level of its concealment according to Girard's criteria by examining to what extent the various cultural and literary mechanisms of mystification are deconstructed in the epic itself.

Signs of a sacrificial crisis permeate the epic. These might include the following:

1. Gilgamesh's obsessive drivenness, which has outraged and exhausted the citizens of Uruk;

2. The "symbolic inversions" of Shamhat the harlot and Siduri the alewife;

3. The intimate relationship between Gilgamesh and Enkidu;[41]

4. The impingement by Gilgamesh and Enkidu on a number of di-

vine prerogatives. The ire of the gods is thereby unleashed. In order for the "innocent" to be spared, it is determined that one of the protagonists must be victimized.

Following Girard's unpacking of mythic symbolism, we see violence in its collective potential when the people faint under Gilgamesh's rough tutelage. We see violence demonized in the form of Huwawa, the foreign monster. And we see violence divinized in the form of Ishtar, the irate goddess who will prevail on Enlil her father to unleash violence on the earth, and in Enlil, who condemns Enkidu to die for the killing of Huwawa.

With scarcely disguised arbitrariness, Enkidu the outsider who has been integrated into society is chosen to play the role of appeasing sacrifice. When he dies by illness, equilibrium should be restored to the community. It is at this point that Gilgamesh should be able to take his rightful place in Uruk society, no longer as overbearing taskmaster who overwhelms his subjects but as a human king who can enjoy his children as well as repair the awe-inspiring walls of Uruk.

Yet this is not the end of the story, but only the end of part I. What follows is a deeply human protest against human mortality, and perhaps against the arbitrariness of Enkidu's death. If we understand the theme of mortality as a revelation of the lie of victimization, then what we have in Gilgamesh is much more than a liminal coming-of-age tale, in which an epic hero comes to grips with the immutable realities of the human condition. We have insight into the falsehood of the scapegoat mechanism. Only at the death of his friend Enkidu, on whom the Middle-Babylonian version lays the blame for the killing of Huwawa, exonerating Gilgamesh, is Gilgamesh able to identify with his double, the foreigner so much like him.[42] He goes out on a quest for immortality which may also be interpreted as a protest against the arbitrariness of fate as decreed by the gods.

Eventually his journey will bring him back to Uruk ready to fulfill his role as king. Along the way there is revealed to him, from wise Siduri the alewife and Utnapishtim the immortalized ark-builder, that he is not above the realities of human relationships—even as king without peer—but personifies them. Although we do not have Gilgamesh offering himself as replacement for condemned Enkidu, Gilgamesh does live out a kind of protest against the mechanism of collective violence, here mythically obscured as divine anger, and eventually lives out the possibilities that would have been Enkidu's.

Our appreciation of this tale may well be determined, then, by the terms in which we choose to define the revelation of the scapegoating mechanism. For Girard, it seems to have taken full expression only in the Passion of the Gospels, even though glimpsed in the religious traditions of Israel in the Old Testament. For some Jewish and Christian *Alttestamentler*, what one finds in the OT is more than just prefiguring. It is the exposure and overcoming of violence already fully realized, though in different terms, an eventuality so aptly demonstrated in Sandor Goodhart's reading of the Joseph narrative.[43]

If we seek only for a Christ figure who voluntarily offers himself up as a victim, then the OT revelation seems preliminary and faint. If instead we seek for a monotheistic tradition which takes a stance of anti-idolatry, and in which the source of violence and redemption is Yahwistic instead of demonic, then the ANE tradition seems inferior. But if we stick to the basic categories, always mindful of historical and critical features, it is possible to see cultures dealing in a rich variety of ways with the underlying hidden violence, sometimes more successfully and other times less successfully. This is true regardless of the intent of myth or epic to hide and obscure the collective complicity in substitutionary victimization.

At the heart of religion and culture is a mimetic principle with both "good" and "bad" forms. Just as bad metaphors help to create the scapegoat mechanism and hide the victim's innocence from view, so too do good metaphors help us to understand our own plight in the plight of the victim. The undoing of this mimetic principle would mean the undoing of human relationships. Further, the essentially positivist expectation that to uncover the scapegoat mechanism is to overcome it overlooks both historical reality and free will. Religious studies scholar and magician Lee Siegel reminds us that

> The mind, by seeking to normalize what it perceives, to make sense and resolve, is deceived, easily and constantly misdirected, and willing to be so for the sake of equilibrium. Our need for order deludes us. We realize this not only at the magic show but while walking through the marketplace. We dare not see what is really going on.[44]

With these reservations, I affirm Girard's insights into the insidiousness of violence and the various ways in which we attempt to hide from ourselves our complicity in violence. This is achieved by using the mimetic principle as a vehicle of all-against-one catharsis, whereby one victim takes on the impurity and guilt of the community and is then "justly" violated and expelled from the community. It is the unmasking of such occultations in literature, in sacred institutions, in false theology, which is the task of the peacemaker. It is a prophetic task, as Goodhart has shown so eloquently in his article, "I am Joseph." It is also a "messianic" task in that it calls on the messenger, the revealer, to stop the chain of violence by voluntarily becoming the victim. Here we have no lasting city. Thus our "sojourning" mentality in any given cultural and political settings keeps us in the pool of "outsiders" and "foreigners" who might adequately put an end to the violence.

THE SIGNIFICANCE OF GIRARD
FOR CONTEMPORARY PEACEMAKING AGENDA

It may seem at first blush that Girard's unmasking of the scapegoat mechanism is readily adaptable to contemporary peacemaking perspectives and initiatives. Indeed, Girard's insights do constitute a powerful theoretical tool for exposing the evils of systemic violence often obscured by the implicit sanction of social convention. Particularly for those who trace their eirenic heritage through the radical Reformation to the Gospels, Girard's culture criticism recalls the social ethic of Anabaptism, with its rejection of sacred violence and its countercultural stance vis-à-vis the secular powers of the established church. Girard's essentially Christian "solution" to the problem created by this inherent violence of the sacred echoes the radical Reformation critique of Western culture and religion, its insistence of the separation of church and state, and its categoric rejection of just war. Furthermore, Girard's understanding of the sacrificial death of Jesus as the exposing and mitigating factor that ultimately disables the inherent violence of the scapegoat mechanism evokes the Anabaptist emphasis on the discipleship of the cross.

An inherent danger of such an assumption, however, is the temptation to appropriate Girard's work as a sophisticated exoneration of narrowly confessional distinctives. To indulge such blandishments would be to reenact the very type of violence that Girard's model intends to expose and undermine. "We dare not see what is really going on. . . ."[45] The implicit locus of critical scrutiny in Girard's analysis is not prospective but introspective.

Girard has constructed a methodology for exposing and nullifying mechanisms of violence and ostracism in our own conceptual framework. By uncovering the victimization of marginalized persons in mythology, in tragedy, in biblical epic, and in anthropological studies, Girard provides a model that enables us to examine our own sacrificial mechanisms. What and whom are we willing to sacrifice to keep our consciences pristine? Our communities stable? Our worldview intact?

Is it possible that we as peacemakers have simply exchanged one set of sacrificial mechanisms for others, and continue to do violence to individuals in our communities who conveniently personify and embody our fears and anxieties and anger and hatred, emotions all the more intense and lethal among us since they cannot be expressed physically? Our victims bear marks, not on their bodies so much as on their psyches. This, as I understand it, is the challenge that Girard places before us as a community of those dedicated to the way of peace.

It is not difficult, for example, to interpret some of our struggles with models of pastoral ministry in terms of Girardian insights into the vulnerability of scapegoats. Pastors often live and work as marginal persons in the congregations they lead, both by virtue of their office (thereby reflecting the sacrificial king image elucidated by Girard) and by their ambiguous status as both outsiders and insiders. Granted that every local situation is characterized by unique factors, it is striking how often pastoral shake-ups and resignations fulfill the purpose of cathartic sacrifice in church communities facing sacrificial crisis.

Girard emphasizes that the choice of a sacrificial victim is arbitrary. He says, "It is futile to look for the secret of the redemptive process in distinctions between the surrogate victim and the other members of the community. . . . The religious interpretations we have considered so far are at fault precisely because they attribute the beneficial results of the sacrifice to the superhuman nature of the victim or of the other participants, insofar as any of these appears to incarnate the supreme violence."[46] This seems to undermine certain Christian views of atonement, especially those that emphasize Jesus' divinity and often go hand in hand with transactional notions of redemption. On the other hand, it lends itself to a theology and ethic of nonviolence and peacemaking if Jesus is the surrogate victim, the human being who voluntarily accepts his status and does not pass on the violence but absorbs it. This provides a model for *Nachfolge* (discipleship) which may be incarnated by a whole community, the "Kingdom of God."

Girard has much to offer, not least of which is a clear framework for self-criticism. It may help move us as peacemakers from the virtue of not killing others and the washing-the-hands mentality which *may* characterize sectarian and holiness communities, to active engagement in the defenseless unmasking of the scapegoat mechanism in our own midst.

I close by paraphrasing two New Testament characters who give expression to some of the ambivalence I have towards the work of Girard. As Agrippa said to Paul in the wake of his narrative defense: "Almost thou persuadest me to be a Girardian" (Acts 26:28, KJV, paraphrased). And finally, as the unnamed father in Mark 9, who comes to Jesus with a devil of a problem, says to him, "If you are able to do anything, have pity on us and help us." *If?* says Jesus. "All things are possible for those who believe." From my reading and encounter with students and colleagues of Girard, I confess with that man: "I believe! Help thou my unbelief!" (Mark 9:24).

NOTES

1. This phrase was used by Eric Gans ("Pour une esthétique triangulaire," *Esprit* 429 [1973], 581) in reference to René Girard's research in anthropology and is quoted by Sandor Goodhart, "'I am Joseph': René Girard and the Prophetic Law," in *Violence and Truth: On the Work of René Girard*, ed. Paul Dumouchel (Stanford: Stanford University Press, 1988), 53, who suggests it may be an understatement.

2. "His work," says Williams, "radically critical and disconcerting on the side of social theory, conservatively radical on the side of theology, offers . . . the basis of a new Christian humanism," James G. Williams, *The Bible, Violence, and the Sacred: Liberation From the Myth of Sanctioned Violence* (San Francisco: Harper Collins, 1991), 6.

3. A summary of the strikingly disparate assessments of Girard's work is offered by Virgil Nemoianu in "René Girard and the Dialectics of Imperfection," in *To Honor René Girard*, ed. Alphonse Juilland (Saratoga, Calif.: Anmi Libri, 1986), 1-16.

4. Girard, *Violence and the Sacred*, trans. Patrick Gregory (Baltimore: John Hopkins University Press, 1977), 31.

5. There are many summaries and critiques of Girard's central ideas, including those found scattered throughout his own writings. I mention as particularly relevant here those by Vern Redekop in *Scapegoats, the Bible, and Criminal Justice: Interacting with René Girard* (MCC Office of Criminal Justice, 1993), 4-16; "Violence and the Sacred Scapegoat," by Edmund Pries in *Essays on War and Peace: Bible and Early Church*, ed. Willard M. Swartley (Occasional Papers #9; Elkhart: Institute of Mennonite Studies, 1986), 46-56; and Williams, *Bible, Violence*, 6-14.

6. See the bibliography in *To Honor René Girard*. I might also mention here that Girard's ideas have been applied to fields such as economics, law, and even biology, as reiterated by Sandor Goodhart in *Violence and Truth: On the Work of René Girard*, ed. Paul Dumouchel (Stanford: Stanford University Press, 1988), 53.

7. In the *Preface* to *What Maisie Knew* (New York: Augustus M. Kelley, Publishers, 1970), xix. The full quote, appropos in this case, is: "To criticize is to appreciate, to appropriate, to take intellectual possession, to establish *in fine* a relation with the criticized thing and to make it one's own."

8. René Girard, *Things Hidden Since the Foundation of the World*, trans. Stephen Bann and Michael Metteer (Stanford: Stanford University Press, 1987), 43.

9. He says, "*Religion* in its broadest sense, then, must be another term for that obscurity that surrounds man's efforts to defend himself by curative or preventative means against his own violence" (*Violence and the Sacred*, 23).

10. Girard, *Things Hidden*, 43f.

11. Ibid., 44. The very notion that collective violence is characterized by a profound and automatic obscuration by means of sacrificial mechanisms suggests a subtle antilogy whereby victimage is apparent wherever it cannot be perceived.

12. Girard's main criticism of contemporary ethnology seems to be its assertion, borne of a tendentious "intellectual scepticism" (*Things Hidden*, 5), that broad theorizing about religion is otiose, passé.

13. Evans-Pritchard, *Theories of Primitive Religion* (Oxford: Clarendon, 1965), 43.

14. Girard's approach also raises the methodological question of how we know the essence of things, whether by discovering their origins and development or by elucidating their functions. And if, as we suspect, this is not an either/or proposition, then how are we to understand and correlate the interrelationship of these factors? How can we know that the sacral complex, which functions to bring peace to the community, is actually an elaborate diversion which masks our complicity in an ongoing holocaust of slain innocents, as Girard claims? In asking this question I intentionally anticipate an issue which will be addressed in the concluding section of this paper, viz., the ideological utility of such a reconstruction of origins for contemporary peacemakers.

15. Girard, *Violence and the Sacred*, 309.

16. Nemoianu, *To Honor*, 1-16.

17. Ibid., 7.

18. Quoted from Millard Lind, "Power and Powerlessness in the Old Testament: A Book Analysis," in *Monotheism, Power, Justice: Collected Old Testament Essays* (Elkhart, Ind.: Institute of Mennonite Studies, 1990), 204. We let this assertion of Schwager's stand for now, despite its oversimplified and admittedly subtle triumphalism, to illustrate one of the temptations Girard's ideas represent for Christian intellectuals in the West. Christianity and Western culture have indeed represented two sides of the same coin since at least the fourth century C.E., and Western secularisms tend to be expressly Christian heresies. But the claim that Christian orthodoxy has now uncovered the root cause of the sacralized violence that has accompanied its leading role in society is unconvincing.

19. Girard, *Things Hidden*, 176.

20. Ibid., 177.

21. Ibid., 176.

22. Ibid., 177f.

23. Ibid., 178.

24. The story, as retold in "'I am Joseph': René Girard and the Prophetic Law" (*To Honor*, 96-97), is this: "A woman is sitting upstairs in an orthodox synagogue while the story of Joseph is being recited. And when they come to the section in Part One where Jacob sends Joseph to Shechem to find his brothers and Joseph ends up 'blundering in the field' as the Torah tells us, before someone directs him to Dothan, the woman cries out, 'Don't go down there! Don't you remember what they did to you last year there! They are going to sell you!'"

25. Sandor Goodhart, *To Honor*, 97f.

26. Girard, *Things Hidden*, 176.

27. Girard, *Scapegoat*, 101.

28. Again, this *use* of Girard seems to reflect a very tightly closed hermeneutical circle.

29. Norbert Lohfink, *Gewalt und Gewaltlosigkeit im Alten Testament* (Freiburg: Herder, 1983), 216.

30. "I am Joseph," in *To Honor*, 109.

31. With echoes of the evolutionary model of development criticized above.

32. The interpretation which follows makes no claims of comprehensiveness, whether from the side of Girardian analysis or in terms of the rich multivalence of the epic itself. It is intended rather to illustrate the potential usefulness of the scapegoat theory for reading Ancient Near Eastern texts, and of the ways in which such texts may also reveal mechanisms whereby the institutions of sacralized collective violence are demystified.

33. The historical evidence is summarized in Jeffrey H. Tigay, *The Evolution of the Gilgamesh Epic* (Philadelphia: University of Pennsylvania Press, 1982), 13-16.

34. Besides slain Tiamat, whose carcass provides the basic building blocks of creation, it is the blood of Kingu from which humanity is created, according to the epic (Tablet VI).

35. (New Haven, 1976), 195-219.

36. See W. L. Moran, "Ovid's *Blanda Voluptas* and the Humanization of Enkidu," *JNES* 50 (1991), 121-127.

37. This represents the "symbolic inversion" of the role of the harlot according to Rivkah Harris, "Images of Women in the Gilgamesh Epic," in *Lingering Over Words: Studies in Ancient Near Eastern Literature in Honor of William L. Moran*, ed. Tzvi Abusch et al. (Atlanta: Scholars Press, 1990), 222-224.

38. Cf. the similar transformation of the hero Achilles in the Homeric tradition. In the Iliad, Achilles' hubris eventually leads to the death of his friend and ritual substitute, Patroklos. In the Odyssey, Odysseus' encounter with the shade of Achilles in Hades is a sobering reversal (Od. XI 489-91); cf.

Greg Nagy, *The Best of the Achaeans* (Baltimore, 1979), 35.

39. Here again there is a symbolic inversion represented by Siduri's role. Rivkah Harris writes, "Siduri, the divinized tavernkeeper, is also depicted in ways which are very unlike the actual tavernkeeper," in "Images of Women," 225.

40. As a model of Girard's methodology applied to tragedy, see "Oedipus and the Surrogate Victim," in *Violence and the Sacred*, 68-88.

41. Concerning this, Rivkah Harris comments, "I think that on a subliminal level, if not overtly, the composers of the epic were critical of so intense a relationship between men," in "Images of Women," 228. Cf. also the Jungian interpretation of Rivkah Schärf Kluger, *The Archetypal Significance of Gilgamesh: A Modern Ancient Hero* (Einsiedeln, Switzerland: Daimon, 1991), 66-71.

42. Cf. Thorkild Jacobsen, *Treasures of Darkness: A History of Mesopotamian Religion* (New Haven: Yale University Press), 201.

43. "I am Joseph," in *To Honor.*

44. Lee Siegel, *The Net of Magic: Wonders and Deceptions in India* (Chicago: Chicago University Press, 1991), 426.

45. Cf. p. 171 above.

46. Girard, *Violence and the Sacred*, 257.

CHAPTER NINE

King as Servant,
Sacrifice as Service:
Gospel Transformations

James G. Williams

THE SIGNIFICANCE OF RENÉ GIRARD'S work for peacemaking is immense. He himself has not dealt with concrete implications and applications of the mimetic theory, which holds much theoretical and practical potential in numerous areas scarcely yet begun, ranging from anthropological field studies to feminist theory and from international relations to group conflict resolution.

Girard's disinclination to offer concrete solutions for problems of conflict and violence does not mean that he disdains them. I think it is rather that he is committed to what he understands as his calling, which is to continue the research and writing generated from his conversion[1] and the "idea" of the mimetic theory that came to him like a revelation. His vocational unwillingness, except in general terms, to address himself to questions of ethics and praxis has a positive side in that numerous fields are left open without the "master's" intervention or supervision.

However that may be, the subject of this chapter is at the heart of what could be characterized as a Girardian understanding of human liberation and the ethics of peacemaking. If I have any kind of grasp of this understanding, it is basically a classical Christian view translated into a new anthropological mode as expressed in the mimetic theory. What I intend to discuss here is the significance of the Gospels' witness to Jesus and to the ethos of Christian discipleship in light of their deep roots in the Jewish Scriptures.

This essay presupposes the affirmation of the Christian tradition: in and through Jesus as the Christ, a transformed expression of the "rule" and "reign" of God comes about through Jesus' role as the bearer of the divine Person. My thesis is that the New Testament Gospels witness to and represent a transformation of sacral kingship.

I will develop the argument that originally the king (or anyone, male or female, holding an office of utmost prestige)[2] is the victim whose power is closely allied to sacrifice, and as such he is the primary cultural difference and differentiator. That the king is the difference and the differentiator means that he is the *sacrificer* but also the *sacrifice* in periods of crisis. (This can be ritualized to the point that a king is regularly slain as a sacrificial victim.).[3] According to the Hebrew Bible, Saul, the first king of Israel, exemplifies the role of sacrificer and sacrifice. David has some of the features of Saul but avoids the victim status through the power that he develops. In the gospels, among which I will focus particularly on Mark, Jesus is the king who does not confirm the sacrificial system but exposes and interrupts it. The meaning of "Kingship" and "Sacrifice" is transformed: kingship becomes servanthood and sacrifice becomes service.

[*Editor's note:* when presented at the 1994 Conference, Williams's paper included a major section on mimetic theory, explicating the relation between sacrifice and ritual and the nature of mimetic desire. Since then this portion has been published in an essay by James G. Williams: "Sacrifice and the Beginning of Kingship," Semeia 67; *Transformations, Passages, and Processes: Ritual Approaches to Biblical Texts,* ed. Mark McVann (copyright © by the Society of Biblical Literature, 1995) 73-92.] For fuller understanding of the Girardian theory that underlies the following analysis, the reader is encouraged to consult this essay. I include three quotations here that are important for basic understandings:

> From the standpoint of the interstices of biblical studies, literary theory, and Girard's mimetic model. . . . I would say that ritual is always, in some mode, concomitant to expressions of the sacred, and the heart of ritual is sacrifice, viz., "to render sacred" (Latin *sacrificare*, French *sacrifier*). (p. 74)

> The *acquisitive* character of human desire lays the groundwork for human conflict. The subject not only seeks to be like the model, the one who is imitated; s/he wants to have what the model has and even to be what the model is. The object of desire is what the model or mediator desires. The result of this relationship of subject to model has a great potential to turn to conflict or violence. The message given off by the model may be "imitate me"—except in this one respect, "don't imitate me." A classical instance of this is Freud's so-called "Oedipus complex." According to Freud,

180 • VIOLENCE RENOUNCED

the child learns that s/he must imitate the parent of the same sex in every respect except one, which is to have the parent of the opposite sex as a sexual partner. However, from the standpoint of the mimetic theory it is the desire to imitate the model/mediator, not sexual attachment to the parent of the opposite sex, that may issue in rivalry. In other words, the child identifies first with a given parent, then imitates her or him in desiring the other parent. This could and sometimes does lead to the child's attempt to displace the parent who is the model to take his or her place with the other parent. But this sort of conflict is not restricted to parent-child relationships. It can occur in all sorts of relationships, including, and perhaps above all, relations with peers.

Of course, in human relationships conflict doesn't always emerge, and in most cultural contexts conflict and violence do not reign most of the time. This is because cultural forms, which cannot be separated from what we now call the religious or the sacred, establish *differences*, such as roles, rules, institutions, etc. These differences function to keep people from destructive rivalries yet enable them to enter into cooperative relations. (p. 79)

What Girard's theory about the originary elements of religion and culture entails, in other words, is that the primitive sacred is violence: the collective violence of the community that is transmitted, transformed, and routinized in such a way that its object is to protect the community from violence. (p. 80)]

SACRIFICE AND THE BEGINNING OF KINGSHIP

To demonstrate the relationship between sacrifice and kingship, I summarize the sacrificial occasions in 1 Samuel. It is striking that 1 Samuel recounts the greatest number of sacrificial occasions of any narrative portion of the Hebrew Bible. I can only think this is so because the emergence of the monarchy is itself a sacrificial event in which the person set apart, the *difference*, must be the polarizer, the *differentiator* who establishes order. If this person fails, s/he becomes the new difference as sacrifice-scapegoat.

1. The piety of Elkanah's family is described with reference to sacrifice and vows at Shiloh (1 Sam. 1).

2. The sons of Eli, priest of Shiloh, are immoral priests who reserve the best portions and raw meat for themselves when worshipers bring animals to offer in sacrifice (2:12-17).

3. The Philistine capture of the ark of the covenant of YHWH occurs during war and occasions further crises (4–7:2). The ark is a sac-

rificial object, and the narrative is replete with sacrificial offerings in the sacrificial crisis.

4. As Saul approaches the city where he will find Samuel, he learns that Samuel is presiding over a sacrifice (9:12-13). Saul, whom Samuel will anoint as ruler, is subsequently placed at the head of the table at the meal that follows the sacrifice.

5. In 1 Samuel 10 Saul encounters a band of prophets descending from what was probably a sacrificial occasion at Gibeath-elohim. He is caught up by the divine spirit in a prophetic frenzy with them.

6. When messengers inform Saul of the Ammonite siege of Jabesh-gilead, the spirit of God possesses him and he cuts a yoke of oxen into pieces, sending them throughout Israel (11:7-8). There is no doubt this is a kind of sacrificial act. The same verb, *ntch,* used for severing an animal, is employed also in Judges 19:29 and 20:6 in the story of the Levite's concubine and the tribal warfare with the Benjaminites; otherwise, it is employed only with reference to cutting up an animal for a burnt offering (Exod. 29:17; Lev. 1:6, 12; 8:20; 1 Kings 18:23, 33).

7. Saul sacrifices a burnt offering at Gilgal. Samuel condemns him for not waiting until he arrives, and announces that Saul's kingship will not continue (13:7-15). Saul's excuse to Samuel is that "the people were slipping away from me" (v. 11), which is to say he could not maintain popular and military support if he did not go ahead with the burnt offering.

8. Saul supervises a sacrificial slaughter of sheep and oxen and calves when he notices that some of his troops are eating animals with their blood (14:31-35). The altar Saul builds is presumably used also to offer an animal for the ransom of Jonathan after he had transgressed Saul's oath and was taken in the casting of lots (14:3-45).

9. Saul disobeys Samuel's command on behalf of YHWH utterly to destroy the Amalekites (15:3). Saul does not say why he spares Agag the Amalekite king, but he does explain to Samuel that the "people" spared the best of the livestock to sacrifice to YHWH in Gilgal (15:15, 21; cf. 15:9). He finally cries out that he disobeyed the Lord's commandment and Samuel's instructions "because I feared the people and obeyed their voice" (15:24). The Amalekites were *cherem* to YHWH (15:21), i.e., to be devoted to utter destruction. This is a sacrificial act. Both the verb *charam* and the noun *cherem* could be used in a manner not directly related to the realm of the sacred and sacrifice, but it is evident that in origin they represent the sacred quality of persons, animals, or things that are set aside for utter destruc-

tion. This is especially the case in the occurrences of the noun. A cherem to YHWH could not be redeemed or ransomed; it must be destroyed or put to death. Every devoted thing is "most holy" (Lev. 27:28-29). In Joshua 7 the people must be sanctified before the lots are cast to find out who has taken of the cherem (Josh. 7:13; cf. 7:1, 11, 15). Passages like these clearly reflect the ancient belief that the sacred is not only life-giving and beneficial but also dangerous and deadly.

When Samuel himself executes Agag, the king of the Amalekites, he does it "before the Lord in Gilgal" (15:33). In other words, Agag, who is cherem to YHWH, is done away with as befits a sacrifice in the form of a cherem.

10. When Samuel visits the house of Jesse in Bethlehem to anoint a new king, he uses sacrifice as his *cover* (1 Sam. 16:1-13). Fearing Saul's reprisal, sacrifice is the justification of his visit. This appears to be simply a ruse to avoid violent retaliation. Yet according to Girard, that is basically what sacrifice is, a "*trompe*-violence," an attempt to maneuver around violence, to "deceive" it.[4]

11. David tries to elude Saul by going to Bethlehem under the pretext of offering a yearly sacrifice with his family (20:6, 29). Again here is a trompe-violence, which is highly ironic when read in conjunction with Samuel's ruse in 1 Samuel 16:1-13. However, David's attempt at deceiving Saul does not work (20:30-34).

12. In the aftermath of Saul's vision of the dead Samuel, who has been conjured from Sheol by the medium of Endor, the latter feeds Saul and his servants. She takes a fatted calf, then, as the text explains, "quickly slaughtered it" (*wattizbachehu*, 28:24). The verb used here, *zabach*, is the most common word in the Hebrew Bible for offering sacrifice. The occasion is probably, therefore, a sacrificial one and an important bit of evidence for the connection of slaughtering an animal, sacrifice, and eating a meal in ancient societies.

Some of these narrative episodes are particularly telling. We encounter here the issue of *who may offer sacrifice*, which emerges over the question of morality (1 Sam. 2:12-17) and authority (1 Sam. 13:7-15). Closely related to this issue is Saul's disobedience in failing to execute the ban (1 Sam. 15). Saul's rise to kingship and final fall are framed by sacrificial occasions (1 Sam. 9:11-30 and 28:24). And his function as monarch is represented in his ability to offer sacrifice, to *differentiate* (1 Sam. 11:7-8; 14:31-35). In one instance this brings him into conflict with Samuel (1 Sam. 13:7-15).

The frequency of sacrifice and sacrificial occasions in 1 Samuel indicates the text's awareness of both the sacrificial roots of kingship and the sacrificial crisis which the selection of a king is intended to resolve. Saul is both the sacrificer, the differentiator, and the sacrifice, the scapegoat. His failure stems from three factors: his inability to handle sacrifice and his mimetic involvement with his people, whom he tries to please; his fascination with Samuel, who is his model-obstacle; and his relationship with David, who becomes his chief rival. Sacrifice and the management of mimetic desire are the obverse of one another in the origin and maintenance of culture. So it is that Saul's failure as sacrificer is closely related to his status as a scapegoat in the narrative. In another study I have argued that the narrative itself begins to take precedence as the "ruler" of the reader-hearer in the tradition.[5] The standpoint of this historiography is that of a witness against the king and sacrifice and a witness for the God of Israel.

The combination of the failure of the first king as sacrificer and the failure of sacrifice itself is generated from the heart of a religious vision that begins to replace kingship with the writing of history and sacrifice with law and Scripture. But this is not achieved without making the first king a kind of sacrifice, a scapegoat offered to the critique of sacrifice.

THE FALL OF THE KING

KING AS TRANSGRESSOR

Saul is presented as a transgressor in 1 Samuel. In the received text, the selection of Saul as king is ominous from the very beginning, according to 1 Samuel 10:20-24, and he ends up by transgressing his own ban of mediums and wizards, according to 1 Samuel 28. If we divide the narratives as "early" and "late" as done in traditional criticism we still find interesting patterns that complement one another. In the so-called early source Saul is possessed by the spirit of YHWH and prophesies; indeed, he is subject to mimetic contagion when he is with the prophets, falling under the influence of his spiritual "father," Samuel (1 Sam. 19:18-24; cf. 10:1-12; see Williams[6]). His end comes when he transgresses his own ban on mediums and wizards (1 Sam. 28:9), undoubtedly because they summon up ancestral *elohim*, gods or divine spirits. The medium does not recognize Saul until she recognizes Samuel as the elohim coming up out of the earth (28:12-13).

I read this as the text's way of pointing out that Samuel is Saul's *double*, the other from whom he cannot distinguish himself. The story of Saul, especially from the standpoint of the "early" source, is a story of possession: when Saul crosses the boundary of the prohibition, he is fully overcome by the one who has been his authoritative other all along. His collapse among the prophets earlier on is a foreshadowing of the final collapse, which plays itself out in the victory of the Philistines and Saul's suicide before the Philistines can kill him (1 Sam. 31).

The "later" source allows the "earlier" narrative of Saul's bitter end to stand, as related in the concluding chapters of 1 Samuel, but makes it clear in the choosing of Saul that he is doomed. Traditional criticism has struggled with the passage in question (1 Sam. 10:20-24). P. Kyle McCarter observes that Saul seems to be somehow blameworthy when he is selected by lot but as yet there is nothing for which he could be guilty. Saul has not committed a criminal offense like Achan, yet "he is an offending party by virtue of the election itself."[7]

THE ANCIENT WAY OF THE WICKED

What all the commentators miss is the paradox of the sacred, and in a monarchic society the king would be one of the primary bearers of the sacred—if not its chief manifestation. The sacred is the power of differentiation that is also the source of the undifferentiation of violence; it is that which must be appropriated but is nonetheless taboo; it is that which is at the very center of existence but is simultaneously most alien to it.[8] The paradoxical bivalency of the sacred can be split and managed in such a way that the paradox is somewhat subdued and becomes less dangerous: the king—or the monarch's office—is divine and good, and evil comes from other sources; the power and the meaning at the center of the community's life is beneficial and benevolent if approached in the right way, through the acts and in the space marked off for such approaches; evil, misfortune, etc., has alien sources, such as the devil, demons, and the like. But there is always a paradoxical ambiguity about the sacred, whose primitive foundation is violence and the channeling of violence.

Girard, in comparing Job to Oedipus, refers to the imaginary crimes of the sacred monarch.[9] Eliphaz asks Job, "Will you keep to the old way/that the wicked have trod?" (Job 22:15). The king or queen is the one available to blame, one to whom to transfer the sin (actual or imminent violence) of the social order in a time of crisis. He or she is the chief insider who is the most marginal, the furthest from what is "common" to the community. In Israel the office and functions of monarchy were relatively de-divinized and separated to some extent from the blatant role of scapegoat. In Psalm 72, for example, the king is praised and exalted as the conduit of divine blessings. Nothing is said about what might happen if things go wrong, if crops fail, if the economy collapses, if foreign enemies triumph. Of course, the strategy of the monarchic leader is classically that of referring the royal scapegoat status to surrogates.

But in ancient Israel rulers could be and were blamed for social, political, and military disasters. Jeroboam I got Israel started on the wrong road in leading the northern tribes to separate from Judah (1 Kings 12-14). David's son Solomon not only levied heavy taxes and corvée labor for his building projects, he "loved many foreign women" (1 Kings 11:1), which is why YHWH tears away the kingdom from his descendants (11:11). Manasseh's abominable practices, including placing an image of Asherah in the Jerusalem temple and sacrificing his own son as a burnt offering, are given as the reason for Judah's eventual downfall before Babylonia (2 Kings 21:1-16).

These instances all have one element in common: the king transgresses by associating with the foreign, the other, the polluting disorder outside the Yahwist realm. The Deuteronomic historian, looking from the standpoint of Judah and the Davidic dynasty, condemns all the northern or Israelite kings, and so Jeroboam is the worst offender in principle because he led the northerners in their rebellion against the house of David.[10] Solomon's sins and the eventual division of the united monarchy is laid at the door of his many foreign women. Manasseh brought foreign cult objects into the temple, as well as reverting to child sacrifice, which Yahwism had long prohibited.

We could easily add other instances of the ruler as the cause of impiety and misfortune. Ahab is similar both to Manasseh and Solomon in that he erected an altar of Baal and made an Asherah, and he married the Sidonian princess Jezebel, who persecuted the prophets of YHWH (1 Kings 18:4) and urged Ahab to make false accusations against Naboth to acquire his vineyard (1 Kings 21). Of course, there is also David, who stands as God's favored one in the later tradition: the narratives in 1 Samuel are somewhat ambiguous but seem to indicate that he worked as a mercenary for the Philistines (1 Sam. 27; 29).

Moreover, the reason given by Nathan the prophet to David for the evil that would rise against David out of his own family was his affair with Bathsheba, wife of Uriah the Hittite (see 1 Sam. 11-12). Because Uriah would not have sexual intercourse with his wife during a rest from battle, thus unknowingly threatening to expose the fact that Bathsheba's pregnancy was due to an adulterous affair, David had him killed in battle. Here we see a combination of sexual transgression and possibly involvement with a foreign woman. But what is emphasized in Nathan's oracle of condemnation is David's arrogance of power (1 Sam. 12:6-9).

THE FALL OF THE KING

This arrogance of power, the pride or *hubris* that leads to "outrages," the gravest acts of transgression, is an essential feature of the fall of the king, who keeps "to the old way/that the wicked have trod." This hubris that leads to a fall is the common element that Hans J. L. Jensen stresses in his comparative study of the fall of the king in various sources: Yima in Ferdowsi's *Shanama*, Indra in *Markandeya Purana*, Yayati in the *Mahabharata*, Kroisus in *Herodotus*, Pentheus in Euripides' *The Bacchae*, Romulus in Livy, as well as various ancient Near Eastern and biblical figures.[11]

Now the ancient Israelite tradition, as represented in the Scriptures, struggled with the sacred and certainly demystified and demythologized it to a great extent, above all in the witness to the Servant in Deutero-Isaiah and through Job's testimony in the dialogues of the book of Job. We see a partial desacralization in the story of Saul. Saul is one of the *Unheilsherrscher* Jensen mentions.[12] But there is a difference in the biblical text: the narratives cast a light on Saul and the social structures attending kingship that humanizes him, that sympathizes with him to some extent. Certainly this is true in the "early" source, where he is more and more swept into a mimetic crisis that overpowers him. In the "late" source the ominous character of the selection of the king is clearly indicated.

Saul is presented in a very unfavorable light, but once his fate is intimated in his selection by lot (1 Sam. 10:20-24), it only remains to seal it. And the sealing of the fate of King Saul is done with a good deal of strain in 1 Samuel 13:7-15 and 1 Samuel 15. He is not presented as personally reprehensible or spiritually arrogant, but simply swayed by the desires of the people (1 Sam. 13:11; 15:24). The depiction of Saul comes so close to the Greek tradition of the tragic hero because he, of all Israelite kings portrayed in the biblical sources, is the most subject to mimesis. He becomes *the* Person, the Subject as king, because he is subject (*subjectum*, "cast under") to Samuel, the prophets, and the people. This is to leave aside his relation to David, a subject in its own right.

The first ruler of Israel had to be a kind of scapegoat or sacrifice to establish an institution that the inner core of the Yahwist tradition inspired many Israelites to distrust (see 1 Sam. 8; 12). It is interesting, however, that besides David's major transgression with Bathsheba, already mentioned, another transgression is recounted in the coda on David in 2 Samuel 21-24. It is as though the cycle of storytelling had to bring David back into the myth of sacral kingship. Although it does not lead to his fall, the incident is presented as a matter so serious that thousands of lives were lost.

In 2 Samuel 24 David is the conduit of YHWH's anger in that he is commanded to take a census of Israel. But when it is completed David is stricken with guilt that he has done this. He seeks an oracle and hears through his prophet Gad that he has three options as punishment for the transgression: three years of famine, three months in which David flees from his foes, or three days of pestilence on the land. David chooses the pestilence, which slays 70,000 people. David sees the destroying angel by the threshing floor of Araunah the Jebusite and implores him/YHWH to cease, confessing his sin abjectly. David purchases the threshing floor, builds an altar there, and offers burnt offerings and peace offerings. "So the Lord answered his supplication for the land, and the plague was averted from Israel" (2 Sam. 24:25).

What are we to make of this story, apparently so full of contradictions? YHWH incites David, yet David is guilty. David chooses a form of punishment that could be construed as self-serving, and it results in as many deaths perhaps as three years of famine would. Yet David also confesses that he alone has sinned, so he builds an altar and offers sacrifices to atone for his guilt to the God who incited the chain of events. We cannot understand this unless we understand the status of the sacred king who is the polarizer, the divider, the differentiator, the bringer of weal and of woe.

JESUS AS KING IN MARK

MARK AND ISRAEL'S SCRIPTURE TRADITIONS

So far I have tried to place kingship and sacrifice in the context of both the ancient Israelite traditions and comparative myth and ritual. Israel's traditions crystallized into several dominant complexes that partly mirror and partly conceal the dynamic process we see in the narratives about Saul and David. Willard M. Swartley has analyzed and interpreted these formative complexes as they influenced the synoptic gospels and were appropriated by the gospel writers.[13] Here I discuss his research, particularly as it bears on Mark; then I supplement it from my own studies of the Jewish Scriptures, the Gospel of Mark, and the mimetic theory.

Swartley delineates the Old Testament faith traditions in keeping with the consensus of biblical scholarship, as follows: Exodus, Sinai, Way-Conquest, temple, and Kingship. Noting that in general these traditions are associated with the north or Israel (Exodus, Sinai, Way-Conquest) and the south or Judah-Jerusalem (temple, Kingship [and Zion]), he articulates the insight that in the synoptic gospels—which probably means first of all in Mark—there is a parallel distinction of Galilee—Jerusalem. In this paper I am not concerned with treating Swartley's poles of Galilee-Jerusalem as magnets for the clustering of the traditions. Rather, my focus is on his thesis about continuity and transformation. He concludes that there is both continuity with the older traditions and transformation of those traditions through the gospel stemming from and representing Jesus as the Christ.

Here I am interested primarily in the kingship tradition. Swartley's discussion of kingship and the passion in Mark concentrates on the question of the high priest, "Are you the Messiah, the Son of the Blessed?" (Mark 14:61) and the repeated phrase "King of the Jews"/"King of Israel" (15:2, 9, 12, 18, 26, 32). He notes that the question about Jesus' identity and the charge that Jesus said he would rebuild the temple are linked.[14] The title "King of the Jews" is used by accusers and persecutors ironically and mockingly, conveying a truth that is denied in the ridicule.[15] The truth of the mockery points to a different sort of king, to which I will return below.

Swartley also discusses three other "royalty indicators."

1. The cry of "Eloi, Eloi" from the cross and the mockery of bystanders. The lament/complaint comes from Psalm 22, a royal psalm.

2. Recurrence of the phrase "kingdom of God" (14:25; 15:43), which is related to Mark 1:14-15 (the nearness of the kingdom), 9:1 (some standing there will not taste death until they see the kingdom), and Jesus' quotation of Zechariah 13:7 in 14:27-28:

"I will strike the shepherd,
and the sheep will be scattered."
"But after I am raised up,
I will go before you to Galilee."

When the resurrected Jesus will have met his disciples again in Galilee (not narrated, but part of the larger story-time of the gospel of Mark), he "not only gathers the scattered disciples physically but also gathers them around the truth from which they fled, i.e., the messianic identity and kingdom reality of the *crucified* Jesus, Son of God."[16]

3. The narrative role of women (14:1-9; 15:40-41; 15:47-16:8). The male disciples have fled, but the women remain and so play an important role in the implied ironic message: "how strange and disarming this kingship!"[17]

Of overriding interest in my reading of Mark is the quarrel of the disciples and Jesus' reply in Mark 10:35-45. Strikingly, Swartley reserves his primary treatment of this passage for his discussion of the Way-Conquest traditions. He cites primary and secondary literature to support the contention that the Son of man ("Son of humanity") comes out of the apocalyptic tradition, which is in turn dependent on the motifs of YHWH as warrior and king. Therefore, the Son of man who is the Servant of the Lord (8:31-33) is a transformation of the divine warrior tradition.[18]

I have some uneasiness about this hypothesis, but in any event I simply observe that Jesus' pronouncement to his disciples in Mark 10:42-45 deals directly with rule, authority, and service. As Swartley notes, "The redeemed, i.e., the followers of Jesus, are linked to Jesus, to the servant-head, who leads the ransomed into servant-living."[19]

TRANSGRESSION, CROWD, AND ARK

Here I would like to supplement Swartley's analysis and interpretation with a few other notes before proceeding to focus on Mark 10:35-45. One issue worth mentioning is the disciples' transgression of the Sabbath laws when they plucked heads of grain (Mark 2:23-28). In responding to the Pharisees' complaint, Jesus cites David and "those who were with him" as a scriptural model. David entered the sanctuary and ate the bread of the Presence. This is not only an appeal to the (future) king as transgressor of taboo, but probably also implies a connection between the leader and the band of followers. As David had companions, those "with him" (2:25), so Jesus appointed the Twelve "to be with him" (3:14). Deciphering this code of allusions results in this message: The one who will rule must transgress the sacred boundaries of his world to become the ruler. Of course, as Swartley shows, though there is a structural and historical continuity of tradition and gospel text, there is also transformation.

At the place in question in Mark the reality of this new kind of "king" and "rule" has not yet been revealed.

A second note is the observation that from a narratological standpoint, the crowd plays a narrative role in Mark—much as in Shakespeare's *Julius Caesar,* where the antagonists are continually thinking of and playing to the crowd.[20] So in Mark the crowds are generally an unstable, threatening phenomenon, easily subject to mimetic contagion (see especially 3:7-30; the demon-legion of 5:1-20; and relation of Jesus and the authorities to crowds in 11:18, 32; 12:13-17; 15:6-15). Pilate "perceived that it was out of *phthonon* [envy or jealousy] that the chief priests had handed him over" (15:10). Envy and jealousy are supremely mimetic phenomena. "Jealousy," as in the NRSV, is probably the better translation here to the extent that it indicates competition for possession of some object or objective that the other desires. "Envy" implies a fascination with the model but not necessarily a direct contesting of the object that mediates the reality or being of the model. The jealousy of the priests is stirred by the desirability of what Jesus has/is—which is popularity and authority with great numbers of people.

We have remarked on the significance of the people/crowd in the story of Saul. Even as Saul sought to act as the leader, the model for others to follow, he was subject to the mimesis of the crowd of people, above all his military. Power exercised is power conferred; there is a continual feedback loop between leader and led, even though in some situations the led may have almost no control if the leadership is armed and ruthless. Saul could not handle it, he was unable to be the differentiator, and so he became the difference, the victim whose demise was the precondition of a new royal dynasty, the House of David.

David himself was a successful charismatic; YHWH was with him (2 Sam. 7:3). When David entered Saul's entourage, Saul came to be in awe of him (1 Sam. 18:12-16); perhaps he brought him into his entourage because he was already in awe of him. First Samuel 17:55–18:5 could be read as intimating Saul's fascination with David, whom "all Israel and all Judah" loved (1 Sam. 18:16). David not only commanded loyalty from many, he was able to perform in a charismatic way (2 Sam. 6:17-19). Yet Absalom, who probably learned not a little from his father, was able to gather a large following and temporarily usurp the throne.

In the moments of crisis for a ruler, the primitive level of the scapegoat mechanism rises to the surface as the monarch faces the threat of loss of power and death. One of the remarkable things about the gospel of Mark is that it indicates so clearly the potential volatility of the human mimetic condition. Even when masses of people are ostensibly positive and friendly, as they sought to be healed by Jesus, there is an ominous note. "He told his disciples to have a boat ready for him because of the crowd, so that they would not crush (*thlibosin*) him" (3:9; cf. 4:35; 6:45; 8:10, 13).

Just as Jesus is a new kind of ruler, so the disciples are to be a new kind of community. But in Mark's narrative they consistently fail to understand this, as for example in the feeding stories (6:34-44; 8:1-10; note 6:37; 8:4; cf. 8:17). The feedings, a preparation for the last meal and a foretaste of the kingdom of God (14:22-25), are the disclosure of the new mimesis of the new kind of ruler. Here the crowds are not threatening; they do not crush Jesus, but are in need. The people gathered allow themselves to be ordered or organized. When they eat the bread and fish there is an enormous amount "left over" (8:8)—as though whatever they are given and share among themselves would keep on feeding them.

There are also some noteworthy similarities between Jesus' entry into Jerusalem and David's transporting of the ark to Jerusalem (2 Sam. 6:1-15. The ark was carried on a new cart (6:3; see 1 Sam. 6:7: the Philistines used a cart with "two milch cows that had never borne a yoke"). David and the people "danced before the Lord" (2 Sam. 6:4; see 6:14). This account leads into the promise of an everlasting dynasty for the house of David (2 Sam. 7:1-16). In the gospel account Jesus rides on an ass's colt on whom no one has ever sat (Mark 11:2). Many people celebrated his arrival and shouted praise and affirmation of "the kingdom of our father David" (Mark 11:10). But David offered sacrifice, an ox and a fatling (2 Sam. 6:13), whereas Jesus himself, rather than an animal substitute, will suffer the very effects of sacred violence which the ark represented and mediated.

Finally, the empty tomb scene in Mark 16:1-8 harks back to the ark narrative in Numbers 10:29-36. The ark, as the throne seat of YHWH, was to lead Israel into the Promised Land (see also Josh. 3, 4, and 6). The ark traveled before the people three days' journey, "to seek a resting place for them" (Num. 10:33). The ark, that is, the sacred Presence, is the divider, scattering the enemies of the Lord, who are the enemies of Israel: "Arise, O Lord, let your enemies be scattered. . ." (10:36). In Mark 16 Jesus is not in the tomb; he has gone before the disciples to Galilee, as he had told them (14:28). Jesus rises, not to scatter enemies but to gather the disciples in Galilee.[21]

The transgression imputed to the scapegoat-king, the mimetic volatility of the crowd (source of violence displaced onto persons and objects), and the ark as repository of sacred violence: these motifs are all present in the gospel account. But they are transformed into witness to a "king" who does not rule by violence, who moves away from the crowd toward divine-human community, and whose differentiating function is love. Here is a "good" mimesis which brings violence only to the extent that subversion of ordinary mimesis, managed by means of the scapegoat mechanism, threatens that world which requires excluding or eliminating the innocent victim.

CONVERGENCE OF CHRISTOLOGY AND ETHICS: MARK 10:35-45

Jesus' response to the disciples' mimetic conflict in Mark 10:35-45 is the central passage in Mark—and in the NT gospels—for understanding how kerygma, Christology, and praxis converge in the revelation of God through human community and the revelation of humanity through the divinely human. The disclosure of the secret of the Son of man in 8:27-33 and the teaching on discipleship have prepared the way for this disclosure. Here the transformation of kingship and sacrifice comes to a head.

James and John want to be Jesus' chief lieutenants in the glory of his coming kingdom. Jesus asks them whether they are able to drink his cup and undergo his baptism, and they affirm that they are able. Whether or not the language stems from ritual practice in the early church, the meaning of the text is clear: Jesus alludes to his death, his voluntary giving of himself, and the disciples still do not comprehend his words. If they did, of course, they would not have asked the question in the first place. The other ten become angry when they hear of James and John's request, repeating the pattern of mimetic conflict that is recounted in 9:33-37. Jesus interrupts with a pronouncement. He reminds them that among the Gentiles the rulers and nobles exercise all the power of the "lord" and all the weight of "authority" that they can muster over their subjects (10:42).

> But it is not so among you; but whoever wishes to become great among you must be your servant, and whoever wishes to be first among you must be slave of all. For the Son of man came not to be served but to serve, and to give his life a ransom for many. (10:43-45)

Here is the "king" who is a servant. The character of this pronouncement-story makes it clear that this servant-Son of man is the model for the disciples who are pioneers of the new community.

As the king becomes servant, sacrifice is transformed into service. Of fundamental import for understanding this is the last clause of 10:45: ". . . and to give his life a ransom (*lytron*) for many." In *The Bible, Violence, and the Sacred*, I discussed *lytron*, "ransom, price of release."[22] It and its cognate verb, *lytrō*, translate the Hebrew *g'l*, "redeem" and *pdy*, "ransom." I noted that this was an obviously sacrificial word that was used to break out of a sacrificial worldview.

Some studies since my book was published have added nuances to my understanding but without changing my interpretation. For example, Swartley notes Sam Williams's explication of the martyr theology in 2 and 4 Maccabees. Particularly interesting is what Eleazar says in 4 Maccabees 6:29: "Make my blood their purification and take my life as a ransom for theirs."[23] Clearly, the vocation of *martyr*, "witness," is fundamental to Mark, but it is not that Jesus is a substitute who removes the disciples from the same fate of suffering and death. Mark is quite clear about that (8:34-38; 10:38-45). The Son of man as "ransom" could, of course, be construed as God's agent (whatever the title) who frees or liberates spiritual prisoners from this age, the world of mimesis, for participation in the age to come, the new life of the kingdom of God. But even so, there is no question that lytron is rooted in the tradition and language of sacrifice.[24]

My recent research and thinking lead me to reaffirm what I said in *The Bible, Violence, and the Sacred*. Yet there is reason to nuance and extend what I presented earlier. The ransom, *lytron*, that which looses, unbinds, liberates, is derived from sacrificial usage, but this is not a substitution—a sacrifice standing-in-stead-of—of one for all that God imposes on humans, who must in turn render the ransom to God to satisfy the divine command or to appease divine wrath. Of course, from the standpoint of "world," i.e., ordinary mimesis, it *is* sacrifice, as are not only the offering of victims in ritual, but all executions also. But from the standpoint *sub specie Dei*, or the kingdom of God, it is God's free offering of release to human beings through Jesus as the divine son, Son of God, Son of man—the king who rules through serving. The ordinary world of mimesis is exposed for what it is through the suffering, death, and resurrection of the divine son.

"A nonviolent deity . . . can only signal his existence to mankind by having himself driven out by violence—by demonstrating that he is not able to dwell in the Kingdom of Violence." [25]

"[T]he Word that may be affirmed as absolutely true never speaks except from the position of the victim in the process of being expelled."[26]

GOSPEL TRANSFORMATIONS

This revising of sacrificial language is a gospel transformation of the meaning of kingship and sacrifice. It renders the "king" as no longer the supreme differentiator through violence, whether the violence of sacrifice, victory in war, or power over the people. Rather, he now is the differentiator through servanthood, through giving oneself rather than sacrificing—or letting the others be sacrificed—in war and ritual. The "king" is no longer the transgressor who brings misfortune on his subjects because of his hubris, but the suffering servant who for the sake of many endures the effects of the scapegoat mechanism that stems from the generative source of transgression, which is originary violence. The spell of ordinary mimesis is broken.

I do not wish to imply, however, that there is no continuity in the movement from the ancient Israelite traditions of kingship and sacrifice to Jesus and the early Christian traditions. The critique of sacrifice already present in 1 Samuel, as indicated in this essay, and the exposure of the mimetic process in the story of David's reign in 2 Samuel[27] are among the sources for indicating that the gospel transformations of kingship and sacrifice should be understood in a dialectic of continuity and discontinuity in the dynamic of ancient Jewish history.

Especially important are the great prophets who called the kings to be subjects to the God properly known only if the cause of the poor and needy is taken up (Jer. 22:16, cf. Ps. 72:1-4). Above all, the prophetic figure of the servant who suffers for many (Isa. 53:12) links the Hebrew Bible and the New Testament Gospels. The revelation of the Servant of the Lord is already present in the Isaiah text. The difference between the Isaiah Servant and Jesus as the Servant is the radical character of the disclosure associated with a known historical figure to whom the gospel texts witness in a sustained way. The Gospels' accounts gather up the full panoply of Israelite traditions and illuminate them through this one person, Jesus the crucified and risen one.

Although the synoptic Gospels, particularly Matthew and Mark, draw on apocalyptic language[28] and occasionally use sacrificial terms, they are remarkably free of the language of the sacrificial tradition. If Luke, like Matthew, drew freely on Mark for narrative structure and content, then it seems likely that he recognized the inadequacy of a sacrificial word like *lytron* and so dropped it. In the Lucan parallel to Mark 10:45, Jesus describes himself as a servant, and, as such, a model for the disciples. But there is nothing about giving his life as a ransom (Luke 22:24-27; cf. Matt 20:20-28).

As for sacrifice as service, Paul catches the transformative sense in Romans 12:1-2, where he appeals to the Romans to "present your bodies as a living sacrifice (*thysian zōsan*). . . . " *Thysia* is now not the victim who must be eliminated, expelled, or killed, but the person who makes his or her life an ongoing offering to God through Christ. This could, of course, entail suffering and death, but suffering and death are not the object. *Life* is the object.

My reading of the New Testament, to this point, leads me to the conclusion that in most of the instances where clear, heavily freighted sacrificial language is used, the sacrificial meaning is transformed.[29] This consistency could only be so because the New Testament has a real transformative center, the innocent victim, Son of man, Son of God, whose actuality cannot be swallowed up either in historicism or intertextuality.

ETHICS AND PRAXIS

In intellectual culture there is a powerful stream of thought that attacks all models of authority, and this means that Christianity and the Bible are the primary objects of intellectual hostility. It has even swept into religious and theological studies. It is an irony of history that the very source that first disclosed the viewpoint and plight of the victim is pilloried in the name of various forms of criticism that have fallen prey to an attachment to all viewpoints, persons, and positions that are "other" than or "different" from the dominant Western ones. I speak here of the antagonism toward patriarchy, hierarchy, racism, one-dimensional language, and so forth. My code word for this ideology is "multiculturalism." (Another code term is "political correctness," but I have never encountered a person who avows it, whereas multiculturalism is often used as a positive descriptive term.)

However, it is in the Western world that the affirmation of "otherness," especially as known through the victim, has emerged. And its roots sink deeply into the Bible as transmitted in the Jewish and Christian traditions. From the stories of Cain and Abel, Joseph, and the Israelites in Egypt, from the prophets and Job, and from the witness to Jesus in the New Testament Gospels, the standpoint of the victim is our unique and chief biblical inheritance. It can be appropriated creatively and ethically only if the *inner dynamic* of the biblical texts and traditions is understood and appreciated. The Bible is the first and main source for women's rights, racial justice, and any kind of moral transformation. The Bible is also the only creative basis for interrogating the tradition and the biblical texts. Why sell this birthright for a stew of multiculturalism?

So it is now of supreme importance for Jews, Christians, and all who are in any sense religious humanists, not to be caught up in the mimetic rivalry of critics seeking to mystify their practices or control their students or audiences, by sacrificially subverting whatever remaining models of authority there may be in their deconstructed world. The reference to a real victim and a real disclosure of the God of victims through the victims, the "least" in whom the divine reality is manifest, is indispensable to faith, understanding, and practice.

The paradigm pericope, Mark 10:35-45, is crucial because it witnesses to the Servant Son of man as the transformative center of the movement of faith and theology into ethics and practice. It witnesses also to the movement of ethics and practice into belief and understanding.[30]

Tony Bartlett, a doctoral candidate at Syracuse University, has nicely described this witness as *interruptive praxis* because it interrupts violent reciprocity. Eschewing "disruption" and "eruption" as words that convey an extreme sense of violent breaking, he opts for *interruption* as connoting a breaking without necessarily intending to do away with the prior reality.

Interruptive praxis interrupts guilt (it is not necessary to blame or scapegoat anyone, including oneself), the process of victimage (the weak or wounded are not to be turned into scapegoats), and personal mimetic conflict (individual mimetic rivalry is interrupted by the gift of new power, a new potential).[31] Jesus is the king who neither confirms nor overturns the sacrificial system but rather exposes and interrupts it. The meanings of kingship and sacrifice are transformed: kingship becomes servanthood and sacrifice becomes service.

NOTES

1. René Girard, *Quand ces choses commenceront. Entretiens avec Michel Treguer* (Paris: Arléa, 1994), 189-95. See also *The Girard Reader*, ed. James G. Williams (New York: Crossroad Herder, 1996), 283-288.

2. Simon Simonse has analyzed the scapegoat mechanism operative in sacral kingship among peoples of southeastern Sudan. He treats both ritually simulated regicide and actual incidents of regicide [*Kings of Disaster: Dualism, Centralism, and the Scapegoat King in Southeastern Sudan.* Studies in Human Society 5 (Leiden: E. J. Brill), 354-73.] The instance of the latter that he reports in detail is the lynching of the queen of the Pari.

3. James George Frazer's material in *The Golden Bough* is replete with instances of ritual regicide and the scapegoating of monarchs (*The New Golden Bough. A New Abridgement*, ed. with notes by T. H. Gaster [1890; reprint, Garden City, N.J.: Doubleday, 1961].

4. Girard calls Abel's animal sacrifice in Genesis 4 a "trompe-violence," an act to deceive violence; see *Violence and the Sacred*, trans. P. Gregory (Baltimore: Johns Hopkins, 1977), 14, and *Violence et le Sacré* (Paris: Grasset, 1972), 4. However, the English translation renders "violence outlet."

5. James G. Williams, "History-Writing as Protest: Kingship and the Beginning of Historical Narrative," *Contagion: Journal of Violence, Mimesis, and Culture* (1994), 91-110.

6. James G. Williams, "The Prophetic 'Father': A Brief Explanation of the 'Sons of the Prophets,'" *Journal of Biblical Literature* 85 (1966), 344-48.

7. P. Kyle McCarter Jr., *1 Samuel: A New Translation with Introduction, Notes and Commentary* (Anchor Bible 8; Garden City: Doubleday, 1994), 196; see survey in V. Philip Long, *The Reign and Rejection of King Saul* (SBL Dissertation Series 118; Atlanta: Scholars Press, 1989), 215-8. David Gunn identifies Saul as a scapegoat and so in some respects comparable to the tragic hero-king, and Oedipus is one of his examples. He does not, however, connect the taking of Saul by lot to Saul as "pawn" or "scapegoat" (David Gunn, *The Fate of King Saul* (JSOT Supplement Series 14; Sheffield: JSOT Press, 1980), 63, 128.

8. For valuable perspectives on the sacred, I recommend particularly Emile Durkheim, *The Elementary Forms of the Religious Life*, trans. J. W. Swain (1915; reprint New York: The Free Press, 1965), whose thesis concerning the relation of the social order to the sacred must be considered in any adequate sociology of religion; Sigmund Freud, *Totem and Taboo*, trans. James Strachey (1913; reprint New York and London: W. W. Norton & Co., 1950), ch. 2, who cites much interesting material to support his position on taboo and emotional ambivalence; and Mary Douglas, *Purity and Danger* (New York and London: Routledge, 1966), who presents a case that the "unclean" ("dirt" as "matter out of place") is part of the symbolic order of the sacred.

9. Girard, *Job: The Victim of His People*, trans. Y. Freccero (Stanford: Stanford University Press, 1987), ch. 14.

10. Jeroboam fled to Egypt when Solomon sought his life (1 Kings 11:40), and after Solomon's death returned to lead the northern tribes in their secession from the Davidic dynasty (1 Kings 12:2, 20). There may be the implication of Egyptian complicity in his revolt.

11. Hans J. L. Jensen, "The Fall of the King," *Scandinavian Journal of the Old Testament* 1 (1991), 121-47.

12. Ibid., 131.

13. Willard M. Swartley, *Israel's Scripture Traditions and the Synoptic Gospels: Story Shaping Story* (Peabody: Hendrickson, 1994).

14. Ibid., 207.

15. Ibid., 208.

16. Ibid., 213, emphasis mine.

17. Ibid., 215.

18. Ibid., 109-11; see also 146.

19. Ibid., 114.

20. René Girard, *A Theater of Envy: William Shakespeare* (New York and Oxford: Oxford University Press, 1991), esp. chs. 20-26 and 30.

21. It is also worth noting that according to 2 Maccabees 2:1-12, when the Babylonians destroyed the temple and took the Jews into captivity, Jeremiah commanded that the Torah, the tabernacle, and the ark be hidden in a mountain. Kiley refers to an amplification of this in the Lives of the Prophets 2:15: in the resurrection the ark will be resurrected first and come out of the rock; see Mark Kiley, "Marcan Ark Typology and the Debate over Jesus' Trip(s) to Jerusalem," in *Chronos. Kairos. Christos II: Essays in Honor of Ray Summers,* ed. Jerry Vardaman (Winona Lake: Eisenbrauns, 1998), 203-10.

22. James G. Williams, *The Bible, Violence, and the Sacred* (San Francisco: Harper Collins, 1991), 223-24, 230-31.

23. Quoted in Swartley, 114, n.55.

24. Swartley raises the question whether *anti*, in *lytrōn anti pollōn*, expresses its root meaning, "face to face," rather than "instead" or "for." In this case the meaning of the phrase would be "ransom before [in front of as representative] many." Jesus would thus be affirmed as representative head rather than as substitute bringing about atonement. Logically, however, the distinction between substitute and representative head is questionable. A representative, one who "makes present again" the symbolic order of the community, is a substitute, one who "stands under" or "stands in the stead of" the others. On the other hand, if the distinction is between someone who pays the price of release one time, without further action on the part of the beneficiaries, and someone who pays the price and also continues to lead and inspire those who are beneficiaries, I think the distinction is valid.

25. Girard, *Things Hidden Since the Foundation of the World,* trans. S. Bann and M. Metteer (Stanford: Stanford University Press, 1987), 219; originally published as *Des choses cachées depuis la fondation du monde* (Paris: Grasset) [my trans. of 1978].

26. Girard, *Things Hidden* (1987), 435 [my trans. of 1978].

27. See Hans Jensen, "Desire, Rivalry, and Collective Violence in the 'Succession Narrative," *Journal for the Study of the Old Testament* 55 (1992): 39-59.

28. It is interesting, indeed striking, that the apocalypse in Mark 13 and parallels does not once say that God is causing the tribulations and distress. The only overt mention of divine intervention is Mark 13:20/Matt 14:22, about foreshortening the days of tribulation for the sake of the elect. Therefore, even though Girard's comments on the gospels are not supported by the usual warrants of contemporary gospel criticism, I think one must give heed to his insight that "Jesus does not credit God with violence" (1987b: 188). The context of this statement is a discussion of the parable of the wicked tenants in Matthew 21.

29. For example, in Romans 3:24-25, the sacrificial offering is given by

God and is put forward (*protithēmi*) as a public display, i.e., the distinction between sacred space and profane space is broken down. Furthermore, the *hilastērion*, Hebrew *kapporet*, is not a sacrifice per se but the place where atonement is brought about (see Lev 16:2, 13-15). I think therefore that there is something to be said for the argument that Paul is speaking of Christ as the place or position from which and in which new life is given. This would fit his message of justification or being "rightwised." Some very similar factors are at work in Ephesians 2:11-21 and Colossians 1:13-20, to cite two other examples. The blood (life) of Christ is divinely offered and breaks down old sacred differentiations. As for the Apocalypse, there is no doubt it poses difficult interpretive questions to a Christology centered in the gospels. Could it, however, be construed as expressing the full unleashing of the violence of the sacred when the old protections of the sacred are dissolved and tyrants seek to impose their will by violence?

30. This transformation is essentially the same as the Gospel of Matthew's version of it, which I have termed "ethical mysticism." See James G. Williams, "Paraenesis, Excess, and Ethics: Matthew's Rhetoric in the Sermon on the Mount," *Semeia* 50 (1990), 163-87, esp. 172-3.

31. Anthony Bartlett, "Blood and Peace," unpublished paper on sacrifice and atonement written for an independent study course, Syracuse University, Spring, 1994. Bartlett's doctoral dissertation "Cross Purposes: The Violent Grammar of Christian Atonement" (Syracuse University, 1999), examines biblical and classical Christian sources in searching for a better way to ground and articulate a nonviolent doctrine of atonement. The thesis is influenced by Girard's mimetic scapegoat theory, but it also offers a critique of it.

CHAPTER TEN

"al lo-chamas asah (*although he had done no violence*)": René Girard and the Innocent Victim

Sandor Goodhart

THIS ESSAY HAS THREE PARTS. In the first, I address the concern Willard Swartley expressed when he invited me to participate in the conference from which this material emerged: "I know that one of the liabilities in biblical scholarship appropriating Girard's work is a potential scapegoating effect of Christians toward Jews. I hope this can be resisted or, if not, that it can be explained as an inherent weakness of his contribution."

In the second, I turn to an examination of Second Isaiah (52:13–53:12) in which I suggest some of the fundamental similarities of Jewish Scripture to Christian Scripture and examine the implications of such similarities—one of which is that we need to read more closely each other's texts.

In the third, and in this spirit of such shared close reading, I turn to a short Talmudic text—from the tractate *Shabbath*—as an example of writing from which such comparisons may begin to be drawn.

René Girard's thinking seems at first glance an ideal focus for a discussion of "peacemaking theology and praxis," the phrase Willard Swartley used when first approaching me for this material. The difference between peace now and violence just a moment ago is at the origin of René Girard's account of the primitive religious community, which is to say, in his view, of all cultural difference. Such a distinction reflects par excellence the successful conclusion to a "sacrificial crisis" in which the distinction between the sacred and violence is lost and in which an end to conflict issues from the effective scapegoating or collective substitution and removal of one member of the community who has come to serve as a surrogate victim for each member in his or her Hobbesian war against all the other participants in the community.

In the modern world, in which we have increasingly lost the capacity to guarantee that sacrificial behavior will not become itself just one more form of violence (and in which, we have to assume in Girardian theory, that other mechanisms are at work to insure cultural survival), the concern for peace and peacemaking becomes even more acute. Sacrificial substitution comes to be replaced by other methods of the management of violence—such as by good deeds, prayer, and reading in the Jewish tradition; by the imitation of positive models in the Christian tradition (for example, the *imitatio dei*); or by the rejection of desire itself in Buddhist and other Eastern traditions.

Nevertheless, it remains the case that in all these traditions, the establishment of peace is primary. Girard's reading of the Christian Gospels as the explication of mimetic and sacrificial violence, and the proposal of a way out of that violence, specifies at once the nature of that disease, its treatment, and the prognosis if the treatment is not adopted.

Such Girardian thinking regarding peacemaking may, I contend, indeed prove decisive for us in responding to the crisis in which we find ourselves in the contemporary setting—but only if we overcome certain obstacles that have recently been placed in our path before its understanding. I refer, of course, to the reputed anti-Semitism of Girard's ideas, his alleged scapegoating of Judaism and/or the Jews, and its ironic correspondence with his use of the idea of the *skandalon*. These obstacles seem from my vantage point to act out the very ideas concerning obstacles and stumbling that Girard is at such pains to expose.

The misreading of Girard's work in this fashion is certainly not without precedent. In literary criticism, for example, where Girard was first noticed for his book on the novel, and in particular for exposing mimetic desire in the work of Cervantes, Stendhal, Flaubert, Proust, and Dostoyevsky, he was accused of promoting mimetic desire.[1] Some critics thought that because he wrote about the romantic lie—by which the great novelists of our European tradition deflected their own appropriation of models for their desire onto myths of external need or internal inspiration—he endorsed it. Similarly in the 1970s, when his work on anthropology appeared, and especially his explanation of the identification of the sacred with violence and of the mechanism of the sacrificial expulsion, he was accused by some critics of promoting such sacrificial expulsion—as if Girard were a closet defender of the Nazi Holocaust against the Jews.[2]

No amount of explanation could forestall such eccentric accounts, although they came for the most part from outsiders to his thought and were largely dismissed by those who worked with Girard (or read him seriously), they did not constitute the majority opinion among critics—which was relatively positive. But with the advent of his work on Christianity, a new type of misunderstanding appeared that could endanger the reception of his work. Some critics continued to misread his work as endorsements of the very materials he was exposing. But now those same misunderstandings began to appear from the inside, among individuals who liked his work and thought they were praising it for his sacrificial views.

Suddenly some readers were saying, for example, not only that René Girard's account of the sacrificial dynamics at work between historical Christianity and Judaism was an endorsement of those dynamics from a Christian perspective, but that such an endorsement was a good thing. Moreover, since Girard declared himself publicly a believing Christian, and since theological anti-Semitism has long been a part of discussion of Jewish-Christian relations, Girard's personal declaration seemed to some a confirmation of those views.

It is this new level of misunderstanding that seems to me to occasion the charges of anti-Semitism about which we spoke earlier ("a potential scapegoating effect of Christians toward Jews" was how Professor Swartley put it). These are charges brought, I suggest, not only by those who oppose his work but by those who would appropriate it as a platform for promoting a sacrificial attack on Christianity's perceived enemies.[3]

Is René Girard's thought anti-Semitic? As early as the 1970s Girard had answered this question—as he did, for example, in "Les Malédictions contre les pharisiens et la révélation évangélique."[4] "You say," Jesus tells the scribes and the Pharisees, according to Girard's understanding, that had you been there (at the stoning of the prophets) you would not have stoned them. But don't you see that in saying as much, in making a sacred distinction between yourselves and those who stoned the prophets, you do the same thing as they do? You stone the prophets once again, and you do so in the very act of denouncing such behavior. Moreover, you are going to do the same to me for telling you this truth of your own desires. And those who come after you will likewise repeat the sacrificial process once again, doing to you what you do to the prophets, what is more, doing so in my name no less, calling themselves "Christians" and calling you "Jews."

The record of historical Christianity as a sacrificial religion, as a triumphalist and supersessionist declaration of the superiority of the last revelation (in which its proponents declare themselves participants) is also the history—whatever its success in promoting the Jewish law of anti-idolatry—of violence.

What is important, in other words, is not the attack on the other but the ownership of our own violence. It is to show us our own violence and where that violence is leading that in Girard's view Jesus taught. When Vatican II was issued, and a statement to the effect that the Jews are no longer to be considered guilty of having killed Jesus was circulated, Girard had a similar response. What the church should have said, he suggested, is not that the Jews are no longer considered guilty of killing Jesus (Who then is guilty? Everyone is now declared innocent!), but that we should have stated that we Christians are just as guilty as we have always accused the Jews of being.

In recent texts, Girard has repeated this view even more trenchantly. Jesus, he emphasizes, condemns sacrificial violence from the outset—from the murder of Abel by Cain as Torah presents it. The Jews are no more responsible for violence than are the pagans or the Christians themselves. And the reason for this claim is that Jesus speaks in the tradition of the Hebrew prophets. In the following text, for example, taken from his interviews with Michel Treguer, Girard writes:

> Les Évangiles affirment donc la culpabilité des juifs comme des païens. Et leurs seuls prédécesseurs dans cette affirmation, ce sont les livres prophétiques juifs qui racontent souvent les violences subie par les prophètes. C'est bien pourquoi Jésus dit qu'il va mourir "comme les prophètes avant lui." Il suffit de lire le récit de la mort du "Serviteur souffrant" dans le Second Isaïe, ou celui des souffrances de Job, ou de celles de Jérémie, ou de l'aventure de Jonas, ou l'histoire de Joseph, pour voir que les bouc émissaires justifiés sont déjà dans l'Ancien Testament."
>
> Une fois qu'on a accepté le christianisme, la seule manière d'écarter la Révélation et de ne pas voir qu'elle met toutes les cultures humaines en cause, tous les êtres humains sans exception, c'est de s'en prendre aux juifs. C'est ce que les chrétiens n'ont pas cesse de faire depuis qu'ils se sont séparés des juifs. Ils doivent donc reconnaître leurs torts qui sont très grands. L'anti-sémitisme

chrétien n'est pas un exemple parmis d'autres de religio-centrisme ou d'ethnocentrism: c'est une defaillance par rapport à la Révélation.[5]

[The Gospels thus affirm the culpability of the Jews as of the pagans. And their only predecessors in this affirmation are the books of the Jewish prophets which often recount the violence undergone by the prophets. That is really why Jesus says that he is going to die "like the prophets before him." It is sufficient to read the narrative of the death of the Suffering Servant in Second Isaiah, or that of the sufferings of Job, or those of Jeremiah, or the fortunes of Jonah, or the history of Joseph, to see that justified scapegoats are already in the Old Testament.

As soon as one has accepted Christianity, the only manner of avoiding Revelation and of not seeing that it puts all human cultures at cause, all human beings without exception, is to blame the Jews. This is what Christians have not ceased to do since they separated from the Jews. They must therefore recognize their wrongs which are very great. Christian anti-Semitism is not one example among others of religio-centrism or ethnocentrism: it is a failing with relation to Revelation.][6]

The criticism Jesus makes is an internal Jewish affair. It is what Isaiah says to his audience, what Jeremiah says, what we learn in the Book of Job, the story of Joseph, and elsewhere in Torah. It is with the tradition of prophetic criticism that Jesus speaks, not as a repudiation of Judaism nor of "the Jews"—of which he is one. As a prophet, Jesus condemns sacrificial violence wherever it comes up, just as the prophets and Judaism as a whole condemn sacrificial violence wherever it crops up.

But to misunderstand Jesus as doing that, to think that Jesus is condemning Judaism or Jews or Israel as violence, is not just any misunderstanding, not just one among other possibilities, Girard tells us. It is the misunderstanding *par excellence*. It is to miss the very point Jesus is making, the point that is to say, of Christian revelation itself. The only way out of this particular misunderstanding—of believing that Judaism is violence—is to become Christian, to adopt the revelation one has evaded by such strategies.

Far from it being the case for Girard, in other words, that to be a Christian one must reject being Jewish, Girard's position is in fact the opposite. From a Girardian perspective, to be a Christian is to recognize the ways in which one has always already been Jewish, and to own the specifically Jewish Toradic critique of sacrificial violence as one's own in order that violence be rejected and peace established.

If we wish to claim, however (as I do), that the Christian revelation for Girard is fully part of the Jewish soil in which it is embedded, and that what Girard is discovering in Christianity is its Jewish filigree—the critique of sacrificial violence from which Judaism started and which has constituted its history from the prophets to the rabbis—then we need to ask about the differences between them. Is Christianity to be regarded from a Girardian perspective as simply an extension of Jewish studies? Or is there rather a specific Christian revelation that marks it as different from Judaism? Girard often speaks of the revelation of the innocent victim as the distinguishing feature of Christianity. In turning to part two of my comments, I take up this theme.

The Innocent Victim in Isaiah 52:13–53:12
Similarity of Jewish and Christian Texts

René Girard's theory of the uniqueness of Christianity is based on his theory of the innocent victim. Jesus of Nazareth is not in his view simply another figure like the hero of Greek tragedy, like Oedipus, for example, who becomes an enemy twin of everyone. Jesus does nothing violent and yet is willing to die to reveal the arbitrariness of scapegoat violence, the lack of efficacy of the sacrificial expulsion about which the Hebrew prophets have been speaking. This is a process which may once have galvanized primitive culture but which has become in the modern context little short of murder.

But careful examination of Isaiah 52–53 reveals that though it appears some six hundred years before texts of the Christian gospel appear, it is entirely conversant with the idea of the innocent victim. There is little that Girard says about the innocent victim that is missing from Isaiah 52–53. Thus I suggest we need to reexamine Girard's claim that the gospel is unique in this particular fashion. Here is the passage in the old standard JPS 1917 translation.[7]

> Behold, My servant shall prosper,
> He shall be exalted and lifted up, and shall be very high.
> According as many were appalled at thee—
> So marred was his visage unlike that of a man,
> And his form unlike that of the sons of men—
> So shall he startle many nations,
> Kings shall shut their mouths because of him;
> For that which had not been told them they shall see,
> And that which they had not heard they shall perceive.

'Who would have believed our report?
And to whom hath the arm of the Lord been revealed?
For he shot up right forth as a sapling,
And as a root out of a dry ground;
He had no form nor comeliness that we should look on him,
Nor beauty that we should delight in him.
He was despised, and forsaken of men,
A man of pains, and acquainted with disease,
And as one from whom men hide their face;
He was despised, and we esteemed him not.
Surely our diseases he did bear, and our pains he carried;
Whereas we did esteem him stricken,
Smitten of God, and afflicted.
But he was wounded because of our transgressions,
He was crushed because of our iniquities:
The chastisement of our welfare was on him,
And with his stripes we were healed.
All we like sheep did go astray,
We turned every one to his own way;
And the Lord hath made to light upon him
The iniquity of us all.
He was oppressed, though he humbled himself
And opened not his mouth;
As a lamb that is led to the slaughter
And as a sheep that before her shearers is dumb;
Yea, he opened not his mouth.
By oppression and judgment he was taken away,
And with his generation who did reason?
For he was cut off out of the land of the living,
For the transgression of my people to whom the stroke was due.
And they made his grave with the wicked,
And with the rich his tomb;
Although he had done no violence,
Neither was there any deceit in his mouth.'

Yet it pleased the Lord to crush him by disease;
To see if his soul would offer itself in restitution,
That he might see his seed, prolong his days,
And that the purpose of the Lord might prosper by his hand:
Of the travail of his soul he shall see to the full, even My servant,
Who by his knowledge did justify the Righteous One to the many,
And their iniquities he did bear.
Therefore will I divide him a portion among the great,
And he shall divide the spoil with the mighty;
Because he bared his soul unto death,

And was numbered with the transgressors;
Yet he bore the sin of many,
And made intercession for the transgressors.

The passage has, of course, sustained a long tradition of commentary in both the Hebraic and Christian traditions. There is no place in the present context to engage all of the issues raised.[8] The passage is part of the sequence of Isaiah from chapters 40 to 55 commonly associated with the "Second" school of prophetic writers whose theme is taken to be comfort after the destruction of the temple and the Babylonian exile (and thus the appellation "Second" or "Deutero").[9] It is the fourth and last of the so-called songs of the Suffering Servant of the Lord. And the central concern of interpretation in both traditions has been the identity of the subject of this song.

In the Jewish tradition the servant is customarily identified with Israel. Meanwhile in the Christian typological tradition the servant is commonly regarded as a prefiguration of Jesus himself. Neither tradition, however, has proved entirely satisfactory to its adherents. Our own concern in this present context is less to rekindle this old debate than to compare the content of the passage—whoever the servant is understood to be—with the content René Girard has attributed to the Christian reading of the sacrificial mechanism. This is a comparison which may in turn then shed light on other significant interpretative matters.

The correspondence between the two is extraordinary. In the first place, the servant is described as an outsider. Thus, in 52:14-15,

Many were appalled at thee—
So marred was his visage unlike that of a man,
And his form unlike that of the sons of men—
So shall he startle many nations

And then again, at the outset of the long middle sequence (53:3),

He had no form nor comeliness that we should look upon him,
Nor beauty that we should delight in him.
He was despised, and forsaken of men,
A man of pains, and acquainted with disease,
And as one from whom men hide their face.

He was "despised" and "forsaken" by others, and the narrator includes himself in the group that took this approach to him ("we esteemed him not"). His face was disfigured along with his body, so much so that people were startled by the disfiguration. He had no beauty or attractiveness to recommend him, and people assumed these blandishments were the product of long suffering and disease.

But the speaker is not satisfied with such an account and will examine in an extraordinary manner the origins of such attributions. Whatever the physical causes of his disfigurement, and whatever others have done to him, we ourselves are not free from implication in his pains. The pains he bears and the disease he carries are the product at least in part of our own behavior toward him—although we commonly deny responsibility for that behavior. It is not simply that he was wounded by another because of what we did. He was wounded by us. And what we did was precisely what wounded him. We blamed him for our transgressive behavior and that constituted his wound.

> Surely our diseases he did bear, and our pains he carried;
> Whereas we did esteem him stricken,
> Smitten of God, and afflicted.
> But he was wounded because of our transgressions,
> He was crushed because of our iniquities:
> The chastisement of our welfare was on him,

Moreover, by his removal from the community, by his sacrifice or expulsion, we told ourselves that our afflictions were ended.

> And with his stripes we were healed.

Each of us continued to engage in our own radical individualism, each turning to his or her own way. And the Lord, who foresees all, caused it to turn out that our iniquity has fallen on him.

> All we like sheep did go astray,
> We turned every one to his own way;
> And the Lord hath made to light upon him
> The iniquity of us all.

Did he complain? Did he object to our treatment of him?

> He was oppressed, though he humbled himself
> And opened not his mouth;
> As a lamb that is led to the slaughter
> And as a sheep that before her shearers is dumb;
> Yea, he opened not his mouth.
> By oppression and judgment he was taken away,
> And with his generation who did reason?

We killed him for what we decided he did to us. Instead of blaming ourselves—where the blame should have been lodged—we blamed him. We called him wicked and buried him with those we considered our enemies—although he was innocent of any wrongdoing and did not protest our behavior toward him. He went to his grave like a lamb to the slaughter.

> For he was cut off out of the land of the living,
> For the transgression of my people to whom the stroke was due.
> And they made his grave with the wicked,
> And with the rich his tomb;
> Although he had done no violence,
> Neither was there any deceit in his mouth.

And what excuse did we offer when we took such action? Did we own what we did to him after we did it? "We did esteem him stricken, / Smitten of God." We told ourselves that "it pleased the Lord to crush him with disease; / To see if his soul would offer itself in restitution, [in order] That he might see his seed, prolong his days, / And that the purpose of the Lord might prosper by his hand."

We told ourselves, in other words, that the Lord did it, perhaps to test him, as God did Abraham, to see whether an exchange was possible. He would get to see his children, we told ourselves. His days would be long. He could make restitution for the wrongdoing of others.

What did he do when we took this action against him? He bore the violence willingly and proceeded to justify God in the act even though he was the victim of our iniquities and our transgressions. "By his knowledge did [he] justify the Righteous One to the many, / And their iniquities he did bear." He took the violence we launched against him and justified God and us in the very act of doing so. Even in the act of dying for what we did to him, he intervened on our behalf.

> He bared his soul unto death,
> And was numbered with the transgressors;
> Yet he bore the sin of many,
> And made intercession for the transgressors.

For all these things, then, the speaker concludes, I will honor him.

> Therefore will I divide him a portion among the great,
> And he shall divide the spoil with the mighty.

He revealed to us in this manner "the arm of the Lord." And although the report of this action is hard to believe ("Who would have believed our report?"), we have to believe that something extraordinary took place, and we have begun to see things that have not been perceived before.

> So shall he startle many nations,
> Kings shall shut their mouths because of him;
> For that which had not been told them they shall see,
> And that which they had not heard they shall perceive.

What element of René Girard's theory of sacrifice is missing from this description? The sacrificial expulsion, the violent removal of the victim who has done no violence, who is removed by (and for) what his persecutors did and by whose removal they are healed—all of it is there.

Indeed, elements appear in this text that are not part of Girard's theory. We learn that this this process seems to have been foreseen by the Lord who caused this to happen: that this servant was willing to be the intercessor on our behalf with God (and perhaps this is why the Lord caused it to take place); that the servant was given the opportunity to make restitution on our behalf; that we are much like sheep who have gone astray; that we buried him among those we considered our enemies; that the servant was willing to undergo this experience in order that the Lord might prosper; and so forth.

But these elements are precisely those that Girard has also left out of his account of the Christian text. Far from undermining the correspondence between the two texts, their presence serves to buttress it. If there are elements that remain mythic in Isaiah 52–53 (in the way that Girard speaks of "myth"), they are the same elements that remain mythic in the gospel. And there may be ways of reading these elements that render them less mythic. Could the lines in 53:6 ("And the Lord hath made to light on him / The iniquity of us all") and in 53:10 ("Yet it pleased the Lord to crush him with disease") reflect less the speech of the narrator than examples of the ways in which "we did esteem him stricken, / Smitten of God, and afflicted"—though in fact "He was crushed because of *our* iniquities" (italics added)?

However, whether or not Isaiah 52–53 matches the gospel in all particulars, clearly it contains all Girard needs to uncover the scapegoat mechanism. There is nothing Girard says about the innocent victim in Christianity, it would appear, that is not already fully present in Isaiah 52–53, some six hundred years earlier. So we need to ask, What are the ramifications of this correspondence for Girard's claim regarding the uniqueness of the Christian gospel in this regard? We seem to be left with a limited number of possibilities, none entirely satisfactory. I will enumerate them, then discuss them in more detail.

The first is that Christianity really *is* unique—as both Girard and Christians say it is—but its uniqueness is not based on the disclosure of the innocent victim before his persecutors as Girard claims (which is in fact already fully a Jewish idea). Rather, the gospel's uniqueness is based on some other consideration still to be articulated—perhaps, for example, the Christian revelation itself. One could imagine acknowledging the Christian revelation of Jesus as the son of God who triumphs over death while continuing to credit the deconstruction of the sacrificial mechanism and the like as entirely coincident with Jewish understanding, an understanding that appears briefly in Isaiah 52–53 and that Christianity considerably expands. The advantage of this reading is that it maintains the revelatory status of the Christian experience, although it does so at the expense of the Girardian understanding of the centrality of the disclosure of the sacrificial mechanism.

The second possibility is that Christianity is *not* unique (although Girard and Christians say it is). Christianity is only an "acting out" of Judaism, so to speak, an episode in the history of the religion which preceded it and of which it remains—in all of its themes and content (and however much it may deny that affiliation)—an unwitting or unwilling extension. This view has the advantage of sustaining a thoroughgoing continuity between the two experiences but at the expense of the distinctive revelatory status of the second.

The third possibility for understanding the connection between Isaiah 52–53 and the Christian gospel is the explanation that Christianity really *is* unique (as both Girard and Christians say), and that such uniqueness *is* rooted in the understanding of the innocent victim (as Girard claims), but that the correspondence between the two—between the innocent victim as presented in Isaiah and the innocent victim as presented in the gospel—is not complete, although precisely the ways in which these texts differ has yet to be elaborated.

Obviously there are problems with each potential interpretation. Although we want to keep the question open, it seems valuable to enumerate the difficulties, if only better to imagine alternatives.

The problem with the first proposal—that Christianity is unique but the deconstruction of sacrifice not central—is that the Girardian explanation is convincing. Although Christians may continue to debate the matter, from a Jewish perspective there is no obstacle to regarding the explanation that Girard offers as entirely compelling, both as an account of primitive culture and as the distinguishing critical feature of the gospel revelation.

The deconstruction of the sacrificial is not new. It is already thoroughly available in Jewish texts. But it has less centrality there than the law of anti-idolatry. Christianity takes up the critique of sacrifice and centralizes it in a way to which Jews and Christians alike, it could well be argued, have failed to pay sufficient attention. A proposal, therefore, which excludes Girard's explanation from a central place in the Christian text seems insufficient.

But the second proposal—that Christianity is simply an episode in the history of Judaism—must similarly be rejected. Whether or not such a claim is acceptable from a Jewish point of view, it is certainly not so from a Christian perspective. And even from a Jewish perspective, we need to grant Christianity its own revelatory experience—just as we would Buddhism, Hinduism, Islam, or any other major world religion.[10]

This leaves us with the third possibility—that Christianity is unique and the Girardian view central but incomplete. This is the most interesting alternative, but even here there are difficulties. This view maintains the revelatory status of Christianity. It also maintains the linkage to Girard's theory. But it depends on a position that remains to be articulated. Precisely what the content of such a future understanding of the innocent victim in the Christian context may be is somewhat difficult to fathom.

Could it be, for example, an expansion of the manner in which Christianity takes up themes of invasion and abandonment in family life? Is it possible that Christianity introduces into the history of the anti-sacrificial what may be termed the "self-sacrificial," or, more precisely, the dynamics of self-formation or self-construction, dynamics that appear fundamental to both Judaism and Christianity (and along precisely the lines of the mimetic and the conflictual Girard has been developing)? Moreover, such dynamics may even be responsible for the appearance of the Christian within the history of Pharisaic Judaism, yet these dynamics are not yet articulated.[11]

Whatever the future direction of these discussions, however, some things are already apparent. The theory of the innocent victim is not new. It is an old Jewish theme. What Girard discovers in the Christian text—whatever else he discovers (which may be a great deal)—is its Jewish filigree. What is new is the focus that Christianity gives to it, the centrality with which the persecutory structure comes to dominate Jesus' life (and the lives of Christians afterwards), a structure which in the Jewish context is subsumed within the more general formulation of the anti-idolatrous.

But that change of focus may reflect the kind of midrashic or interpretative impulse that Judaism *would* recognize: namely, the delineation of the power of Toradic insight for a particular time and place. With its emphasis on mediated desire, violence, and the sacrificial scapegoat mechanism, Christianity in Girard's interpretation may well extend an analysis already present in Judaism to a new and vital context, to a family setting in which the phenomena of invasion and abandonment assume an importance not hitherto imagined within Jewish culture. If so, then it is on such a basis that we may at once regard Christianity within a larger Jewish perspective—an "episode in the history of the Judaic"—and sustain the historical specificity and revelatory impact that Christians have always felt to be endemic to their experience.

COMPARING EACH OTHER'S TEXTS: *SHABBATH* AS EXAMPLE

To gain further comparative insight between midrashic Judaism and early Christian understanding, I refer as example to tractate *Shabbath* in the Babylonian Talmud (30b-31c). This text concerns one of the famous episodes of the ongoing debate between the house of Hillel and the house of Shammai regarding the teaching of Torah to outsiders, a topic that is not without interest to a dialogue in which it is asked whether Judaism can open its inner portals to outsiders. Further, the anecdotal tale that Jesus of Nazareth was a disciple of the house of Hillel might be of interest here.

A heathen once approached a representative of the house of Shammai with the following request: Make me a proselyte on condition that you teach me Torah while I am standing on one foot. (The "house of Shammai" is taken to be the more orthodox school of religious practice, and the request of the would-be novitiate is understood to be the inquiry of an outsider who presumably has no understanding of Torah—as opposed to a child growing up in the community of that understanding). The heathen was in effect asking, Can you teach me Torah while I am standing on one foot? Can you teach me Torah in a way that I can commodify it, carry it around with me, the way one might be able to do with the knowledge or skill or wisdom one would get from one of the roaming Greek Sophists against whom Plato wrote? One can imagine the response of this orthodox teacher. He will not even consider the request of his visitor. He shoos him out of the house—"with the builder's cubit which was in his hand."

The would-be novitiate—not to be put off—then approaches a representative of the house of Hillel with the same request: Make me a proselyte on condition that you teach me Torah while I am standing on one foot. Hillel is taken as the representative of the more liberal school of ritual practice. Here he receives what appears to be a more positive response. Hillel will answer him. Moreover, Hillel will do so in terms of the request he has made. But here as well, in the response he receives from Hillel, is a commentary he perhaps did not expect.

> When he went before Hillel, he [Hillel] said to him, "What is hateful to you, do not to your neighbor: that is the whole Torah, while the rest is the commentary thereof; go and learn it." [31a]

Can we hear in this little exchange a lesson for our own dilemma? The similarity of Hillel's dictum to the formulation of Jesus' golden rule—"do unto others as you would have them do unto you" (which in fact also appears in this form in Torah)—is unmistakable. Can we learn from the difference in formulation? You think, Hillel says, that in approaching me with your request—that I teach you Torah while you are standing on one foot—that you are putting something over on me. What poses as a request is really a form of attack. Shammai recognized that attack immediately and would not play your game (and therefore ushered you out without engaging you about it). I recognized the same baiting strategy (and on this point, Shammai and I are in agreement). But it occurs to me that I can use where you are as a beginning, that I can stage your strategy against me before you, so to speak, as a way ironically of teaching you that the Torah—whose wisdom you say you seek—has never been any other.

In making your request of me (Hillel)—to teach you Torah while you are standing on one foot—you in fact retract the offer on which it is based in the act of extending it. If the wisdom of Torah is to be valuable, it will hardly be the kind of wisdom that could be commodified in such a way that it could be so offered. The Torah that I could teach you in such a fashion is not Torah. Moreover, your very asking of the question in that manner betrays an orientation that exceeds a request for knowledge, that slips into an attack. Why do you think I don't see what you are doing? Do you think we are that different? You would not want that kind of exclusionary behavior enacted against you. So why do you do it to me? On the other hand, I can take the tactics from which you do start and work with them. I can show you that such tactics are in fact the text's very subject matter, and that you've come to the right place after all.

Hillel reads the individual's extraordinary psychological insight. He sees that the would-be novitiate is projecting a self-defeating strategy, an impossible demand, on his interlocutor, perhaps because he has experienced the same betrayal himself in his own past and is now repeating that behavior against others—behavior hardly far removed from the text. What Hillel is suggesting is that instead of acting out that betrayal he might take stock of it, that he might own his own violence, even the violence that has been done to him and that he would now repeat.

Moreover, the questioner needs to grasp that the Torah he says he wants—and has dismissed—offers in fact the same teaching: that the words are insufficient by themselves (and could be replaced by others), and that to read them requires a teacher. What is needed, in other words, is a relationship that does not betray you, one that allows you to take stock of your own behavior in a way that both makes it clear to you and does not harm you. Perhaps this short Talmudic text—which offers the Jewish reader a way into Torah—teaches the same lesson, the presentation of what appears to be two options which are in fact the same option, one which concerns betrayals we have experienced and would foist on others.

Does this sequence not have a bearing on Jesus' golden rule in the texts of Matthew and Luke? And is it not more generally applicable to a history in which betrayal has been felt so keenly on both sides. This is a history in which Jews have felt fundamentally betrayed by Christians, who have arisen from within their ranks, so to speak, and defied their parental affiliation and parental progeniture. It is a history by the same token in which Christians have felt similarly betrayed, disapproved for efforts they thought eminently worthy of approval, entirely Jewish in their understanding, and as a result of which disapproval their resentment and anger have been kindled.

Does this history not sound like the life of Paul, even the life of Luther, and perhaps of others, if only we would view the context broadly enough? Are Adolf Hitler's speeches to the Reichstag at the end of the 1930s, in which he speaks repeatedly of the laughter he perceives among the Jews against him, not part of the same profound sense of betrayal and humiliation with consequences we now know too well? Humiliation and betrayal are powerful human motivators, perhaps the most powerful, as a writer like Dostoyevsky certainly knew. What if the history of sacrificial violence as it concerns Jewish-Christian relations is really the same history? What if the anti-Semitism we attach to René Girard's thought, either because we approve of it or because we wish to attack it, is but another version of the same dislocation?

Such reflections could render the distant and sometimes hostile relations between Judaism and Christianity something of a family quarrel. As in all families, there may be difficulties, even bloodshed. But considering Judaism and Christianity as part of a family—and not as a set of independent perspectives—we also open the potential for reconciliation and consequently for hope.

I suspect we are far from ready to embark on such a path. But that does not diminish the value of imagining it. The experience of each community may only be enriched by such fundamental speculation as each in turn highlights threads operating in the other in ways individually less visible. In that coming debate, the innocent victim as René Girard presents this figure at the heart of the Christian gospel, like the analysis of sacrificial violence on which it is based, will no doubt be one of the Jewish filigrees that continue to enliven the Christian text and render discussion of that text and its relation to Judaism especially valuable.

NOTES

1. René Girard, *Deceit, Desire, and the Novel*, trans. Yvonne Freccero (Baltimore: John Hopkins, 1965); originally published as *Mensonge romantique et vérité romanesque* (Paris: Grasset, 1961).

2. René Girard, *Violence and the Sacred*, trans. Patrick Gregory [French, 1972] (Baltimore: John Hopkins Press, 1977). See, for example, Hayden White's essay, "Ethnological Lie and Mythical Truth," *Diacritics* 8, no. 1 (1978): 2-9.

3. For an example of the kind of heated controversy to which discussion of Girard's work has given way, see Robert G. Hamerton-Kelly's *Sacred Violence: Paul's Hermeneutic of the Cross* (Philadelphia: Fortress Press, 1993) and articles edited by Ted Peters in *Dialog* 32, no. 4 (Fall 1993) under the title, "Paul and Luther: A Debate over Sacred Violence," 247-288, in which Hamerton-Kelly restates his view and is answered by Krister Stendahl, Hayim Goren Perelmuter, David Frederickson, René Girard, and Gerhard O. Forde. For another response by a Pauline scholar, see Daniel Boyarin's review of Hamerton-Kelly's book in his article, "The Subversion of the Jews: Moses's Veil and the Hermeneutics of Supersession, *Diacritics* 23, no. 2 (Summer 1993): 16-35, as well as his book, *A Radical Jew: Paul and the Politics of Identity* (Berkeley/Los Angeles/London: University of California Press, 1994).

4. See René Girard, *Bulletin du Centre Protestant d'Etudes* (Geneve, 1975), 5-29.

5. René Girard, *Quand Ces Choses Commenceront . . . Entretiens avec Michel Treguer* (Paris: Arléa,1994), 118-19.

6. My translation.

7. *The Holy Scriptures. A New Translation* (Philadelphia: Jewish Publication Society, 1917), 543-44.

8. For the Jewish tradition, see Rabbi A. J. Rosenberg, *Isaiah, vol. 2: A New English Translation* (New York: The Judaica Press, 1983). For the Christian tradition, see the Anchor Bible series volume, John McKenzie, *Second Isaiah* (New York: Doubleday and Company, Inc., 1979).

9. Cf. Isaiah 40.1-2.

10. Christian exegete Norbert Lohfink has written about the possibility of a double revelation from a Christian perspective. See Norbert Lohfink, *The Covenant Never Revoked: Biblical Reflections on Christian-Jewish Dialogue*, trans. John Scullion (New York: Paulist Press, 1991).

11. Michel Foucault seems to have been working on this problem at the moment of his death.

CHAPTER ELEVEN

Discipleship and Imitation of Jesus/ Suffering Servant: The Mimesis of New Creation

Willard M. Swartley

INTRODUCTION: PERSPECTIVE AND FOCUS

The Gospels and the New Testament do not preach a morality of spontaneous action. They do not claim that humans must get rid of imitation; they recommend imitating the sole model who never runs the danger—if we really imitate in the way that children imitate—of being transformed into a fascinating rival:

> He who says he abides in him ought to walk in the same way in which he walked (1 John 2, 6).

> On one side are the prisoners of violent imitation, which always leads to a dead end, and on the other are the adherents of non-violent imitation, who will meet with no obstacle.—René Girard, *Things Hidden*.[1]

In this statement Girard speaks of positive mimesis. But overall Girard says relatively little about this,[2] although at numerous points he speaks of good mimesis and occasionally commends Jesus as the good model.[3] Usually, Girard focuses simply on mimetic *desire*, which for him is desire that leads to rivalry. Thus, "Following Christ means giving up mimetic desire" (431). By this he means mimesis that is *generated by acquisitive desire*. But giving up either *mimesis* or *desire* is impossible. Rather, what is necessary is a double transformation: that by transcendent provision we are given an object for mimesis whose very nature and action does not lead to rivalry when imitated, and that through the empowerment of this One our human desire(s) be transformed so that we will *desire* to imitate the nonrivalous, nonviolent Person.

In this chapter I seek to show that major strands of NT teaching are directed specifically to just this reality: transformation of desire that enables a positive, *nonacquisitive mimesis*. This study seeks to show how foundational and ubiquitous this idea is in the New Testament.

Further, I develop this thesis: that the NT use of imitation/discipleship language carries contextual emphases that prevent, even repudiate, *the mimesis of acquisitive desire*. Rather, this stream of NT paranesis (i.e., counsel, exhortation, instruction) sets forth another type of mimesis, one antithetical to the mimetic desire that generates rivalry and in turn leads to violence. The mimesis enjoined by the NT canonical literature is grounded in the Jesus cross event, an event that exposes violence and, from Jesus' side, manifests the freedom and power of new creation.

In developing this thesis, this chapter also sheds fresh light on the long-standing issue in biblical studies of the role of *imitation* in Christian character formation, a point in the modern debate initiated by Martin Luther's strong reaction to *imitatio Christi* because it threatened to undermine his central and precious doctrine of justification by faith alone.[4] Any effort to imitate Christ, says Luther, invites through the side door a works righteousness into the salvation experience, and thereby mitigates God's grace and salvation *extra nos*.

Much Protestant exegesis has continued in Luther's footsteps, spurred additionally by atonement theology that sets off Jesus' suffering and death as so unique in its salvific purpose that it disconnects discipleship from salvation. This produces lamentable moral results and invites through the side door the old acquisitive mimesis under the guise of protecting salvation. Consequently, the liberating gospel of peace is substituted with a self-serving redeemer myth. Further, one or both of these factors often play into the exegetical comments that argue down the importance of NT *imitational/example* language.

The influential article by Michaelis in Kittel's *TDNT* work demonstrates the point. Disagreeing with Oepke and Larsson in their important and full-length studies of the topic,[5] Michaelis argues against any genuine imitation in Paul:

First, there is simple comparison. The older example seems to be imitated, but there is no conscious imitation. This type occurs in 1 Th. 2:14 and 1 Th. 1:6. Then there is the following of an example. This use is found in 2 Th. 3:7, 9; Phil. 3:17, and Paul is always the example. Recognition of the authority of Paul is plainly implied in these passages, so that following his example carried with it obedience to his commands. In the third group obedience is predominant, so exclusively so in 1 C. 4:16 that the thought of an example is quite overshadowed, and in 1 C. 11:1; 1 Th. 1:6; Eph. 5:1 it is quite obvious that the main stress falls on the element of obedience. In this third group alone are Christ and God associated with Paul as authorities in relation to whom one must be a μιμητής [mimētēs].[6]

Given this reductionism of mimēsis in Paul to a command-obedience paradigm, it is easy to see why Elizabeth Castelli, in her recent study of Paul's imitation language,[7] concludes that Paul's call/command to imitation functions to imprint the hierarchical structure of power on Christian thought and conduct. But, as Fodor points out, Castelli's wider study of mimēsis in Greek literature, and her own caution against reductionism of its meaning, should have prevented her narrow conclusion.[8]

In view of this mimetic error in NT scholarship, one purpose of this chapter is to resolve this problematic by doing fresh exegetical commentary on the mimēsis texts in light of Girard's theory. Indeed, if Girard's theories are correct, mimesis in the NT can be very bad news, given Castelli's thesis that it reinforces a conservative hierarchical power structure, or it might also be very very good news, if the call to imitation is securely linked with renunciation of acquisitive mimetic desire, through Jesus' own model, so that the spiral of rivalry and violence is decisively broken.

If the Girardian thesis is correct, that mimetic rivalry is the generative power behind the scapegoating mechanism that led to Jesus' violent death, and if Jesus' life-death breaks this spiral of violence empowered by rivalry—the thesis that I will argue—then it should be possible to show exegetically that Jesus' teachings on discipleship and the early church's teaching of imitation (later called imitatio Christi, see also note 8) function as antidote to aspirations of rivalry. They are analogous to Jesus' own refusal to play the mimetic game that feeds destructive impulses and leads to violence, sacralized under the guise of having made peace (a counterfeit to true peace). Further, if it is exegetically possible to demonstrate this point, then theological quarrel among biblical scholars about the relationship between discipleship and imitation in the NT will be resolved via a fresh perspective on the topic.

The first part of this chapter thus takes up Paul's and the wider NT use of imitation language and paranesis with brief expositional comment on the passages. The second part then examines the Gospel narratives that emphasize Jesus' teachings on discipleship—i.e., the call to follow Jesus. The third part of the article casts a still larger net in considering a wider set of *correspondence* and *identification* language. This will set the stage for final comments to clinch the thesis developed. In this way this study seeks to provide a fresh understanding of *imitation and discipleship* in the NT.

Methodologically, a word about the order of these three parts is necessary. The atonement (see Miller's chapter as well as Collins's) is the precondition theologically and practically for all imitation, "in Christ," and identification or correspondence paranesis. The potential of a new mimesis rests on God's inauguration of a new creation reality through the cross and, most significantly, the resurrection of Jesus Christ. Theologically, then, the three parts of this essay should be presented in reverse order, for in that order one is foundational for the other.[9] But since the basic topic focuses on imitation and mimesis, I follow this order, building to the climax of the foundation of the new reality. Hence, to play on Girard's book title (see note 1), this essay is about "Things Designed (in Christ Revealed) before the Foundation of the World" (Eph. 1:4ff.).

ANALYSIS OF IMITATION TEXTS

And you became *imitators* of us and of the Lord, because you received the word with much affliction/persecution/suffering with joy of the Holy Spirit, so that you have become a *type/example* to all the believers in Macedonia and in Achaia. (1 Thess. 1:6-7, WMS trans.)[10]

This text is crucially important for two reasons: first, it is likely the earliest extant Christian writing. Second, this early paranesis sets up an identity grid by which the Thessalonians believers are assured of their authentic Jesus character. Daniel Patte, in his structural analysis and explication of Paul's letters, regards this second factor as most crucial. That these believers received the word in suffering marks them in *type* (*typon*, the word translated *example*). The fact that they suffered like their Lord Jesus, and like Paul and his coworkers before them (note the plural *us*, referring back to "Paul, Silvanus, and

Timothy" in the salutation)[11] marks them as genuine. It certifies and assures them that they belong to Jesus.[12]

My translation suggests that *en thipsei pollē* should be taken as an instrumental of manner, i.e., *in affliction* denotes the manner in which they received the gospel. This *affliction* specifies the mimetic relationship (*mimētai* in 6a) to the Lord Jesus. There is, as it were, a double marking, first in *mimētai*, in that their experience stands in continuity with that of Jesus, and second, in *typon*, in that they become a type for others who likewise undergo similar suffering in receiving and living out the gospel.

> "For you, brothers and sisters, became *imitators* of the churches of God in Christ Jesus that are in Judea, for you suffered the same things from your own compatriots as they did from the Jews, who killed both the Lord Jesus and the prophets. . . ." (1 Thess. 2:14)

This text, standing in the tradition of the Hebrew prophetic critique, as Craig Evans has shown,[13] similarly denotes *suffering* (*epathete*) as the identifying mark of Christian experience.

In both these early texts, the Christians knew who they were in relation to Christ in that they shared his victimage experience. Their suffering certified their character, as those who did not mimetically counter-respond but experienced typologically the fate of Jesus.

> Now we command you, beloved, in the name of our Lord Jesus Christ, to keep away from believers who are living in idleness and not according to the tradition that they received from us. For you yourselves know how you ought to *imitate* us; we were not idle when we were with you, and we did not eat anyone's bread without paying for it; but with toil and labor we worked night and day, so that we might not burden any of you. This was not because we do not have that right, but to give you an *example* to *imitate*. (2 Thess. 3:6-9)

Again, as in 1 Thess., the model to be imitated is not Paul alone, but Paul, Silvanus, and Timothy, the leadership team. This appears to reflect the assumed pattern of Greek education, *paideia*, in which learners imitate the model of noble leaders.[14]

Three features of this text are especially noteworthy: first, it begins with a command (*parangellomen*) that appeals to *tradition* (*paradosis*) for its authorization. In the universally recognized Pauline writings (2 Thess. is often considered duetero-Pauline), the appeal to tradition (paradosis) is associated with central tenets of the gospel (notably 1 Cor. 15:3; 11:1; cf. 1 Thess. 4:1-2). Second, this text reflects the hebraic *halakahic* concept of the moral life in its use of *walk* (*peripateō* in 3:6, which the NRSV translates *living*). On this basis we might observe that the NT concept of imitation is likely derived in part from the Hebrew tradition in which *way (derek)* and *walk (halak)* are foundational to paranesis on the moral life.[15]

Third, of all the NT uses of imitation language, only this one is not linked to the conceptual field of love, forgiveness, servanthood, humility, and suffering. Work as such, avoiding idleness or unruliness, does not necessarily fit the paradigm to which the other imitation texts conform.

> To the present hour we are hungry and thirsty, we are poorly clothed and beaten and homeless, and we grow weary from the work of our own hands. When reviled, we bless; when persecuted, we endure; when slandered, we speak kindly. We have become like the rubbish of the world, the dregs of all things, to this very day. I am not writing this to make you ashamed, but to admonish you as my beloved children, for though you might have ten thousand guardians in Christ, you do not have many fathers. Indeed, in Christ Jesus I became your father through the gospel. I appeal to you, then, be *imitators* of me. (1 Cor. 4:11-16)

This passage reflects Paul's conflictual relationship with some in the Corinthian congregation and comes at the end of a sarcastic outburst in which the Corinthian believers are "rich" and "kings," while Paul and company are spectacles of death. Whereas *they* are wise, strong, and honored, Paul and company are fools, weak, and in disrepute. Clearly, here Paul is risking his "cool" for the sake of making clear that the gospel of Jesus Christ is not a *theologia gloria* but a *theologia crucis.* Literarily, these verses anticipate Paul's classic description of his sufferings for the gospel in 2 Corinthians 4:6ff. (the "treasure in earthen vessels" text).

Preceding immediately Paul's call to "imitate me," Paul uses the metaphor of father. This personalizing of his relation to the young believers explains the shift from the plural (vv. 8-13) to the singular (vv. 16-21). The father metaphor intends to convey intimacy and care, descriptive of his relation to the community. The profile of experience in vv. 10-13 clearly denotes personal deprivation, suffering, and abuse. When the father-image is blended with this list of hardships, the pattern that emerges is willingness to take on personal anguish because of caring love for others. Thus Paul voluntarily foregoes his own rights for the cause of the gospel and the welfare of the faith-communities. This forms the model of attitude and action that Paul now calls the believes to imitate.

So, whether you eat or drink, or whatever you do, do everything for the glory of God. Give no offense to Jews or to Greeks or to the church of God, just as I try to please everyone in everything I do, not seeking my own advantage, but that of many, so that they may be saved. Be *imitators* of me, as I am of Christ. (1 Cor. 10:31–11:1)

The context of this summary depiction of Paul's effort to please others in order not to impede the gospel's salvific effect among both Jews and Gentiles focuses on whether or not to eat meat offered to idols (ch. 8) and whether or not to participate in (cultic) feasts in the temple shrines of pagan gods (ch. 10). While his counsel on the former is yes and his command on the latter is no, the bottom-line principle is not to become a stumbling block/scandal (*skandalon*) to another believer's conscience. Then one deliberately avoids scandalizing another brother or sister (*scandalisō*, 8:13d; cf. *egkopēn* in 9:12b, translated *obstacle* in NRSV). That this becomes the model to imitate is most provocative in view of Girard's extensive attention to the role of *scandal* in the gospel narrative.

Girard treats the point of *scandal* numerous places, most provocatively in his essay on Peter's denial in *The Scapegoat*[16] and in his 1992 AAR speech, "How Can Satan Cast Out Satan?"[17] In his essay on Peter, Girard claims: "The convergence of the content of the [Passion] narratives with the theory of the *skandalon*—theory of mimetic desire—cannot be fortuitous."[18] He observes that Jesus says to his disciples, *"You will all scandalize yourselves because of me this night"*[19] (Matt 26:31). Earlier, he notes, Jesus had severely reprimanded Peter, "'Get behind me, Satan! You are an obstacle in my path'; [*you scandalize me*] (Matt. 16:23)."[20]

Girard rightly contends that mimetic desire (a.k.a. Satan) drives Peter in both cases and that it causes Peter to be a scandal to Jesus and Jesus to be a scandal to Peter and the other disciples. This mimetic desire, of course, is *acquisitive desire,* the exact opposite of those desires and impulses that occur in the contexts of Paul's paranesis that exhorts believers to imitate him, Christ, and God. In my analysis of the Markan discipleship pericopes below, this contrast between the way of Jesus and the desires of the disciples will be further elucidated.

A surface reading of Paul's admonition to imitate him and Christ in the context of the Gospel's portrait of Jesus as a skandalon raises an apparent contradiction. Paul's self-denying actions have as their express purpose avoidance of scandal/offense that causes another to stumble. And he attributes this pattern to Christ, from whom he learned it.

But the gospel story portrays Jesus occasioning scandal. The resolution hinges on two crucial points. First, acquisitive mimetic desire of the disciples in the Gospels is the real reason Jesus becomes a scandal. Second, Paul's concern in this text is that young believers are not scandalized by other believers. At the same time, this epistle begins by marking the gospel's proclamation as a skandalon to unbelieving Jews and *foolishness* to refusing Gentiles (1 Cor. 1:23). Paul does not court the illusion that it is possible to strip the gospel of its *scandalizing* edge to those oriented to acquisitive mimetic desire.

> Brothers and sisters, join in *imitating* me, and observe those who live according to the *example* you have in us. For many live as enemies of the cross of Christ; I have told you of them, and now I tell you even with tears. (Phil. 3:17-18)

The context of this admonition is Paul's counting as loss his Jewish credentials and achievements—which he labels as "confidence in the flesh"—and then he owns a righteousness based on the faith of Jesus Christ, a righteousness which is from God based on faith (3:9). What Paul then desires, as mark of this righteousness, is to know the power of Jesus' resurrection and to share in Jesus' sufferings, thus "becoming like him in death" (3:10). These twin points of analogous experience are pursued further in vv. 11-16. Then follows this language of imitation and example in vv. 17-18.

Clearly, given the preceding context of sharing in the sufferings of Christ and the immediately following reference to the cross of Christ, this use of *imitation* and *example* is oriented to the cross and suffering. It is also striking that Paul completes this thought by pointing to a heavenly reward for this kind of earthly life (vv. 20-21). He then addresses a conflict between two sisters in the community, Euodia and Syntyche, a manifestation of mimetic rivalry in the sisterhood. He speaks highly of their contribution to the missionary enterprise and is confident that this conflict can and will be resolved.

> Let the *same mind* be in you that was in Christ Jesus, who, though he was in the form of God, did not regard equality with God as something to be exploited, but emptied himself, taking the form of a slave, being born in human likeness. And being found in human form, he humbled himself and became obedient to the point of death—even death on a cross. Therefore God also highly exalted him. . . . (Phil. 2:5-11)

Even though this text does not use either of the key terms, *imitation* or *type*, it clearly portrays the believers patterning their conduct after the suffering and obedience of Christ Jesus. Hence this important text takes its place in this list. Further, this text is joined to *imitation* in Philippians 3:17 (see p. 225) by the similar exhortation, "be of the same mind" (*touto phroneite* in 2:5 and *touto phronomen* in 3:15).

The context of this foundational confession on Jesus' self-emptying and humbling to the cross is Paul's admonition in vv. 3-4 to put away conduct that proceeds from mimetic rivalry: "Do nothing from selfish ambition or conceit, but in humility regard others as better than yourselves. Let each of you look not to your own interests, but to the interests of others." Then follows: "let the same mind be in you that was also in Christ Jesus."

> . . . and be kind to one another, tenderhearted, forgiving one another, as God in Christ has forgiven you. Therefore be *imitators* of God, as beloved children, and live in love, as Christ loved us and gave himself up for us, a fragrant offering and sacrifice to God. (Eph. 4:32-5:2)

The longer context exhorts believers to put off old pagan ways of conduct and to put on the new clothing of attitude and action that accords with their having been recreated in the image of God (4:23-24). Here, the admonition to imitate is linked not to Paul, or even to Christ, but to God (echoing the Sermon on the Mount's injunction to be perfect in indiscriminate love as God is, Matt. 5:44-48). This is a singular use of imitation in the NT; nowhere else are believers explicitly told to imitate God.

The dispositions identified are kindness, being tenderhearted, forgiving others, and loving, which is specifically linked then to Christ and his example in giving himself for us as a fragrant offering and sacrifice to God.

Here is one of numerous cases where the word *sacrifice* is used in a sense quite different from the Girardian use. A synonym might be "costly gift" or "thank offering." In my judgment, Schwager is correct when he distinguishes different meanings in the word *sacrifice* as used in Scripture, not all of which can be reduced to a sacrificial crisis generated by violence.[21] Indeed, there is a distinct metaphorical use of the term (as Girard recognizes[22] and that can be seen in Psalms 50:14, 23; 51:17; Rom. 12:1; 1 Pet. 2:4-5; Heb. 13:15-16—cf. the use of the word *offering* in Isa. 66:20 and Rom. 15:16). It is striking also to realize that Paul does not refer to Jesus' death as a *sacrifice* even though

he has a wide repertoire of images for explicating the salvific meaning of Jesus' death.[23]

OTHER NT EXAMPLE/IMITATION TEXTS

> For to this you have been called, because Christ also suffered for
> you, leaving you an **example**, so that you should *follow in his
> steps*. "He committed no sin, and no deceit was found in his
> mouth." When he was abused, he did not return abuse; when he
> suffered, he did not threaten; but he entrusted himself to the one
> who judges justly. He himself bore our sins in his body on the
> cross, so that, free from sins, we might live for righteousness; by
> his wounds you have been healed. (1 Pet. 2:21-24)

Although the Pauline terms for *example/type (typos)* and *imitation
(mimēsis/mimeomai)* do not occur in these verses, similar ideas are
present in Peter's distinctive vocabulary. The word for *example
(hupogrammon)* occurs only here in the NT and carries the connotation of a sketch or imprint.[24] This idea is then joined to the memorable phrase, *in his steps (tois ichnesin autou)*. Clearly, Jesus is set forth
as a pattern that is to guide the formation of the believers' thought
and conduct.

The *content* of the example is unambiguously the nonretaliatory
conduct of Jesus when he was threatened and abused. Mary Schertz's
chiastic and stichometric analysis of this hymn shows that v. 23b
forms the center, with six syllables: *paschōn ouk epeilei* ("when suffering he did not retaliate").[25] That this same paranetic emphasis occurs
throughout the NT and forms a significant unity to the NT canon has
been persuasively argued and demonstrated by William Farmer.[26]
This injunction not to retaliate, i.e., not to repay evil for evil, is present
also in two Pauline texts (Rom. 12:17-21 and 1 Thess. 5:15), although
it is not joined there to the *example* or *imitation* language. But it is con-
gruous with and even provides theological foundation for Paul's
other exhortations, as noted above.

> so that you may not become sluggish, but **imitators** of those who
> through faith and patience inherit the promises. (Heb. 6:12)

> Therefore, since we are surrounded by so great a cloud of wit-
> nesses, let us also lay aside every weight and the sin that clings so
> closely, and let us run with perseverance the race that is set before
> us, **looking to Jesus the pioneer** and perfecter of our faith, who for
> the sake of the joy that was set before him endured the cross, dis-
> regarding its shame, and has taken his seat at the right hand of the

throne of God. Consider him who endured such hostility against himself from sinners, so that you may not grow weary or lose heart. (Heb. 12:1-3a)

Remember your leaders, those who spoke the word of God to you; consider the outcome of their way of life, and *imitate* their faith. (Heb. 13:7)

Although 6:12 and 13:7 use *imitate*, 12:1-3a employs distinctive vocabulary to portray Jesus as a model by which believers form moral conviction and character. Here, in the context of the chapter 11 catalog of the those who lived by faith—from Abraham onward—and did not see the promise fufilled, Jesus is set forth as the Leader or Pioneer (*Archēgos*) of the train of the faithful. The pilgrimage image of chapter 11 now shifts to that of a race (*agōna*) that lies ahead of the faithful. Immediately, this is linked to Jesus' own endurance of the cross and the hostility of sinners against him. This in turn is the motive or rationale for believers to not grow weary in doing good.

When this injunction to *look to Jesus*, literally *fix one's eyes on* or "be glued to" (to use modern colloquium), is joined to the description of Jesus as the *Pioneer of the faith*, a strong case for Jesus functioning as a model for the shaping of our desire emerges. But again, Jesus is linked to the cross, and only through it to an exalted position at the right hand of God. The short phrase "disregarding the shame" (of the cross) arrests our attention on two counts. First, what really does this mean, especially when earlier versions translated it (*aischunēs kataphonēsas*) as "despising the cross"? Second, how does this meaning square with a Girardian interpretation of Jesus' attitude toward the cross?

Although the translation "despising" is the more natural meaning, the NRSV translators, apparently failing to see sense in this, took the less likely connotation, "disregarding" the shame, i.e., putting up with it to move on to the next phase of exaltation (Phil. 2:5-11 *may* but need not be interpreted to concur with this meaning). The weakness of this solution lies in its tendency to "slide over or through" the cross to get on to glory. But this is hardly in keeping with the larger emphasis of Hebrews (as well as Paul's emphasis on *theologia crucis*).

The more natural meaning of "despising the cross" acquires special significance when informed by the Girardian understanding of the cross as exposure of human violence and the culmination of acquisitive mimetic desire against the innocent victim. The *shame* of the cross lies precisely in its function as death for criminals. To identify the *shame* factor in the experience is to expose its injustice, to say clearly that Jesus was killed like a criminal, and that this *shameful* action is one Jesus despised and despises today when human violence scapegoats the innocent. The good of Jesus' death—even the divine necessity (*dei*), therefore, does not justify or whitewash the violence. It was and is *shameful*. In this light, there is important reason to retain the older translation (KJV, RSV).

> So if I, your Lord and Teacher, have washed your feet, you ought to wash one another's feet. For I have set you an ***example***, that you also should do as I have done to you. Very truly, I tell you, servants are not greater than their master, nor the messengers greater than the one who sent them. (John 13:14-16)

In John's Gospel account, Jesus memorializes the moral injunction to humble service in ritual enactment. The discourse, in which this exhortation to follow Jesus' example (*hupodeigma*), concludes with denoting the mark of the disciples' identity: "By this everyone will know that you are my disciples, if you have love for one another" (13:35). Indeed, even though John's Gospel is distinctive in its account of Jesus' ministry, it too speaks the same voice as the Pauline imitation paranesis, the 1 Peter *example*, the Hebrews *Pioneer* of faith amid hardship, and the Synoptic's dramatic presentation of Jesus' repeated efforts to enable the disciples to see and walk a new way. This new way of willingness to suffer the rejection and violence of humanity against the righteous One diverges decisively from that of acquisitive mimesis.

MIMESIS IN THE SYNOPTICS' PASSION NARRATIVE

"The convergence of the content of the [Passion] narratives with the theory of the *skandalon*—theory of mimetic desire—cannot be fortuitous." —Girard, *The Scapegoat* [27]

"That same day Herod and Pilate became friends with each other; before this they had been enemies." —Luke 23:12

Girard gives considerable space to analysis of the Passion narrative, since it shows how the players in the story depict the mimetic rivalry: the disciples; Judas; the chief priests, elders, and scribes; the Council; and Pilate and Herod. Even though crowds are initially favorable to Jesus, the religious leaders maneuver them to their side so that the story moves to the climax of "all against one," summed up deftly in Acts 4:27, "For in this city, in fact, both Herod and Pontius

Pilate, with the Gentiles and the peoples of Israel, gathered together against your holy servant Jesus, whom you anointed. . . . "[28]

Due to length and time constraints, my work in this section is limited to Mark's central section, for there the two types of mimesis are starkly contrasted.[29] The same content and emphasis is present in Matthew and Luke as well, with slightly different accent. Mark's prepassion section is carefully crafted, interweaving Jesus' teaching on his forthcoming passion (8:31; 9:31; 10:32-34) with depiction of the disciples' failure to understand (8:32-33; 9:32-34; 10:35-41) followed immediately by Jesus' teaching on cross-bearing (8:34-37), valuing the child (9:35-41) and self-giving service (10:32-45). This pattern of thinking contrasts sharply to the disciples' persisting acquisitive mimesis and rivalry: messianic rule by oppressive power—Peter voices Satan's thoughts—(8:29-33); seeking prestige—"who is the greatest?"—in the coming kingdom (9:33-34); and clamoring for top positions in the messianic cabinet (10:35-37).

Using Girard's analyses, the object of desire progresses in this section into ever greater specificity, with mounting rivalry and latent violence. Further, the second cycle of teaching is followed by extended admonition (in 9:38-50) to avoid *scandalizing* little ones and to cut from one's life those *desires* that cause offense and stumbling (*be scandalized*). The section ends (v. 50) by urging the disciples to be at peace with one another, possible only when they have repudiated their acquisitive mimetic rivalry and have learned to avoid the skandalon.

Probing yet to another level, Mark frames his journey section with the *hodos* motif, which echoes Israel's earlier journey to the land of promise, the movement from old life in Egypt's slavery to new life in the land promised as God's gift and their inheritance.[30] The theological significance of Mark's weaving of Jesus' announced passion and resurrection into the recurring exodus and way-"conquest" motifs is far-reaching. Many scholars have recognized that Mark's hodos is indeed the *way* of suffering. *Hodos* in 8:27-10:52 not only narrates Jesus' journey to Jerusalem, but it marks both the *way* of Jesus in his passion and the *way* of disciples who follow him. It will be a way of suffering.[31] In this hodos-narrative of 8:27-10:52 Jesus concentrates his *teaching* on discipleship.[32] Indeed, Mark uses *hodos* as a hermeneutical tool to contemporize Jesus' past history so that Mark's readers—and us—now hear the call to follow on the way.[33]

From these three cycles on Jesus' passion and teachings on discipleship we can grasp the essential conditions of entrance into the kingdom of God, the goal of Jesus' hodos teachings *a la* Mark. In the first cycle Jesus as the suffering Son of humanity-Messiah rebukes the disciples for their too-eager acclaim of Peter's confession of Jesus as Messiah (*epitimaō* is used already in 8:30). In v. 32 Peter rebukes Jesus for speaking about suffering. Then in v. 33 Jesus sternly rebukes Peter and identifies Peter's thinking with Satan.

It is clear that two opposing views of the Messiahship have locked horns. Peter's view is most likely the Maccabean model, in which the Messiah will crush the power of the enemy nations.[34] Jesus' view is the way of the suffering Son of humanity; indeed, the way of the Servant of the Lord (Isa. 53). The call to take up the cross means nothing less than willingness to die, to be crucified, for the sake of Jesus' gospel (v. 38), i.e., the kingdom he proclaimed. It means losing one's life and not being ashamed of Jesus' gospel even though threatened with death (vv. 34-38).

The second opposition between Jesus' and the disciples appears in 9:33-34, where the disciples are quarreling over who is the greatest. Although Mark does not narrate the substance of their dispute, it appears that the disciples were imagining themselves as part of a new ruling government of Palestine and thus were discussing the ranking of each in the new administration. The third round of discussion in 10:37 makes this point more specific. This time James and John ask for the top seats of power: one on the right and one on the left.

To these queries Jesus turns aspirations to greatness upside down. He sets forth new identity images for life in the kingdom of God: child and servant. To enter the kingdom we must regard a child as important. Ranked at the bottom of the pecking order in their social stratification, the child is precisely the one who merits care and love. To receive the child in "my name" is to receive me, says Jesus. To follow Jesus on the way requires, absolutely and thoroughly, a revisioning of greatness.

The following pericope then juxtaposes acts of power (exorcism) and humble service (giving a cup of water). Both are equally significant when done in Jesus' name! Then the narrative takes up the topic of *offense* (skandalon). Harsh words of judgment fall on those who cause "one of these little ones who believe in me to sin." The cause of offense (skandalon) to the "little one" or to one's own transformed *desires* must be purged to enter the kingdom of God (v. 47; cf. "life" in vv. 43, 45). Drawing on the imagery of well-prepared salted sacrifices (Lev. 2:13), Jesus calls for the self to be salted,[35] purified of evil and acquisitive desires, and for his followers to live peaceably with one another (vv. 49-50). This exhortation, to live peaceably with one another, contrasts to the segment's initial portrait of the disciples disputing with one another over who is the greatest. To walk in the way of Jesus means giving up rivalry over greatness and passionately desiring relationships that do not offend others, but, rather, yield the fruit of peace.

In the third round of hodos teaching, Jesus enunciates even more clearly his messianic mission's transformation of "conquest" theology. Having presented the rigorous demands of the kingdom in relation to marriage, possessions, and family ties (10:1-31), and having reiterated again his impending suffering (vv. 32-34), Jesus now responds to the *acquisitive desires* of James and John to be granted right- and left-side seats to him in glory. What exactly they had in mind is not clear, but the point of their desiring to share in Jesus' misconceived future is clear.

Williams comments perceptively on this matter and the effect this portrait of the disciples had on the early Christians:

> The mimetic desire and rivalry of the disciples and their corresponding inability to comprehend the call to Jesus as the Christ, Son of man, and Suffering Servant is the most difficult aspect of Mark for the Christian tradition to understand and assimilate. Surely, this depiction of the disciples was a scandal and a primary factor occasioning the writing of . . . Matthew and Luke.[36]

After exposing the intensity of their desire, Jesus shocks them—subverting their assumptions—by promising they will share in the cup (of suffering) he will drink (see Mark 14:36) and the baptism with which he will be baptized, but their wish is not his to grant. The ten are indignant, their own mimetic desire flashing, presumably because they think the two have gotten an edge over them. Then Jesus, calling them together, speaks words that sum up his kingdom way:

> "You know that among the Gentiles those whom they recognize as their rulers [RSV, to rule/*archein*] lord [*katakurieuousin*] it over them, and their great ones [*megaloi*] are tyrants [RSV, exercise authority/*katexousiazousin*] over them. But it is not so among you; but whoever wishes to become great [*megas*] among you must be your servant [*diakonos*], and whoever wishes to be first among you must be slave [*doulos*] of all. For the Son of man came not to be served but to serve [*diakonēsai*], and to give his life a ransom for many [*lytron anti pollōn*]. (Mark 10:42-45)

The verbal and grammatical links between these sentences are crucial. The first sentence speaks of political power and rule, denoted by verb forms of "to lord" (*katakuriō*) and "to exercise authority" (*katexousiazō*); both verbs carry overtones of oppressive rule. Those who so rule are so-called *great people*! The second sentence is hooked to the first by the word *great* and a mild adversative (*de*). *Great* is sharply redefined: to be great is to be servant! The point is reinforced by restatement, using the image of *first* (*prōtos*), which here means "the head of things." The head must be the slave of all.

The second and third sentences are linked by the crucial connective *For* (*gar*), used with the intensive *kai*, which here is likely best translated *also* (as in RSV). This construction puts into parallel relationship the way of the Son of humanity and the way of his disciples. The service (*diakonēsai*) of the Son of humanity matches and is the ground for that of the disciples (who are called to be *diakonoi*). Jesus and the disciples are indissolubly linked in this new creation of transformed desire. For the Son of humanity, this life-giving service has ultimate benefit: a ransom for many.

Whether *ransom for many* should be considered part of the parallel structure between Jesus and the disciples is debatable. Although numerous aspects of the belabored exegesis of this saying lie outside the scope of this study,[37] the essential point is that Jesus' giving his life as a ransom means victory for the benefit of many. Although the element of substitution is present,[38] the overall context demands that we stress the binding relationship between the Redeemer and the redeemed. The redeemed, i.e., the followers of Jesus, are linked to Jesus as the servant-head who leads the ransomed into lives of servant-living. Certainly this was one of Mark's primary aims in writing the Gospel: to set forth Jesus' life, death, and resurrection as a call to and an empowerment for faithful discipleship.[39] This discipleship is to consist of transformed desires so that the natural human acquisitive desire is refused in the name and power of Jesus as the Servant of the Lord who leads us into the new creation. Williams puts it well:

> I think Mark probably intends to say, in effect, "The human condition is such that only the price of the Son of man's suffering and death will have the effect of loosing the bonds of the sacred social structure, enabling human beings to see what their predicament is and the kind of faith and action that will bring liberation."[40]

The inclusio images to Jesus' teaching in this section are *hodos*-cross (8:34) and *giving his life as a ransom* (10:45). Both point to suffering and death; both point also toward gaining life and ransoming life. The way of the Messiah's, Son of humanity's own victory and the way of victory for his followers are bound together by the cross and resurrection. The section as a whole shows that God's victory[41] comes in a most unsuspecting way: the way of self-denial, humble service, and the very giving of one's life for others.[42] This is the *way of Jesus*. Jesus' resurrection is indeed a vital part of every passion prediction on the way. Jesus' hodos is not only a way to death, but a way also to God's victory (note *proagei* in 16:7). This victory is assured by Jesus' death as a "ransom for many." For Jesus and his disciples the way of faithful warfare was and is that of humble service, even unto death. Victory comes through God's vindication of the faithful.

This emphasis lies at the heart of the model/imitation-pattern found in Luke-Acts where Jesus' conduct before authorities inspires the persecuted in their testimony to the gospel before rulers. I regard Richard Cassidy's thesis tenable: that Acts serves the cause of strengthening allegiance to Jesus and witness before political authorities. Luke's primary goals were, first, to write out of his personal allegiance to his Lord and strengthen believers in their allegiance and, second, to shape the conduct of believers in their daily interactions with people generally but especially with government officials in accord with the gospel. Luke-Acts thus provides models for believers in their own "Christian witness in their trials before Roman officials."[43]

Revelation shows the same pattern. Believers are challenged to conquer the beast (2:7, 11, 17, 26; 3:5, 12, 21; 21:7)—the epitome of mimetic violence—just as the Lion (5:5)-Lamb (17:14) has already conquered and other brothers and sisters have conquered as well (12:11; 15:2). Hence the pattern of mimesis appears to permeate NT thought.

THE WIDER NEW TESTAMENT PERSPECTIVE

In addition to this more narrow scope of an *imitation/discipleship* pattern defining the manner in which believers relate to Jesus, a much wider set of language and concepts develops *correspondence* logic between the believer and Jesus as Leader or Prototype. John H. Yoder develops the correspondence logic around three main categories of thought.[44]

1. THE DISCIPLE/PARTICIPANT AND THE LOVE OF GOD

Yoder quotes a series of texts that speak of believers sharing the divine nature: in light and purity (1 John 1:5-7; 3:1-3; 4:17); in holy living (1 Pet. 1:15f., citing Lev. 19:2;); and putting on a new nature and being constantly renewed in the image of its Creator (Col. 3:9;

4:23-24). To these might be added 2 Peter 1:3ff., which explicitly speaks of believers sharing in the divine nature.

In a second subsection, Yoder identifies numerous texts that enjoin believers to forgive as God in Christ forgave us (Eph. 4:32; Col. 3:13; Matt. 6:12/Luke 11:4; Matt. 6:14f.; 18:32ff.). To this list others might be added: Mark 11:25 and especially the Johannine form of the Sending Commission, John 20:23, although in these texts the correspondence is only implied.

Yoder's third subsection focuses on Jesus' command to love indiscriminately, thus including the enemy, just as God is indiscriminate in sending sun and rain on the just and unjust (Matt. 5:43-48 and Luke 6:32-36).

2. THE DISCIPLE/PARTICIPANT AND THE LIFE OF CHRIST

The subsections here refer to being "in Christ" (1 John 2:6—many others in Paul could be cited[45]) and the texts that speak of dying with Christ and sharing in his risen life (Rom. 6:6-11; 8:11; Gal. 2:20; cf. 5:24; Eph. 4:20-24; Col. 2:12-3:1). To this he adds "Loving as Christ loved, giving himself" (John 13:34; 15:12; 1 John 3:11-16; cf. 4:4-10 already cited; and Mark 12:28ff. par.). Related to this, the next category is "Serving others as he served" (John 13:1-17; Rom. 15:1-7; 2 Cor. 5:14ff.; 8:7-0; Eph. 5:22-28) and finally "Subordination," where he refers to another entire chapter under the title, "Revolutionary Subordination," in which, through citation of the several *Haustafeln* texts, Yoder puts forward his thesis:

> Subordination means the acceptance of an *order*, as it exists, but with the new meaning given to it by the fact that one's acceptance of it is willing and meaningfully motivated.[46]

Throughout the chapter Yoder shows how the appeal for subordination is rooted "in the example of Jesus Christ or in the nature of Christ as shared by the believer."[47]

3. THE DISCIPLE/PARTICIPANT AND THE DEATH OF CHRIST

To document his first major point that suffering with Christ defines apostolic and Christian existence, Yoder cites many of the *imitation/example* texts I cited above, as well as 2 Cor. 4:10; 1:5; Col. 1:24. Phil. 2:3-14 is his key text for documenting the point that believers are expected to share in the divine condescension and to give their lives as Jesus did (Eph. 5:1 and texts cited above). Then in several subsections Yoder focuses on suffering: suffering servanthood replaces dominion (Mark 10:42-45 par.); the believer is to accept innocent suffering without complaint (1 Pet. 2:20ff.; 3:14-18; 4:12-16; John 15:20f.; 2 Tim. 3:12; Phil. 1:29; 1 Pet. 4:13). Death is then viewed as liberation from sin's power (1 Pet. 4:1f.; Gal. 5:24), as the fate of the prophets (Matt. 23:24; Mark 12:1-9; Luke 24:20; Acts 2:36; 4:10; 7:52; 23:24; 1 Thess. 2:15ff.), and as victory (Col. 2:15; 1 Cor. 1:22-24; Rev. 12:10f.; cf. 5:9ff.; 17:14).

To complete the chapter, Yoder enumerates many actions, lifestyle features, and cultural particularities that believers are never told to emulate or copy, then concludes provocatively,

> There is but one realm in which . . . imitation holds—but there it holds in every strand of the New Testament literature and all the more strikingly by virtue of the absence of parallels in other realms: this is at the point of the concrete social meaning of the cross in its relation to enmity and power. Servanthood replaces dominion, forgiveness absorbs hostility. Thus—and only thus— are we bound by New Testament thought to "be like Jesus." [48]

Yoder's treatment and summary are reductionistic, since the correspondence logic is extended to include other features of God or Christ in certain uncited passages,[49] most notably 2 Pet. 1:3ff., which correlates a string of Christian virtues with the goal, "that you may become participants in the divine nature" (v. 4c). The constituent qualifications of this identification with the divine nature are the divine empowerment of life and godliness—to escape corruption through this world's lusts—and many virtues ($aret\bar{e}$): faith, goodness, knowledge, self-control, endurance, godliness, mutual affection, and love. Paul also lists vices (below) that contrast with these virtues.[50]

Col. 3: 5-9	Rom. 1	Gal. 5	Eph. 4-5	1. Cor 5	1 Cor. 6	1 Pet. 2, 4	Rev. 22
Fornication		◆	◆	◆	◆		◆
Impurity	◆	◆	◆			◆	
Passion	◆	(◆)				◆	
Evil desire	◆	(◆)	(◆)			(◆)	
Greed	◆		◆	◆	◆		
(Idolatry)		◆	◆	◆	◆	◆	◆
Anger		◆					
Wrath		◆	◆			◆	
Malice	◆		◆			◆	
Slander		◆					
Abusive (filthy) language		◆					
Lying	(◆)		◆			(◆)	◆

Pauline ethical injunctions, which are often introduced by "put off/ on" wording, connect the "new creation" with practical life and with Girard's view of *desire* and its causal relation to rivalry and violence.

It is striking to see the prevalence of *evil desire (epithumian kakēn), greed* or *covetousness (RSV; pleonexian)*, and *idolatry (eidololatria;* Gal. 5 also includes *witchcraft* [NIV] or *sorcery* [NRSV], Gr. *pharmakia*) and that *anger, wrath, malice* are close associates in a few texts. The argument that these lists have kinship to (perhaps origin in) Hellenistic usage does not detract from, but adds to, the force of Girard's emphasis regarding the human condition. These vices that characterize the "old life," the life displeasing to God, are all interrelated aspects of what Girard identifies as acquisitive mimetic desire and its evil works. Especially noteworthy is the prominence of *covetousness* (or greed) in this list (echo Gen. 4) and its equivalence with idolatry (echo Gen. 3) in both Colossians and Ephesians.

In contrast to this list, the virtues are compassion, kindness, lowliness, meekness, patience, forbearing one another, and forgiving each other (Col. 3:12-14). The ninefold fruit (sing.) of the Spirit—love, peace, joy, patience, kindness, goodness, faithfulness, gentleness, self-control—is also a gospel description of the new life, in sharp contrast to the works (pl.) of the flesh (Gal. 5:16-24). These vice/virtue lists in the NT epistles thus corroborate Girard's theses regarding the human plight.

But not only is the believer's life to be modeled ethically after virtues that flow from the new life in Christ, but the destiny of believers is interconnected to a process of change, as 2 Cor. 3:17-18 describes it.

> Now the Lord is the Spirit, and where the Spirit of the Lord is, there is freedom. And all of us, with unveiled faces, seeing the glory of the Lord as though reflected in a mirror, are being transformed into the same image from one degree of glory to another; for this comes from the Lord, the Spirit.

Here the image that functions as the object of desire is the exalted Lord Jesus who significantly (see 1 Cor. 4) is never unhooked from the suffering Jesus Christ. But this also means that the model of mimetic desire in the new creation is not only the Jesus of suffering, forgiving, and humble service, but also the exalted, vindicated Jesus, victorious over the powers of evil.

The fundamental conception in Pauline thought that unites believers to their Savior Jesus Christ is the "in Christ" stream of emphasis, so pervasive that entire epistolary discourses are shaped by it (Rom. 6 and 8; Eph. 1).[51] Paul also uses numerous *co*-constructions (with the Greek prefix *sun*): co-buried (*sunetraphēmen*, Rom. 6:4), united with him (*sumphutoi*, 6:5), co-crucified (*sunestaurōthē*, 6:6), co-died (*apethanomen*, 6:8), co-live (*suzēsomen*, 6:8), co-inherit, co-suffer, and be co-glorified (all in 8:17). The grand climax to this co-participation language comes in Rom. 8:29: "in order that we might be conformed (co-formed, *summorphous*) into the image (eikonos) of God's Son, in order that he might be the firstborn (protōtokon) among many brothers and sisters."

This identification with Christ as model is so strong that in some texts Jesus Christ is said to be (manifest) in the believers: the life of Jesus is manifest in our dying bodies (2 Cor. 4:10-12), Christ's sufferings abound in us (2 Cor. 1:5-7); Christ is glorified in my (our) body (Phil. 1:20); that Christ be formed in you (pl.; Gal. 4:19); Christ in you (pl.), the hope of glory (Col. 1:27); and that Christ dwell in your (pl.) hearts by faith (Eph. 3:17a).

Although this language, part and parcel of the massive *in Christ* emphasis, has generated much debate over whether this relationship is to be understood mystically—and if so, what kind?—its obvious connection to the core emphases on *imitation/example/following Jesus* should not be missed. If there is a mysticism here, it is moral and mimetic at its core.[52] It is linked to *desire* and assumes that thought, conduct, and aspiration are governed by new *desires*. The point is put most sharply in Paul's exposition on the first and second Adam (in Rom. 5:12ff.) and his depiction of the new Christ reality as a *new creation*: "So if anyone is in Christ, there is a new creation: everything old has passed away; see, everything has become new!" (2 Cor. 5:17).

Grounded in the life, death, and God's resurrection of Jesus, this new reality makes possible "Things Destined (Now Revealed) before the Foundation of the World." The "in Christ" person dies to the old *acquisitive mimetic desire* and lives by the power of a new mimesis, *imitating the pattern of Jesus Christ and seeking to be conformed to his image.* Jesus in the fullness of his work enables renunciation of the natural human desire for reward or glory.

This desire is "cross-fired," refined through transformation. Through this experience, solely possible through the *Pioneer* of the faith, we learn a new pattern of *mimetic desire*, one that leads not to rivalry and violence, but to building others up, avoiding scandal, preferring one another, empowering the other, and nonretaliation against evil in order that as members of the community of the new creation we break the spiral of violence and become the strands of yarn that by God's Spirit are knitted into the display of love, justice, and shalom.

SUMMARY AND CONCLUSION

A mimesis pattern lies at the heart of NT thought. Any theology or ethics of the NT should make this point foundational, but few do. Just as world culture generally manifests energy via mimetic desire, so life in the kingdom of God, the new creation, is animated and empowered also by a mimetic model. The key difference is that the lead Model is the new Adam precisely because he was tempted with the acquisitive mimeses in all ways such as we are but did not yield to that mimetic pattern that generates rivalry and violence. Jesus as faithful Servant of the Lord has opened up for us a new world of hope and potential; we are saved by his transforming of our desire. We seek then to follow in his steps and be conformed to his image.

Precisely in this context we can grasp anew the full significance of the gospel's declaration that "Christ is our peace" (Eph. 2:14) and that Christ is our reconciliation and entrusts to his followers the ministry of reconciliation (2 Cor. 5:18-20). Further, the pervasive NT teaching on "love of enemy" and "nonretaliation against evil" is the outworking of this new mimesis in an ethic for conflictual relations. To pursue these themes adequately requires another paper. Some of this work has already been done.[53]

Finally, I suggest that the evidence of this paper witnesses analogically to the correctness of Girard's analysis of the human condition and culture. If indeed the life of Jesus' followers is so profusely and consistently described as a relation between Jesus as *Model* and his followers as *imitators-disciples* in self-giving love, service, and suffering, then from the standpoint of this gospel revelation we can deduce also the nature and dynamic of the shadow-model that rules the world: acquisitive mimetic desire, rivalry, and violence (indeed, the Gen. 3-4 depiction).

The element of sacrificial scapegoating that enshrouds the violence in a halo-lie cannot be adduced analogically from the evidence of this paper (though with more work on "atonement" in Mark 10:45; Eph. 5:2; Heb. 12:2; and Rev. 5:9, this may be possible also). However, the ubiquity and reign of the persecutors' myths might be inferred logically from the predominant suffering-martyr experience of the Paracletic community. But as Luke-Acts testifies, the gospel witness of the believers exposes the persecutor's myth and manifests, in life and martyr-death, the proclaimed incarnation of the "gospel of peace" (Luke 10:5-9; Acts 10:36, quoting Isa. 52:7).

NOTES

1. *Things Hidden Since the Foundation of the World* (Stanford, Calif.: Stanford University, 1987), 430.

2. I consider this a neglected area in Girard's work and in writings on Girard. Raymund Schwager has written briefly on this, but quite inadequately. He confines most of his remarks to John's Gospel, emphasizing the significance of Jesus calling his disciples no longer servants, but friends, thus inviting them into full unity with himself and with God his Father. This means renouncing selfish ambitions and striving to be like Christ and God in true love (*Must There Be Scapegoats? Violence and Redemption in the Bible* [San Francisco: Harper & Row, 1987], 176-80). Michael Hardin has also utilized this theme in his analysis of Maximus Confessor's explication of growth into spiritual maturity; see "Mimesis and Dominion: The Dynamics of Violence and the Imitation of Christ in Maximus Confessor," *St. Vladimir's Theological Quarterly* 36, no. 4 (1992): 373-85. More recently, James Alison has added significantly to this emphasis in his profound theological monograph, *Raising Abel: The Recovery of Eschatological Imagination* (New York: Crossroad, 1996).

3. In his more recent writing Girard speaks more of this possiblity and need. See his comments in "How Can Satan Cast Out Satan?" *Biblische Theologie und gesellschaftlicher Wandel*, ed. G. Braulik, W. Gross, S. McEvenue (Norbert Lohfink Festschrift; Freiberg: Herder, 1993), 128, and in an Interview article by Rebecca Adams, "Violence, Difference, Sacrifice: A Conversation with René Girard," *Journal of Religion and Literature* 25, no. 2 (1993): 22-26.

4. This, however, is not the first time that *mimēsis* plays a crucial role in Christian theological dispute. Jim Fodor, in a manuscript, "Imitation and Emulation: Training in Practical Christian Judgment" (For Stanley Hauerwas, The Divinity School of Duke University), observes that Augustine's controversy with the Arians hinged on the issue of the Incarnate Son's relation to the Father, as to whether or not the Son's being is a true mimesis or only a pale reflection. Further, the issue arises in describing the interrelation of the Father, Son, and Spirit more broadly, and is thus intrinsic to the disputed doctrine of *perichorēsis* (Fodor, 40).

5. A. Oepke, *Nachfolge und Nachahmung Christi im NT*, AELKZ 71 (1938), 853-69, and Edvin Larsson, *Christus als Vorbild: Eine Untersuchung zu den paulinischen Tauf- und Eikontexten*, Acta Seminarii Neotestamentici Upsaliensis XXIII (Lund-Uppsal: C. W. K. Gleerup, 1962).

6. *Theological Dictionary of the New Testament,* trans. G. Bromiley (Grand Rapids: Eerdmans, 1967), 4.671-72.

7. Elizabeth A. Castelli, *Imitating Paul: A Discourse of Power* (Louisville, Ky.: Westminster/John Knox, 1991).

8. Fodor, "Imitation and Emulation," 47-48. Worth noting in this regard is that clearly in the thought and life of Ignatius (early second century), who profoundly emulates Paul, the concept of *imitatio Christi* is central. See Willard M. Swartley, "The Imitatio Christi in the Ignatian Letters," *Vigiliae Christianae* 27 (1973), 81-103.

9. For these comments about method and theological order, I am grateful to Diana Culbertson's in absentia written response to my paper at the Colloquium, in stressing that rebirth and daughter/sonship precedes imitation.

10. In the printed Scriptures I normally follow the NRSV. The bold print for imitation and example language is mine.

11. Elisabeth Castelli, in her effort to reduce *imitation* to a rhetorical strategy that utilizes Paul's position of power in a hierarchical structure in order to valorize *sameness*, resists the true import of this plural construction. Even though she recognizes it, she shifts back to the singular: "became imitators of me and of the Lord" (*Imitating Paul*, 95, 91-92). Obviously, this first use of the concept in the plural, which puts *imitation* in a communal *type* context threatens her entire project, to argue that Paul's exhortations, as well as this reference to historical experience, function so that "he constructs a hierarchical community of sameness" (p. 117).

12. Patte, *Paul's Faith and the Power of the Gospel: A Structural Introduction to the Pauline Letters* (Philadelphia: Fortress, 1983), 134-40.

13. Craig A. Evans, "The New Testament and First-Century Judaism," in *Anti-Semitism and Early Christianity: Issues of Polemic and Faith* (Minneapolis: Fortress, 1993), 1-20 (see p. 3 for citation of this Pauline text).

14. Werner Jaeger, *Paideia: The Ideals of Greek Culture* (2nd. ed.; New York: Oxford University, 1945), 1.310. For wider survey in Greek literature, see Castelli, 81-85.

15. See, e.g., James Muilenberg, *The Way of Israel: Biblical Faith and Ethics* (New York: Harper & Brothers, 1961) and Waldemar Janzen, *Old Testament Ethics: A Paradigmatic Approach* (Louisville: Westminster/John Knox, 1994). Janzen's use of the word *paradigm* is similar to the concept of a *model* that one follows.

16. *Scapegoat*, 157-62.

17. In *Biblische Theologie*, ed. G. Braulik et al., 125-41. See also his section, "Beyond Scandal," in *Things Hidden*, 393-431.

18. Girard, *Scapegoat*, 159. Girard then questions whether the Gospel writers fully understood this point. He thinks not, but that they simply repeated what Jesus has said, in all its mysterious detail, specifically the crowing of the cock (twice—mimetically—in Mark, but which in Matthew and Luke is only once). Not understanding the import of this, the story of the cock becomes a kind of miracle fetish, says Girard. On this, Girard is speculative, as he himself suggests (*Scapegoat*, 160).

19. Girard, *Scapegoat*, 158.

20. Girard, *Scapegoat*, 157.

21. On this see Raymund Schwager, "Christ's Death and the Critique of Sacrifice," in *René Girard and Biblical Studies; Semeia* 33; ed. Andrew J. McKenna (Decatur, Ga.: Scholars Press, 1985); also Robert North, "Violence and the Bible: The Girard Connection," *CBQ* 47 (1985), 1-27, esp. pp. 8-10 and his summary of this point on p. 26: "Sacrifice is inadequately equated with simple violence rather than 'self-deprivation for an ulterior goal.'" In *The Bible, Violence, and the Sacred: Liberation from the Myth of Sanctioned Violence* (San Francisco: Harper, 1991), James G. Williams has a good survey of the various (anthropological) theories of sacrifice (pp. 14-20).

22. Girard, *Things Hidden*, 243; in Adam's Interview, 28-31. For an extensive critique of Girard's use and understanding of the word *sacrifice*, see Bruce Chilton, *The Temple of Jesus: His Sacrificial Program within a Cultural History of Sacrifice* (University Park, Pa.: Penn State University Press, 1992), 15-42.

23. On this see Bradley H. McLean, "The Absence of an Atoning Sacrifice in Paul's Soteriology," *NTS* 38 (1992), 531-53. McLean convincingly shows that *sacrifice* is not a category in Paul's explication of Jesus' death, even though metaphors of *redeeming, delivering, expiating, dying/rising* abound.

24. In 2 Macc. 2:28 the word is used to denote the "outline" of a sketch that the artist fills in with detail. But the use by Clement of Alexandria (*Strom.* v.8.49) to denote a "master copy" that pupils use to imitate is more common. Thus Christ sets a pattern to be reproduced. See Charles Biggs, *Epistles of St. Peter and St. Jude* (ICC; Edinburgh: T. & T. Clark, 1901), 145-46. See also G. Schrenk, *TDNT* 1.772-73.

25. Mary H. Schertz, "Nonretaliation and the Haustafeln in 1 Peter," in *The Love of Enemy and Nonretaliation in the New Testament*, ed. Willard M. Swartley (Louisville, Ky.: Westminster/John Knox, 1992), 268-69.

26. William R. Farmer proposes that those books that made it into the canon did so because they nurtured and empowered Christians amid suffering. It is striking how prominent that theme is in virtually all the New Testament writings. See Farmer, *Jesus and the Gospel: Tradition, Scripture and Canon* (Philadelphia: Fortress, 1982), 177-221. Farmer, after showing the correlation between emerging lists of books and persecution, concludes: "That the reality of Christian martyrdom in the early church and the selection of Christian writings for the New Testament canon stand in some vital relationship to one another is as certain as anything that can be conjectured on this complex historical question" (221). See also Farmer and Denis M. Farkasfalvy, *The Formation of the New Testament Canon: An Ecumenical Approach* (New York: Paulist, 1983), 7-95.

27. Girard, *The Scapegoat*, 159.

28. The longer analysis of Girardian perspectives in this story are to be found in Girard, *The Scapegoat* (100-64) and his essay, "How Can Satan Cast Out Satan?"; Williams, *Bible, Violence, Sacred* (185-258); and now in Hamerton-Kelly's work on Mark, *The Gospel and the Sacred: Poetics of Vio-*

lence in Mark (Fortress, 1994).

29. See here Hamerton-Kelly's discussion, *Gospel and Sacred*, 103-11.

30. My book, *Israel's Scripture Traditions and the Synoptic Gospels: Story Shaping Story* (Peabody, Mass.: Hendrickson, 1994) develops broader theses on this point for each of the Synoptics' travel narratives (see ch. 4).

31. For discussion and documentation of this point, see Swartley, *Israel's Scripture Traditions*, 111, n. 50.

32. Again see Swartley, ibid., for discussion, p. 111, and notes 51 and 52 for documentation.

33. In this interpretation, *hodos* leads from Jesus' own history to the suffering experience of Mark's Christian community in the late sixties C.E. See K. G. Reploh, *Markus—Lehrer der Gemeinde: Eine redaktionsgeschichtliche Studie zu den Jüngerperikopen des Markusevangeliums* (SBM 9; Stuttgart: Katholisches Bibelwerk, 1969), 96, 107, 141, 222, 226.

34. It is striking that the various conceptualizations of evil in and behind biblical thought link war and military weapons to evil itself: in the "Watchers Myth" Asael (Azazel) gives to humans the knowledge of weapons for war (1 Enoch 8:1, OTP, I.16); in Genesis 6 the *nephilim* that come from the union of gods and humans are Israel's later giant military foes; in the Isa. 14 and Ezek. 28 arrogant king traditions, which provide much of the later imagery for the devil, the kings are dethroned because of oppressive military power and self-deification; in the early *satan* tradition, Satan incites David to take a census for military enlistment (1 Chron. 21:1ff.). For extensive treatment of the origins of the conceptions of evil reflected in scripture see Neil Forsyth, *The Old Enemy: Satan and the Combat Myth* (Princeton, N.J.: Princeton University Press, 1987), 44-191.

35. Might this be an anti-sacrificial pun?

36. Williams, *Bible, Violence, and Sacred*, 225.

37. See here Williams' discussion of *lytron* (in *Bible, Violence and Sacred*, 190-92, 223-24, and his essay in this volume, 193, 198 n. 24). The phrase may also have its background in the Macabbean martyr theology (see 2 Macc. 7; 4 Macc. 6 and 21). In accepting torture and death, Eleazar says, "Make my blood their purification and take my life as a ransom for theirs" (4 Macc. 6:29; *OTP* I, 552). Similarly, "let our punishment be a satisfaction on their behalf" (v. 28). For an analysis of this tradition as background to the early church's view of atonement see Sam K. Williams, *Jesus' Death As Saving Event: The Background and Origin of A Concept* (HTR Diss. 2; Chico, Calif.: Scholars Press, 1975), 76-90, 165-202, 230-34; John Pobee, *Persecution and Martyrdom in the Theology of Paul* (JSNTSS 6; Sheffield: JSOT Press, 1985), 13-46.

The meaning of *anti* also needs examination. Does it mean *instead* (hardly in 1 Cor. 11:15 and Matt. 5:38), which too easily leads from vicarious to substitutionary, or does it mean *face to face*, the root meaning of *anti*? If the latter, followers are linked to Jesus in identification with the representative head (see Vincent Taylor, *The Atonement in New Testament Teaching* [London: Epworth, 1945], 182-96). The person ransomed is bound to the

Ransomer as disciple and servant. This view fits well Mark's correspondence logic in which Christology forms the basis of discipleship. Nonetheless, it is *Jesus* who gains the victory *for us (extra nos)*; we benefit from and participate in his victory (*Christus Victor*). See Thomas N. Finger, *Christian Theology: An Eschatological Approach*, vol. 1 (Scottdale, Pa.: Herald Press, 1985), 303-348.

38. John R. W. Stott cites Mark 10:45 and the similar phrase in 1 Tim 2:6 for support of his emphasis on the substitutionary element of the atonement (*The Cross of Christ* [Downers Grove: InterVarsity, 1986], 146-48, 177-79). Whereas he and the exegetical tradition that stresses the "in place of, instead" meaning of *anti* are correct, the root meaning of *anti* as "face-to-face" should not be lost. Otherwise this teaching on the atonement tends to disconnect atonement from discipleship, a link that is fundamental to the Mark 10:42-45 context, and to the nature of the Gospel narrative as a whole, in which Jesus' self-giving life and death function prototypically for discipleship. Leonhard Goppelt has commendably emphasized this interconnection in *A Theology of the New Testament*, vol. 1 (Grand Rapids: Eerdmans, 1981), 194-99.

39. This climactic instruction on the way (*en tē hodō*) set as it is within the "conquest" (exodus) imagery of the Old Testament, leaves no doubt that Jesus is presenting a counter model to *acquisitive desire and mimetic rivalry* for the ordering of social and political relationships. If entering and living within the kingdom are guided by this new empowering imagery, which subverts prevailing empire images, then the "way-conquest" tradition, which provided prominent imagery for this section of Mark's presentation of Jesus, has undergone significant transformation. The Divine Warrior Son of humanity Messiah attains the victory, ransoming many, through suffering and death.

40. Williams, *Bible, Violence and the Sacred*, 224.

41. In the only exorcism in this section (9:14-30), Jesus sharply rebukes the disciples for their lack of faith. This story makes it clear that Mark's Jesus does not avoid the fight against evil. Cross-bearing and servanthood are not substitutes for or bypasses around the task of overcoming evil.

42. This accords with atonement theories that emphasize Jesus' humiliation and death as tricking the devil (cf. 1 Cor. 2:6-8).

43. Richard Cassidy, *Society and Politics in Acts of the Apostles* (Maryknoll, N.Y.: Orbis Books, 1989), 159-60.

44. John H. Yoder, *The Politics of Jesus* (Grand Rapids: Eerdmans, 1972), ch. 7, 115-34 (2d ed., 1994: 112-33).

45. For a complete list see Albert Schweitzer, *The Mysticism of St. Paul the Apostle* (New York: Seabury, 1968 [Germ. orig., 1931]), 123-27, and Lewis Smedes, *Union with Christ* (Grand Rapids: Eerdmans, 1983), esp. 55-135.

46. Yoder, 175 (2nd. ed., 172).

47. Yoder, 180 (2nd. ed., 177).

48. Yoder, 134 (2nd. ed., 131).

49. Michael Griffiths selects a broader set of texts in his helpful work, *The Example of Jesus* (Downers Grove, Ill.: InterVarsity, 1985).

50. Modified from Ernest Martin, *Colossians-Philemon*; Believers Church Bible Commentary (Scottdale, Pa.: Herald, 1994), 163.

51. On this see A. Schweitzer, *Mysticism*, 120-30; Smedes, *Union with Christ*, 55-85; and the several treatments by Lucien Cerfaux, *The Christian in the Theology of St. Paul* (London; G. Chapman Ltd., 1967); *Christ in the Theology of St. Paul* (New York: Herder & Herder, 1959); *The Church in the Theology of St Paul* (New York: Herder & Herder, 1959).

52. For a survey of the various interpretations, see Smedes, *Union*, 58-67.

53. See the three volumes in the Studies in Peace and Scripture series with Westminster/John Knox Press published in 1992. These include *The Gospel of Peace* by Ulrich Mauser; *The Meaning of Peace: Biblical Essays*, ed. by Perry B. Yoder and Willard M. Swartley (esp. the essay by Erich Dinkler); and *The Love of Enemy and Nonretaliation in the New Testament*, ed. by Willard M. Swartley (see esp. the article by Luise Schottroff).

CHAPTER TWELVE

Christian Discipleship as Participative Imitation: Theological Reflections on Girardian Themes

Jim Fodor

INTRODUCTION

The pride of place given to discipleship and its accompanying notion, imitation (*mimesis*), is perhaps the one feature that most characterizes Christian devotion throughout the centuries. Christians have long acknowledged and affirmed the central role imitation plays in their lives as faithful followers of Jesus, in their spiritual development and ascent to God. Although discipleship proves extremely difficult, if not impossible, without the exercise of our imitative capacities, Christians are at the same time aware that our mimetic desires often generate negative, personally distorting, and socially destructive forms of life—all of which is to say that without further qualification imitation (emulation or modeling) is not, in itself, virtuous.

Indeed, what crucially distinguishes Christian mimesis from all other forms of imitation cannot be measured apart from its specific, unsubstitutable object and its peculiarly peaceable, nonviolent character, both of which are displayed in the action and suffering, the life and death of Jesus of Nazareth. In this regard, Christians owe a great debt to René Girard, whose fascinating analyses of the scapegoat mechanism help unmask the intrinsically violent proclivities structurally embedded in our unredeemed, mimetic desires. Without question, a Girardian hermeneutic has much to offer, enriching not only our understanding of the texts of the New Testament in general but the Pauline texts in particular.

In his wonderfully rich and suggestive essay, "Discipleship and Imitation of Jesus/Suffering Servant: The Mimesis of New Creation" (reproduced as a chapter in this book), Willard Swartley provides concrete detail and specificity to the Girardian thesis that in the life and death of Jesus Christians are given an imitative pattern, a model of nonacquisitive, nonviolent mimesis that decisively breaks the spiral of violence and enmity that so characterizes unregenerate human life.

To be sure, following Jesus as his disciples does not call for obliterating our mimetic desires; on the contrary, it demands that they be redirected, reoriented, and refashioned away from selfish, acquisitive, and violent forms of mimesis to patterns of imitation that are forgiving, other-regarding, peaceable, loving, and marked by humble service. Indeed, embarking on the way of Jesus, being made part of the life of Christ through incorporation into his body, the church, is precisely to have our mimetic desires so ordered, disciplined, shaped, reformed, and reeducated that we become, in fact, what we have already been made; namely, a new creation (2 Cor. 5:17).

Following Jesus means, of course, entering particular types of association and adopting a peculiar set of complexly related activities and behaviors—but at its center lies an unmistakable mimetic pattern.[1] This becomes evident not only in Swartley's examination of Paul's language of mimesis but also his comparison of a number of Pauline passages with wider New Testament paranetic teachings, especially those Gospel narratives that deal specifically with Jesus' instructions to his disciples.

Although the focus of Swartley's essay is on the relation between discipleship, suffering, and imitation—in particular what that means in light of Jesus' designation as Suffering Servant—he nevertheless offers the reader a much wider panoramic display of the qualities, characteristics, and habits that constitute a life of Christian discipleship. Suffering, of course, is intimately related to Paul's use of mimesis and thus plays a central role in the formation of Jesus' disciples. The imitation/suffering theme cannot be understood in isolation but must be situated in, linked to, and integrated with a whole cluster of related ideas, including "the conceptual field of love, forgiveness, servanthood, [and] humility. . . ."

Indeed, the cogency of Swartley's argument is strengthened precisely to the extent that broader soteriological themes are related to, and thus made to bear on, the language of imitation and discipleship, perhaps the most important of which include the notions of "correspondence" and "participation," "conformity," and "identification." That we are to "identify" with Christ is a motif that appears in numerous places throughout the New Testament, such as in those texts that speak of believers participating in the divine nature, of being "in" Christ, of putting on a new nature, of sharing in Christ's risen life, and so on.

Furthermore, our understanding of imitation and discipleship is also qualified by a certain logic of 'correspondence' or analogy. Scripture, after all, speaks of believers forgiving as God in Christ forgave us, of loving indiscriminately as God loved us, of serving others even as Christ became a servant of all, of suffering innocently yet without complaint, just as Jesus did. By setting the subject of imitation in a matrix of ever-expanding and increasingly elaborate connections, Swartley finds corroboration for his central thesis; namely, that "the New Testament language of mimesis/discipleship carries contextual emphases which prevent, even repudiate, *the mimesis of acquisitive desire*" (p. 219 above).

The import of Swartley's essay is both singularly clear and impressive. He has persuasively demonstrated that despite their somewhat different understandings of what is entailed in following Jesus, the several New Testament writers nonetheless speak with one voice. Indeed, the full amplitude and depth of the imitative aspects of Christian discipleship can only properly emerge in the rich polyphonic discourse of the New Testament as a whole. Although not every New Testament voice sings the melody, they all nevertheless contribute their own individual tones and timbres so as to produce a fully rounded, if not always a perfectly agreeable harmony.

The purpose of this essay is twofold. First of all, I wish to respond to Swartley's chapter by elaborating and extending—more theologically and hermeneutically than exegetically—a number of themes and relations his essay helpfully delineates.[2] By developing some of Swartley's ideas in a more wide-ranging and intentionally theological manner, I hope to set the notion of imitation and discipleship in a Trinitarian framework that will encourage a distinctively Christian appreciation of Girard's insights regarding mimesis and imitative desire. This is the second part of my twofold objective. In other words, I intend to show the following: first, a Trinitarian understanding of God, supported by the careful exegetical/theological work exhibited in Swartley's essay, at once allows for—indeed invites—a Girardian reading. Second, however, a Trinitarian understanding at the same time carefully circumscribes, limits, and interrogates such a reading. By elaborating and refining in an explicitly Trinitarian fashion particular exegetical points and theological insights introduced in Swartley's chapter, a certain point of vantage will be gained from which to explore specific problem areas in Girard's work, critical queries that have been provoked in part by Swartley's work and also by my own rather limited reading of Girard.

EXEGETICAL, THEOLOGICAL, AND HERMENEUTICAL CONSIDERATIONS

I begin by isolating what I consider to be Swartley's singular contribution to our understanding of Christian discipleship and how it accords with Girard's theory of sacred violence and acquisitive mimetic desire—though it may not depend on or be derived from it. First, Swartley is right in exhorting biblical scholars to engage in fresh exegetical investigations on the mimesis texts, given the often truncated and misleading views of mimesis that have dominated the discipline in the past—even the not so distant past.[3]

Although Swartley appreciates the value of Girard's theory of mimetic desire—that it may serve, in some respects, as a useful corrective to past abuses—he also knows it represents no panacea. Hence his appropriation of Girard is not only cautious and judicious but importantly suggestive. This is the case insofar as he attends closely to the actual *shape* of Jesus' life and death by carefully examining the particular *idioms* in which the life and passion of our Lord find expression in the biblical texts. In this regard, Swartley makes up for what is lacking in Girard's theory and thereby indirectly corrects him.

Although Girard is undoubtedly right to emphasize Jesus' refusal of violence, he allows little place for the distinctive, concrete forms taken by Jesus' nonviolent practice.[4] Mimesis is a universal human proclivity, according to Girard, and thus identifiable with culture itself. However, because his thesis is articulated at such a high level of abstraction, it is difficult to see precisely what Jesus' preaching of the kingdom could really amount to, what positive content it might convey, other than the negative gesture of refusal of acquisitive desire.

In short, Girard's theory is all too formal; he does not take the care to elaborate in any great detail the positive, alternative practices, ways of life, or patterns of behavior enjoined by the gospel. But what is finally compelling, I would contend—and I think Swartley would agree—is not the mere idea of nonacquisitive mimesis but how it is that one might become initiated in and apprenticed to a particular way of life that actually manifests nonacquisitive, nonviolent mimesis. In other words, unless and until nonacquisitive desire expresses itself in particular habits of attention, practices, patterns of behavior, and forms of worship and praise, it is hard for anyone to understand its character, let alone experience its power, be persuaded of its virtues, assess its merits, or gauge its veracity. It is precisely at this point that Swartley's careful exegetical work becomes so indispensable.

Establishing indissociable connections between discipleship and suffering is one of Swartley's foremost contributions. Not only are the themes of suffering and mimesis integrally connected in the Pauline corpus, but the fact that some of these texts are among the earliest in the New Testament suggests just how important imitation is to the identity, character, and self-understanding of Christians. Indeed, for many early believers the fact that they received the gospel in adverse circumstances meant that suffering and affliction were intrinsic to their relation to the Lord Jesus and therefore constitutive of the Christian faith.

Suffering, then, becomes perhaps one of the most determinative, identifying marks of the church. Suffering certified the disciples' witness as Christians; it marked them as followers of Jesus. In one important respect, then, mimesis is not only something that Christians *do* as much as it is something that Christians *undergo*; mimesis is something they *suffer*. That point cannot be lost if we are properly to understand the nonacquisitive, dispossessive, nonviolent mimetic desire that informs our own life and practice as disciples of Jesus.

DISCIPLESHIP AND THE "WAY" OF SUFFERING

Swartley's reading of the central section of Mark's Gospel complements and supports this unmistakably Pauline emphasis. Indeed, suffering characterizes not only the way of Jesus in his passion, but also the way of the disciples who follow him. For Jesus' very life and teaching represent an invitation to embark on a distinctive journey, a different "Way," a new *hodos*.[5] The Suffering Servant motif also coalesces with those of discipleship and "the Way." This fusion of the hodos theme with those of imitation, discipleship, and suffering accords nicely with the Girardian thesis regarding the nature of sacred violence. If we are to avoid the *skandalon* that violent, acquisitive mimesis produces, we must not only repudiate those desires but actively learn (and relearn, because we are still on the Way) new ways to live at peace with one another according to the nonviolent pattern set forth in Jesus' life and death. Hence, learning the peaceful demeanor and irenic practices of Jesus precisely *is* to repudiate acquisitive mimetic desire.

MARK'S STORY: A HERMENEUTICS OF "THE WAY"

The hodos theme in Mark's Gospel—the Way of discipleship and of suffering, the way of the cross—requires greater theological elaboration if we are to appreciate fully the sense in which mimesis is both a literary and a social praxis.[6] Telling a story can never be fully distinguished from its enactment—simply because any engagement with a story never leaves everything exactly as it is, not least the reader/hearer of the Word. All readership, therefore, presupposes some form of discipleship. And to the extent that all serious reading of Scripture entails a set of disciplined practices embodied in specific, identifiable forms of life, it too exhibits that general relation.

Mimesis, therefore, mediates a complex reality that is at once in yet beyond the text. In this regard, Mark's Gospel "not only imitates the character and teaching of Christ in it, but provokes and engages *our* imitation of the character and teaching of Christ (our discipleship) beyond it."[7] To engage the gospel story, in other words, is to "become part of a performance that draws disciples and readers into its suggestive depths."[8] Reading the scriptural texts aright results in—or, better, is coextensive with—an initiation into or instruction in the way of discipleship. To "follow" the biblical text correctly is to be enabled on the Way. For to perform an act of reading is already to obey, to be disciplined by and thus empowered to act in accordance with, a particular set of protocols. Discerning the meaning of the biblical text is thus less decoding it—as if the text were an extrinsic object standing over against the reader—and more entering the life or the world or the Way of the Bible.

Construing meaning as mimesis, then, underscores the active, participative, self-reflective sense in which disciple-readers have been taken up in the Way of the Lord as that manifests itself in the gospel narratives. Accordingly, it is more true of meaning to say that it "shows" or "exhibits" itself in our lives than to say of meaning that it presents itself as something over which control might be exercised, because it is contained "in" a text.

In a very profound, albeit paradoxical sense, following Jesus is likewise less a matter of choosing than of being chosen.[9] To be sure, Christian discipleship continually calls for choices and decisions, many of which are extremely difficult and costly, but this in no way diminishes the sense in which discipleship is just as truly a matter of recognition and consent, that is, an acknowledgment that we have already been on the Way well before we have consciously and deliberately chosen that way as our own. Here the New Testament language of being made partakers with Christ, of being "co-opted" or incorporated into his body, is especially pertinent.

The mimetic process, of course, like that of discipleship, is always *in media res*, always on the Way. And this is how it should be, if the structure of Mark's Gospel is testament at all to what it means to follow Christ. Indeed, one curious feature of the Gospel of Mark is that it has structurally neither a real beginning nor a "proper" ending. As Graham Ward notes,

> The opening of Mark's Gospel draws attention to the fact that it is no beginning at all. The first word, *Arche*, is anarthrous and the noun or verbal form reoccur[s] throughout the narrative (31 times in Mark; 17 times in Matthew). One could either say the narrative is always trying to define a beginning (and cannot) or that all "beginnings" are pragmatic for Mark (i.e., there is no true beginning at all). In the opening fourteen verses of the Gospel there are no less than five beginnings.[10]

Similarly, Mark's Gospel comes to an abrupt end, which is no real ending either. Any final end is deferred and the reader is instead forced to double back on the story.

> There is in the "end" no final release from the rhythm of the narrative. The book cannot be closed and put away as if the tale is completed. We, like the disciples and as contemporary representations of discipleship, return to Galilee to learn again, to reinterpret. We, like the disciples, remain caught in the nets of the Christian story (and its telling and re-telling). And in doing so we continue the story, represent it anew in our lives. . . .[11]

Discipleship, then, means being inscribed in the story even as the story orchestrates the rhythmic patterns, habitual cadences, and recurrent patterns of practice and behavior that uniquely shape Christian faithfulness.

Discipleship, imitation, and participation are thus mutually defining categories, principally in Mark's Gospel, but also in the New Testament's overarching mimetic structure of redemption. Since the economies of salvation and discipleship are one and the same, it is not by accident that Swartley should be led to Mark's Gospel in developing the interconnected themes of suffering, imitation, discipleship, and the Way. That the hodos on which Jesus' disciples have embarked should also be the way of suffering touches on important questions regarding the atonement.

DISCIPLESHIP, ATONEMENT, AND SUFFERING

Although I want to elaborate these connections a little more fully below in conjunction with my critique of Girard, it is important at this juncture to set the broad parameters of the discussion to highlight the crucial and weighty theological implications of Swartley's exegetical analyses. By stressing the life-giving service of the Suffering Servant for all humanity, the way Jesus lay down his life as a ransom for many, Swartley astutely balances two ingredients. One is the traditional emphasis on the substitutionary aspects of the atonement (Jesus died *instead of* or *in place of* us). The other is the equally important but sadly neglected emphasis on the deep, bonding relation, the "face to face" encounter, formed between Redeemer and redeemed.

Accentuating the substitutionary aspects of the atonement at the expense of the ransom motif has the unwelcome effect of disconnecting atonement and discipleship, thereby underwriting a noxious form of cheap grace. In other words, Jesus' life-giving life and death function prototypically for discipleship to the extent that his followers are now bound to Jesus as one who is our leader, our pioneer, our servant-head who introduces us to a life of servant-type living. But more than this, we are bound to Jesus as friends. Friendship is indispensable to understanding the salvific work of God in Christ

Articulating the rich complexity of God's redemptive activity without at the same time obscuring, neglecting, or doing injustice to one or other of its manifold aspects, is probably one of the most vexing problems attending Christian theology. Even the most cursory glance at the major attempts to construct a doctrine of redemption will reveal a number of these one-sided approaches.[12]

Part of the problem, of course, is that no one theory or model appears fully capable of circumscribing God's reconciling activity, of rendering one aspect of it without at the same time concealing, distorting, or diminishing another. In short, the challenge is to avoid losing the "theo-dramatic tension" of the whole.[13] Confusion over the nature of imitation, not to mention the role of suffering[14] and the intractable temporal/eschatological dimensions of redemption (the fact that salvation continually happens on the Way), compounds this already formidable task. My purpose here is not to become embroiled in the continuing theological debates about atonement, but to register the fact that themes of imitation, suffering, participation, and the Way are indispensable to that discussion.

That imitation has received renewed attention of late, thanks partly to the work of Girard, is both a promising sign and a subtle danger. Girard's conception of mimesis is promising, I will argue, because it is neither strictly Platonic nor Aristotelian in character, and hence remains open to inflection by Christian practice and biblical faith. It continues to present a danger, however, precisely because it tends to entrench rather than debunk prevailing notions of mimesis.[15]

Reinvigorated interest in mimesis, then, presents a temptation to theology precisely insofar as the notion is made to carry conceptual burdens far greater than it can bear. Or, better put, a Christian construal of imitation is faulty and incomplete to the extent that it is not properly related to a wider supporting cast of theological motifs. Given its central, dominating role in Girard's theory of the scapegoat mechanism, mimesis tends to obscure the other vitally important structures of exchange, participation, sociality, fellowship, incorporation, and union which are crucial to Christian existence.

Historically, Christians have found considerable difficulty establishing a satisfactory relationship between grace and morality, justification and sanctification.[16] Indeed, once the Christian life of discipleship is set in the broader context of participation in the benefits of Christ's finished work of salvation, two (characteristically Protestant) reservations about mimetic language emerge. First, imitation tends to imply a deficient Christology to the extent that language of mimesis appears to reduce Jesus Christ to the status of an exemplar. Second, imitation tends to shift attention away from God's prior agency in forgiveness and reconciliation and refocus it instead on the salvific efficacy of our own actions. This is especially problematic when themes of imitation and participation are conjoined.

The great fear is that "imitation language may make it acutely difficult to state the distinction between Christ and the Christian, since it may imply that human morality is in some sense an extension or continuation of his work rather than a testifying to it in properly human and derivative action."[17] Christians are, to be sure, rightly wary of advocating the idea that believers are simply absorbed into or merge with Christ, rendering all differences between them superfluous. However, Christians at the same time feel compelled to do justice to the force of the biblical affirmation, not only that there are profound somatic connections between Christ and his followers,[18] but that Jesus' followers are, in some deep sense, truly and actively work-ing at the same reconciliation as their Lord (2 Cor. 5:14-21).

Moreover, given the strong participatory dimension to Christian life, it seems to follow that suffering is also an unavoidable compan-ion to discipleship.[19] Disciples, after all, are those whose lives are be-ing conformed to the pattern of Christ's suffering and death. Paul's letters in particular are replete with language of this sort. Paul says that "we share abundantly in Christ's sufferings" (2 Cor. 1:5, RSV); that he is "always carrying in the body the death of Jesus" (2 Cor. 4:10, RSV); that his purpose is to "share his sufferings" (Phil. 3:10, RSV). The crux of the matter, however, comes at Colossians 1:24, where the author speaks of how in the sufferings of his own flesh he is "completing what is lacking in Christ's afflictions" (RSV).

The Colossians passage, while underscoring the indissoluble connections between the believers' life and the life of Christ, has nonetheless produced endless controversies about the sufficiency of Christ's work of redemption vis-à-vis the Christian's own need to participate in (and ostensibly "complete" by imitating) Christ's suf-ferings.[20] Without fully entering the seemingly intractable exegetical problems generated by this Colossians text, I do wish to suggest that if a satisfactory account of the relation between mimesis, suffering, and atonement is forthcoming, it must be placed in a broader Trinitarian framework. For the doctrine of the Trinity is "the ever-present, inner presupposition of the doctrine of the Cross" (and here "Cross" is always used to include the Resurrection, which is the Pauline-Johannine practice, but also that of the Synoptics). "In the same way, and symmetrically to it, the doctrine of the covenant or of the Church . . . must not be regarded as a mere result of the Cross-event but as a constituent element of it."[21]

To be sure, simply because Girard has not developed these inte-gral Trinitarian, covenantal, and ecclesial dimensions in his descrip-tion of the scapegoat mechanism does not in itself preclude theolo-gians from availing themselves of his important insights. What it does suggest, however, is that appropriating Girardian ideas *without considerable modification and supplementation* will result in an under-standing of mimetic desire that is highly deficient for Christian theol-ogy for reasons hopefully apparent below.[22]

THE TRINITARIAN CHARACTER OF CHRISTIAN DISCIPLESHIP

Although Girard is surely right to alert Christians to the perva-sive role that mimetic desire plays in human life, what remains underdeveloped is the sense in which desire, if it is to be properly Christian, must be grounded in the life of God as Trinity. Failure to explicate mimesis adequately in a Trinitarian framework has the unwelcome effect of leaving intact, rather than problematizing and displacing, the human "will" as central to discipleship. Indeed, any model that separates the will from prayer, contemplation, and dispossession is woefully inadequate.[23] As it stands, most accounts of mimetic desire (Girard's included) presuppose a notion of human agency predicated on the idea of the individual as self-constituted through willful choice and decision.

In light of the gospel, such a view simply will not do. For the disciple is not first and foremost one who constructs herself or himself in the process of performance; if that were the case, the meaning of our actions would unavoidably and exclusively terminate in the will's success.[24] Not only that, but given what Girard rightly describes as the competitive, Hobbesian-like character of unregenerate human life, any attempt to extricate ourselves from unredeemed human structures of desire would inevitably fail. We would remain trapped in a never-ending, downward spiral of animosity, conflict, rivalry, and violence.

Discipleship, however, is grounded in God, not in our own will or desire. External autonomous achievement does not secure our status as Jesus' disciples. On the contrary, the disciple's adequacy or excellence or attunement to God lies, in its most determinative sense, outside the agent's control.[25] Our actions, in the final analysis, are grounded in God rather than in our own desires. In that respect human acts of faithfulness always show more than the life of the agent: they show the character of the Creator.[26]

The first word that needs to be spoken about discipleship, then, is not mimesis but *kenosis*, self-emptying, a "relinquishing" or "giving over."[27] The initial kenosis in the Godhead that underpins all subsequent kenosis is, of course, the Father's self-utterance in generation of the Son.[28] God the Father must not be thought to exist prior to this self-surrender; rather, he *is* the movement of self-giving that holds nothing back. Likewise, the Son's answer to the gift of Godhead can only be eternal thanksgiving to the Father, a thanksgiving as selfless and unreserved as the Father's original self-surrender. Proceeding from both, as their subsistent "We," there breathes the Spirit who is common to the Father and the Son. As the essence of love, the Spirit maintains the infinite difference between Father and Son, seals it, and, since he is the one Spirit of them both, bridges that difference.

The doctrine of God as Trinity, therefore, is essentially about a God who is *perichoresis*: "an unceasing dialectically corrective movement."[29] God as Trinity signifies the self-giving or self-dispossession that marks the divine life, not in terms of some impassive, eternal substance, but as a "giving away" or "giving place." In other words, God's life is eternally generative of difference, but a "difference that is still conceivable as communion or continuity."[30] Indeed, because the fellowship of Father, Son, and Spirit is distinguished by continuous self-dispossession and self-giving, a certain space is opened up whereby we, as God's creatures, are enabled to share in God's Trinitarian life—which is but another way to speak of human friendship with God.

That God invites our friendship, our participation in God's own peaceable life, is the most astounding, extravagant, but wonderfully remarkable fact of salvation.[31] Since we have been made friends of God, our lives—if they be truly godly—must mirror the self-dispossessive features which characterize the Trinitarian relations of the Godhead. That is to say, if faithful Christian discipleship genuinely exhibits God's love, then our lives must become transparent to the self-giving life of God as revealed in the Lord's Christ who gave himself up on our behalf. Our desire for God, then, is not fundamentally acquisitive and violent but dispossessive, self-emptying, peaceable.[32]

The task that remains peculiar to theology is to articulate and strengthen the epiphanic quality of Christian discipleship; that is, to show how our lives manifest God's character. This is another way of saying that discipleship is finally not about obedience or submission but rather about manifestation and witness—disclosing, making visible, making palpable, making present the purposes of God in the world in order that God might be glorified.[33] As Rowan Williams puts it, as disciples "we are to act in such a way that the nature of God becomes visible, in the way it was visible in the life and death of Jesus."[34]

Given the unceasing dispossessive movement that constitutes God's Trinitarian life, discipleship cannot be reduced to a choice between mimesis and participation. Rather, discipleship means maintaining these two central ideas in motion, keeping both in elliptical orbit around one another. If Christian mimesis is unavoidably participatory, so too participation in God's life proves inescapably mimetic—for the simple reason that we only know what it means to participate in God's life by imitating the pattern set forth in his Son.

To be sure, our ability to imitate the sufferings of Christ presupposes our having first experienced the power of his resurrection. But this must not obscure or override the fact that such power only manifests itself in us as we become like him in his death. As Paul puts it, "For his sake I have suffered the loss of all things . . . that I may know him and the power of his resurrection, and share his sufferings" (Phil. 3:8b, 10a, RSV). As disciples, therefore, we participate in the divine activity of redemption to "show God's glory and invite or attract human beings to 'give glory' to God."[35]

The imperative force of Christian imitation remains, to be sure, but given its epiphanic *telos* the character of that imitation is radically altered. Far from being driven by desires which are antagonistic or competitive, the true disciple is impelled by what John Dunne calls "heart's desire," theological rationale of which is to act in such a way that our action might become a vehicle of God's glory.

The crucial aspect of Christian discipleship, then, the one thing that Girard's understanding of mimetic desire cannot account for, is this radical renunciation or *kenosis*.[36] For as long as mimetic desire is construed in terms of the strictly immanent social bonds and structures that found, form, and maintain human societies, Girard cannot find a place for self-dispossesive or self-emptying love. Because his construal of the scapegoat mechanism remains too immanent, too anthropologically centered, he fails to attend to the ways in which imitation, for the Christian at least, presupposes participation in a more determinative, saving economy.

In short, mimetic desire as espoused by Girard is not yet a properly theological account because it is insufficiently Trinitarian. Girard's theory of mimetic desire is not so much wrong as it is partial and incomplete. A truly adequate expression of the relation between imitation, suffering, and discipleship—either in Paul or the New Testament generally—requires "a Trinitarian structure of discourse about the eternal life of God."[37]

SPECIFIC CRITICISMS OF GIRARD

Let me turn, in this second section, to a few further criticisms of Girard's theory of sacred violence, criticisms which have only indirectly emerged in the course of my constructive theological elaborations and proposals, but which nonetheless require sharper definition, if not explicit formulation. I have already indicated how Girard's inadequate Trinitarian display of the atonement renders his account of the scapegoat mechanism less than compelling theologically.

I want to touch on two additional but related problem areas, each of which is afflicted with questionable substantive claims as well as suspect methodological assumptions. The first has to do with Girard's understanding of the relation between mimetic desire and sin. The second concerns his Christology. Given the methodological problems that bedevil both areas, let me first say a word or two about Girard's methodology in general.

METHODOLOGICAL INTERROGATIONS

Perhaps the most deeply troubling and debilitating feature of Girard's theory of sacred violence—at least from a philosophical perspective—is that it remains positivistic in outlook.[38] In Girard's view, religion legitimates and secures culture. Indeed, because religion can be explained in terms of (and to that extent is reducible to) social scientific categories, its secondary, derivative status is more or less assured. In fact, it is methodologically predetermined.

Religion, in other words, can only be a later, secondary phenomenon whose invention is necessary to safeguard the relatively smooth and stable functioning of human societies. Its task is more or less one of generating mechanisms that will cope with cultural crises, correct political instabilities, restore social imbalances, and generally insure order and equilibrium.[39] Religion does not so much *found* the social order as *regulate* the components of an already given, pre-existing reality. The difficulty with this view, of course, is this: apart from the insuperable problem of establishing culture's ontological priority to religion (not to mention their possible symbiotic coexistence[40]), it is not even clear whether there is such a thing as "religion." It is uncertain whether religion is "univocally definable in such a fashion as clearly to distinguish it from culture in general."[41]

Apart from his positivistic and essentialistic proclivities, many critics chide Girard for his speculative conceit, for advancing an overly ambitious "scientific" theory which purports to account for the vital function of religion in all societies.[42] Indeed, Girard is not unaware of these criticisms and has a ready response. In the first place, what he means by "scientific" is nothing more than a certain ability or explanatory power that enables one to account for all the data.

Girard's project is scientific, in other words, "because it allows for a rigorous definition of such key terms as *divinity, ritual, rite,* and *religion.*"[43] Although frequently employing the language of "hypothesis," "science," "law," and so on, Girard's use of "explanation" does not exactly fit the standard scientific model. Far from explaining in any scientific sense of the term, Girard is more accurately "re-describing"—that is, "drawing attention to certain recurrent patterns."[44] Hence, for those who ridicule the excessive ambition of *le systeme-Girard* and its grandiose claims, Girard has the following reply: "What they mistake for an encyclopedic appetite is the single insight that I pursue wherever I can recognize *it*."[45]

But exactly what is the "it" that Girard claims single-mindedly to pursue and recognize? Is it "sacrifice," "the scapegoat or victimage mechanism," "acquisitive mimetic desire," "violence"? Whatever Girard takes "it" to be, his assertion is surely contestable. For whatever phenomenon "it" signifies, what is in view is clearly *not* a single, homogeneous, uniformly identical reality, transparent and obvious to all.

In this regard, Girard betrays a tendency to be seduced, held captive, by his own use of abstract terms. His habit is to employ, for example, such notions as violence, sacrifice, and mimetic desire, as if each named some self-identical constant or essence. But even on Girard's own terms, we can only know what sacrifice or violence or mimetic desire is relative to the forms of life in which they are embedded. What these phenomena are, how they are recognized, identified, and thus named—that is, how they are explained or re-described—will vary across cultures and communities of readers. These essentializing tendencies raise questions about the singularity and ubiquity of Girard's insight regarding *the* scapegoat mechanism.

GIRARD ON MIMETIC DESIRE

A similar homogenizing tendency, which obscures important differences and erases significant contrasts, also infects Girard's account of desire. According to Girard, desire is entirely arbitrary; it is never for the objectively desirable but only for what others deem to be desirable. We copy or mimic the desires of others, not because desire is innate but because it is something we learn. It is part of our psychosocial formation. Thus desire is not linear or binary, moving from the person desiring to the thing wanted. Rather, desire is triangular, moving between the desiring self, the object, and the other who also desires.

The operative presupposition, therefore, is that the "original" state of society, the primordial condition of culture, is always one of competing equals set in a realm of scarcity. All cultural differences are in principle generated from dualistic oppositions arising out of mimetic antagonism. This rather Hobbesian view of the original human condition implies that we are inevitably caught in a universal, reciprocal violence of all against all.

It is not clear, however, that all desire is objectless, that no thing or person or idea or practice has intrinsic value. Nor is it the case that all desires that others have necessarily intensify my desires.[46] What others desire may disgust, annoy, or, on more than a few occasions, entirely disinterest me. From the fact that we are caught up with each other and become models for each other, it does not follow that all human desires can be explained in terms of what others desire.[47] To be sure, Girard's theory of mimetic desire is not a purely structuralist account. Although his theory of mimetic rivalry is largely synchronic, it is not strictly so. For anterior to the whole process he posits a "primal human scene of which no record has been preserved, yet which we must suppose really to have occurred."[48]

Positing this purportedly "original human condition," however, does not quite get Girard off the hook. For even if we were to grant Girard his "primal scene," which would allow him to circumvent the problem of infinite regress, it is not entirely clear in what sense it could be said that imitation or desire *as such* precedes particular desires for specific objects. The final and perhaps most acute objection, however, is that it is not readily apparent that Girard's understanding of mimesis can actually do the work necessary to support his theory of sacred violence. This is elaborated below in conjunction with Girard's structural understanding of sin.

In addition to his rather narrow, one-dimensional understanding of mimesis, Girard is hampered by the notion of a relatively autonomous, self-sufficient, desiring agent.[49] Because Girard's theory of imitative violence does not quite dispel the illusion of self-possession, the idea of nonidentical repetition as more determinative than simple mimicry in explicating the character of Christian discipleship is never entertained.[50] To be sure, "imitation can readily suggest something purely mechanical and/or derivative, so that it can readily acquire a cheapening sense."[51]

Although Girard rightly rejects such a naive view, it is not clear that his account of mimesis is sufficiently nuanced to display the reciprocal relations between imitation and repetition—something clearly required by Christian accounts. As all faithful disciples know, any attempt to repeat *exactly* the content of Christ's life is to repeat it *differently*.[52] In other words, the nonidentical repetition that inheres in any true mimesis, any genuine following, is more complex and nuanced than what could be embraced in Girard's vision. As Milbank persuasively argues, the other is not only a repository of values to be imitated, but has also a life of goals, longings, and quests. The other is continuously in process so that his or her desires cannot be specified precisely at any given time. Copying another, who is first agent in her own right can never occur "in an automatic, predetermined relation to the object of the . . . [other] person's desire." Thus before or as one imitates another, his relation to the uncertain *telos* of the other will have supervened.[53]

Whereas Girard's account of mimesis is certainly alert to the complex, intersubjective patterns of sociality and rapport, conflict and rivalry that characterize social life (precluding thereby any simple equation of mimesis with duplication), his explanation nonetheless excludes the possibility of any *direct* supervention of a *telos* over and above the network of mimetic relations.[54] In short, Girard's account of mimetic desire remains locked in immanent structures of human social life in a way that precludes transcendent irruption. This has crucial implications for a Christian understanding of sin, especially if the repudiation of desire as such is structurally ruled out. There are implications as well for Christology, especially if salvation is merely a matter of realigning or redirecting human desire.

SIN AND THE ONTOLOGICAL NECESSITY OF DESIRE

Underwriting mimesis with a metaphysics is always a very dangerous enterprise. Girard admirably displays little or no compunction to provide a philosophical foundation to his understanding of mimetic desire. At the same time, however, there is a sense in which metaphysical convictions are unavoidably, if only tacitly and unreflectively, embraced.[55]

Although Girard does not advance an explicit ontology of his own, he does attempt to offer some sort of transcendental grounding to his understanding of mimetic desire. For on the one hand, Girard characterizes mimetic activity as a more or less universal trait of human societies. On the other hand, Girard speaks of mimetic desire as having psychosocial rather than biological roots.[56] Mimetic desire, therefore, appears to be at once contingent but also an ontological necessity, at the same time part of the human condition, yet learned and acquired. In theological language, sin appears structurally lodged in human subjectivity per se, in the patterns of mimetic relations that constitute our intersubjective, social life. But this is too nearly a gnostic reading which demonizes an entire aspect of human nature. From the outset, our very creaturely condition appears infected with sinful desire.

GIRARD'S CHRISTOLOGY

If sin is gnostically lodged in our finitude, as Girard seems to suggest, then salvation becomes, for the Christian, more a matter of listening to Christ's wise diagnosis than actually following him in a peaceable path, being schooled by him in the way of nonviolence.[57] Girard's interpretation of redemption, moreover, not only tends to be psychoanalytical but gnostic. He speaks of Christ "uncovering," "unveiling," "laying bare," and "seeing through" the hidden mechanisms of violent mimesis.

On a more charitable reading, Girard is advocating a type of natural theology which concedes that although desire is fundamental and unavoidable it is evil only when inordinate; that is, desire is evil only when allowed to follow the violently acquisitive impulses of its own unconstrained dynamism. Ordered to its true end, however, mimetic desire is good and "salvific."

Nevertheless, Girard is careful not to espouse a Pelagian view of salvation, which would make redemption more or less a matter of human effort. Like the early Barth, Girard separates naturalism and theology. Human desire is totally corrupt in principle, having absolutely no bounds and unleashing a war in which everyone is struggling against all. Thus naturalism and theology are not even linked by an ethics. Yet Girard also wishes to affirm the exclusivity and uniqueness of Christian revelation—namely, that only in and through Christ do we have the final unmasking of the victimage mechanism, the repudiation of all violent mimetic desire.[58]

Not only does this appeal to divine revelation introduce "an ineradicable contradiction into his system,"[59] it fails to account for the actual specificity—the incarnation, the life, death, and resurrection— of Jesus. If mimetic desire is, as Girard claims, a universal feature of the human life, if it is a historical, psychosocial constant, then one is hard-pressed to specify exactly what redemptive contribution the life and death of Jesus of Nazareth makes. In short, the so-called "Christ event" is swallowed up, assimilated into, and subsumed in a wider explanatory structure. Jesus' life and death become an epiphenomenon on the surface of a more inclusive philosophical anthropology: the victimage mechanism.[60] Within a Girardian schema, it is hard to find any other role for Jesus than that of a gnostic bearer of true "enlightenment," one who by his example unmasks the scapegoat mechanism.

In this regard, Girard's theology of salvation is reminiscent of Kant, who attempted to give philosophical respectability to Christian religion by universalizing it, by exchanging the contingencies and particularities of the historical Jesus for a universal "Christ-idea." This approach risks rendering irrelevant the historical Christian community in which knowledge of discipleship is displayed, inculcated, and transmitted. Of course, both Kant and Girard recognize the value of living exemplars and specific concrete models in making the Christ-idea (or, in the case of Girard, the idea of nonacquisitive, nonviolent mimetic desire) more understandable and comprehensible. But this does not yet explain Jesus' uniqueness, his divinity, or indeed the necessity of the incarnation.

On Girard's account, Jesus' divinity amounts to little more than a demonstration of the possibility of nonviolence in a particular pattern of existence, and not the actual intrusion of extra-human enabling capacities.[61] But as Swartley rightly points out with regard to Christian teaching on atonement, discipleship and imitation are inextricably linked with God's work of redemption in Christ. Without being bound to Jesus as the ransomed are bound to their ransomer, without becoming friends of God in Christ, without actually taking up, participating in, being conformed to, and living out an atoning way of life, the whole point of the incarnation is thwarted. In other words, the incarnation is more than just the communication of the *idea* of reconciliation. The incarnation includes actual training and participation in particular peaceable relations and reconciling patterns of existence. It means learning a whole new *idiom*, a completely different set of skills and practices and language games.

As John Milbank aptly puts it,

> the *modus vivendi* of the Church . . . is an "atoning" way of life. It is highly significant that from Paul, through Origen to Augustine, the early Christians seem to have thought in terms of a "continuing" atonement. Paul talks of "filling up what is lacking in the sufferings of Christ," Origen of the *logos* "suffering to the end of time," Augustine of the Church, the whole body of Christ, as the *complete* sacrifice to God which is yet identical with Christ's own offering.[62]

Here the Western church would do well to take seriously an emphasis long recognized by the Eastern Christian tradition: namely, that in the proclamation "the Word became flesh" lies the true source, the ultimate joy, of the Christian faith. The full significance and the ultimate purpose of human existence, in other words, is revealed and realized in and through the incarnation.

As Irenaeus puts it: "the son of God became the Son of man, that man also might become the son of God." Set in its proper Trinitarian economy, this means that

> the descent (*katabasis*) of the divine person of Christ makes human persons capable of an ascent (*anabasis*) in the Holy Spirit. It was necessary that the voluntary humiliation, the redemptive *kenosis*, of the Son of God should take place, so that fallen men might accomplish their vocation of *theosis*, the deification of created beings by uncreated grace. Thus the redeeming work of Christ . . . is seen to be directly related to the ultimate goal of creatures: to know union with God. If this union has been accomplished in the divine person of the Son, who is God become man, it is necessary that each human person, in turn, should become God by grace, or "a partaker of the divine nature" (2 Pet. 1:4).[63]

However, as Paul rightly recognized, to partake in the divine nature also means to share in the Lord's sufferings, to be crucified together with Christ, to bear his wounds. As is shown by the phrase "I complete what is lacking in Christ's afflictions" (Col. 1:24, RSV), there is both a closeness *and* a distance here. Whereas Paul's crucifixion is clearly not that of the Lord's, his (and our) suffering nonetheless constitutes its prolongation.

The sufferings of the God-man are all-sufficient, but in those sufferings a place has been left for the disciples; thus Jesus predicts that those who are his will share his destiny (John 16:1-4; Matt. 10:24f.). "Through grace" a fellowship of suffering and resurrection is created, and this fellowship only has meaning if the *pro nobis* is extended to the participants.[64] Here we see connect again the unending dialectical interplay between imitation and participation which is so vital to a proper understanding of Christian discipleship.

Conclusion

Regrettably, an unqualified Girard-like emphasis on the ideational or conceptual aspects of mimetic desire has the unwelcome effect of downplaying, mitigating, and ultimately obscuring the peculiar contours, the actual ecclesial shape, the specific practices of Christian discipleship. An abstract attachment to nonviolence of the sort that Girard propounds is not finally fully satisfactory. As

Christ's followers we need to be trained and apprenticed. We need to be schooled in the idiom of peace by taking on the life of Christ, by imitating him, by following him in the Way. As Christians, we can only do this as part of his body, as it finds enfleshment in the church.

Clearly Girard's Christology lacks any serious ecclesiological dimension. Swartley's exegetical interventions provide a healthy corrective inasmuch as they direct our attention away from *the idea* of mimetic desire and more to *the actual idioms* of our imitation of and participation in the life of Christ as revealed in Scripture and disclosed in the life of the church. Thus, whereas Swartley's analysis does not directly challenge or contradict Girard's work, it nonetheless exposes the limitations and the weaknesses of Girard's otherwise intriguing theory of nonacquisitive mimetic desire.

Christians gladly acknowledge that "Girard's 'scapegoat mechanism' can prove helpful to some degree"[65] and to that extent his argument is well worth rescuing[66]—but not without qualification, expansion, correction, and readjustment. Theologians and biblical exegetes alike must be ever vigilant in their task of insuring properly *theological* readings of the faith—in this case, discipleship, suffering, atonement, and reconciliation.

Christians may, no doubt, find in Girard an important ally, for his work on sacred violence in general and the scapegoat mechanism in particular casts valuable light on Christian self-understanding. In these matters, however, the ore always comes mixed with clay. This means Girard's work must be subjected to a good deal of smelting, refining, and purging to be useful to those who claim to be disciples of the one whom Christians have pre-eminently identified as the Suffering Servant.

Notes

1. "Mimesis"—or, more accurately, the *mimesthai* word group—conveys much of what Christian discipleship entails, although no single notion or concept can adequately capture its nuanced richness and complex diversity. Yet at the same time, one also has to concede that without recourse to mimesis the character of Christian discipleship could not be properly displayed. Mimesis, in other words, constitutes but one aspect of a larger, more elaborate constellation; this means that even while discipleship always remains larger than mimesis (imitation), mimesis nonetheless lies at the heart of discipleship.

2. My purpose in drawing out the theological implications of Swartley's work is partly methodological and partly substantive. It is crucial, of course,

that one appreciate on an exegetical level how Paul's understanding of the relation between imitation, suffering, and discipleship develops and matures. But it is also important that one recognize how these themes have continued to unfold, insofar as they are re-appropriated and redescribed, not only within the wider Christian canon but also within subsequent Christian tradition. Indeed, a properly *theological* understanding of the relation between imitation, suffering, and discipleship is never satisfied with any strict division between the so-called exegetical work on the biblical texts and the hermeneutical retrieval, recapitulation, and deployment of those texts in the ongoing life of the church. My contention, in short, is that from the very outset exegetical work is incipiently theological. Since exegesis is always already theologically informed, it is incumbent on responsible expositors of Scripture either to acknowledge their theological presuppositions or explicitly develop those theological ideas as they bear upon their exegetical work.

3. Compare, for example, Elizabeth Castelli, *Imitating Paul: A Discourse of Power* (Louisville, Ky.: Westminster/John Knox Press, 1991). In her fascinating but finally unconvincing monograph, Castelli argues that operative in "Paul's use of the rhetoric of mimesis is not simply the benign call to emulate a laudable ethical model," but a subtle political strategy that dissimulates the actual relations of power and authority that obtain between Paul and his readers. Paul's exhortation to the churches to imitate himself as he imitates Christ, for example, represents a covert and coercive rhetorical strategy that effectively masks Paul's will to power (pp. 16, 87). That is, in his exhortation to imitation Paul implicitly claims for himself a privileged position by re-inscribing a confusion of identity between Christ and himself (p. 32). Collapsing this distinction allows Paul to legitimate, preserve, and reinforce certain power relations. In the end, according to Castelli, Paul's rhetoric of mimesis is of one piece with his conservative political strategy, the internal workings of which come to light in two important ways.

First, Paul's insistence on imitation—the valorization of sameness over difference—indicates that he is interested in promoting "the hegemony of the identical" (pp. 16, 41). Consequently, the diffusion and specificity of the diverse social groups that constitute the early church are replaced by a singularity of purpose and a universalism, both of which undercut and indict particularity and difference (p. 56). Second, the exhortation to imitation not only underwrites the apostle's demand for the erasure of difference, but it links that erasure to the very possibility of salvation (pp. 17, 53).

Christians, therefore, live under the implicit but constant threat of being deprived of their salvation if they do not imitate Paul as he imitates Christ. At this juncture Paul's scheme becomes particularly pernicious (but also, ironically, exposed as self-refuting) by virtue of a built-in mimetic hierarchy that can never quite be surmounted. For while the mimetic relationship is motivated by the drive to erase the difference between divine original and human copy, to create sameness, it can never actually succeed since there will always be that unbridgeable gap between the model and the copy (p.

68). Although sameness is valued above difference, sameness can never be realized because of the nagging difference that will, by definition, always obtain between the eternal model and the mortal copy. Christians are therefore caught in a double bind out of which they can never successfully extricate themselves. Given her understanding of mimesis, the very practice of which dooms one to failure (p. 13), Castelli cannot but characterize Christians trying to emulate their exemplars in anything but despairing terms.

Although Castelli's analysis is extremely useful in bringing to the fore (by virtue of Michel Foucault's insights) the question of the power relations inherent in all human discourse, her approach is finally defective because it ascribes to Paul and his readers a simplistic Platonic understanding of imitation, according to which all copies are, by definition, derivative of and thus ontologically inferior to their originals. As Castelli puts it, mimesis is for Paul "constituted through a hierarchy in which the model is imbued with perfection and wholeness, and the copy represents an attempt to reclaim that perfection" (p. 86).

But surely to attribute to Paul an understanding of mimesis that incorporates, relatively intact, an entire set of Greek metaphysical presuppositions, is irresponsible. This rather naive understanding of mimesis is all the more surprising given Castelli's close attention to the use and meaning of the word-group in Plato and Aristotle, as well as early Greek sources generally. Although she concedes that a survey of uses of mimesis in ancient Greece and the Hellenistic period yields no single, monolithic definition, that mimesis "evades precise definition and reduction" (p. 59), Castelli nevertheless proceeds to ascribe to Paul and his readers a rather vulgar, one-dimensional understanding of mimesis. This facile equation of a Platonic mimeticism with Paul's use of the term, combined with the assumption that the primary motive of imitation is the "erasure of difference" or the "valorization of sameness over difference," prevents Castelli from actually attending to *Paul's* use of the term.

I single out Castelli's work not because it deserves special censure but because it is representative of no small segment of recent scholarship, which, though offering helpful insights in understanding Paul's language of mimesis, is nevertheless fraught with difficulties, some of which are intractable precisely to the extent that assumptions operative in one domain or discipline are transferred and appropriated uncritically in another. This is but another way of underscoring the need to insure that scholarship, if it is to be of truly Christian import, must be properly *theological*.

4. Of course, in one sense Girard does provide several very fascinating and helpful close readings of biblical texts that speak to Jesus' nonviolence. I do not wish to deny this. My point, however, is to query whether Girard's readings are more determinatively informed by literary-critical skills as acquired within the academy and according to the disciplinary rigors of the modern university classroom rather than the practical-theological skills as procured within the church according to the disciplinary habits and prac-

tices that spring from a life of Christian discipleship. By making this distinction I do not, of course, wish to discount the contributions that the former set of skills and practices bring to our understanding of the biblical texts or the Christian faith in general. Nor do I wish to challenge the importance of the institutional setting in which those literary-critical skills are exercised and promoted or what bearing these skills can have on a life of faith.

My only point is to underscore the indispensable importance of ecclesial forms of life in the formation and cultivation of actual nonviolent practices that mark Christian existence as peaceable and from which theological reflections of a constructive and critical sort issue. Indeed, without the narrative mediation of Jesus Christ, both textually but also actually (i.e., as that narrative is embodied in the life of a community of his disciples), the very possibility of mimesis remains ungrounded. Just as the textual mediation of Jesus provides grounds for the very possibility of mimesis, so too mimesis provides grounds for the very possibility of the church. I am indebted to Graham Ward for this later formulation. See Graham Ward, "Mimesis: The Measure of Mark's Christology," *Literature and Theology 8* (March 1994): 1-29; 5.

5. "*Hodos,*" of course, "gathers a density of pedagogical, ethical, geographical and eschatological reference as the narrative proceeds" (ibid., 17).

6. As Ward notes, the insight is essentially Aristotle's, for whom "'imitation' was both what the text did *vis-à-vis* the world 'out there' (Poetics 1448a) and an anthropological *a priori* whereby human beings were educated and socialized (*Poetics* 1448b 5)." Ibid., 3.

7. Ibid., 4.

8. Ibid., 12.

9. Discipleship, in other words, is a gift and not simply a call.

10. Graham Ward, "Mimesis: The Measure of Mark's Christology," 5.

11. Ibid., 10.

12. Ted Peters helpfully sketches six models of atonement that have appeared in the history of Christian thought: Jesus Christ as (1) the teacher of true knowledge; (2) our moral example and influence; (3) *Christus Victor*; (4) our satisfaction; (5) the happy exchange; and (6) the final scapegoat. "Atonement and the Final Scapegoat," *Perspectives in Religious Studies* 19 (Summer 1992): 151-181; 152. Peters' sixth model, the final scapegoat, is of course a reference to René Girard's account of the scapegoat mechanism as applied to Christian theology. However, this should not obscure the fact that it was Rupert of Deutz (d. 1135) who was the first medieval theologian to apply to Christ the image of the scapegoat. See Hans Urs von Balthasar, *Theo-Drama*, Vol. IV trans. Graham Harrison (San Francisco: Ignatius Press, 1994), 291-292, and also Georges Florovsky, *Creation and Redemption*, Vol. III (Belmont, Mass.: Nordland Publishing Company, 1976), 165-167.

13. Balthasar, *Theo-Drama*, 244.

14. As Peters puts it, "the trick of the task of theology is to try to understand the atonement without hiding from the horror of Golgotha" ("Atonement," 152).

15. This does not of course invalidate its usefulness to theology nor is this observation intended as a complaint against Girard. After all, there is nothing about Girard's agenda that holds it accountable to theological strictures. I make this observation, rather, as a cautionary warning to those who too quickly and too enthusiastically appropriate Girard's work for theological purposes.

16. For a clear, succinct account of the issues surrounding imitation and atonement, see John B. Webster, "The Imitation of Christ," *Tyndale Bulletin* 37 (1986), 95-120.

17. Ibid., 103.

18. Paul's language of the church as the body of Christ, for example, clearly underscores the real, intimate, sacramental bonds between believers and their Lord. Partaking of the Lord's Supper, for example, means to participate in the body and blood of Christ. (1 Cor. 11:27ff.). As C. Merrill Proudfoot puts it, *"soma tou christou* makes the strongest possible tie between soteriology and ecclesiology" (Proudfoot, "Imitation or Realistic Participation? A Study of Paul's Concept of 'Suffering With Christ,'" *Interpretation* 17 [April 1963], 140-160; 145). Equally fundamental to Paul's thought is the truth that Christ died and rose again, not merely as an individual but as the embodiment and representative of all people. Here the ancient Hebrew notion of "corporate personality," made prominent by the work of H. Wheeler Robinson and others, is also essential to Paul's concept of the role of Christ. Like Adam, Christ too is a "corporate personality," a new Adam (1 Cor. 15:22, 45-49; Rom. 5:14-19). See Barnabas Mary Ahernn, "The Fellowship of His Sufferings (Phil. 3:10): A Study of St. Paul's Doctrine on Christian Suffering," *Catholic Biblical Quarterly* 22 (January 1960), 1-32; 9. Of course, the idea of solidarity by itself is insufficient. It must be complemented with that of representative (vicarious) suffering if we are to do justice to biblical affirmation. See Balthasar, *Theo-Drama*, 297.

19. John's Gospel comes most immediately to mind: "'A servant is not greater than his master.' If they persecuted me, they will persecute you" (John 15:20, RSV).

20. The classic study of this passage is Jacob Kremer's, *Was an den Leiden Christi Noch Mangelt: Eine Interpretationsgeschichtliche und Exegetische Untersuchung zu Kol. 1,24b*, (BBB 12; Bonn: Hanstein, 1956). A useful summary of and commentary on Kremer's work, as well as subsequent exegetical study on Col. 1:24, is provided by John Reumann, "Colossians 1:24 ('What is Lacking in the Afflictions of Christ'): History of Exegesis and Ecumenical Advance," *Currents in Theology and Mission* 17 (December 1990), 454-461.

21. Balthasar, *Theo-Drama*, 319. Elsewhere Balthasar cautions: "We must not forget that the work of redemption is not the work of the Son in isolation but of the entire Trinity" (ibid., 357; see also p. 314).

22. This criticism should not obscure one of the major strengths of Girard's account of the scapegoat mechanism; namely, its dramatic, narrative structure. Balthasar is surely right to characterize Girard's work as "the

most dramatic project to be undertaken today in the field of soteriology and in theology generally" (ibid., 299). To be sure, any adequate theology of atonement requires a narrative rather than a strictly systematic display for the simple reason that systems, by their static nature, tend to exclude or give insufficient weight to one element or another that individually and in conjunction with others proves essential to the complete dramatic plot. No element, in other words, can be excluded; all elements are simultaneously operative—each has its role, each belongs on the stage. Because all systematic construals of the atonement invariably fail to hold all these elements together in dramatic tension, the theologian's task is not so much to erect a system ("for the Cross explodes all systems," ibid., 319) as to bring the work of conceptual reflection to bear upon the drama of salvation. Putting it this way has the virtue of acknowledging the necessary place of conceptual, reflective work in theology while at the same time underscoring its limited role *vis-à-vis* the narrative structure of the Christian faith.

23. Rather than viewing this as a serious omission, theologians ought to embrace Girard's "undeveloped" views as a wonderful opportunity to develop distinctively Christian understandings of imitation. For much of what follows concerning the importance of a Trinitarian framework in understanding the character of Christian discipleship, I am indebted to the reflections of Rowan Williams, particularly his response to Ellen Charry's *By the Renewing of Your Minds: The Pastoral Function of Christian Doctrine* (New York: Oxford University Press, 1997). Williams's remarks come in the form of a conference paper, "Responding to Ellen Charry," delivered at a symposium on "The New Testament and Ethics: Problems and Prospects" at Duke University, March 30-April 2, 1995. (Hereafter, references to this paper will be designated "Williams." Page references are those of the manuscript copy.)

24. The goal of faithful Christian discipleship, in other words, is not "the self-construction of the righteous agent by successful performance" (Williams, 11).

25. Williams, 14.

26. Ibid., 15.

27. The intimate connection between "submission" and "dispossession" is not always fully appreciated. Given the current climate of suspicion in the broader culture, language of self-emptying (especially when used in conjunction with "sacrifice") is almost immediately equated with bad faith. For feminists and other theologians of liberation such discourse smacks of ideological distortion, abuse, and repression. To be sure, the language of submission or consent often signals dehumanizing subjugation, especially when the dominant mimetic model is, as Girard describes it, antithetical, conflictual, exclusionary, violent, full of strife. However, this should not make theologians shy to employ the term in a proper theological sense, in relation to the Trinity and our life in God. There are, after all, points at which all Christians must confess, if their relation to God is genuine, "I submit because I recognize here that I have been touched by something much

more profound than my own will or my desire." For a considered view of the theological importance of self-sacrifice, see John Milbank, "The Ethics of Self-Sacrifice," *First Things* No. 91 (March 1999), 33-38.

28. For the following brief summary of the Trinitarian understanding of God, I am indebted to Balthasar, *Theo-Drama*, 323-324, and to Rowan Williams.

29. See Nicholas Lash, *Easter in Ordinary: Reflections on Human Experience and the Knowledge of God* (London: SCM Press, 1988). As Lash explains, "It is only *in* this movement, and not apart from it, that the oneness or unity of him whom we triply worship is apprehended" (271).

30. Williams, 9. In this respect, speaking of the *perichoresis* that characterizes the life of the Trinity as "an unceasing dialectically *corrective* movement"—as in Lash's formulation—is perhaps not quite right. Or at least the notion of "correction" must be understood in a very peculiar sense, one which suggests not so much the idea of "over-againstness" as endless generativity arising from a source that is differential in its singularity, manifold in its oneness.

31. David Burrell succinctly captures the astonishing but vitally integral connection between mimesis and divine friendship as follows: "What proves remarkable . . . is the way in which Jesus' call to erstwhile disciples to follow him is carefully crafted to circumvent the conflict potential to all *mimesis*. As the gospel of John articulates so clearly, the call to follow him is in fact an invitation to enter into the very same relationship which obtains between Jesus and the Father. And since the object is not to gain the Father's approval, but rather to receive Jesus' own gift of friendship, and thereby enjoy intimacy with God, desire is transformed from striving to an 'active receptivity.' Discipleship, then, is a far cry from 'imitating Jesus,' but rather an invitation to enter into something entirely gratuitous and hence quite unanticipatable: friendship with God" ("René Girard: Violence and Sacrifice," *Cross Currents* 38 [Winter 1988-89], 443-447; 445).

32. John Milbank helpfully relates this theme of self-emptying to the Christian doctrine of creation, which is, of course, intimately linked to (better, co-extensive with) the doctrine of redemption. In the case of biblical faith, "creative giving is not loss but a self-emptying *in order* to be, and sacrificial response is, in return, a total giving back which is the only possible mode of continuing to participate in Being. Since, according to the logic of creation *ex nihilo, to be* is entirely to receive, a constant 'giving up' of oneself is the only way to receive oneself back again, and so to remain. No 'thing' here is given up for a greater something, but rather *everything* is given up in order to be received back differently and only, thereby, as 'the same.'" See "Stories of Sacrifice," *Contagion: Journal of Violence, Mimesis, and Culture* 2 (Spring 1995): 75-102; 100. (An expanded version of this essay is published as "Stories of Sacrifice" in *Modern Theology* 12 [January 1996], 27-56. For purposes of this essay, I draw upon the article published in *Contagion*.)

33. Disciples are not finally asked to choose between mimesis and participation, given the unceasing *perichoresis* that is God's Trinitarian life. Nor

are they asked to give priority to one over the other. Rather, they are required to keep these in balanced motion, in dialectical tension. In short, a life of Christian discipleship is equally about imitation and participation.

34. Williams, 5. Ultimately, the quality of our discipleship is judged "according to its fidelity to the character of God, its 'epiphanic' depth" (ibid., 19).

35. Williams, 5.

36. Once again, this criticism is not registered as a fault intrinsic to Girard's program as much as it serves as a warning to theologians who too readily and too uncritically adopt Girardian views. In this regard, John Dunne's distinction between mimetic desire and heart's desire offers a salutary corrective. See John S. Dunne, *The Peace of the Present: An Unviolent Way of Life* (Notre Dame: University of Notre Dame Press, 1991), ix, 13, and "Myth and Culture in Theology and Literature: A Conversation with John S. Dunne," *Religion & Literature* 25 (Summer 1993), 77-104; 98-99. The challenge of the Christian life, according to Dunne, is to find the true way of desire. "Finding the true way is a matter of discerning between heart's desire and mimetic or competitive desire, between what we truly want and what we think we want, seeing what others want." There are, of course, many ways of desire, many paths along which the heart can be lost, many blind alleys, many dead ends. However, there is a center to heart's desire the entrance to which Dunne calls "the beginning of desire." "If all desire is mimetic, as Girard says, then the center has to be a peace that comes of renunciation" *(Peace of the Present,* 2).

37. Williams, 9.

38. Here I am following the criticisms of John Milbank, *Theology and Social Theory: Beyond Secular Reason* (Oxford: Basil Blackwell, 1990), 394. Milbank identifies seven thematics in Girard akin to those found in nineteenth-century scholars of a positivistic bent (e.g., Julius Wellhausen, William Robertson Smith, James Frazer, Henri Hubert, and Marcel Mauss) who sought to account for religion in terms of a logic of sacrifice and who, on that basis, were determined to erect a general theory of society.

> First of all there is the attempt to posit a decisive emergence of religion from a pre-religious and yet human past; second is the idea of an ambiguous character of 'the sacred' prior to and independent of divinity; third the notion of a univocal 'essence' of all sacrifice; fourth the idea that sacrifice precedes religion rather than being inscribed within it; fifth the claim that animal sacrifice substitutes for human; sixth the idea that sacrifice is a perfectly rational although inadequate response to a pre-religious predicament. Finally there is even in Girard a certain reworking of the idea that the true 'end' of sacrifice (both termination and conclusion) is pure individual self-renunciation ("Stories of Sacrifice," 97-98).

39. In this respect, Girard's project is clearly postmodern in that "it acknowledges the critical unavoidability of the theological" (Fergus Kerr,

"Rescuing Girard's Argument?" *Modern Theology* 8 [October 1992], 385-399; 386.

40. Kerr maintains that Girard, far from espousing a view of religion as something superimposed upon a more fundamental social or cultural reality, argues for religion's existence at the foundations of every society. As Kerr puts it, "there is no culture without religion, no society without sacrifice" ("Revealing the Scapegoat Mechanism: Christianity after Girard," in *Philosophy, Religion and the Spiritual Life*, ed. Michael McGhee [Cambridge: Cambridge University Press, 1992], 161-175; 167). But even if one grants to Girard the Durkheimian intuition concerning the virtual identity of the social and religious domains, this still leaves unanswered the more fundamental problem regarding religion's purported "essence."

41. Milbank, "Stories of Sacrifice," 75.

42. See, e.g., Charles Davis, "Sacrifice and Violence: new perspectives in the theory of religion from Rene Girard," *New Blackfriars* 70 (July/August 1989), 311-328.

43. René Girard, *Violence and the Sacred*, trans. Patrick Gregory (Baltimore: Johns Hopkins University Press, 1977), 315.

44. Kerr, "Rescuing Girard's Argument?" 395-396.

45. René Girard, "Violence, Difference, Sacrifice: A Conversation with René Girard," *Religion & Literature* 25 (Summer 1993), 11-33; 21. Emphasis mine.

46. David Stevens gives the mundane example of items put on sale at auction. Although it may be true to say that such objects tend to increase in value relative to the number of bidders interested, there are a number of factors that qualify this phenomenon, one of which is the perceived intrinsic value of the object itself ("Unmasking the Gods of Violence: The Work of René Girard," *Studies: An Irish Quarterly Review* 77 [Autumn, 1988], 309-320; 310). Girard, however, might respond to Stevens by pointing out that even the notion of "the perceived intrinsic value of the object itself" is always already socially constructed. Nevertheless, this leaves intact the question of the adequacy of Girard's account of mimetic desire.

47. As Milbank puts it, "a commonsense view of this matter would seem to suggest that sometimes we desire things because people we envy have them or want them; while at other times we emulate people because they are successful in getting the things we want. Girard's reduction of all instances of the latter to instances of the former seems somewhat high-handed" ("Stories of Sacrifice," 93).

48. Ibid., 91.

49. The notion of mimesis within the Greek philosophical tradition was a much more complex, multivalent notion than Girard's use of the term suggests. His understanding of mimesis is indebted to, albeit in different ways and in varying degrees, both Aristotelian and Platonic accounts. Girard clearly borrows freely from both traditions, even though his own position finally eludes characterization under either rubric. On the one hand, Girard's understanding of mimesis has a strong Platonic bent; but it is not

quite Platonic insofar as there is no original, pre-existing form or objectively given object to copy. Rather, objects of mimetic desire are invented or produced; they are arbitrary and contingent—constructed according to historically variable and socially inconstant determinations. On the other hand, the strong ethical and political cast of Girard's theory brings him in close proximity to an Aristotelian understanding of mimesis. But here too there is an important difference. Insofar as Girard does not countenance the possibility of objects or actions being objectively good, or which warrant imitation because of their inherently virtuous character, his notion of mimetic desire ultimately falls outside an Aristotelian purview.

50. The same is true of Walter Ong, who sets up an unwarranted contrast between "imitation" and "following" and makes overmuch of the fact that "in the Gospel accounts Jesus never says to anyone that they should 'imitate' him, although he does say, over and over again, 'Follow me'" (Walter J. Ong, "Mimesis and the Following of Christ," *Religion & Literature* 26 [Summer 1994], 73-77; 73).

51. Ibid., 74.

52. See Milbank, "Can a Gift be Given? Prolegomena to a Future Trinitarian Metaphysics," *Modern Theology* 11 (January 1995), 119-161; 150.

53. Milbank, "Stories of Sacrifice," 92-93.

54. Jean-Michel Oughourlian, a collaborator and disciple of Girard, has been instrumental in developing the notion of the "interdividual." This view rejects any psychology oriented toward radical individualism and stresses instead the inherent mutual involvement between the individual and either other individuals or the culture and society as a whole. For a helpful discussion, see Eugene Webb, *The Self Between: From Freud to the New Social Psychology of France* (Seattle: University of Washington Press, 1993).

55. The specific thrust of our objection is *not* that Girard fails to produce an ontological theory for his account of mimetic desire (the scapegoat mechanism). Rather, the objection is that Girard's account is patient of a number of readings, not all of which are self-consistent, or readings that are mutually exclusive if pushed to their logical conclusions. The crux of our objection, then, is not that Girard fails to give sufficient theoretical status to his implicit ontology, but more with the fact that his account lacks the concrete specificity to be fully persuasive.

56. As Robert Hamerton-Kelly puts it, "mimesis operates initially below the level of consciousness, but it is not a biological drive like Freud's libido. Mimesis is rather an interpersonal attraction rooted more in psychosocial reality than in biology, although it has a power comparable to a biological drive" (*The Gospel and the Sacred: Poetics of Violence in Mark* [Minneapolis: Augsburg/Fortress Press, 1994], 4).

57. Milbank, "Stories of Sacrifice," 99.

58. The crux of the matter, theologically speaking, is whether Girard's Christ is the same as the Christ of Christian life and faith.

59. Balthasar, *Theo-Drama*, 309. Balthasar argues that Girard, by acknowl-

edging Christ's divinity, posits "a theological dimension that explodes his allegedly pure scientism" (309). See also Charles Davis, "Sacrifice and Violence," 313.

60. Here Milbank's warning is both timely and appropriate; namely, that "Girard represents for religion and theology a temptation to be resisted, namely sacrificially to concede to science a right to explain, in order to receive back from science 'a demonstration' of Christocentricity" ("Stories of Sacrifice," 99). Whenever Jesus' life and death are understood within broader, more determinative narratives (like that of Girard's story of the scapegoat mechanism and mimetic desire), the specificity, unsubstitutable identity, and irreplaceable uniqueness of Jesus is seriously jeopardized if not in danger of being lost altogether. That is, when the story of Jesus of Nazareth is subsumed within a Girardian framework, the life, death, and resurrection of Jesus cannot help but appear as derivative of, secondary to, and thus a mere exemplification of, a more foundational narrative.

61. Milbank, *Theology and Social Theory*, 397.

62. Ibid., 397.

63. Vladimir Lossky, *In the Image and Likeness of God* (Crestwood, N.Y.: St. Vladimir's Seminary Press, 1974), 97-98.

64. Balthasar, *Theo-Drama*, 388.

65. Ibid., 334.

66. Kerr, "Rescuing Girard's Argument?" 385-399.

CHAPTER THIRTEEN

Loving Mimesis and Girard's "Scapegoat of the Text": A Creative Reassessment of Mimetic Desire

Rebecca Adams

RENÉ GIRARD IS PROBABLY BEST KNOWN as a theorist of violence. In his work of the last four decades he has developed a powerful hermeneutic of suspicion and a compelling theory of culture derived from his reading of literary texts, myths, other theorists (such as Freud), and the Judeo-Christian Scriptures. Alongside his general intellectual project, moreover, he has developed a religious and ethical interpretation of the human condition.

Most of us find that when we try practically to understand why there is violence in our world, however, we need more than a theory of violence: we need an alternative vision of what human beings could be, or are meant to be. What is Girard's contribution to this constructive enterprise? How can a theorist concerned with the deep structure of violence help us to discover a way to transcend violence?

Girard has developed insights that have profound implications for theology, peacemaking, and social transformation. His influence and following, especially among theologians and those in pacifist traditions, attest to this. At the same time, as many have noted, there are problems with his theory related to the nature and exclusivity of his claims about the Christian revelation, even with the very claim that his theory constitutes a comprehensive thesis about violence and culture.

Girard's theoretical account of how human subjectivity[1] and social relationships may have originated in prehuman times, as well as how they function in the present, can be understood anthropologically as an origin myth. His work can also be read in a theological sense as an interpretation of the Genesis creation and garden stories, as well as a commentary on such basic theological categories as original sin, salvation, and atonement. Girardian theory has seemed to many to offer a powerful anthropological and theological understanding of violence and its relation to human subjectivity. I believe the theory could, in a reconstructed form, also provide a constructive paradigm of human relations and spiritual reality that is truly nonviolent and able to offer a philosophical basis for a praxis of peacemaking and social renewal.

In this chapter I reconsider the basic conception of *mimetic desire* from which all else in Girard's work derives, addressing hard questions many have raised regarding the ultimate adequacy of Girard's theory as a comprehensive theory of human consciousness and culture. In essence, I am proposing that we examine the Girardian theory itself as a metanarrative to see how it performs according to its own insights about violence. We must ask what happens when we read the theory itself as a myth, in the general sense of a paradigm that seeks to offer universal anthropological and theological claims. Does it have a scapegoat? If so, what is it and where is it? I believe the answers lie in a careful analysis of what Girard and others have said about mimetic desire, together with a positive reassessment of that central concept. As I will indicate, this reassessment has far-reaching implications for theology, politics, and theory and practice of peacemaking.

GIRARD'S "SCAPEGOAT OF THE TEXT"

When we feel we understand a large number of connected phenomena, except for one that keeps occurring again and again and does not quite fit the general picture, the chances are that our whole system of representation has already failed. In order to discover a better one, we should not shove under the rug the phenomenon that stubbornly resists our efforts—this the myths themselves already do. We should actively focus our attention on it. —René Girard, Violent Origins

Objections to Girard's mimetic hypothesis seem to have a common theme, which suggests a systematic distortion, and possibly a "scapegoat," in Girardian theory itself. The basic objection to the theory seems to be something like that stated by Jonathan Smith, in dialogue with René Girard in *Violent Origins*:

I guess what I want to know is, what can't you account for? I have no problem with the fact that there are an enormous number of myths that have what you're calling a scapegoating pattern, but there are a great many myths, at least to my eyes, that bear no resemblance to them. And they are often found simultaneously in the same cultures, told about exactly the same object, in exactly the same situation. So what I really want to know is, is this a partial theory? . . . Or is there a way of reducing all of the mythic strategies to one?[2]

To this question, Girard answers, admirably, "I don't know." However, the same objection raised by Smith recurs repeatedly in different forms. George Frear Jr. argues, for instance, that Girard's theory describes "not the origin of religion and culture as he maintains, but distortions in religion and culture" and points to "legitimate desires, the social nature of humanity, wholesome expressions of the sacred and sacrifice, and Christianity's embeddedness in the world."[3] Theological objections, such as those I raised in a 1992 interview with Girard, take the form of understanding the theory as implying absolute original sin, with no account of the primordial goodness of human beings, as represented by their biblical creation in the "image of God" (in fact, the creation of human subjectivity through mimesis in Girard's thought is logically conflated with its "fall" into violence.)[4]

This systematic pattern of objection to the Girardian theory also converges on Girard's central generative conception of mimetic desire, which many find inadequate.[5] Especially psychoanalytic feminist critics of Girardian theory have claimed that, like Freud's, the Girardian schema excludes the "feminine" or the "Mother" and all she represents. Such critics mean that in Girard's paradigmatic triangle of desire as currently conceived, his theory does not consider the desire represented by the psychoanalytic Mother, who could function for the "Father" (i.e., mediator and subject) and the "Infant" (the one who does the imitating)—not only as an *object* of desire but also as a *subject* in her own right *and thus crucially as another potential model of desire*. In degendered language, their critique is that Girard cannot account for positive, nonviolent desire, what they call *feminine* desire or *the Feminine*.[6]

Taken together, those who object to the universal pretensions of the Girardian hypothesis and who quarrel with his fundamental concept of mimetic desire might express an appreciation for the explanatory value of much of Girard's analysis of violence. However, they ultimately reject violence as *the* primordial generating principle of human subjectivity and culture, "the origin and father of all."[7] Conversely stated, all of the above examples boil down in some fashion to the critique that Girard does not adequately account for a truly ethical, constructive type of desire—at least not in any originary sense such as he assigns to the "founding murder" or the scapegoat mechanism. For these critics, such desire, or genuine Love, is the partly visible and only partly demystified scapegoat of the Girardian hypothesis. Thus in choosing to defend this scapegoat in the interest of an adequate ethics, these critics are forced to reject or expel the current formulation of Girardian theory, at least as a metanarrative.

I believe this "scapegoat" of constructive desire in the current Girardian text is real and problematic. I also believe this "scapegoat" is not central to the structure of the mimetic hypothesis but is, ironically, an effect created by not following the hypothesis through to its logical conclusion. I will not claim that Girard himself ends up having a scapegoat because he evades speaking centrally of positive desire, nonviolence, or love as *the* fundamental metaphysical and/or ethical reality. This he actually does. Rather, I will analyze Girard's tendency to conceptualize and speak in a way that remains in the very violent system of representation he seeks to undo. In doing so, he inadvertently relegates love, and thus ethics, and ultimately even his own concept of mimetic desire, to the realm of what he calls *the Sacred*.[8]

My contention is that when Girard's insights about violence and the scapegoating mechanism are applied to his own theory, its "scapegoat" disappears and Girard's theoretical framework becomes self-referentially consistent: That is, when applied to itself, the theory passes its own test for truth as an overarching hypothesis or metanarrative about the origin and nature of violence.[9] I also believe that revealing and rehabilitating the theory's scapegoat actually strengthens the general claim of the Girardian theory as an explanatory model and a practical framework for ethical action in the world, providing what the theory currently lacks: an adequate model of a genuine, nonviolent sacred, of the human person, and of love.

My thesis will be that Girard *can* account for constructive, nonviolent desire as a fundamental generative principle but has yet to find a way to do so that is itself conceptually nonviolent, as well as logically, anthropologically, and theologically coherent.[10] Girard's recent remarks regarding the fundamentally good nature of mimetic desire are in my view not yet arguments but statements of intent, of commitment to understand mimetic desire more constructively. In fact, Girard has been making suggestions of this type for some time. In *Violent Origins* he states, "violence does not play a primordial role in my perspective; only mimesis does. This point is often misunderstood."[11] Unfortunately, however, since he himself and others have reiterated the "inevitable" connection between violence and mimesis so many times, statements such as these seem simply to have no meaning or to be directly inconsistent with his previous analysis of mimetic desire as primarily conflictual. The task I undertake here is to logically detach violence and the scapegoating mechanism from mimetic desire itself. I will show that this connection, though as real a danger as Girard says it is, does not inevitably arise *logically* from within the nature of mimesis itself, and that there is a singular set of conditions under which mimetic desire is nonviolent, even primordially *creative*.

Girard himself has been responsible for some of the misunderstanding surrounding his central term of mimetic desire because of misleading terminology he has used and inconsistent statements he has made. Willard Swartley, for instance, in his original conference paper, pointed out one of the key contradictory (and much-quoted) statements by Girard regarding the nature of mimetic desire, from the final pages of *Things Hidden Since the Foundation of the World*:

> The Gospels and the New Testament do not preach a morality of spontaneous action. They do not claim that humans must get rid of imitation; they recommend imitating the sole model who never runs the danger—if we really imitate in the way that children imitate—of being transformed into a fascinating rival. . . . On the one side are the prisoners of violent imitation, which always leads to a dead end, and on the other are the adherents of nonviolent imitation, who will meet with no obstacle. . . . *Following Christ means giving up mimetic desire* (italics added).[12]

This passage contradicts itself. What Girard must mean is that "following Christ" means giving up scapegoating, or violence, or participating in the victimage mechanism. But because Girard occasionally asserts yet never consistently explains how mimetic desire *itself* can be positive or creative in a fundamental sense, the contradiction does not appear glaring and it is easy to miss it: it appears that giving up these things does indeed logically entail giving up mimetic desire. This is a conceptual leap. Many readers, friends and foes of Girardian theory alike, however, appear to have taken the italicized sentence at face value without going on to think through the contradiction and to decide the last sentence must be an erroneous statement.

In recent years Girard has expressed frustration at having mimetic desire repeatedly misunderstood. In a 1992 interview he clarifies his terminology and states his position on the subject.

> R[ebecca] A[dams]: At the end of *Things Hidden* you make the statement that to follow Christ means to "give up" or renounce mimetic desire, yet the hominization section [on Fundamental Anthropology] implies that mimetic desire is the only kind of desire there is.

> R[ené] G[irard]: A simple renunciation of desire I don't think is Christian; it's more Buddhist. . . . As to whether I am advocating "re-

nunciation" of mimetic desire, yes and no. Not the renunciation of mimetic desire itself, because what Jesus advocates *is* mimetic desire. Imitate me, imitate the Father. So the idea that mimetic desire itself is bad makes no sense. *It is true, however, that occasionally I say "mimetic desire" when I really mean only the type of mimetic desire that generates mimetic rivalry and in turn is generated by it....* I would say that mimetic desire, even when bad, is intrinsically good, in the sense that far from being merely imitative in a small sense, it's the opening out of oneself.

RA: Openness to others.

RG: Yes. Extreme openness. [*Mimetic desire] is everything. It can be murderous, it is rivalrous; but it is also the basis of heroism, and devotion to others, and everything....* I hear this question all the time: "Is all desire mimetic?" Not in the bad, conflictual sense. Nothing is more mimetic than the desire of a child, and yet it is good. Jesus himself says it is good. *Mimetic desire is also the desire for God."* (italics added)[13]

The theological ramifications of this statement seemed to suggest a surprising turn of emphasis in Girard's thought at the time. Since then some scholars have begun arguing for and developing a fuller understanding of a constructive mimetic "imitation of Christ" (as Swartley and Fodor develop biblically and theologically in their much-needed treatments in this book).[14] Key for our purposes is to point out that in this statement Girard provides a crucial clarification of his terms. In effect he admits he has at times split and verbally as well as conceptually scapegoated the term *mimetic desire* itself by forgetting to stress that mimetic desire is also sometimes, or even fundamentally, good.

Because Girard's positive conception of mimesis is not only undeveloped in his work but inconsistently stated, others similarly continue to "split" and scapegoat the concept (i.e., "forgetting" about good mimetic desire) by simply designating it as inherently violent or by inconsistently referring to it as violent but then (as in the interview) admitting its fundamentally dual "good/bad" nature. Narrative theologian John S. Dunne, for instance, contrasts mimetic desire, which leads to violence, with his positive conception of "heart's desire," which is non-mimetic, authentic, and peaceful.[15] Biblical scholar Kirsten M. Anderson sets up a similar dichotomy between Girardian violent mimetic desire and positive non-mimetic desire. Yet she quickly problematizes this understanding of Girard's work by admitting he is the critic who best understands that mimesis is paradoxically both commanded and forbidden in the Genesis garden story with respect to God.[16]

Girard's remarks in the interview illuminate why there has been so much confusion about the "good" versus "bad" nature of mimesis itself. This passage, as we shall see in more detail, however, also provides a clue that the problem goes deeper than the mere use of terminology and lies in the current actual formulation of the concept itself. Splitting involves more than mere confused usage. It involves dividing a concept in half, then expelling the undesirable half while at the same time obscuring and/or mystifying the remaining half. Yet in this process, it proves impossible to rid oneself entirely of the evidence of the inconsistent, divided usage or of the concept's original unity.[17]

Both Girard's and Anderson's statements about mimetic desire reveal traces of a dualistic and inconsistent pattern of thought characteristic of the textual distortions of scapegoating: the term *mimesis* or *mimetic desire* or even *acquisitive mimesis* has *already* undergone a process of splitting and expulsion revealed by contradictory uses of the term in the same text. The tendency to equate mimetic desire with violence and something "bad," a temptation to which even Girard sometimes yields, presupposes a good/bad dichotomy in which half the concept, the "good," "feminine," "ethical," "nonviolent" half, has been either obscured, diminished, or mystified in Girard's work (Figure 1)

FIGURE 1: MIMETIC DESIRE

| |

(*splitting/expulsion = scapegoating*) __ __ __ __ __ __

| |

BAD DESIRE ←	VS	GOOD DESIRE
acquisitive	*Things Hidden*	nonacquisitive
rivalrous	*Things Hidden*	nonrivalrous
internal mediation	DDN	external mediation
imitation of Satan	*Things Hidden*	imitation of Christ
renounce? yes	Interview	renounce? no
"Eros"	*Things Hidden*	"Agape"
death	*Things Hidden*	life
human reason,"myth"	*Things Hidden*	divine rev., gospel
violence	*Things Hidden*	peace
human culture (+ nature)	*Scapegoat*	divine nature
lies of persecutors	*Scapegoat,*	truth of victim
	Things Hidden	
"The Sacred"	*Violence & Sacred,*	Christ
	Things Hidden	

PROFANE		SACRED

In the split conceptual schema illustrated by Figure 1, we can see how everything on the bad side of this representation is sharply contrasted with and then expelled (demonized, rejected, or erased) in favor of affirming (divinizing, making central, or elevating) everything on the "good" side. The theory itself therefore harbors a paradigm of warring doubles, rivalry, and expulsion at the level of general theoretical and theological concepts! The good side supposedly represents nonviolent imitation and the bad side violent imitation or mimesis, but as we shall see below, Girard offers no real account of good mimetic desire *of a type human beings could possibly have or even imitate with God as mediator.* Thus it is easy to slip into the simple equation of mimetic desire with violence and something "bad." This is why many people, to defend human ethics, have expelled the concept of mimetic desire altogether and even the Girardian hypothesis itself.

When his critics do this, Girard objects to being misunderstood. He attempts to defend the concept by claiming that mimetic desire "itself" is "good." Clearly, as Girard points out, merely designating mimetic desire "bad" is inadequate: Jesus himself says mimetic desire is "good," and our intuitions seem to confirm the possibility of constructive imitation. More importantly, however, to think otherwise is implicitly to resort to a mythical and expulsive conceptual schema of the very type that Girard critiques. Conversely, however, it is easy to see on closer analysis that to simply call mimetic desire fundamentally "good," as Girard has more recently tried to do, simply participates in the same splitting and mystification of the term: *although the term is retained it cannot be referring any longer to anything on the bad side, nor for that matter on the good.* The point here is that although mimetic desire might conceivably be the desire *for* God (as an object)[18] in the schema illustrated in Figure 1, it cannot, as we shall see, be the desire *of* God, which is what we are supposed to be "imitating" when we engage in good mimetic desire.

"Good" mimetic desire in this split framework ends up being a type of divine desire which by definition excludes the human and the left side of the dichotomy. Girard's current schema requires maintaining an absolute distinction between violent imitation "on the one side" and nonviolent imitation "on the other." The crucial objection to this construct, however, is whether God's "desire" in this scenario (if truly "nonacquisitive") is really desire in any recognizable sense, and how we could possibly "imitate" it. Girard must suppose God's good and nonacquisitive desire to be so utterly metaphysically different from violent, acquisitive human desire to maintain metaphysical distance between God and us and thus ensure lack of rivalry. But it is then hard to understand what this imitation of God could consist of. At best, this imitation seems to have little content. So it seems that either this godly desire cannot really be imitated by human beings or that it could only be imitated by them at the cost of having to expel their own humanity. Worst of all, this divine order ultimately implies the expulsion of mimetic desire itself, since desire which cannot really be imitated or which can only be imitated though some act of expulsion cannot be good mimetic desire. Girard's "solution" to the problem of violence and mimesis remains in the very double bind the solution is trying to transcend.

"Good" mimetic desire thus cannot be describing the nonviolent, nonacquisitive desire of God *itself*, as Girard must intend. Instead, this desire of God is implicitly represented in this split schema as being something *other* than mimetic desire, which is once again (covertly) expelled onto the bad side of the dichotomy. Accordingly, escape or "salvation" from the victimage mechanism and sin as violent desire in Girard's current theological framework is always conceived as *conversion* to an entirely separate divine order as represented by the right hand of this dichotomy. Because there is an insuperable metaphysical gap between the two sides of the dichotomy, mimetic desire as a concept is propelled out of the realm of recognizable human life and understanding and into the realm of the "sacred" (in Girard's negative sense) by being expelled at times as purely demonic (bad, acquisitive, and human) and elevated at others as purely divine (utterly good, nonacquisitive, and of God).

Simply calling mimetic desire *either* of these, as we have seen, however, logically makes no sense. Throughout his work Girard theoretically understands mimetic desire as a power which fundamentally transcends the good/bad dichotomy (even though he himself lapses sometimes into equating mimetic desire with violence). However, whenever he talks about the solution to the problem of violence as coming solely from a realm of nonviolent divine love which is wholly Other, he is forced onto one side of the dichotomy or the other, neither of which is satisfactory. In his own recent remarks about mimetic desire as fundamentally "good," the concept of mimetic desire has been just as mystified/expelled as in the thought of those who "misunderstand" him, but this time it has been divinized by Girard instead of demonized by his detractors. Girard, ironically, ends up repeating an opposition of a kind he explicitly repudiates in Nietzsche (only with the values reversed) between good desire (the "will to power") and a bad one ("*ressentiment*" or reactive "love," with which Nietzsche associated Christianity and thus dismissed it as the religion of slaves).[19]

These objections, along with Girard's own inability adequately to correct them, point toward the lack of a genuine creative sacred in Girard's work as well as toward theological conceptions of both sin and salvation which continue to fall into a mythical, scapegoating structure. In fact, the way Girard currently conceives a nonviolent religious orientation and social reality logically entails insisting on absolute difference between human love and divine love,[20] between human reality and divine revelation, then scapegoating everything human.[21] The injunction at the end of *Things Hidden* to "imitate Christ" and share in nonviolent love ("good" mimetic desire in Girard's thought) thus entails renouncing or expelling a fundamentally violent human nature/culture. This deep, structural, conceptual scapegoating at the most basic metaphysical and theoretical level, glaring to many, seems invisible to Girard himself, even though his work unmasks so many similar constructs.

FURTHER REVELATION OF THE SCAPEGOAT: PROBLEMS IN THE "IMITATION OF CHRIST"

Girard's answer to violence, as I have noted, is always theological. In particular, Girard claims that the Christian gospel uniquely exposes the scapegoat mechanism as the foundation of human culture and disarms it through gradual historical revelation. Robin Collins addresses in detail both strengths and problems with this thesis in the context of the Christian doctrine of the atonement and offers his own reassessment on this point. Others, including Swartley, Fodor, and James Alison, have critiqued and extended Girard's positive notion of the "imitation of Christ" in ways helpful not only for understanding Girard's claims but also more generally in understanding this often misused concept.[22]

I believe, however, that I can clarify some of the logical and theological problems which remain unexamined in this latter concept as it functions in Girard's framework, by adding some observations. First, from both a feminist point of view and from within the standpoint of his own theory, Girard's current solution to the problem of violence by appealing to the imitation of Christ is problematic for those who actually occupy the position of "victims" in the violent, most general system of representation (i.e., that of human culture itself) his theory is trying to unmask. Feminist theologians have long pointed out the problem for historically victimized peoples with interpreting this imitation as submission. They have identified problems as well with those related traditional formulations of sin and salvation which tend to leave deeper levels of violence unchallenged, or even inflict more violence through conceptual exclusion. As Andrew Sun Park, a Korean theologian, points out, "traditional doctrines of sin and salvation [which] focus primarily on the moral agency of the sinner . . . fail to deal adequately with the pervasive *reality* of the suffering of the victims of sin."[23] Park argues that

> the traditional doctrine of sin has been one-sided, seeing the world from the perspective of the sinner only, failing to take account of the victims of sin and injustice. . . . To bring the good news to the poor and downtrodden, we need to develop a proper analysis of the problems of the world viewed from the perspectives of both the sinner *and* the victim.[24] [italics added]

In the context of the Girardian framework, this critique points to the problem of conceiving of the imitation of Christ as simply the "giving up" of power, agency, and desire, or, conversely (and more subtly), as voluntarily taking on the position of the victim *in the sense of giving up one's position as a persecutor/perpetrator of violence*. This injunction paradoxically leaves *actual* victims disempowered, with no possibility of agency or desire of their own, and reifies them in exactly the same social, political, and metaphysical position as before—in the position of *victims*. The particular problems of actual victims of violence therefore go unrecognized in this formulation, because it fails to see their genuine difference within historical experience in relation to violence, and thus their different subjectivity.

If we consider the perspective of historically victimized peoples, we begin to see the indispensable need for an adequate understanding of nonviolent empowerment rather than a dichotomous choice between violent power on the one hand and a nonviolent "resignation" or vague acquiescence to the will (desire) of God on the other. Neither option effectively speaks to and has the capacity of liberating actual victims from real violence. This dichotomous choice is one I believe Girard would not want to maintain, yet within his current formulation it forces itself on actual victims of violence simply through sustained omission.

Second, the (current) Girardian solution to the problem of violence not only suffers from this omission of the victim's perspective, it renders it invisible while retaining telltale traces of its absence/presence. This leads to the interesting conclusion that the entire theory is (in its unreconstructed form), in Girard's own terminology and according to his own criteria, still partly a "myth" or "persecution text." In other words, it remains a story told from the point of view of the persecutor (i.e., those with relatively more power in the system of representation assumed by the theory), a story which hides the viewpoint and innocence of real victims (i.e., those with relatively less power in this system). Note that the "solution" offered by the theory speaks mostly to and from the position of the powerful. After all, it is primarily those more likely to play the role of persecutors/perpetrators of violence than that of victims in this system of representation who need to "give up" excessive or inappropriate desire and "repudiate [the] will to power" through "renunciation of divinity."[25]

Note, however, that those with relatively less power do not exactly need to give up their desire to agency and subjectivity. Instead, they need to give up their *lack of will* to *appropriate* subjectivity, desire, and agency as those made in the Image of God.[26] Self-emptying, *kenosis*, and suffering are still meaningful terms for historically victimized peoples, but their meaning, it is important to note, is quite different for someone who enjoys relatively little social power or for those who have been repeatedly scapegoated. Kenosis for such persons will entail their giving up the falsely constructed subjectivity, abject will, and captive agency created by the false system of representation they have been forced to inhabit.

In Girard's thought, anomalous statements regarding "giving up" the desire for power, agency, or *being* continue to betray an understanding still partly situated in a mythical framework unconsciously informed by a persecutor/powerful perspective.[27] Critiques of traditional theologies of original sin and guilt similarly point out that these theologies scapegoat humanity by presupposing that all human beings are equally, unproblematically, and ahistorically guilty in having a fundamental *desire for self*. The reality is that some people are genuinely more victimized than others. Such people have a different and positive relationship to this desire for selfhood, power, agency.

As Park and many others have noted, theologies that tend to reduce sin to guilt and individual moral agency overlook the genesis and consequences of sin as a cultural system that enmeshes people, *often against their will*, in violent social and ideological structures. (At the same time, it should be stressed that the concept and reality of guilt remains valid for understanding some of the ways in which everyone *willfully* turns away at times from this creative intersubjective reality by engaging in violence against self and/or others.) In Girard's antidote to the problem of violence, he leaves the assumption of universal human "guilt" unquestioned, though from the standpoint of his own theory he ought to be suspicious of this "story" of culture as having all the marks of a "persecution text."

If, as Girard argues, we must uncover and take the viewpoint of those excluded from/within a system of representation to discover its "truth," any genuine solution to the problem of violence must account for how the actual victims of history can be nonviolently empowered. How can they be brought to subjectivity, gain appropriate agency, and exercise desire in a framework that benefits both them and others? A genuine solution, theoretically speaking, would also need to account for how such "victims" already to some extent experience themselves as something other than or reducible to victims, how they already partly escape this system of representation which is really a myth. As Girard himself perceives, the entire mythical system of representation, with its fixed categories of "persecutor/victim" or "master/slave" and its "good/bad" dichotomies, is precisely what we see from the true perspective of the victim.

This means that a solution to the problem of violence must centrally include an account of constructive desire, the taking on of a new, nonvictimizing, *and nonvictimized* perspective. Girard clearly understands these two latter principles in theory, and in fact they are one of the key themes of his work. Yet he has been unable clearly to see his own scapegoat and split system of representation, as well as how his own theory fails to achieve this solution because of his own viewpoint in relation to the theory.

The imitation of Christ thus must mean something strong, active, and liberative, simply to include, let alone privilege, the perspective of those who have been real victims. In addition, to be truly intellectually compelling and practically useful, a complete theory of violence must not only *tell* us that we can take on this new perspective, but it must also *show us how* those who have been victims can actually cease to be victims *by ceasing to identify with their victim position*. This account is lacking in the Girardian theory as a whole, so it cannot (in its present form) be a universal theory of culture or provide a satisfactory theological account of the human predicament. Girardian theory fails itself to escape the kind of mythical structure it seeks to expose. Like the Mother in the psychoanalytic triangle, the victims in Girard's representation of the structures of culture and religion are incompletely recognized as subjects: They are not recognized as occupying this special point of view in relation to the entire system and thus offering (even demanding) another potential model of (constructive) desire. The theory still unwittingly expels the victims in its very formulation of the solution to the victimage mechanism.

LOVING MIMESIS: A CREATIVE REASSESSMENT OF MIMETIC DESIRE

Thus far I have laid out the self-referential problem in the current Girardian theory and located the theory's own "scapegoat," which is a nonviolent, nonscapegoating, constructive concept of mimetic desire. Next I will offer what I believe is a solution, a way forward which arises from inside the logic of the mimetic theory itself. The crucial question I believe Girard never explicitly asks is this: What does God desire? This is the question Girard's current account of mimetic desire and originary violence cannot answer in a satisfactory way. Yet the answer is the key to following Girardian theory through to its logical conclusion to make the theory itself nonviolent.

It is crucial to understand that uncovering any scapegoat—even Girard's own—amounts to challenging the entire Manichean system of representation which breaks reality into dualistic oppositions, including that of "good" and "bad" themselves. Such dualisms are a construct which Girard recognizes as suspect from the beginning in *Deceit, Desire and the Novel* and later persuasively links with scapegoating in his analysis of "doubling." The *Good*, or what some feminists have called *the Feminine*, or what I will call the genuinely Ethical or *Sacred* therefore *cannot be defined from within this violent dualistic type of system* but instead must be understood as belonging to an act of undivided thinking before the act of conceptual splitting/expulsion.

To ask what God desires and what we are imitating when we imitate this desire—to ask, in other words, how mimetic desire could be truly nonviolent—means being willing to give up this split system of representation itself, that is, to see it as *already* a *mis*representation. To see if mimetic desire could be understood in a way that does not once again replicate this system of representation, we need to return to the fundamental paradigm of mimetic desire and its variations (Figure 2).

FIGURE 2: FOUR CONFIGURATIONS OF MIMETIC DESIRE

2a. Classic Triangular Desire

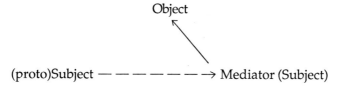

2b. "Coquette" phenomenon; romantic "love"

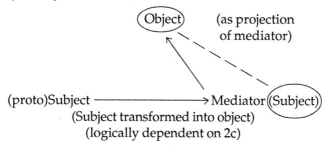

2c. Colonization

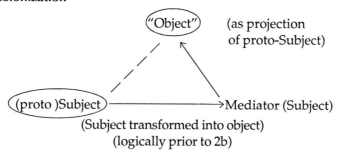

2d. Love

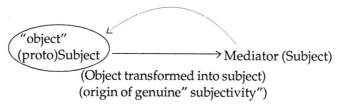

Figure 2a represents that paradigm of triangular mimetic desire with which we are all familiar. Here imitation of the mediator (subject) by the proto-subject[28] automatically leads, as Girard has demonstrated, to rivalry, then doubling, then escalation and the mimetic crisis of undifferentiation, and ultimately the scapegoat mechanism.

Figure 2b shows a fascinating and gender-relevant variation of this basic triangle, the phenomenon of the "coquette."[29] The coquette, as a mediator, desires her/his own body or self *as an object*. The triangular structure of mimetic desire, though less obvious than in the original model, is still present in 2b, because the the mediator's subjectivity is split into a subject who desires and the desired imaginary, projected object. Other proto-subjects, or"suitors," then imitate the coquette's desire for her/his body and/or self, resulting in rivalry with the mediator for possession of the object, and so forth. (In some ways Figure 2b offers a clearer picture of rivalrous mimetic desire than 2a, since, as Girard makes clear, the object in triangular desire is relatively unimportant in itself and gains its value primarily as a projection of the perceived *being*—i.e., subjectivity and capacity for agency—of the mediator.[30])

In Figure 2b, the mediator coquette's desire is narcissistic. But the coquette's narcissistic subjectivity (which Freud construed as the natural state of the female psyche!) conceals a further hidden violence and a further configuration of mimetic desire which logically precedes it. How could the coquette (here, for convenience, considered female) desire herself as an object if she had not already imitated someone else's desire for herself as an object? Before the scenario described by 2b, the coquette was herself a proto-subject. Figure 2c thus illustrates another extension of mimetic desire which Girard has not explicitly analyzed but which provides the blueprint for colonization of all kinds.

As in Figure 2b, the object in 2c is a projection of a split desiring subject, but this time it is a projection of/on the proto-subject, who is desired by the mediator *as an object*. The proto-subject then imitates the mediator's desire and desires himself or herself *as an object*. This responsive action simultaneously creates the coquette phenomenon and a split, inauthentic, and/or derivative subjectivity "colonized" by the subjectivity of the mediator. In fact, Figures 2b and 2c are simply two halves of the same scenario, seen from the two different perspectives: that of the colonized (coquette) and the colonizer.

Figure 2c shows why the Girardian theory is potentially such a valuable resource for historically victimized peoples, for it has the power to theoretically describe the process through which internalized oppression is actually generated and propagated, via the specific mechanism of mimetic desire. On the other hand, this scenario seems more than ever to leave historic victims stranded in the persecutor/victim dichotomy, seemingly with no way out.

Or is there? If we look more carefully at this last case of scenario 2c, it is important to take note that violence (to the subjectivity of the proto-subject) *arises in mimetic desire prior even to a formal scapegoat mechanism, preempting its function,* which is to establish order and difference. Is mimetic desire therefore even more insidious than we thought, rather than less? I think not. In fact, mimetic desire as represented in Model 2c suggests that violence is somehow bound up with the nature of *objects,* or the nature of *turning things into objects.* I believe mimetic rivalry and the scapegoat mechanism, though as real and as generative as Girard claims, are themselves but logical expressions of this more primordial violence, that of "object"-ifying.

Kirsten Anderson comes near to something like this conclusion in her analysis of the mimetic imperative regarding the imitation of God in Genesis 1-3. Though Anderson tries to talk about the two creation texts (P and J) "negotiating" between two different *kinds* of desires, she seems to admit the problem really lies elsewhere. She observes, in a way actually inconsistent with her thesis, that

> No doubt mimesis is a highly ambiguous category. René Girard seems to be the one critic, who most appropriate to P and J, describes humanity as caught in a double-bind, a contradicting double-imperative, whereby every command: *Imitate me!* immediately is followed by another command: *Don't imitate me!* In Girard's terms that really means, *don't appropriate my object.*" [31] [Last italics added; Anderson is quoting here from *Violence and the Sacred.*]

Now I would argue that in paradigms 2a-2c, it is clear we are *already* dealing in a realm (a system of representation) in which objects are assumed. How do objects, or acts of objectifying, generate violence? Girard says that "appropriation [presumably of objects] is the domain where imitation is conflictual."[32] Here he reiterates his basic view that objects and their appropriation, and not the nature of imitation (mimesis) *per se,* is the locus of violence in mimetic desire.

In *Violent Origins,* Jonathan Smith makes the observation that origin myths ask the fundamental question of how we "get" something.[33] Let's put Anderson's and Smith's observations together and ask the question, Under what condition do we genuinely get something without appropriating it (as an object)? In the language of the double bind, how do we acquire an object *without* acquiring it? I suggest that there is one instance of mimetic desire that can simultaneously answer this question, solve the double bind, and make the scapegoat of the Girardian framework disappear, thus transforming the entire theory by rendering it a self-referentially consistent "myth of origins."

Model 2d illustrates a case of mimetic desire I have not seen discussed by anyone to date, including Girard. What happens if the object desired by the mediator is the *subjectivity* of the proto-subject? After all, the proto-subject, being unformed and thus not yet truly a subject, *is* a kind of "object." In this scenario, if the proto-subject were to imitate the desire of the mediator, then the proto-subject would desire his or her own subjectivity. *Model 2d thus creatively fulfills both conditions of the double bind* (Imitate me! Don't imitate me!), *which are really a seamless simultaneous command.* That is, if proto-subjects fulfill the first half of the command and desire their own subjectivity, they also by definition fulfill the second: They will not merely imitate the mediator's subjectivity.

Furthermore, no rivalry ensues from this act of mimetic desire, since the object of desire by definition is that which cannot be appropriated by (reduced to the subjectivity of) the mediator. Yet the mediator and proto-subject both get or acquire something through this act of acquisitive mimesis—that is, greater subjectivity, desire, and relationship than either had before. Also in this case, if the mediator reciprocally imitates the proto-subject's desire, once again they both end up desiring the proto-subject's subjectivity.

The case of model 2d suggests mimesis as an event that generates between subjects an escalating circle of desire, but not a vicious one, as once again no rivalry ensues. In fact this idea of circular movement is really a way of describing something that is not a dialectic between two autonomous subjects at all but a single, unified dynamic of intersubjectivity which has generative power.

What of the idea that our own natural desires are selfish and we must adopt a somehow foreign, yet morally superior selfless attitude in relation to others (often called altruism or theologically equated with the imitation of Christ)? We have already seen how this notion makes little sense for those downtrodden as real historical victims; it also offers little motivation for those who enjoy relative positions of power. In this new scenario, however, if I am the mediator, I will be inclined to desire another's subjectivity (even assuming that desire comes out of my own lack or self-interest) because it enriches *both* of us to do so. It is *both* selfless (altruistic) and self-interested (selfish, narcissistic) to desire the subjectivity of the other, since I also desire my own subjectivity in the process. By definition, in desiring your subjectivity I get or acquire an intersubjective relationship with you, the proto-subject, but I do so without acquiring you as an *object*.[34]

This paradigm of intersubjective participation through self-reflexive mimetic desire does not negate or replace but transforms our understanding of classic triangular desire. If I as proto-subject imitate the mediator's desire more generally (i.e., imitate the mediator's desire for the subjectivity of third, external objects), I end up desiring not only myself but others and indeed potentially *everything around me* as a subject—as something alive with its own irreducible being, yet in dynamic, loving, intersubjective relation to me. Entering into and participating in this dynamic relation could be understood theologically as adopting the same unconditional relation of love that Christ exemplifies in relation to the Father, or imitating him.[35]

Model 2d demonstrates that the source of violence is not in mimesis itself. Rather, violence originates in the very split way of thinking that conceives of subjects as autonomous and in opposition to one another and therefore allows things, including human beings, to be conceived as objects of appropriation. The essence of the scapegoating process is that someone or something is turned into an *object*. This temptation to turn things into objects instead of subjects, even ourselves or God, might be called Idolatry. In a violent or mythical system of representation, something or someone must play the role of object so something or someone else can be a subject.

Though Girard sees through this exclusionary logic at the textual level over and over again, his current theology reaffirms this conceptual violence at the most general level with regard to the human self and God as mediator/Other. Model 2d suggests a system of participation (not representation) that gets beyond a false and violent subject/object dualism and the splitting characteristic of mythical thought. This dualism generates violent and misleading representations because it already does a more primordial violence to a unified intersubjective reality.

Mimetic desire in the case of Model 2d, however, particularly undoes many traditional theological and philosophical dichotomies. Some of the most compelling are those between self versus other, Eros versus Agape, persecutor (and the active will to power) versus victim (and *ressentiment* or love as renunciation of active desire for self), and humanism versus Christianity. This model allows for both/and. It suggests that subjects need not be conceived as emerging out of an inevitably violent opposition and exclusion but could be understood as the creative product of the dynamic of loving mimesis itself. Idolatry might be perceived as the attempt to quash this dynamic of creative mimesis by dividing the world up into subjects who act and objects who are acted on, perhaps out of fear, or to try to control things by giving them fixed meanings. Note that the scapegoat mechanism seems to work by putting things back in their "proper" place, then representing this distorted order of things as "natural." Perfect love, however, casts out (that is, transforms) this fear of mimetic play.

Theologically, I believe this new paradigm of mimetic desire describes genuine love, not as still conceived from within a split system of representation as mere nonviolence, a set of prescriptive ethics, or self-renunciation, but love conceived as a truly creative, revolutionary force. The concept of creative mimetic desire puts ethics (love) and power back together. Unlike Nietzsche, who tried definitively to take them apart and who rejected Christianity in the process, I claim that this paradigm makes possible a more adequate interpretation of true power as the will to intersubjective creative love of Self *and* Other.

This fourth configuration of mimetic desire fully meets the criteria Girard exhaustively sets out as characteristic of mimetic desire: it is "acquisitive"; it leads to doubling; it escalates in a feedback loop; it transforms subjects and objects; it has a metaphysical character; and it even describes a "twin narcissism" (wherein desiring you is really desiring myself).[36] Yet in this case all these characteristics are not only nonviolent but actively constructive.

Mimetic desire can be understood therefore as fundamentally positive, or more accurately, *creative*, not only in the sense that it is capable of generating new forms (which Girard claims of the scapegoat mechanism) but also in the sense that it is theoretically capable of doing so without violence. Yet real love is not mere peace or harmony, and creativity is not merely positive or pretty. Real love is the powerful force which liberates victims and perpetrators as well, which will not allow us to remain small or static, a prospect which can indeed be frightening. Real love continually brings new things into being.

How is this ethical, loving mimetic desire creative in practical human relationships? From within this new paradigm we can see that intersubjective relationships must continually be created. Moreover, new experiences, responses, and solutions to problems between people or groups must be negotiated and created in ways that honor the reality of this fundamental intersubjectivity—meaning without expelling someone as a scapegoat. This means not scapegoating even those we see as enemies or perpetrators of violence. This is the most difficult step in giving up our entrenched violent patterns of thought, because—for victims especially— it will be tempting to believe that renouncing the false power to scapegoat also jeapardizes power to identify and resist evil. So how do we prosecute evil without scapegoating, or on the other hand, forgive without excusing evil?

Marjorie Suchocki has given a fine analysis and definition of forgiveness which suggests how this is possible: Forgiveness is the transcending of this false system of representation, its violent reciprocity, and even its false and inappropriate indifferentiation between perpetrators/persecutors and victims, by "willing the well-being of the victim and violator in the fullest possible knowledge of the nature of the violence. . . . Forgiveness [is] living and acting from the will toward well-being."[37] This could also be interpreted here as living from within the paradigm of mimetic desire I have offered, or living out of "the mimesis of new creation" (Swartley) or following in "the way" of discipleship (Fodor).

Understood in its fullest sense, however, living from this will toward well-being involves more than forgiveness, reconciliation, and healing of the wounds of sin (with which Suchocki is concerned). Such an orientation must ultimately be understood as participating in an ongoing, active power toward and from the divine Good. What I call this "will to love" expresses itself not only in transcending (renouncing) one's previous imprisonment and identity as a perpetrator or victim. In addition, as suggested by the experience of real victims of violence, it also will result in appropriate anger and resistance in the face of new violence. The will to love becomes the impetus toward justice; creative negotiation with people or things that might have previously been obstacles; and finally, experiences of discovery and joy leading to ever deeper and more complex experiences of subjectivity and relationship with God and others. Living out of this new dynamic is to be an active co-creator with God in the divine and originally good created order of things (the kingdom of God), which might also be called the Order of Love.

THEOLOGY, POLITICS, AND PEACEMAKING: SOME THEORETICAL CONCLUSIONS

Despite fears and objections we might have regarding how any kind of totalizing theory, even of violence or liberation, tends to reinscribe violence, there is an emerging, even urgent sense, among theologians and philosophers as well as ordinary people that we need a new global myth or paradigm. What would be on a wish list for such a paradigm?

A general consensus seems to be forming: this paradigm needs to be nonviolent; it needs to be cross-cultural, affirming both our diversity and common life; it needs to have deep spiritual and/or psychological insight, yet not be reductive to human realities; and it needs to be capable of practical application in concrete, immediate terms helpful to us in dealing with the growing threat of physical, environmental, economic, and ideological violence rising everywhere around us.

It is easy to see why the sweeping claims and explanatory power of René Girard's theory of religion and culture, combined with the theory's tremendous fruitfulness in a diversity of applications, have made his work compelling to many, even those who have been put off by his totalizing claims. With the revisions I have proposed, the mimetic theory becomes much more convincing as a general theory, one on which we might build a common ethic, understanding of human beings, and practice of peacemaking.

In addition, I believe that taken as a metanarrative, Girard's overarching philosophical/theological paradigm now not only escapes the problem of replicating violence but actively promotes an ethic of peace, understood in a strong sense as human flourishing in the interconnectedness of all life and as the unfolding of God's creative life and purposes. I will just briefly touch on a few further consequences of my reassessment, the ramifications of which are far-reaching.

THEOLOGICAL IMPLICATIONS

I have already suggested above how this revised account affects general theological categories such as sin, salvation, and sacraments (or participation in divine reality), as well as the Christian concept of love. It can be seen as a corollary conclusion of my analysis that although Girard also has tended to split/scapegoat such terms and concepts as *myth*, the *sacred*, and *sacrifice*, this reconstructed concept of loving mimesis makes constructive interpretations of all of these possible. Indeed, this reassessment provides a powerful basis for a theology and worldview (*myth*) in which all of life and human relations may be viewed and treated as *sacred*, a gift offered back to God as a *sacrifice* of praise and thanksgiving. And though Girard has often focused on the Paraclete as the "defender of innocent victims and *the destroyer of every representation of persecution*"[38] (italics his), we might also remember that the Holy Spirit is first of all the divine energy which brings forth creation and life.

In addition, this reconstruction makes the Girardian theory compatible with theologies of historically victimized peoples. The theory now provides an adequate philosophical underpinning to the claims and prophetic challenges of theologies with a liberation emphasis (which stress justice for the oppressed) as well as feminist theology and theory (which are concerned with understanding and transcending the violence toward women and other victimized peoples embedded in both thought and social structures).[39]

This new paradigm also is more truly in keeping with Girard's fundamental theological stress on the prophetic nature of the Gospels. It also overcomes the tendency of his current formulation to fall back into an Augustinian "City of God" versus "City of Man" dichotomy with regard to human nature/culture. Such a dichotomy reinforces an excessively eschatological understanding of the kingdom of God and pessimism regarding human beings. Jesus says that the kingdom is among us, and it is now, for those who have "eyes to see and ears to hear" in a new way. This change of perspective involves a type of conversion, but not a conversion away from mimetic desire or to a sacred which is wholly Other. Rather, it is the conversion to a new viewpoint which recognizes the *already existing reality* of the deeply intersubjective, interdependent, and unfolding nature of human relationships and life.

The needy already see this more naturally than the socially powerful. Taking into account the viewpoint or corrective perspective of those who have tended to be the "victims" of others' violence, we must come to the conclusion that original sin must not be desire itself, especially the desire for selfhood, agency, and subjectivity, as is often claimed in traditional theologies of pride. Rather, original sin can be understood as a powerful name for the refusal or loss of this open system of intersubjective and unconditional relation to God and others by which we are constituted. That is, original sin is a description of the perversion and enslavement of mimetic desire in representations of idolatry, *within which it inevitably leads to violence.*

POLITICAL IMPLICATIONS

Girard's current religious views still partly participate in a dualistic and implicitly violent theology which has actually obscured his fundamental early insight about the mimetic, social nature of desire and the human person, as well as the brilliant extrapolation of his literary textual readings into a variety of anthropological domains. Though I believe I have shown this particular theology to be inadequate, I do agree with George Frear Jr. that Girard's current analysis clearly and powerfully describes those cultural and religious distortions, and the violence they engender, traditionally named *sin*. It also describes the system of representation feminists call *patriarchy*. For this reason, the theory has a potentially revolutionary character in its ability to identify victims, the mechanism of their internalized oppression, and the violent political, social, and ideological structures which engender injustice.

At the same time, the general political implications of this theory have seemed reactionary to some. The pessimistic view of human nature and institutions it proposes might be interpreted as reinforcing the political status quo. Some have seen it as advocating the largely passive awaiting of a historical evolutionary process of revelation, with an implied need for law and order—or even scapegoats—until this new order comes into being. Although Girard may not intend for his theory to be interpreted in a politically conservative way, it contains elements making such an interpretation possible, even likely.

A reconstructed view of the Girardian theory, however, maintains that the victimage mechanism, though a social and political reality, is not the foundation of culture; rather, mimetic desire is. Though this may seem a simple clarification, it in fact changes much of what Girard and his followers have said about human institutions such as religion (ritual) and the law (taboo). In Girard's current thought, these cultural institutions arise from and are means of holding back and regulating violence. On the other hand, in the revised view these institutions have an ambivalent and not simply negative relationship to love and freedom. Our common sense tells us human institutions serve both to regulate violent mimesis *and* to express and propagate our highest ideals. This suggests they are founded on mimetic impulses which originate both in scapegoating and in creative love.

Our job as Christians or citizens, then, is to desire the subjectivity of these and all human institutions to embody the redemptive reality that humans are made in God's image and to nurture and reflect our common life. The task then will be prophetically to call institutions to become what the better ones claim to be and to challenge those with an inadequate and violent ethic to become what they are not. Thus my reconstructed model, rather than allowing the theory to remain open to authoritarian politics, as some have charged of Girard's work, aligns itself with the best impulses of democracy. This better befits the theory's truly radical nature.

IMPLICATIONS FOR PEACEMAKING

A theory and praxis of peacemaking implicitly or explicitly relies on a theory of human nature, agency, and desire, since it presupposes that we engage in violent acts to get what we want, but that either these desires or these acts must be curtailed. This implies that a general theory of human relations must adequately understand subjectivity and desire. The notion of loving mimetic desire I have proposed has direct consequences for our conception of a practice of nonviolence and reconciliation, whether in formal conflict mediation or in the more general circumstances of our lives.

In peacemaking, a theory and practice of mere nonviolence that allows the system of representation that generates violence to itself go unchallenged is not enough. When dealing with real and powerful conflict, the threat of violence and scapegoating of actual people or things, we need a correspondingly powerful theory of subjectivity and agency to effectively address these practical conflictual situations and call for alternatives.

We have seen how any concept of the imitation of Christ or Christian "love" as mere self-sacrifice or servanthood on behalf of others, even if understood as "positive" mimetic desire or discipleship, can tend to encourage actual victims of violence to keep scapegoating themselves and encourage others to do so. It can even encourage self-scapegoating of the peacemakers themselves. Girard's work, however, if taken to its logical conclusion as I aim to have done, can challenge and empower the Christian theologian and peacemaker as well as those who have experienced victimage. In overcoming evil, peace as "the will to love" is an active, even a powerful concept, able not only to confront injustice but to create new realities, yet without itself lapsing into violence or scapegoating. In addition, this powerful love as mimetic desire will be just as contagious when whole and creatively directed as it was when split and inclined to violence.

What of Girard's claim that the Christian gospel uniquely reveals the scapegoating basis of human culture? As I have said, mimetic desire reconceived as love overturns the claim that violence and scapegoating form the basis of human experience. It is not hard to see theologically that love of this type cannot be confined to the special revelation of Jesus. Thus it cannot be, as Girard currently claims, *the* unique claim of Christianity to unmask the violent victimage mechanism and reveal nonviolent love in its place, though of course Christianity does this.

In fact, this love, and God, are already partly revealed in our common experience, in what has been conceded even by conservative theologies stressing sin and depravity as "general revelation" and "common grace." Such grace is possible in our most intimate family relationships, where we learn how and what to desire, as well as the larger social realm, not only in some separate metaphysical realm. These realms are all one. The words of 1 John are the Christian affirmation of the simple unity of familial, social, and divine realms, and our intimate human access to creative desire: "Beloved, let us love one another. For love is of God, and he who loves is born of God, and knows God. He who does not love does not know God for God is love" (1 John 4: 7-8).

From a reassessed Girardian point of view, the implication is that to imitate (follow in the way of) love in the way I have described *is* to "imitate Christ." To participate in an intersubjective dynamic of loving creativity with others through mimetic desire *is* to imitate, image, or reflect God. I do not believe it is essential to have the Judeo-Christian Scriptures to understand, or more importantly, to participate in this truth.[40] However, I do believe Christianity does have a unique claim regarding the gospel revelation from a Girardian point of view, a claim which has been made by no other religious tradition or human system of thought: that is that Jesus is the full, historical incarnation of this love which is both fully human and fully divine, and this love is stronger than any system of death which tries to contain it.

NOTES

1. I use the terms *subject* and *subjectivity* in my discussion to refer to one's sense of selfhood, as well as the point of view from which one perceives, desires, and acts in the world. In the broadest sense it also refers simply to the sense of human existence and/or consciousness which seems to need explanation and whose origin and nature can be speculated upon.

2. Walter Burkert, René Girard, and Jonathan Z. Smith, *Violent Origins: Ritual Killing and Cultural Formation*, ed. Robert Hammerton-Kelly (Stanford, Calif.: Stanford University Press, 1987), 136.

3. George Frear Jr., "René Girard on Mimesis, Scapegoats, and Ethics," *Annual of the Society of Christian Ethics* (1992), 115-133.

4. "Violence, Difference, Sacrifice: An Interview with René Girard," *Violence, Difference, Sacrifice: Conversations on Myth and Culture in Theology and Literature*, ed. Rebecca Adams, *A Special Issue of Religion and Literature* 25, no. 2 (1993), 11-33 (henceforth, Interview, R&L). See also Fodor's summary of this problem in Jim Fodor, "Christian Discipleship as Participatory Imitation: Theological Reflection on Girardian Themes" (246-276 in this volume).

5. See, for instance, Robert Greer Cohn, "Desire: Direct and Imitative," *Philosophy Today* 34, no. 4 (1989), 318-329, who objects that "Girard's concept of desire which heavily features imitation is excessively unidimensional" and argues, as have others, that there must be other—and more constructive—kinds of desire.

6. See Sarah Kofman, "The Narcissistic Woman: Freud and Girard," *Diacritics* 10, no. 3 (1980), 36-45, and Toril Moi, "The Missing Mother: The Oedipal Rivalries of René Girard," *Diacritics* 12, no. 2 (1982), 21-31.

7. Girard particularly uses language of this type, or makes explicit claims about violence as an originary principle within human culture, in discussions linked with the principle of Satan as the "Father of lies"; see, for instance, *The Scapegoat*, trans. Yvonne Freccero (Baltimore: Johns Hopkins University Press, 1986), 165-6.

8. The *sacred*, like the term *myth* and usually *sacrifice*, is always negative in Girard's thought and refers to the religious and/or metaphysical (mis)representation created by scapegoating, and the mystifying process by which the scapegoat is simultaneously demonized and expelled from this system of representation, yet also divinized and paradoxically made the cornerstone of the system. The scapegoat, therefore, is that thing the sacred system excludes, yet without which the system cannot be what it is and whose presence and true nature it cannot entirely efface.

9. This kind of self-reflexive confirmation is essential in maintaining the validity of any general or universal claim, but it is especially crucial that any theory about violence would itself be nonviolent. What would be simply a logical problem in some other theories would also become an ethical problem within a theory of nonviolence.

10. Girard does make reference to positive forms of mimetic desire in his work, but I believe they are inadequate or even self-refuting. In his early work, Girard speaks of external mediation as the key to nonviolence, in which rivalry becomes impossible through sheer distance and the impossibility of appropriating the mediator's "object." Girard's argument about God as ideal external mediator depends on maintaining a strong, even absolute "spiritual" (metaphysical) distance/difference between human and divine, in particular with regard to God himself as the object in question. Thus if this distance were to begin to collapse, rivalry would ensue. In fact, this collapse into rivalry with God is what we see in stories about the fall of Satan and human beings, who experience the double-bind (Imitate me! Don't imitate me!) in a mimetic imperative with respect to God as an object of desire; they try to appropriate and *become* God.

In his later work, Girard seems largely to abandon the terminology of *distance* as a satisfactory solution to the problem of rivalry and instead insists upon maintaining a distinction *in kind* between God's desire and human desire. This distinction (which is really just another kind of distance) is implicit in his understanding of the Imitation of Christ, which involves the idea both of God as proper (distant) object of mimetic desire *and* as proper mediator of (divine) desire. The Imitation of Christ therefore can be seen as a modified form of external mediation (a conversation with Paul Nuechterlein helped clarify this issue). The distance/difference so essential to the whole idea of external mediation is not only unstable, however, it leads to an unresolvable dilemma within the theory. If there is not enough "spiritual distance" between created beings and God, external mediation lapses into rivalry; on the other hand, if this distance/difference is maintained absolutely, the theory itself lapses into conceptual expulsion and scapegoating of the concept of mimetic desire itself, and specifically of human desire and subjectivity, as I show

304 • VIOLENCE RENOUNCED

later in the text. Thus all Girard's current formulations of positive forms of mimetic desire/mediation are both logically and theologically highly problematic, and come at the cost of the theory itself having a "scapegoat."

11. Girard, *Violent Origins*, 123.

12. René Girard, *Things Hidden Since the Foundation of the World*, trans. Stephen Bann and Michael Metteer (Stanford: Stanford University Press, 1987), 430-1.

13. Interview, *R&L*, 24-25.

14. Willard M. Swartley, "Discipleship and Imitation of Jesus/Suffering Servant: The Mimesis of New Creation" and Fodor, "Christian Discipleship as Participatory Imitation" (218-276 in this volume).

15. John S. Dunne, C. S. C., *The Peace of the Present: An Unviolent Way of Life* (Notre Dame, Ind.: University of Notre Dame Press, 1991), 2.

16. Kirsten M. Anderson, "*Imago Dei* and Desire in Genesis 1-3: To Eat or Not to Eat; or Rather To Eat or What to Eat," *Literature and Theology* 6, no. 3 (1992), 254-267; 255.

17. As a systematic distortion, Girard's anomalous remarks regarding the "good" versus "bad" nature of mimetic desire appear almost exclusively in contexts that deal with the issue of finding a solution to or escape from the violence entailed by mimetic desire. I want to reiterate that this splitting of the term and concept, a systematic distortion which, as we shall see, can be observed in the interview and elsewhere, is anomalous within Girard's general intellectual project. That project is exactly in the business of analyzing such splitting and expulsion phenomena (particularly textually) as evidence of scapegoating. Furthermore, this distortion is contrary to his general conception of mimetic desire as fundamentally "ambiguous" (hence his stress upon the double-bind, and the simultaneous "good"/"bad" character of mimesis it implies). Therefore, what is at stake here is whether the theory is self-referentially inconsistent, or to use Girard's own terminology and criteria, whether his theory is itself a "myth" which founds itself upon a scapegoat and then conceals its own violence.

18. Girard's remarks about God as the *object* of desire do not really solve the problem of rivalry at all and lead to illogicalities. In Girard's current analysis, he claims that God is the only safe object of desire (the only object which does not lead to rivalry), presumably because God is an *infinite* object. This idea, however, leads to two major problems. First, the idea of God as infinite object tends readily to collapse, as I point out in a related discussion in footnote 10, into one of God as finite object that one then attempts to possess or even displace, as in the extreme case of Satan in the temptation story of Jesus. Examples such as this set up God and created beings as rivals much as the coquette is in a "love/hate" rivalry with her suitors for impossible possession of his or her person (my Figure 2b). Thus it may be that the idea of God as an infinite object is simply an oxymoron which still conceals the double-bind. Finally, I would point out that even if it were possible to desire God as an infinite object as Girard proposes, this solution provides no help in obtaining positive desires directed outward toward the world. Without such positive

desire, we are left with the dilemma of being able to engage with the world only through "bad" mimetic desire, or with having to renounce desire from and toward the world altogether, which Girard refers to as a "living death" (*Things Hidden*, 399).

Taking God as object of desire would imply the need to imitate someone else who desires God as object, which leads naturally to the idea of the "Imitation of Christ." Christ (God the Son) is to mediate desire for God (the Father) and also our imitation of God the Father's desire itself. Yet how can Christ's imitation of God not be rivalrous if Satan's is? It must not just be because Christ takes God as the object of desire, which Satan also does, and not only because Christ perfectly imitates the desire of the Father, *in the sense of taking God as a mediator*, which Satan also does. Girard's remarks about the imitation of Christ and God as an object of desire are therefore really only a logical detour which ends in a *cul de sac* and which misleads the reader from his central claim, which is about the nature of God as a mediator of desire *and specifically about the nature of God's desire*. It is exactly here that Girard makes a conceptual leap by claiming that God's desire is of a different *nature* from mimetic desire, that is, it is *nonacquisitive*, whereas Satan's, and the rivalrous disciples, and human desire in general, is violent (even if God is the "object") because it is *acquisitive*. This confused and partially concealed conceptual leap constitutes an act of conceptual splitting and expulsion, as I go on to demonstrate in detail in my text and in Figure 1.

19. See *Things Hidden*, 426, where Girard rejects Nietzsche's "sacrificial and victimary distinction" and also the desire to differentiate between the "guilty" and the "innocent."

20. In this he follows a traditionally constructed dualistic theology of love such as that elaborated by Anders Nygren in *Agape and Eros*, trans. Philip Watson (Philadelphia: Westminster Press, 1953); see *Things Hidden*, 277.

21. See René Girard, *Deceit, Desire and the Novel: Self and Other in Literary Structure*, trans. Yvonne Freccero (Baltimore: Johns Hopkins University Press, 1965), 142-146, where according to his own definitions his theoretical position on Christianity can be characterized as "romantic criticism" which falls prey to "Manichean" thinking and "absolutes," and which still unwittingly participates in what he himself has called the illusion of "romantic singularity."

22. In addition to Swartley and Fodor's discussions, see James Alison's treatment of the Imitation of Christ as what he calls "pacific mimesis" in *The Joy of Being Wrong: Original Sin Through Easter Eyes* (New York: Crossroad, 1998).

23. Andrew Sun Park, *The Asian Concept of Han and the Christian Doctrine of Sin* (Nashville: Abingdon Press, 1993).

24. Ibid., 11, 13.

25. Girard, *Deceit, Desire and the Novel*, 292 and 294, respectively.

26. In fact, Girard says something very like this at the end of *Deceit, Desire and the Novel* in his discussion of the "conversion" of the protagonist, where Proust's Marcel must give up "seeing himself in the role of the eternal vic-

tim," (p. 299) "in an act of "creative renunciation" (p. 307); and Girard even hints at some positive notion of empowerment ("resurrection") in the sense that the novelist gains the ability to act in the world by writing the novel.

27. This is the point made in the feminist critique of the Girardian theory made by Susan Nowak, to which Girard has seemed unable, or has not seen the need, to make a satisfactory response. Because Nowak's analysis of this problem is presented in feminist categories and terminology instead of terms intelligible solely from within the theory itself, this point apparently has remained unclear; conversely, Nowak's critique lacks a developed constructive proposal for fixing this problem in the theory. See Susan Nowak, "The Girardian Theory and Feminism: Critique and Appropriation," *Contagion: Journal of Violence, Mimesis and Culture* 1, no. 1 (1994), 19-29.

28. I call the imitating "subject" the "proto-subject" because his or her subjectivity is unformed or incomplete prior to the act of imitation represented in the paradigm. The paradigm attempts to describe the mechanism by which subjectivity is created and thus, in effect, itself qualifies as a myth of origins.

29. See Girard, *Things Hidden*, 370-371; and *Deceit Desire and the Novel*, 105.

30. Girard, *Deceit, Desire and the Novel*, 53.

31. Anderson, 255. See René Girard, *Violence and the Sacred*, trans. Patrick Gregory (Baltimore: Johns Hopkins University Press, 1977).

32. René Girard, *"To Double Business Bound": Essays in Literature, Mimesis and Anthropology* (Baltimore: Johns Hopkins University Press, 1978), 201.

33. Girard, *Violent Origins*, 136-137; "How did something that wasn't come to be?" (130).

34. As I have shown, it is not wrong or dangerous to want to acquire the right things under the right conditions. I therefore propose using the terms *appropriate* and *appropriative* desire instead of the misleading term *acquisitive* desire, the latter of which is another term that has been "split" and scapegoated within the Girardian framework. I have demonstrated that *acquisitive* mimetic desire can be nonviolent, nonrivalrous, creative, and *appropriate*. *Appropriative* desire, on the other hand, is the term I will use for wanting to take something that is *not* appropriate with regard to maintaining a loving relationship with oneself and with others.

35. David Burrell, John Dunne, and James Alison all make this point, but without offering an explanation of what conditions exactly constitute this relation as I have done. For instance, James Alison asserts the reality of this imitative relation as different and constructive rather than providing an explanation of the mimetic mechanism for what he calls "pacific" mimesis. His treatment also overlooks the logical problems posed by external mediation and God's desire as different in kind. As such, his treatment is not so much wrong as incomplete, and it suffers from very much the same problems as Girard's original statement. (One can see how Alison's discussion of pacific mimesis is subject to the same subtle splitting and expulsion I have described in Girard's work, this time of the word/concept of "peace," which I believe still appears in his treatment as somewhat in opposition to power and thus

still implicitly tied to ideas of subordination.) See David Burrell, "René Girard: Violence and Sacrifice," *Cross Currents* 38, no. 4 (1988-89), 443-447; 445.

36. See Girard, *Things Hidden*, 8-9; *Violence and the Sacred*, 161; *Deceit, Desire and the Novel*, 96-98; 17 and 19; 67, 77 and 119; and 108, respectively.

37. Marjorie Hewitt Suchocki, *The Fall to Violence: Original Sin in Relational Theology* (New York: Continuum, 1995), especially the discussion on pp. 148-150.

38. Girard, *The Scapegoat*, 207.

39. I believe Girardian theory, though certainly still partially patriarchal in its current formulation, could provide an invaluable resource for feminist analysis if it took into account the reassessment I have outlined. Furthermore, Girard's conception of mimetic desire provides not only a gender-neutral term and concept, but also a fruitful description of the *mechanism* by which a desire of *difference* is generated and an ethics that could be immediately graspable in concrete, practical terms. For an analysis of the relationship of Girardian theory to feminist theory generally, and the possibility of a beneficial mutual critique, see Susan Nowak and also Jennifer Rike, "Mimesis and Scapegoating: René Girard on the Violent Origins of the Sacred and Feminist Constructions of Selfhood," *Contagion: Journal of Violence, Mimesis and Culture* 3, no. 2 (1996), 21-42.

40. My religious conclusions regarding mimetic desire, since less exclusivistic than Girard's, might seem to call for jettisoning theology altogether and understanding mimetic desire in purely philosophical or anthropological terms. This is not the case. Whereas my new paradigm may be understood as coherent and consistent on a purely logical or humanistic level, I believe there are good reasons also to retain a specifically theological understanding of these issues. For instance, given the new model I have proposed, it is reasonable to propose that love as the dynamic of intersubjective creative mimesis is itself personal (participates itself in subjectivity) rather than impersonal. I also accept Christian theological formulations such as the Trinity and the incarnation (properly understood) not only as valid but rich elaborations of this paradigm; see for instance, Catherine Mowry La Cuna, "God For Us: The Trinity," in *Freeing Theology: The Essentials of Theology in Feminist Perspective* (San Francisco: HarperSanFrancisco, 1993), 83-114; and Robin Collins's treatment of incarnation and atonement as necessary for our participation in the divine life (132-153 in this volume.)

At the same time, I believe that my reassessment provides a strong basis for dialogue with other religious traditions and points of view. Others have noted Girard's tendency to overlook both religious and literary texts that portray constructive or ambiguous cases of mimetic desire. These texts, however, clearly exist, as do loving religious and cultural practices outside of, or prior to, contact with Christianity.

CHAPTER FOURTEEN

Violence Renounced

Response by René Girard

UNFORTUNATELY I COULD NOT ATTEND the symposium at which the papers in the present volume were first presented and discussed. When Professor Willard Swartley, able organizer of this event as well as editor of its proceedings and a participant, kindly sent me all the manuscripts and invited me to comment on them, I was confronted with a difficult choice. The quality of all these contributions is such that I wanted to say something about each. Such a course, however, would limit my observations to statements so brief and inconsequential that they would do justice neither to the individual papers nor the volume as a whole.

I decided to focus on the main subject of the symposium, which is also my one real field of competence, the "mimetic theory." Some of what follows applies to many papers in *Violence Renounced*, some applies to only a few or even to a single one, as in the case of Sandor Goodhart. Many contributors are not mentioned. Their essays are not necessarily those I enjoyed least; rather, they often are the ones from which I learned the most.

• • •

I begin with a general observation regarding the overall summarizations of the mimetic theory. There are several examples of it in this volume and, as a rule, they are remarkably accurate. I observe, however, that frequently in the descriptions of the "scapegoat mechanism" it is difficult to avoid the misleading language of conscious purpose.

In the first paper, for instance, Marlin E. Miller seems to suggest that the "foundational murder" was deliberately planned by archaic communities to deflect internal violence against a scapegoat for the purpose of avoiding violence within the community: "Girard posits that the way to resolve the mounting crisis is to select a victim onto whom the violence of the entire community can be projected."

This language is legitimate, I believe, in the case of ritual sacrifice, but not appropriate in the case of the original scapegoating, which must be completely spontaneous, unplanned, and even unconscious in the sense of the victim being misunderstood for a real culprit, a powerful troublemaker responsible for the ills from which the community suffers. If the victimizers realized that their victims are arbitrary, they would not be unable to transfer their hostilities on them, and peace would not be restored. Effective scapegoating, it is evident, entails unanimous self-deception.

In archaic communities, this self-deception must have been so monolithic that it produced not one but two illusions in quick succession. First the scapegoat phenomenon, properly speaking, turned the victim into the dangerous malefactor portrayed at the beginning of many foundational myths. Then came the reconciliation, so sudden and so miraculous, it seemed, that the beneficiaries apprehended it not as their own doing but as the work of the scapegoat once again. This scapegoat was therefore mistaken for an all-powerful benefactor as well as a malefactor. Instead of canceling each other, these two opposite transfigurations persisted side by side. The result was the "ambivalent" notion of the sacred and its divinities, which brought peace as well as violence to the community.

In the description of this generative process, I myself have not always avoided an excessively transitive and voluntaristic language. We must do our best, however, to portray scapegoating as the delusional experience that it still is even in its weakened modern versions. Scapegoaters never see through their own scapegoating: they interpret it as the legitimate punishment of a bona fide culprit. This is why even and especially the worst scapegoaters never acquire a real awareness of their own scapegoating. To perceive this is an exceptional experience and a great spiritual upheaval which we call a Christian conversion.

There are two striking examples of this in the vicinity of the cross, Peter's return to Jesus after his triple denial, which may be regarded as a second and deeper conversion, and Paul's famous encounter on the road to Damascus. Paul distinctly hears this question from Jesus' own mouth: "Why do you persecute me?" Peter must have heard the query as well. All awareness of our own scapegoating (unlike our awareness of our neighbors' scapegoating) comes from God's own Spirit, the Paraclete, the Defender of victims.

Most of the time Miller represents accurately the self-deluded dimension of scapegoating. And he himself, I believe, might well have modified the formulation I have just questioned had not his untimely death interrupted his work.

• • •

In his own essay, Willard Swartley handles a theme with important implications both for mimetic theory and Christian theology: imitation in the letters of Paul. He observes that Protestant theologians traditionally have de-emphasized *imitatio Christi*, fearing that it might lead to an emphasis on works at the expense of faith.

This neglect of imitation is difficult to justify in view of the fact that not only the Gospels but Paul himself, whose importance for Protestant theology is paramount, insists on the positive role of imitation in Christian life. Swartley shows that the mimetic understanding of desire can help us better grasp the role of imitation in Paul.

According to the mimetic theory, no existence is free from imitation, and the alternative to imitating Christ or Christ-like models is the imitation of our neighbors whose rivalrous impulses are usually as easily aroused as our own. As soon as we pattern our desires on our neighbors' desires, we all desire the same objects and we become entangled in mimetic rivalries.

Comically as well as tragically, human beings keep turning each other into obstacles to the fulfillment of the very passions they keep transmitting mimetically to one another. This is why peaceful relations among neighbors are rare.

The mutual entrapment of mimetic desires has its own name in the New Testament, *skandalon*, the best translation of which is the old "stumbling block." It designates an obstacle so fascinating that the more it repels the more it attracts and vice-versa. Skandalon is a metaphor for the paradox of a mimetic desire that keeps intensifying as a result of being thwarted by its own model. This phenomenon explains the addictive nature of mimetic rivalry and its formidable potential for violence and destruction. Scandals are discussed at length by Jesus himself in the synoptic Gospels.

Paul does not discuss the word as such, but he uses it with tremendous effectiveness. He keeps warning his readers that the imitation of Christ is necessary to avoid scandals. Instead of desiring avidly and s imitates the pure generosity of his Father who "makes and his rain fall on the just as on the unjust." As soon as mitate Jesus instead of our neighbors, the power of scan-

Paul often makes the two-sidedness of mimetic desire visible by juxtaposing the bad imitation of rivalrous models and the good imitation of Christ. Since Paul imitates Jesus just as faithfully as Jesus imitates his Father, he is almost as good a model as Jesus himself and since he is still around, unlike Jesus, he advises his converts to imitate him. This recommendation is not a symptom of Paul's narcissism, or of his "will to power"; it is practical advice to people who get bogged down in scandals.

Swartley quotes a passage that marvelously summarizes Paul's entire doctrine:

> Give no offense [do not become a scandal] to Jews or to Greeks or to the Church of God, just as I try to please everyone in everything I do, not seeking my own advantage, but that of many, so that they may be saved. Be imitators of me, as I am of Christ. (1 Cor. 10:31-11:1)

The effort to show that the imitation of Christ protects us from mimetic rivalries is very much needed to counteract the tendency to suppress the problematic of imitation, under the influence of the pseudo-individualism that dominates our time and multiplies scandals endlessly.

And yet, more than ever today, theologians avoid the word *imitation*. Dazzled by the worldly prestige of hyperindividualism, they blind themselves to the prevalence of bad imitation and *ressentiment* at the moment of their greatest triumphs.

Even people sympathetic to the mimetic theory sometimes resort to language tricks to avoid this dreadful word imitation. It is impossible to reconcile the mimetic theory with fashionable ideologies which are nothing but symptoms of the very disease the mimetic theory alone truly defines. We should not try to minimize the clash between the mimetic perspective and these ideologies. The favorite substitute for imitation is mimesis, an excellent word, no doubt, but only because it means the same thing as imitation. Being Greek, it sounds better to our snobbish (mimetic) ears than its lowly Latin and English equivalent.

• • •

To examine the mimetic theory from the standpoint of its usefulness to theology is what Jim Fodor and many other authors do in their essays. Theologians would like mimetic theory to answer many theological questions to which I confess I have no answers.

I understand very well that theologians would ask these questions—regarding the church, for instance, and above all the matter of redemption—to understand atonement theories. Their answers interest me greatly. Yet it always takes me by surprise that such questions should be asked before the repercussions of the mimetic theory on our understanding of the relationship between mythology and the Judeo-Christian tradition are really assessed and assimilated.

In our world, more and more people believe that the mythical status of Christianity is or soon will be a scientific certainty. When undergraduate students show up at such places as Stanford, they know little about either mythology or Christianity, but most of them never utter such a phrase as "the Christian religion." They find it cool to say "the Christian myth" in a tone of complete self-assurance, as if they really know what they are talking about.

The confusion of the Judeo-Christian tradition with mythology is rooted in the very real similarities between the central drama of myths and the central drama of the crucifixion as well as of many biblical texts. The same collective ganging up against a single victim occurs in countless myths, often as a form of lynching, and also in the Hebrew Bible, most notably in the collective lynching of the Suffering Servant in Isaiah 52–53. The crucifixion is not a lynching, but Pilate is supposed to act under the pressure of a crowd.

As soon as we understand that all these similarities are rooted in "scapegoating," i.e., mimetic violence, mob phenomena—we also understand why they all resemble one another, regardless of where and when they occur. It is understandable that observation of these similarities would lead modern observers to assume that the Christian religion is nothing but "one more myth of death and resurrection."

It must be confessed that Christian believers have always eluded this problem, and that is a terrible mistake. Once we see the universality of scapegoating, it is not difficult to spot the enormous significance of the one constant difference between the mythical and the Judeo-Christian modalities of the scapegoat drama, the difference in the distribution of innocence and guilt, between the victims and their persecutors.

Even though myths ultimately divinize their victims, they first and foremost represent them as real culprits, authentic troublemakers the community is entitled to victimize and murder. It is clear, therefore, that myths are taken in by their own scapegoating processes. The mythical perspective is the perspective of the deluded community, unable to question its own persecutional delusion.

In Judeo-Christian scapegoating the reverse is true. Instead of being guilty the victims are innocent; instead of being innocent, the persecutors are guilty. Unlike myths, therefore, the Bible and the Gospels portray scapegoating truthfully as the mechanism of collective self-deception that it really is. The authors are not the persecuting mob but a few heroic dissenters, or the disciples of these dissenters, who unravel the lie of scapegoating instead of surrendering to it. They lucidly perceive the mimetic contagion which overwhelms the entire crowd, including themselves at the beginning, i.e., Peter's triple denial.

This tremendous difference is enhanced rather than erased by the many similarities among mythic and Judeo-Christian dramas. Contrary to what the deconstructors assume, we are not dealing here with fictional stories unrelated to one another, mere "narratives."

It is not an arbitrary preference for this or that type of fiction that is responsible for the difference I am talking about. It is the ability of biblical and evangelical dissenters to do what mythical communities never manage to do, to resist the contamination of scapegoating, to see through the mimetic delusion of the mob.

Myths embody the perspective of communities unanimously duped by the tidal waves of mimetic contagion that must have occurred, periodically, in all archaic societies, as a result of the irresistible human propensity to mimetic conflicts.

The Bible and the Gospels justly rehabilitate the type of victims myths falsely indict and vice versa: they justly indict those victimizers myths falsely justify. That is why our religious tradition is so unpopular with its beneficiaries. Human beings prefer the reassurance of mythology to the biblical and evangelical denunciation of our collective illusions.

When our religious tradition rehabilitates wrongly accused scapegoats, it reveals the lie of scapegoating and by the same token demystifies or de-mythifies mythology. Each foundational myth ultimately is an example of essentially the same riddle that was solved twenty-five centuries ago in Isaiah 52–53 and again twenty centuries ago, in the accounts of the crucifixion.

Our religious tradition is more genuinely scientific than our science of mythology. The biblical revelation (exposure) of mythology is no "mystical" insight. It rests on commonsensical observations. It requires no religious commitment to be understood. This anthropological vindication of the Judeo-Christian tradition is the first and foremost consequence of the mimetic theory. Far from being an ethnocentric prejudice in favor of our own religion, the Judeo-Christian claim to unique truthfulness, almost universally reviled and ridiculed these days, is objectively, verifiably true.

To make the evidence crystal clear, one can compare the biblical victory over mythology to what happens in the modern world when an instance of scapegoating is successful enough to generate its own kind of mythology in some community. Then one must continue to observe what happens until it is victoriously challenged by dissenters perceptive and courageous enough to fight against almost everybody to vindicate the innocence of the victim, which they alone perceive, at least for a while.

Take the Dreyfus case in France: it is nowadays only a bunch of old texts. But these texts are not what deconstructors and other relativists claim all texts are: they are not merely "stories" or "narratives" that can become the object of ten thousand different interpretations, none of which is really true, none of which is really false. These texts are all accounts of the same real drama, with a real flesh and blood victim. This drama can only be interpreted in two fundamentally opposed manners: one is the scapegoat way, which is absolutely false; the other is the undoing of scapegoating, which is absolutely true.

From a scientific viewpoint the difference between myths and the biblical/evangelical dramas is comparable, mutatis mutandis, to the difference between the innocence of Captain Dreyfus, which was the truth, and his supposed guilt, which was a lie. The lie was almost universally believed for a while but was nevertheless a lie, a typical scapegoat delusion nurtured by popular anti-Semitism.

If myths are really structured by a scapegoating which remains unperceived due to the unanimous self-deception, the Judeo-Christian tradition is as uniquely true, in the one crucial respect I just defined, as the pro-Dreyfus literature is and always will be. Myths, on the contrary, are and always will be as deceptive as the anti-Dreyfus literature. If and when the Judeo-Christian deconstruction of mythology becomes common knowledge, the whole post-Enlightenment culture of naive contempt for our Judeo-Christian heritage will crash to the ground.

This possibility is so momentous that the most urgent task, for those who believe in the validity of the mimetic theory, is to make people aware of its consequences. The beneficiaries must be not this or that Christian church, not even Judaism or Christianity as a whole, but the whole global culture in which we live.

The traditional problems that divide Christian believers among themselves and even Christians from Jews pale into insignificance, it seems to me, compared to the intellectual and spiritual revolution that the palpable proof of the Judeo-Christian truthfulness entails. The mimetic theory turns the supposedly "scientific" basis for religious skepticism into its very opposite. It does not demonstrate the religious truth of the Judeo-Christian tradition, which cannot be done, as we all know, but it does the next best thing: it demonstrates its anthropological truth.

This power for truth in Judeo-Christian Scripture can be made visible in the nonreligious context of the social sciences. At a time of precipitous decline in religious faith, this fact is so stupendous, the Judeo-Christian power to solve the mythical riddle is so precious that, in the very interest of all our religious traditions, theologians should refrain from making use of the mimetic reading for parochially ecclesiastical interests. If the intellectual independence of the mimetic theory is obscured, if it is perceived as a mere servant of this or that theology, *ancilla theologiae*, its effectiveness is nullified.

• • •

The demystification or deconstruction of scapegoating begins with the Hebrew Bible. The story of Joseph, for instance, repeatedly rehabilitates a wrongly accused scapegoat. It is a continuous struggle against false persecution. This process of intellectual and spiritual cleansing is also present in the Psalms, in the book of Job, and, more explicitly than anywhere else, in Isaiah 52–53, which portrays the death of an unknown prophet, Yaweh's Suffering Servant.

In his essay, Sandor Goodhart perceives this truth. He explicates the prophet's collective lynching to show its revelatory value in regard to the falsity of scapegoating. If the text were a myth, the Servant's death would be justified as the punishment of a real culprit, as the just expulsion of an individual harmful to the community, something like the expulsion of that well-known delinquent, Oedipus, who, in addition to his principal crimes, parricide and incest, gives the plague to all his fellow citizens!

The Servant must be accused of similar crimes, but his death is portrayed as the completely unjust lynching of an innocent man by a deluded mob. The text contains a clear allusion to the mimetic disruption that turns human communities into mobs and triggers their scapegoating urge: "All we like sheep did go astray, we turned every one to his own way."

Sandor goes straight to the all-revelatory passage, notably the one on the prophet's lowly status in his community. The Servant is somewhat of an outcast, due in part to his mediocre and unimpressive appearance which, in addition to his gentleness, makes him a likely choice as a scapegoat. He is the type of individual to whom persecutors in search of a victim are irresistibly drawn:

For he shot up as a root out of dry ground;
He had no form or comeliness that we should look on [him].
Nor beauty that we should delight in him.
He was despised, and forsaken of men,
A man of pains, and acquainted with disease,
And as one from whom men hide their face;
He was despised and we esteemed him not. (JPS, 1917)

If we survey a great number of myths we will discover that a high percentage of their hero/victims, just like the Servant of the Lord, possess one or more features of the type that tend to attract scapegoaters: these include physical or cultural features that arouse the fear, anger, or contempt of archaic communities, unpleasant infirmities, abnormalities, repulsive illnesses, a foreign accent, foreign customs. In *The Scapegoat*, I grouped these features together under the label of preferential signs of victimization. Whoever possesses one or several of them will not necessarily be selected as a scapegoat, but his/her chances are increased.

Sandor is aware that the four accounts of the Passion also reveal the process of scapegoating. He is aware, therefore, that the Bible and the Gospels have something essential in common. He is not one of these people who claim that the expression "Judeo-Christian" is meaningless and should be abandoned.

The Songs of the Servant were written six centuries, probably, before the Gospels, and Sandor raises the question of the Gospels' singularity or lack of it in relation to the Jewish Bible:

> There is nothing that Girard says about the innocent victim in Christianity, it would appear, which is not already fully present in Isaiah 52–53. We need to reexamine Girard's claim that the gospel is unique in this particular fashion.

His reexamination leads Sandor to conclude that the singularity that I, like other Christians, attribute to Christ and Christian Scriptures cannot be real, unless we root it in something different from the revelation of the scapegoat mechanism.

Just as Sandor does, I believe that Isaiah 52-53 fully reveals the same scapegoat mechanism as the Gospels. The description is as concrete and realistic as in the four accounts of the Passion. There are several differences, nevertheless, between Isaiah 52–53 and the Gospels' account of scapegoating. I will discuss only the one I regard as essential.

In the Gospels, not only is the revelation of scapegoating repeated once again but, for the first time, this revelation reflects on itself, it talks about itself, and it comments on its own significance for all human beings. Far from refusing to acknowledge the historical priority of the biblical revelation, the Gospels repeatedly acknowledge it and invoke the authority of the Scripture to explain the significance of what is going on in the Passion.

An essential part of this self-referential dimension of the scapegoat revelation lies in the many quotes from the Bible, not only from Isaiah 52–53 but from many other texts which have revelatory value in regard to scapegoating. The Gospel of John (15:25) quotes a statement from Psalm 69:4 (cf. 35:19) that, at first sight, seems rather banal and unimpressive. In this Psalm, the narrator complains that, even though his enemies are as numerous as the hair on his head, they hate me, he says, "without a cause."

Our modern psychological and textual bias suggests that it must be his psychic abnormality, his paranoid tendencies perhaps, that lead the narrator of this Psalm to imagine a huge alliance against him. We never even wonder if he might not be saying the truth, if, in a chaotic community, he might not be really threatened with lynching, just like the Servant of the Lord. Our long tradition of idealism and our tendency to dissolve reality prevent us from even conceiving the possibility of a real violence outside the text. For our fashionable critics all violence is textual.

The phrase "without a cause" is applied to Jesus precisely because it defines the most characteristic feature of scapegoating: if the victimizers have a cause, it is a nonsensical one, a "preferential sign of persecution." The "without a cause" senseless mimetic hostility of scapegoating is everywhere in evidence around Jesus; it contagiously affects even his closest disciples. Peter's triple denial is nothing but this "hating without a cause" which the apostle unconsciously absorbs as soon as he is engulfed in a crowd already hostile to Jesus, and he immediately imitates this hostility. This denial is a most eloquent testimony to the mimetic nature of scapegoating in general and the Passion in particular.

Long believed irrelevant and nonsensical, the idea of christological prophecy makes sense in the context of scapegoat revelation. The Gospels not only provide us with the most complete revelation of scapegoating ever written, more complete and specific than even Isaiah 52–53, but the quotes and comments surrounding the crucifixion make this revelation still more complete and explicit. Even some of the titles given to Jesus are part of the scapegoat revelation. To say that he is the *lamb of God* is the same as saying that he is a scapegoat in the modern sense. The Gospel expression is more effective in conveying the innocence of the unjustly sacrificed victim.

The Gospels not only reveal scapegoating but reflect on their own revelation and its future effects on the world, the apocalyptic violence, for instance, that might be unleashed when the sacrificial protection that pre-Christian cultures still enjoy is completely withdrawn.

In the Jewish Bible the scapegoat revelation, as Sandor himself observes, does not occupy a central place. It remains marginal and does not underline its own importance. That is why the attention of commentators is never focused directly on it. The central theme, as Sandor also observes, is the struggle against idolatry.

If we reflect on idol worship, however, once again we will be confronted by scapegoating which is the true cause of idolatry. The only way to fulfill the struggle against idolatry is to reveal its origin in the invisible, undisclosed scapegoating of mythology. The essence of archaic religion, I recall, is the people's gratitude toward their scapegoats they mistake for divine benefactors.

An idolater is an individual who worships his own victim in the mistaken belief that far from being an innocent scapegoat, he/she is a real malefactor who deserves to be killed; then the unanimous violence, mysteriously, turns the scoundrel into a divine reconciler of the community.

I am not inclined to believe, therefore, that by placing the emphasis on "anti-idolatry" as Sandor does, one can effectively regard the revelation of scapegoating as something of secondary importance. Thus, the rejection of idolatry is impossible unless scapegoating is fully revealed as the mimetic self-deception that dominates mythology and sacrificial rites.

● ● ●

The entire history of religion, I feel, can be summarized in terms of the relationship between scapegoating and the scapegoaters. In archaic religions scapegoating itself is sacralized because it remains forever unintelligible. Archaic religions and their sacrificial systems are an economy of scapegoating that violently evacuates internal violence and, through the endless repetitions of ritual, slowly generates cultural institutions.

The tremendous achievement of the Jewish Bible is that, for the first time in history, it de-divinized victims and it de-victimized God. It replaced the thousands of scapegoat idols with the one monotheistic Yahweh who is totally alien to human scapegoating. That is why in the

Jewish Bible, for the first time, scapegoating is portrayed truthfully as scapegoating. Instead of being first demonized, then divinized—in the sense that Oedipus is—Joseph is admirably humanized.

Jewish monotheism is so essentially characterized by this mutual separation of scapegoating and the divine that it tends to perceive Christianity only as a regression into the bad mythical habit of divinizing scapegoats. Is not Jesus a divinized scapegoat, just as Oedipus?

Indeed he is, but if we carefully examine Jesus' relationship to scapegoating, we will see that, far from being the same as in mythology, it is the very reverse. Instead of being divinized by the people who turn him into a scapegoat and persecute him without being aware of his innocence, Jesus Christ is God to those who realize he is an innocent victim and accepts playing the role of the scapegoat to reveal once and for all how scapegoating operates in human culture, how all human beings ultimately share in scapegoating. *Jesus willingly and knowingly accepts to undergo the fate of the scapegoat to achieve the full revelation of scapegoating as the genesis of all false gods.*

The absolute separation between God and scapegoats, such as we have it in the Jewish Bible, is a most important step in the revelation of what God really is, but it is not the end of the story. The Bible teaches us that the true God is not dependent on the scapegoat mechanism. As a matter of fact God dislikes that mechanism so much that, again and again, God sides with the victims against their persecutors. In the book of Job the essential question is whether or not God is on the side of the crowd, with the persecutors, or on the side of the victim, with the innocent scapegoat. The final answer is that God is on the side of the victim, not of the persecutors.

Already in the Jewish Bible, therefore, a new rapprochement is taking place between God and victimized scapegoats, but on a basis entirely different from the old mythical confusion. Here the basis is revealing and neutralizing mimetic victimization.

What the Gospels and Christian theology really do is take this rapprochement as far as possible, which means all the way to a complete identification. God and the scapegoat become one once again in the death of a Jesus who is as fully divine as he is fully human. God willingly becomes the scapegoat of his own people not for the purpose of evacuating internal violence through the old mythical misunderstanding but for the opposite reason, for clearing up once and for all all such misunderstandings and raising humankind above the culture of scapegoating.

Far from dismissing as necessarily "mythical" and "sacrificial" the attempts to define the mysterious proximity between the Servant and God in the Servant Songs, we must try to understand the text as part of an effort which, half a millennium later, will produce such Christian ideas as the incarnation and redemption through the cross. Some of my earlier statements on the subject were rash and inadequate, I now believe. I am still groping toward a more satisfactory understanding. I hope that the younger researchers such as Sandor and all the authors in the present volume will reach some day the goal that keeps eluding me.

Girard: Biblical
Studies and Theology

WORKS BY RENÉ GIRARD (CHRONOLOGICAL ORDER, IN ENGLISH)

Deceit, Desire, and the Novel: Self and Other in Literary Structure. Trans. Yvonne Freccero. Baltimore: Johns Hopkins Univ. Pr., 1965. Originally published as *Mensonge romantique et vérité romanesque* (Paris: Grasset, 1961).

"Les Malédictions contre les pharisiens et la révélation évangélique." *Bulletin du Centre Protestant d'Etudes.* Geneva (1975): 5-29.

Violence and the Sacred. Trans. Patrick Gregory. Baltimore: Johns Hopkins Univ. Pr., 1977. Originally published as *La violence et le sacré* (Paris: Grasset, 1972).

"To Double Business Bound": Essays in Literature, Mimesis, and Anthropology. Baltimore: Johns Hopkins Univ. Pr., 1978.

"Peter's Denial and the Question of Mimesis [Mark 14:66-72]." *Notre Dame English Journal* 14 (Summer 1982): 177-89.

"History and the Paraclete." *Ecumenical Review* 35 (January 1983): 3-16.

The Scapegoat. Trans. Yvonne Freccero. Baltimore: Johns Hopkins Univ. Pr., 1986. Originally published as *Le Bouc émissaire* (Paris: Grasset, 1982).

Job: The Victim of His People. Trans. Yvonne Freccero. Stanford: Stanford Univ. Pr., 1987. Originally published as *La route antique des hommes pervers* (Paris: Grasset, 1985).

Things Hidden since the Foundation of the World. Trans. Stephen Bann and Michael Metteer. Stanford: Stanford Univ. Pr., 1987. Originally published as *Des Choses cachées depuis la fondation du monde* (Paris: Grasset, 1978).

Violent Origins: Walter Burkert, René Girard, and Jonathan Z. Smith on Ritual Killing and Cultural Formation. Ed. Robert G. Hamerton-Kelly. Stanford: Stanford Univ. Pr., 1987.

A Theatre of Envy: William Shakespeare. New York: Oxford Univ. Pr., Inc., 1991.

"A Girardian Review of Hamerton-Kelly on Paul." *Dialog* 32 (1993): 269-74.

"How Can Satan Cast out Satan?" In *"Biblische Theologie und gesellschaftlicher Wandel: für Norbert Lohfink SJ,* ed. Georg Braulik, Walter Gross, Sean McEvenue, 125-41. Freiberg: Herder, 1993.

"Is There Anti-Semitism in the Gospels?" *Biblical Interpretation* 1, no. 3 (1993): 339-52.

"Violence, Difference, Sacrifice: A Conversation with René Girard." In *Violence, Difference, Sacrifice: Conversations on Myth and Culture in Theology and Literature,* ed. Rebecca Adams. A Special Issue of *Religion and Literature* 25, no. 2 (Summer 1993): 11-33.

Quand ces choses commenceront: Entretiens avec Michel Treguer. Paris: Arléa, 1994.

"Mythology, Violence, Christianity." *Paragrana: International Zeitschrift für Historische Anthropologie* 4, no. 2 (1995): 103-116.

"Sacrifice in Levenson's Work." *Dialog* 34 (1995): 61-62.

"Are the Gospels Mythical?" *First Things* 62 (April 1996): 27-31.

"Reconciliation, Violence and the Gospel." In *Visible Violence: Sichtbare und verschleierte Gewalt im Film,* ed. Franz Grabner, Gerhard Larcher, and Christian Wessely, 211-221. Thaur: Druck- und Verlagshaus Thaur, 1998.

Je vois Satan tomber à l'éclair. Paris: Grasset, 1999.

WORKS ON RENÉ GIRARD AND ON HIS THEORIES
(ALPHABETICAL ORDER, BY AUTHOR)

Adams, Rebecca, ed. *Violence, Difference, Sacrifice: Conversations on Myth and Culture in Theology and Literature.* A Special Issue of *Religion and Literature* 25, no. 2 (Summer 1993).

Alison, James. *Knowing Jesus.* Springfield, Ill.: Templegate Pubs., 1993.

————. *Raising Abel: The Recovery of the Eschatological Imagination.* New York: Crossroad Pub. Co., 1996.

————. *The Joy of Being Wrong: Original Sin through Easter Eyes.* New York: Crossroad Pub. Co., 1998.

Anderson, Kirsten M. "*Imago Dei* and Desire in Genesis 1–3: To Eat or Not to Eat; or Rather to Eat or What to Eat," *Literature and Theology* 6, no. 3 (1992), 254-267.

Bailie, Gil. *Violence Unveiled: Humanity at the Crossroads.* New York: Crossroad Pub. Co., 1995.

Baudler, Georg. *Die Befreiung von einem Gott der Gewalt: Erlösung in der Religionsgeschichte von Judentum, Christentum und Islam.* Düsseldorf: Patmos, 1999.

Boyarin, Daniel. "The Subversion of the Jews: Moses's Veil and the Hermeneutics of Supersession." *Diacritics* 23 (Summer 1993), 16-35.

Bellinger, Charles I. *The Genealogy of Violence: Reflections on Creation, Freedom, and Evil.* New York: Oxford University Press, 2000.

Burrell, David. "René Girard: Violence and Sacrifice." *Cross Currents* 38 (Winter 1988–89): 443-47.

———. "Violence, Sacrifice and the Gospel of Jesus." *Books and Religion* 16 (Winter 1989): 6, 13.

Chauvet, Louis-Marie. "Le sacrifice de la messe: un statu chrétien du sacrifice." *Lumière et vie* 29 (1980): 85-106.

Chilton, Bruce. *The Temple of Jesus: His Sacrificial Program within a Cultural History of Sacrifice.* University Park: Pennsylvania State Univ. Pr., 1992.

———. "René Girard, James Williams and the Genesis of Violence." *Bulletin for Biblical Research* 3 (1993): 17-29.

———. "Sacrificial Mimesis." In *Religion* 27, no. 3 (1997): 225-30.

Cohn, Robert Greer. "Desire: Direct and Imitative." *Philosophy Today* 34, no. 4 (Winter 1989): 318-29.

Darr, John A. "Mimetic Desire, the Gospels, and Early Christianity: A Response to René Girard." *Biblical Interpretation* 1, no. 3 (1993): 357-67.

Davis, Charles. "Sacrifice and Violence: New Perspectives in the Theory of Religion from René Girard." *New Blackfriars* 70 (July/August 1989): 311-28.

Dewey, Joanna. A Response to René Girard: 'Is There Anti-Semitism in the Gospels?'" *Biblical Interpretation* 1, no. 3 (1993): 353-56.

Dominach, Jean-Marie. "Voyage to the End of the Sciences of Man." Trans. Mark R. Anspach. In *Violence and Truth: On the Work of René Girard,* ed. Paul Dumouchel. Stanford: Stanford Univ. Pr., 1988.

Duff, Paul. "René Girard in Corinth: An Early Christian Social Crisis and a Biblical Text of Persecution." *Helios* 22 (1995): 79-99

———. "Murder in the Garden? The Envy of the Gods in Genesis 2 and 3." *Contagion: Journal of Violence, Mimesis, and Culture* 3 (Spring 1996): 1-20.

———. "The Sacrifical Character of Earliest Christianity: A Response to Robert J. Daly's 'Is Christianity Sacrificial or Anti-Sacrificial?'" *Religion* 27, no. 3 (1997): 245-48.

Dumouchel, Paul, ed. *Violence and Truth: On the Work of René Girard.* Stanford: Stanford Univ. Pr., 1988.

Dupuy, Jean-Pierre. "Totalization and Misrecognition." Trans. Mark R. Anspach. In *Violence and Truth: On the Work of René Girard,* ed. Paul Dumouchel. Stanford: Stanford Univ. Pr., 1988.

Dunne, John S. *The Peace of the Present: An Unviolent Way of Life.* Notre Dame: Univ. of Notre Dame Pr., 1991.

———. "Myth and Culture in Theology and Literature: A Conversation with John S. Dunne." In *Violence, Difference, Sacrifice: Conversations on Myth and Culture in Theology and Literature,* ed. Rebecca Adams. A Special Issue of *Religion and Literature* 25, no. 2 (Summer 1993): 77-104.

Frear, George, Jr. "René Girard on Mimesis, Scapegoats, and Ethics." *Annual of the Society of Christian Ethics* (1992): 115-33.

Golson, Richard. *René Girard and Myth: An Introduction.* New York: Garland Publishing, Inc., 1993.

Goodhart, Sandor. "'I Am Joseph': René Girard and the Prophetic Law." In *Violence and Truth: On the Work of René Girard,* ed. Paul Dumouchel. Stanford: Stanford Univ. Pr., 1988.

———. "From Sacrificial Violence to Responsibility: The Education of Moses in Exodus 2-4." *Contagion: Journal of Violence, Mimesis, and Culture* 6 (1999): 12-31.

———. "Prophecy, Sacrifice, and Repentance in the Story of Jonah," *Semeia, an Experimental Journal for Biblical Criticism* 33 (1985): 43-63.

———. "René Girard," *The Johns Hopkins Guide to Literary Theory and Criticism,* ed. Michael Groden and Martin Kreiswirth. Baltimore: Johns Hopkins Univ. Pr., 355:356.

———. *Sacrificing Commentary.* Baltimore: Johns Hopkins Univ. Pr., 1996.

Green, Alberto R. W. *The Role of Human Sacrifice in the Ancient Near East.* ASOR Dissertation Series. Missoula: Scholars Pr., 1975.

Grote, Jim. "The Imitation of Christ as Double-Bind: Toward a Girardian Spirituality." *Cistercian Studies* 29, no. 4 (1994): 485-98.

Gudorf, Christine E. *Victimization: Examining Christian Complicity.* Philadelphia: Trinity Pr. International, 1992.

Hamerton-Kelly, Robert G. "A Girardian Interpretation of Paul: Rivalry, Mimesis and Victimage in the Corinthian Correspondence. *Semeia* 33 (1985): 65-81.

———. "Sacred Violence and the Messiah: The Markan Passion Narrative as a Redefinition of Messianology." In *The Messiah,* ed. James Charlesworth. Philadelphia: Fortress Pr., 1992.

————. *Sacred Violence: Paul's Hermeneutic of the Cross*. Minneapolis: Fortress Pr., 1992.

————. "Biblical Interpretation, Mythology, and a Theory of Ethnic Violence." *Scriptura* 50, no. 1 (1994): 23-39.

————. *The Gospel and the Sacred: Poetics of Violence in Mark*. Minneapolis: Fortress Pr., 1994.

Hamerton-Kelly, Robert G., ed. *Generative Violence*. Stanford: Stanford Univ. Pr., 1987.

Hardin, Michael. "The Biblical Testaments as a Marriage of Convenience: René Girard and Biblical Studies." Unpublished paper presented to Colloquium on Violence and Religion. Annual meeting of American Academy of Religion/Society for Biblical Literature, November 1990.

————. "Mimesis and Dominion: The Dynamics of Violence and the Imitation of Christ in Maximum Confessor." *St. Vladimir's Theological Quarterly* 36, no. 4 (1992): 373-85.

————. "Violence: René Girard and the Recovery of Early Christian Perspectives." *Brethren Life and Thought* 37 (Spring 1992): 107-20.

————. "The Scapegoat: Christologies in Conflict." Paper presented to the International Bonhoeffer Society, August 1992.

Hunsinger, George. "The Politics of the Nonviolent God: Reflections on René Girard and Karl Barth." *Scottish Journal of Theology* 51, no. 1 (1998): 61-85.

Jay, Nancy. *"Throughout Your Generations Forever": Sacrifice, Religion, and Paternity*. Chicago: Univ. of Chicago Pr., 1992.

Jensen, A. E. *Myth and Cult among Primitive Peoples*. Chicago: Univ. of Chicago Pr., 1963.

Jensen, Hans. "The Fall of the King." *Scandinavian Journal of the Old Testament* 1 (1991): 121-47.

————. "Desire, Rivalry, and Collective Violence in the 'Succession Narrative.'" *Journal for the Study of the Old Testament* 55 (1992): 35-59.

Juergensmeyer, Mark, ed. *Violence and the Sacred in the Modern World*. London: Frank Cass & Co., 1992.

Juilland, Alphonse, ed. *To Honor René Girard*. Saratoga, Calif.: Anmi Libri, 1986.

Kaptein, Roel. *Freedom in Relationships*. Belfast: The Queen's University of Belfast, 1993.

————. *On the Way of Freedom*. Introduction by René Girard. Dublin: Columba Press, 1993.

Kerr, Fergus. "Rescuing Girard's Argument?" *Modern Theology* 8 (October 1992): 385-99.

———. "Revealing the Scapegoat Mechanism: Christianity after Girard." In *Philosophy, Religion and the Spiritual Life,* ed. Michael McGhee, 161-75. Cambridge: Cambridge Univ. Pr., 1992.

Knott, Garland. "The God of Victims: René Girard and the Future of Religious Education." *Religious Education* 86, no. 3 (1991): 399-412.

Kofman, Sarah. "The Narcissistic Woman: Freud and Girard." *Diacritics* 10, no. 3 (1980), 36-45.

Lefebure, Leo D. "Victims, Violence and the Sacred: The Thought of René Girard." *The Christian Century* (December 11, 1996), 1226-28.

Lind, Millard. "Power and Powerlessness in the Old Testament: A Book Analysis [of Norbert Lohfink, ed., *Gewalt und Gewaltlosigkeit im Alten Testament.* Freiberg: Herder, 1983]." In *Monotheism, Power, Justice: Collected Old Testament Essays,* Text Reader Series, no. 3, 203-10. Elkhart, Ind.: Institute of Mennonite Studies, 1990.

Lohfink, Norbert, ed., *Gewalt und Gewaltlosigkeit im Alten Testament.* Freiberg: Herder, 1983.

Mabee, Charles. "Before the Law: Un/rivaling the Old Testament." In *Curing Violence,* ed. Theophus H. Smith and Mark I. Wallace. Forum Fascicles 3, 100-117. Sonoma, Calif.: Polebridge Pr., 1994.

———. "René Girard and Rudolph Bultmann: The Problem of Myth." Unpublished paper.

Mack, Burton. "Introduction: Religion and Ritual." In *Generative Violence,* ed. Robert G. Hamerton-Kelly, 1-70. Stanford: Stanford Univ. Pr., 1987.

McBride, James. "Capital Punishment as the Unconstitutional Establishment of Religion: A Girardian Reading of the Death Penalty." *Journal of Church and State* 37 (Spring 1995): 263-87.

McCracken, David. *The Scandal of the Gospels: Jesus, Story, and Offense.* New York: Oxford Univ. Pr., Inc., 1994.

McEntire, Mark. *The Blood of Abel: The Violent Plot of the Hebrew Bible.* Macon, Ga.: Mercer University Press, 1999.

McKenna, Andrew J., ed. "René Girard and Biblical Studies." *Semeia* 33 (1985): 1-171.

———. *Violence and Difference: Girard, Derrida, and Deconstruction.* Urbana: Univ. of Illinois Pr., 1992.

Michaud, Jean-Paul. "Le passage de l'Ancien au Nouveau, selon l'Epître aux Hébreux." *Science et Esprit* 35 (1983): 33-52.

Milbank, John. *Theology and Social Theory: Beyond Secular Reason.* Oxford: Basil Blackwell, 1990.

———. "'I Will Gasp and Pant': Deutero-Isaiah and the Birth of the Suffering Subject: A Response to *Social Class and Ideology in Isaiah 40-55*, by Norman K. Gottwald." *Semeia* 59 (1992): 59-71.

———. "Stories of Sacrifice." *Contagion: Journal of Violence, Mimesis, and Culture* 2 (Spring 1995): 75-102. Expanded version in John Milbank, "Stories of Sacrifice." *Modern Theology* 12 (January 1996): 27-56.

Moi, Toril. "The Missing Mother: The Oedipal Rivalries of René Girard." *Diacritics* (Summer 1992): 21-31.

Nemoianu, Virgil. "René Girard and the Dialectics of Imperfection." In *To Honor René Girard*, ed. Alphonse Juilland, 1-16. Saratoga, Calif.: Anmi Libri, 1986.

North, Robert. "Violence and the Bible: The Girard Connection." *The Catholic Biblical Quarterly* 47 (1985): 1-27.

Nowak, Susan. "The Girardian Theory and Feminism: Critique and Appropriation." *Contagion: Journal of Violence, Mimesis, and Culture* 1 (Spring 1994): 19-29.

Ong, Walter. "Mimesis and the Following of Christ." *Religion and Literature* 26, no. 2 (Summer 1994): 73-77.

Pattery, George. "Mimetic Desire and Sacred Violence: Understanding René Girard from the Indian Context." *Vidyajyoti. Journal of Theological Reflection* 58, no. 1 (January 1994): 15-32.

Pattison, George. "Violence, Kingship and Cultus." *Expository Times* 102, no. 5 (1991): 136.

Peters, Ted. "Atonement and the Final Scapegoat." *Perspectives in Religious Studies* 19 (Summer 1992): 151-81.

Peters, Ted, ed. "Paul and Luther: A Debate over Sacred Violence." *Dialog* 32 (1993): 242-44, 247-96. A special thematic issue, with articles by Robert G. Hamerton-Kelly, David E. Fredrickson, Krister Stendahl, Hayim Goren Perelmuter, René Girard, Gerhard O. Forde, Everett R. Kalin.

Pippin, Tina. *Death and Desire: The Rhetoric of Gender in the Apocalypse*. Louisville: Westminster John Knox Press, 1992.

Pries, Edmund. "Violence and the Sacred Scapegoat." In *Essays on War and Peace: Bible and Early Church*. Occasional Papers, no. 9, ed. Willard M. Swartley. Elkhart, Ind.: Institute of Mennonite Studies, 1986.

Pyper, Hugh. "The Reader in Pain: Job as Text and Pretext." *Literature and Theology* 7, no. 2 (June 1993): 111-29.

Redekop, Vern. *Scapegoats, the Bible, and Criminal Justice: Interacting with René Girard*. MCC U.S. Office on Crime and Justice/Victim Offender Ministries Occasional Papers, no. 13. Akron, Pa.: Mennonite Central Committee, 1993.

———. "A Hermeneutic of Deep-Rooted Conflict: An Exploration of René Girard's Theory of Mimetic Desire and Scapegoating and its Applicability to the Oka / *Kanehsatà:ke* Crisis of 1990." Unpublished dissertation, 1998.

Regensburger, Dietmar. *Bibliography of Literature on the Mimetic Theory.* Innsbruck: Girard-Dokumentation, Institut für Dogmatik, 1994.

Ricoeur, Paul. "Religion and Symbolic Violence." *Contagion: Journal of Violence, Mimesis, and Culture* 6 (Spring 1999): 1-11.

Rike, Jennifer. "Mimesis and Scapegoating: René Girard on the Violent Origins of the Sacred and Feminist Constructions of Selfhood." *Contagion: A Journal of Violence, Mimesis and Culture* 3, no. 2 (1996): 21-42.

Rohr, Richard. *Love Your Enemy: The Gospel Call to Nonviolence.* Sound recording of lecture based on the books *Violence and the Sacred*, by René Girard, and *Violence Unveiled*, by Gil Bailie. Cincinnati: St. Anthony Messenger Pr., 1997.

Schwager, Raymund. "Christ's Death and the Prophetic Critique of Sacrifice." *Semeia* 33 (1985): 109-23.

———. "La Mort de Jésus: René Girard et la Théologie." *Recherches de Science Religieuse* 73, no. 4 (1985): 481-502.

———. *Der Wunderbare Tausch.* Munich: Kösel-Verlag GmbH & Co., 1986.

———. *Must There Be Scapegoats? Violence and Redemption in the Bible.* San Francisco: Harper & Row, Publishers, 1987. Originally published as *Brauchen wir einen Sündenbock?* Munich: Kösel-Verlag GmbH & Co., 1978.

———. Review of *The Bible, Violence and the Sacred*, by James G. Williams, and *Sacred Violence*, by Robert G. Hamerton-Kelly. *Zeitschrift für Katholische Theologie* 115, no. 3 (1993): 339-41.

———. *Jesus of Nazareth: How He Understood His Life.* New York: Crossroad Pub. Co., 1998.

———. *Jesus in the Drama of Salvation: Toward a Biblical Theology of Redemption.* New York: Crossroad Pub. Co., 1999. Originally published as *Jesus im Heilsdrama: Entwurf einer biblischen Erlösungslehre* (Innsbruck-Wien: Tyrolia, 1990).

Scubla, Lucien. "The Christianity of René Girard." Trans. Mark A. Anspach. In *Violence and Truth: On the Work of René Girard*, ed. Paul Dumouchel. Stanford: Stanford University Press, 1988.

Stevens, David. "Unmasking the Gods of Violence: The Work of René Girard." *Studies: An Irish Quarterly Review* 77 (Autumn 1988): 309-20.

Taylor, Simon J. *Sacrifice, Revelation, and Salvation in the Thought of René Girard*. Ph.d. Diss., University of Oxford, 1998.

Tissot, Georges. "Bibliographie: René Girard." *Studies in Religion/Sciences Religieuses* 10, no. 1 (1981): 109-112.

Volf, Miroslav. *Exclusion and Embrace: A Theological Exploration of Identity, Otherness, and Reconciliation*. Nashville: Abingdon Press, 1996.

Wallace, Mark I. *Fragments of the Spirit: Nature, Violence, and the Renewal of Creation*. New York: Continuum, 1996.

Wallace, Mark I., and Theophus H. Smith, eds. *Curing Violence*. Sonoma, Calif.: Polebridge Pr., 1994.

Ward, Graham. "Mimesis: The Measure of Mark's Christology." *Literature and Theology* 8, no. 1 (March 1994): 1-29.

White, Hayden. "Ethnological Lie and Mythical Truth." *Diacritics* 8 (Spring 1978): 2-9.

Williams, James G. "The Innocent Victim: René Girard on Violence, Sacrifice, and the Sacred." *Religious Studies Review* 14, no. 4 (October 1988): 320-26.

———. *The Bible, Violence, and the Sacred: Liberation from the Myth of Sanctioned Violence*. San Francisco: HarperCollins, 1991. Paperback edition, Philadelphia: Trinity Press International, 1995.

———. "Sacrifice, Mimesis, and the Genesis of Violence: A Response to Bruce Chilton." *Bulletin for Biblical Research* 3 (1993): 31-47.

———. "History-Writing as Protest: Kingship and the Beginning of Historical Narrative. *Contagion: Journal of Violence, Mimesis, and Culture* 1 (Spring 1994): 91-110.

———. "'Steadfast Love and Not Sacrifice': A Nonsacrifical Reading of the Hebrew Scriptures." In *Curing Violence*, ed. Mark I. Wallace and Theophus H. Smith, 71-99. Sonoma, Calif.: Polebridge Pr., 1994.

———. "Introduction: 'Christianity: A Sacrificial or Nonsacrificial Religion?'" *Religion* 27 (1997): 219-24.

Williams, James G., ed. *The Girard Reader*. New York: Crossroad Pub. Co., 1996.

Wink, Walter. *Engaging the Powers: Discernment and Resistance in a World of Domination*. Minneapolis: Fortress Pr., 1992.

Yoder, John H. "Review of *The Scapegoat*, by René Girard." *Religion and Literature* 19, no. 3 (Fall 1987): 89-92.

OF TOPICAL SIGNIFICANCE RELATED TO GIRARDIAN THEORY

Appleby, R. Scott. *The Ambivalence of the Sacred: Religion, Violence, and Reconciliation*. Lanham, Md.: Rowman & Littlefield Publishers, 2000.

Balthasar, Hans Urs von. *Theo-Drama*. Vol. 4. San Francisco: Ignatius Pr., 1994.

Bloch, Maurice. *Prey into Hunger: The Politics of Religious Experience*. New York: Cambridge University Press, 1992.

Boyarin, Daniel. *A Radical Jew: Paul and the Politics of Identity*. Berkeley: Univ. of California Pr., 1994.

Castelli, Elizabeth. *Imitating Paul: A Discourse of Power*. Louisville: Westminster John Knox, 1991.

Chauvet, Louis-Marie. "Le sacrifice comme échange symbolique." In *Le sacrifice dans les religions*, ed. Marcel Neusch. Sciences théologiques et religieuses 3. Paris: Beauchesne, 1994.

Chester, A. N. "Hebrews: The Final Sacrifice." In *Sacrifice and Redemption: Durham Essays in Theology*, ed. Stephen W. Sykes. Cambridge: Cambridge Univ. Pr., 1991.

Daly, Robert. *The Origins of the Christian Doctrine of Sacrifice*. Philadelphia: Fortress Pr., 1978.

Dunn, J. D. G. "Paul's Understanding of the Death of Jesus as Sacrifice." In *Sacrifice and Redemption: Durham Essays in Theology*, ed. Stephen W. Sykes. Cambridge: Cambridge Univ. Pr., 1991.

Fodor, Jim. "Imitation and Emulation: Training in Practical Christian Judgment." Unpublished manuscript.

Gans, Eric. *The Origin of Language*. Berkeley: Univ. of California Pr., 1981.

———. *The End of Culture*. Berkeley: Univ. of California Pr., 1985.

Gorringe, Timothy. *God's Just Vengeance: Crime, Violence, and the Rhetoric of Salvation*. New York: Cambridge University Press, 1996.

Konkel, August. "The Sacrifice of Obedience." *Didaskalia* 2 (April 1991): 2-11.

Levenson, Jon D. *The Death and Resurrection of the Beloved Son*. New Haven: Yale Univ. Pr., 1993.

Lohfink, Norbert. "Altes Testament—Die Entlarvung der Gewalt." *Herder Korrespondenz* 32 (April 1987): 187-93.

———. *The Covenant Never Revoked: Biblical Reflections on Christian-Jewish Dialogue*. New York: Paulist Pr., 1991.

Marshall, Christopher. *Christ and Crime*. Grand Rapids: Eerdmans, forthcoming.

McGrath, Alister. *What Was God Doing on the Cross?* Grand Rapids: Zondervan Publishing Hse., 1992.

McLean, Bradley H. "The Absence of an Atoning Sacrifice in Paul's Soteriology." *New Testament Studies* 38 (1992): 531-53.

Milbank, John. "Can a Gift be Given? Prolegomena to a Future Trinitarian Metaphysic." *Modern Theology* 11 (January 1995): 119-61.

———. "The Ethics of Self-Sacrifice." *First Things* (March 1999): 33-38.

Milgrom, Jacob. *Leviticus 1-16: A New Translation with Introduction and Commentary.* Anchor Bible 3. New York: Doubleday, 1991.

Murphy, Nancey. "John Howard Yoder's Systematic Defense of Christian Pacifism." In *The Wisdom of the Cross: Essays in Honor of John Howard Yoder*, ed. Stanley Hauerwas, Chris K. Huebner, Harry J. Huebner, Mark Thiessen Nation. Grand Rapids: Eerdmans, 1999. Pp. 45-68.

Schwartz, Regina M. *The Curse of Cain: The Violence Legacy of Monotheism.* Chicago: University of Chicago Press, 1997.

Schweiker, William. "Beyond Imitation: Mimetic Praxis in Gadamer, Ricoeur, and Derrida." *Journal of Religion* 68 (1988): 21-38.

Swetnam, James. "Sacrifice and Revelation in the Epistle to the Hebrews: Observations and Surmises on Hebrew 9:26." *Catholic Biblical Quarterly* 30 (April 1968): 227-34.

Sykes, Stephen W., ed. *Sacrifice and Redemption: Durham Essays in Theology.* Cambridge: Cambridge Univ. Pr., 1991.

Thompson, James W. "Hebrews 9 and Hellenistic Concepts of Sacrifice." *Journal of Biblical Literature* 98 (December 1979): 567-78.

Vanderhaar, Gerard A. *Beyond Violence: In the Spirit of the Non-Violent Christ.* Mystic, Conn.: Twenty-Third Publications, 1998.

Webster, John B. "The Imitation of Christ." *Tyndale Bulletin* 37 (1986): 95-120.

White, Vernon. *Atonement and Imagination: An Essay in Universalism and Particularity.* New York: Cambridge University Press, 1991.

Williams, James G. "The Prophetic 'Father': A Brief Explanation of the 'Sons of the Prophets.'" *Journal of Biblical Literature* 85 (1966): 344-48.

———. "Paraenesis, Excess, and Ethics: Matthew's Rhetoric in the Sermon on the Mount." *Semeia* 50 (1990): 163-87.

Young, Frances M. *Sacrifice and the Death of Christ.* London: SPCK, 1975.

NOTE: Also all articles in *Contagion: Journal of Violence, Mimesis, and Culture*, vols. 1-6 (1994-1999), are directly or indirectly related to Girardian theory.

The Bulletin of the Colloquium of Violence and Religion (COV&R), published semiannually, contains regular updating of extensive bibliography related to Girard.

The Index

A

Abel, 107, 111, 126

acquisitive mimetic desire, 135, 179, 218-220, 224, 229-232, 238-239, 283-284. *See also* mimesis, appropriative desire

Adams, Rebecca, 23, 25, 140, 143

Alcoholics Anonymous, 152 n29

Alison, James, 23, 26-27, 136-137, 286, 306 n35

Anakim, 76-77

Anderson, Kirsten M., 282-283, 293

anti-idolatry, 23, 163, 171, 318

anti-Semitism, 201-204, 216, 314

appropriative desire, 143-147, 150 n24, 306 n34. *See also* acquisitive desire, mimesis

atonement, 41, 46, 148, 173, 221, 264

  and discipleship, 243 n38, 253-255

  and legitimation of violence, 45

  doctrine of, 22, 44, 149 n1

  theology, 26, 32, 123, 219

  theories of, 31, 132-153, 149 n1, 269 n12, 312

Augustine, 113

B

Babylon. *See* empire, Roman

Bailie, Gil, 95

baptism, 146

Bartlett, Anthony, 196

Becker, Ernest, 141

Benjamin, tribe of, 93-94

biblical narrative, 20

  and scapegoating mechanism, 25

  and violence, 24, 50-51

Braulik, Georg, 83 n11

Brown, Joanne Carlson Brown, 26, 27-28 n7

Buchanan, George, 110

Buddhism, 137-138, 146-147

Burrell, David, 272 n31, 306 n35

C

Cassidy, Richard, 234

Castelli, Elizabeth, 220, 267-268 n3, 241 n11

Chauvet, Louis-Marie, 122

cherem, 181-182. *See also* herem

Childs, Brevard, 71

Christianity, 23, 210-216, 301, 312

Christology, 263-266

Christus Victor, 123, 148

Collins, Robin, 22, 286

communion, 146

community, 35, 43-44, 87, 91-92, 104, 143, 191

coquette phenomenon, 291-292

correspondence logic, 234-236, 248

supersessionism, 130 n32
Swartley, Willard, 193, 247-253,
    264, 266, 281-282, 286, 297,
    310-311
  on Mark, 187-189

T
Taoism, 146-147
temple, Jerusalem, 52-56, 65
Ten Commandments. *See*
    Decalogue
Torah, 36, 71-76, 90, 97, 152 n30,
    213-215
Treguer, Michel, 203
Trinitarian theology, 248-249,
    255-258, 272 n30

U
unmasking theory, 135-137

V
victim(s), 33, 90, 104, 107, 195-
    196, 205, 309, 312-313, 319
  Jesus as, 38, 114-116
  king as, 179
  of violence, 286-290, 294, 297-
    301
  voice of, 20, 26
victimage mechanism, 37, 108-
    109, 113, 115, 301. *See also*
    scapegoat mechanism
violence, 132, 135, 260, 287-289
  and biblical narrative, 24, 50-
    51
  and cultural exclusivity, 57
  exposed, 52, 55
  in Bible, 50-51
  Joshua, 87-88, 93-94, 97-99
  responsibility for, 108, 203
  source of, 295
  spiral of, 49, 51, 62-66, 80, 220,
    239

W
Ward, Graham, 252, 269 n4
warfare, 81, 90-92, 96-98
Way. *See* hodos motif
will of God, 114, 143
Williams, James, 22, 112, 116 n2,
    121, 125, 232-233
Williams, Rowan, 257, 271 n23
Williams, Sam, 193
Wink, Walter, 25, 50-51, 64, 99,
    138, 148
works of law, 57-61, 68 n29
wrath of God, 24-25, 37, 41-42,
    51, 105-108, 127-128, 151
    n27, 193
Wright, G. E., 79

Y
Yadin, Yigael, 127
Yoder, John H., 234-236

The Contributors

Rebecca Adams, Grantham, Pennsylvania; M. A. in English, University of California, Santa Barbara; doctoral study in English, University of Notre Dame, Notre Dame, Indiana; independent scholar and adjunct lecturer in Women's Studies, Messiah College, Grantham.

Robin Collins, Grantham, Pennsylvania; Ph.D. from University of Notre Dame, Notre Dame, Indiana; Associate Professor of Philosophy, Messiah College, Grantham.

Diana Culbertson, Kent, Ohio; O.P. and Ph.D. Professor of Comparative Literature and Religious Studies at Kent State University; President for the Colloquium on Violence and Religion.

Jim Fodor, St. Bonaventure, New York; Ph.D. in Theology, University of Cambridge; post-doctoral fellow at Duke University (1992-1994) and currently Associate Professor of Christian Ethics/Moral Theology, St. Bonaventure University; managing editor of *Modern Theology*.

Sandor Goodhart, West Lafayette, Indiana; Ph.D. in English Literature from the State University of New York at Buffalo; Director of the Jewish Studies Program and Associate Professor of English Literature, Purdue University.

René Girard, Stanford, California; Andrew B. Hammond Professor of French Language, Literature, and Civilization at Stanford University.

Ted Grimsrud, Harrisonburg, Virginia; Ph.D. in Christian Ethics, Graduate Theological Union; Assistant Professor in Theology and Peace Studies, Eastern Mennonite University, Harrisonburg.

Michael Hardin, New York City; graduate student in Bible and Religion.

Loren L. Johns, Elkhart, Indiana; Ph.D. in New Testament, Princeton Theological Seminary; until recently Associate Professor of Religion, Bluffton (Oh.) College, now Dean of Associated Mennonite Biblical Seminary.

Paul Keim, Goshen, Indiana, Ph.D. in Near Eastern Studies and Civilizations, Harvard University; Academic Dean, Goshen College.

Charles Mabee, Detroit, Michigan; Ph.D. from Claremont Graduate School; Professor of Old Testament and Director, M.Div. Program at Ecumenical Theological Seminary, Detroit.

Gordon H. Matties, Winnipeg, Manitoba; Ph.D. in Old Testament from Vanderbilt University; Associate Professor of Biblical Studies/Theology, Concord College, Winnipeg.

Marlin Miller, Th.D. from Heildelberg University; former President and Professor of Theology, Associated Mennonite Biblical Seminary; deceased 1994. Daughter **Rachel Miller Jacobs**, who transcribed several taped lectures and edited them into the article in this volume, has received an M.Div. from Associated Mennonite Biblical Seminary.

Willard M. Swartley, Elkhart, Indiana; Ph.D. from Princeton Theological Seminary; Professor of New Testament at Associated Mennonite Biblical Seminary; until recently, Academic Dean, AMBS.

James G. Williams, Jones, Oklahoma; Ph.D. from Hebrew Union College-Jewish Institute of Religion; Professor Emeritus of Religion at Syracuse (N.Y.) University.

The Editor

WILLARD SWARTLEY IS PROFESSOR OF New Testament at the Associated Mennonite Biblical Seminary, Elkhart, Indiana. He has served as seminary dean 1979-81, 1990, and 1995-2000. He has been a Bible teacher in congregational settings and churchwide conferences, in both North America and overseas. His special interests are in the Gospels, the peace teachings of the Bible, and biblical interpretation. He is a graduate of Eastern Mennonite College (B.A.), Goshen Biblical Seminary (B.D.), and Princeton Theological Seminary (1973 Ph.D.).

Swartley is the New Testament editor for the Believers Church Bible Commentary Series and New Testament editor for a book series on Studies in Peace and Scripture. Swartley earlier taught at Eastern Mennonite University and served as interim dean there also. He directed the AMBS Institute of Mennonite Studies from 1979-1988. He also taught at Goshen College, Eastern Mennonite College and Seminary, and at Conrad Grebel College.

Among Swartley's publications are *Mark: The Way for All Nations* (Herald Press, 1979, rev. 1981); *Slavery, Sabbath, War and Women: Case Issues in Biblical Interpretation* (Herald Press, 1983); editor of *Love of Enemy and Nonretaliation in the New Testament* (Westminster/John Knox, 1992 [available at Sigler Press]); *Israel's Scripture Traditions and the Synoptic Gospels: Story Shaping Story* (Hendrickson, 1994); "War and Peace in the New Testament," in *Aufstieg und Niedergang der römischen Welt* (ed. W. Haase and H. Temporini, Part II, Vol. 26.3: 2298-2408); and co-editor, with Donald Kraybill, of *Building Communities of Compassion* (Herald Press, 1998).